Contents

Introduction by Professor J. D. Omer-Cooper

The geography of Africa — I
Africa north of the Sahara — I
The Sahara desert — 2
The Nile valley — 2
Caravan routes across the Sahara — 3
The Sudanic belt in West Africa — 3
The West African forest belt — 3
The Ethiopian highlands — 4
East and Central Africa — 4
South Africa — 5
The peoples of Africa north of the Sahara — 5
Egypt before the nineteenth century — 5
The civilisations of the upper Nile valley — 8
The origins and development of the Ethiopian Empire — 9
The Maghreb before 1900 — 10
The peoples of Africa south of the Sahara — 13
The kingdom of Kush — 16
States of the western Sudan — 16
West African forest kingdoms — 18
Kingdoms of the Congo — 19
The East African trading cities — 20
Civilisations of East Africa — 21
Civilisations of Central Africa — 21
External influences on Africa before 1800: Islam and the Arabs — 23
The Prophet Mohammed and the founding of the Islamic community — 23
The development of Islamic civilisation — 24
The caliphate and the nature of the Islamic political system — 25

The Sufi brotherhoods 26
The impact of Islam in Africa 27
European influence on Africa before 1800 27
The Portuguese 27
The slave trade 29
The Cape Colony 30
The changed situation in the nineteenth century 30
Internal movements in nineteenth-century Africa 31
Content and divisions of the two volumes 31

Part one
Northern Africa E. A. Ayandele

1 Egypt from the Napoleonic Invasion to the British Occupation

Egypt from the Napoleonic Invasion to the British Occupation 35

Egypt, an Arab nation 35
The Copts 35
The Mamelukes 1249-1517 36
Egypt under the Ottoman Empire 36
Napoleon invades Egypt 37
Consequences of Napoleon's invasion 39
The British force Napoleon to leave Egypt 41
The rise of Mohammed Ali 42
Mohammed Ali's policies 43
Destruction of the Mamelukes and social reforms 43
Military reforms: the creation of a national army 44
Attempts to modernise the Egyptian economy 44
Mohammed Ali's foreign policy 47
Occupation of Syria and conflict with the Ottoman Sultan 48
European intervention 49
Achievements of Mohammed Ali 49
Abbas I 50
Said and the Suez Canal agreement 51
Ismail Pasha and his extravagance 51
Towards self-government 52
British purchase of Suez Canal shares 53
International control of Egyptian finances 54
Nationalist reaction and the rebellion of Arabi Pasha 55
British occupation of Egypt 56

The Growth of African Civilisation

The Making of Modern Africa

1 The Nineteenth Century to the Partition

J. D. Omer-Cooper M.A.
Professor of History, University of Zambia

E. A. Ayandele B.A., Ph.D.
Senior Lecturer in History, Ibadan

R. J. Gavin M.A., Ph.D.
Senior Lecturer in History, Ibadan

A. E. Afigbo B.A., Ph.D.
Lecturer in History, Nsukka

Humanities Press

HUMANITIES PRESS INC.
303 PARK AVENUE SOUTH
NEW YORK, NY 10010

Library of Congress Catalog Card Number 68–8756

Printed in Hong Kong by
Sheck Wah Tong Printing Press

2 The Sudan and Ethiopia in the nineteenth century 57

The Funj Sultanate in the Sudan 58
Turko-Egyptian conquest of the Sudan 60
Turko-Egyptian administration 1820-81 60
Unpopularity of the Turko-Egyptian government 61
Muhammad Ahmad, the Mahdi 63
Collapse of the Turko-Egyptian regime and triumph of the Mahdi 64
The Sudan under the Khalifa 1885-98 68
The British conquest of the Sudan 1898 70
The Ethiopian Empire at the beginning of the nineteenth century 73
Emperor Theodore 75
The reign of Emperor John IV 78
Emperor Menelik II and the Italians 80

3 The Maghreb and European intervention 85

The land 85
Foreign invasions 85
The Turkish Maghreb 87
European influence in the Maghreb before 1830 88
The French occupation of Algeria 90
Abdel Kader and resistance to the French occupation 92
The French occupation becomes permanent 93
Development of French policy in Algeria 94
Tunisia 96
The reign of Ahmed Bey 96
Mohammed es Sadek and the growth of European influence 97
The French occupation of Tunisia 99
Morocco 100
Moulay Suleiman 101
Moulay Hassan 101
The French occupation of Morocco 103
Libya 104
The Senussiya 105
The Italian invasion 106

Part two
West Africa A. E. Afigbo

4 West Africa to 1800   109

Trans-Saharan trade routes   109
Islam   111
Development of European trade   112
The influence of European trade on West African states   114
Rise of the Atlantic trade   117

5 The growth and changing nature of European
  influence (c. 1800–61)   119

The campaign against the slave trade   122
The British anti-slavery movement   123
International agreements   125
The Equipment Treaties   126
The African view   128
West African treaties   129
The founding of Sierra Leone   130
American settlement of Liberia   133
The American Colonisation Society   134
Liberian independence   135
European penetration of West Africa   136
British attempts at penetration   138
Mungo Park   141
The Landers   142
The benefits of exploration   143
French attempts   146
African reaction   148
The coming of the Christian missions   149
The educated elite   153

6 Revolutions and Wars   155

The jihads of the western Sudan   155
Fulani Muslims   158
Uthman dan Fodio   158
Reasons for the success of the jihad   161
Repercussions of the jihad   163
Hamad in Macina   164

Al-Hajj Umar   165
Effects of the jihads   167
Samori Toure   170
The collapse of the Oyo Empire   172
The Yoruba wars   174
British intervention   176
The Dahomean invasions of Yorubaland   178
The Egba stand   179
The Anglo-Asante wars   181
British administration on the coast   186
The end of Asante independence   188

Part three
Southern and Central Africa
J. D. Omer-Cooper

7 Southern and Central Africa at the beginning
  of the nineteenth century   193

The geographical features   193
The Khoisan peoples in South Africa   193
The Bushmen   194
The Hottentots   194
The Bantu-speaking peoples   196
The southern Bantu: important subdivisions of the group   196
The central Bantu   198
Social and political organisation of the Bantu-speaking
people   198
The Mwene Mutapa Empire and the Portuguese   200
Foreign influence in Southern and Central Africa   202
The establishment of the Cape Colony   202
Expansion of the white settlement at the Cape   205
The growth of race prejudice in the Cape Colony   206
Reaction of the Khoisan peoples to the expansion of the
Cape Colony   207
Origin of the Cape Coloured people   208
Migration of the Korana   208
Origin of the Griquas   208
Resistance of the Bushmen to white expansion   209
White settlers and Bantu-speaking peoples encounter one
another   209

Republic of Graaf Reinet 209
First British occupation of the Cape 210

8 The great nineteenth-century migration 211

Two great folk movements 211
Origin of the Mfecane 211
Military grouping in Zululand 212
Origins of the Swazi nation 213
Death of Dingiswayo and rise of Shaka 213
Shaka's military reforms 214
Shaka defeats Zwide 215
Shaka's kingdom 215
English traders in Natal 216
The assassination of Shaka, 1828 216
Succession of Dingane 217
The Wa-Tuta 219
The Gwangara and the Maseko 219
Mpezeni's and Mbelwa's Ngoni 219
The Mfecane on the South African highveld 220
The migration of the Kololo to Barotseland 220
Kololo kingdoms in the Shire Valley 221
Moshesh and the Basuto kingdom 221
Mzilikazi and the Ndebele 222
The Fingos 222
Development of the Cape Colony 222
The Hottentot uprising 223
British missionaries 223
The Dutch at the Cape 1803-6 224
Second British occupation, 1806 224
The Black Circuit 225
The Xhosa driven from the Zuurveld 225
Makana and the 1818 war 226
The 1820 settler experiment 226
Missionary agitation and the 50th Ordinance 227
The emancipation of slaves 228
The expanding frontiers 228
The commissie trekke 228
The Xhosa resistance war of 1835-6 229
The Trek begins 230
The course of the Trek 231
Conflict with Mzilikazi 231

The Trekkers and the Zulu   233
The coup that failed   234
The Blood River Campaign   234
Zulu civil war   236

9 South Africa from the Great Trek to the first Anglo-Boer war   237

Consequences of the Great Trek   237
The dilemma of British policy   237
The first stage of British reaction to the Trek   238
Conduct of the Natal Republic   239
The Boers and their neighbours   239
British annexation of Natal   241
The treaty policy on the eastern frontier and in Trans-Orangia   241
Moshesh, the British, and the Trek Boers   243
Failure of the treaty policy   244
The 1846 Xhosa resistance war on the eastern frontier (The War of the Axe)   245
Annexation of British Kaffraria and the Orange River Sovereignty   245
Reactions to the annexation of the Orange River Sovereignty   246
Warden and Moshesh   247
The Xhosa resistance war of 1850   248
British reactions – war renewed in South Africa   248
The Sand River Convention   249
Moshesh and Cathcart   249
The Bloemfontein Convention   250
The Orange Free State   250
The disadvantages of the conventions   250
Constitutional development of the Cape   252
Grey and settlement in British Kaffraria   253
The cattle killing   254
The Griquas' Great Trek   254
Grey's federation scheme   255
The first Free State – Basuto war 1858   255
British rejection of federation   256
Renewed tension between Boers and Basuto   256
The second Free State-Basuto war   257
British annexation of Basutoland   258

The diamond fields   260
The British annexation of the diamond fields   261
Carnarvon's confederation policy   262
Cape resistance to Carnarvon's plan   263
British annexation of the Transvaal   263
Reactions to the annexation of the Transvaal   264
The Xhosa resistance war of 1877   264
The 'War of the Guns'   265
The Zulu war   266
First Anglo-Boer war   267
The Pretoria Convention 1881   268

Part four
Middle Africa R. J. Gavin

10 The Prelude   271

The Bantu-speaking peoples   271
The kingly states   272
The kingdom of Kongo   274
The Lunda Empire, Kazembe   274
Peoples of the Congo Basin   275
The inter-lacustrine kingdoms   276
The Zande states   278
Ganda and Nyoro   278
The Hima aristocracies   279
Peoples of the east   281
Firearms from abroad   283
Maritime peace   284
Rising foreign trade   285
Commerce in Middle Africa   286

11 Men and Arms   287

Coastal traders   290
Sayyid Sa'id and Zanzibar commerce   290
Arab and Nyamwezi traders   292
The Angoni   293
Angoni imitators   294
The Ruga-Ruga   295
Mirambo   296

M'siri 297
Arabs in the Congo 298
Tippu Tip 299
The northern trade routes 300
Ganda expansion 301
Egyptian pressure 302
Middle Africa in perspective 303

List of maps

page

1 Africa at the beginning of the nineteenth century *facing p.* 1
2 Egypt in the nineteenth century 39
3 The area of the Funj Sultanate and the Nile confluence 59
4 Sudan under Egyptian rule 62
5 The Mahdist State 67
6 The European advance on the Sudan 70
7 The provinces of Ethiopia 73
8 Napier's march from Zula to Magdala 77
9 The Italian campaign in Ethiopia 83
10 The Maghreb in the nineteenth century 88-9
11 The European advance into the Maghreb 103
12 West African peoples mentioned in the text 116
13 States, towns and physical features of West Africa 116-7
14 European forts and trading posts 120
15 Sierra Leone and Liberia 133
16 European exploration of West Africa 140
17 The spread of missionary activities in West Africa 151
18 The Fulani Jihad 160
19 The empires of al-Hajj Umar and Samori Toure 169
20 Yorubaland at the time of the wars 175
21 Asante and the coastal states 185
22 Peoples of southern Africa 197
23 Mozambique 203
24 The main movements of people during the Mfecane 218
25 Routes followed by the Boers in the Great Trek 232
26 Boer-Zulu and Boer-Ndebele battlefields 235

27 The Trekkers' Republic   240

28 British annexations in southern Africa up to 1848   246

29 South Africa after the Sand River and Bloemfontein
   Conventions   251

30 Basutoland showing the territorial effect of repeated
   attempts to annexe the territory   259

31 The diamond yielding areas of South Africa. The political
   problems described in the text resulting from the bordering
   of three separate territories on the diamond area are
   clearly seen   261

32 The area which the first Boer and the Zulu wars were
   fought over, showing the positions of the major battles.
   Battles in the Zulu war are underlined   267

33 The larger groups of Middle African peoples mentioned in
   the text   273

34 Population density in eastern Africa. The map is in two
   parts as information from the different countries does
   not in all cases agree   280

35 Popularity density in the Congo (Kinshasa). Note the low
   population density in this heavily forested area   281

36 Trade routes in Middle Africa   292

ACKNOWLEDGEMENTS The publishers are grateful to the following
for permission to reproduce photographs:

*British Museum, pp. 23, 291; Vincent Brown, p. 62; W. H. Gagne & Sons,
Canada, p. 318;*
Historical Picture Service, Chicago, pp. 305, 315;
Illustrated London News & Sketch Ltd., pp. 68, 94;
Mansell Collection, pp. 53, 54, 57, 82, 143, 211, 274, 299 (top left), 307;
*Radio Times Hulton Picture Library, pp. 58, 71, 79, 81, 88, 91, 96, 108, 113, 127,
273, 282, 296, 298, 299 (top right and bottom), 320;*
Royal Commonwealth Society, p. 137; Royal Geographical Society, p. 159;
South African Department of Information, Pretoria, pp. 220, 228, 246, 268;
Merlyn Severn from 'Congo Pilgrim' (Museum Press, 1952), p. 293;
Captain A. D. Shorey, p. 230; Van Riebeeck Society, Cape Town, p. 271;
*Weidenfeld and Nicolson 'Africa—History of a Continent' by B. Davidson,
p. 205; Werner Forman, pp. 172, 293 (right); Witwatersand University, p. 247.*

COVER PHOTOGRAPH by *A. R. Willcox*
MAPS by *Maureen Verity* based on roughs by Robin Laurent.
Different sources were used in preparing the roughs, particularly
J. D. Fage's 'Atlas of African History', published by Edward Arnold.

Publisher's Note

Dr. A. E. Afigbo is Lecturer in History at Nsukka. He has specialised in the study of indirect rule in West Africa and his book 'Warrant Chiefs in Eastern Nigeria' is to be published soon. He has contributed the section on West Africa.

Dr. E. A. Ayandele is Senior Lecturer in History at Ibadan. He teaches the course on the history of Northern Africa. His book 'The Missionary Impact on Modern Nigeria' was published in 1966 and he has also written many articles for different journals, including 'Tarikh'.

Dr. R. J. Gavin is Lecturer in History at Ibadan. He has specialised in the history of Aden and the Horn of Africa. He has contributed the section on Middle Africa.

The helpful advice of Dr. Terence Ranger, University of Tanzania; Dr. A. A. Boahen, University of Ghana; and Dr. J. Wansbrough, School of Oriental and African Studies, is gratefully acknowledged.

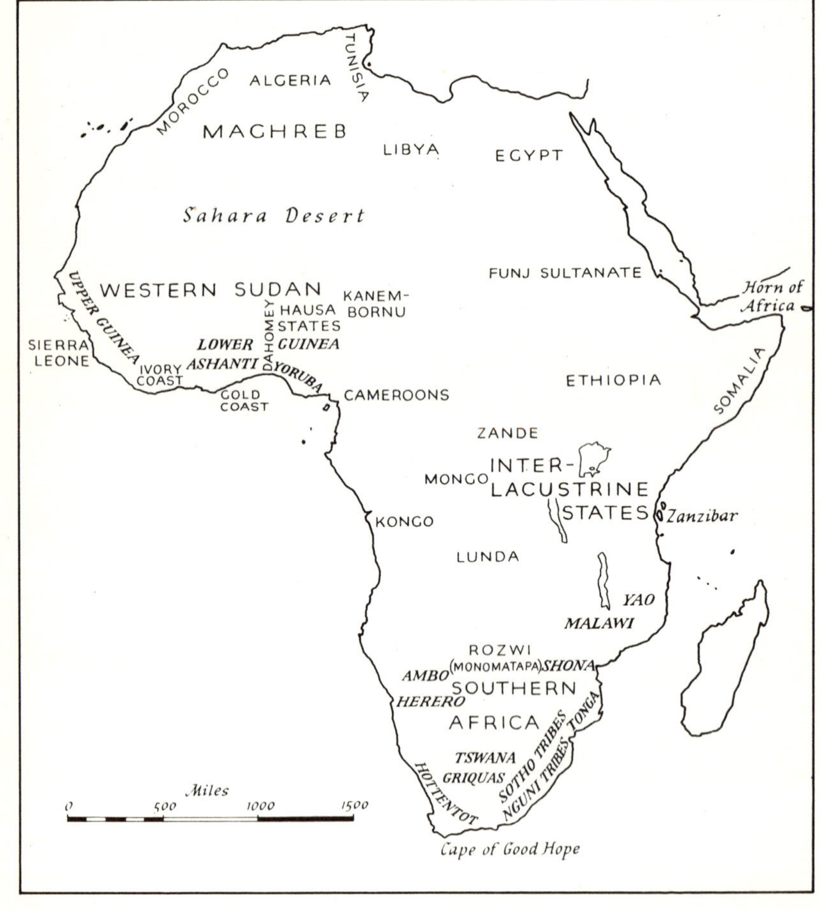

1 Africa at the beginning of the nineteenth century

Introduction

In size the African continent, with its 11,673,000 square miles, may be compared with Asia (10,654,000 square miles), and the USSR (8,649,000 square miles). This vast land mass straddles the equator, facing the Mediterranean Sea in the north and the Antarctic in the south. Its wide variety of climates and natural conditions has greatly influenced the development of its inhabitants.

The geography of Africa

One characteristic of Africa is the striking regularity of its coastline, which has relatively few bays and inlets or promontories and peninsulas reaching out to sea. This has meant that the African peoples have not had the same opportunities and incentives for the development of navigation on the sea, whether for long- or short-range trade, as have the peoples of Europe and Asia. Thus, except for the countries bordering the Mediterranean, they have not until comparatively recent times been brought into close and frequent contact with other continents. Until the nineteenth century African development was relatively self-contained, though this does not mean that there were no contacts with other nations, nor that such contacts were unimportant.

Africa north of the Sahara

The northern part of the continent lies along the Mediterranean Sea and enjoys a climate similar to, though warmer and drier than, that of southern Europe. This Mediterranean area is a narrow coastal strip varying in width according to geographical circumstances.

It is widest in the north-west corner of the continent, known as the Maghreb (Arabic word for west), where the modern states of Morocco, Algeria and Tunisia are situated. There the Atlas mountains cause winds from the Mediterranean and the Atlantic to deposit their moisture and the soil has been noted for its fertility from ancient times.

The Sahara desert

Behind this narrow strip of fertile country with its Mediterranean climate lies the vast desert of the Sahara, greater in extent than the whole of Europe and by far the largest desert in the world. This huge area—which is now almost entirely uninhabited outside the occasional oases which provide welcome islands of green in the almost endless wastes of barren rock and burning sands—was once very different. In remote prehistoric times it enjoyed a reasonable rainfall and supported a considerable population. Gradually, for reasons which are still not well understood, it dried up and its peoples congregated around the oases or moved further afield. By the times of the ancient Greeks and Romans it was in much the same condition as today. But though the Sahara is such a vast and formidable desert it must not be thought that it separated the northern part of the continent from all contact with the centre and south.

The Nile valley

On the eastern side of the continent the river Nile, starting from two sources, one in the highlands of Ethiopia (the Blue Nile) and the other in the Lake region of East Africa, (the White Nile) threads its way across the desert to reach the sea through the many mouths of its delta in Egypt. Every year the rains in Ethiopia and East Africa cause the river to overflow its banks, and as the water subsides it leaves behind a layer of fertile mud which it has brought from the Ethiopian highlands. Along the banks of the Nile there is a narrow cultivable strip containing some of the richest agricultural land in the world. Though it is often no more than a few miles wide it can support a dense population and it gave rise to one of the world's most ancient and elaborate civilizations. Navigation is possible along great stretches of the river, and the winding thread of water and the vivid strip of green beside it form one of the strongest links binding the history of the peoples north and south of the Sahara.

Caravan routes across the Sahara

In the central and western parts of the Sahara the mountains of Tibesti Air and the Hoggar capture sufficient rain to make agriculture possible. In other places underground water provides wells and springs to nourish oases. These provide natural staging posts on the caravan routes which from ancient times have criss-crossed the desert, bringing the peoples of West Africa and the Maghreb into contact with each other.

The Sudanic belt in West Africa

To the south of the Sahara in the west, desert conditions gradually give way to increasing vegetation nourished by the rains brought by warm equatorial winds from the Atlantic. A great belt of savannah stretches across the continent which is called the 'Sudanic belt'.

The West African forest belt

South of the Sudanic belt, along the coast of much of West Africa, stretching inland to varying distances, lies the great West African rain forest which, with a few gaps, meets the dense forests of the Congo to form one of the largest tropical forests in the world.

Thus the pattern of West African geography consists of a fairly regular succession of belts of vegetation, from the Sahara desert, across the grasslands of the savannah belt to the lush forests of the coastal strip. But this pattern is broken by major rivers which have had a significant influence on history, such as the complex Niger-Benue river system which might be described as the Nile of West Africa. Rising in the mountains of the Futa Jallon range in modern Guinea, the river Niger makes a great northward loop almost into the Sahara before turning south into modern Nigeria where it links up with the Benue, another mighty river which rises in the mountains of the Cameroun. The combined waters finally find their way to the sea through the maze of creeks and rivers of the Niger Delta. In its northward path the Niger runs for part of its course over level ground where it overflows its banks every year when the rains in the Futa Jallon bring down the flood waters to form what is often called the inland Delta of the Niger. A relatively dense population can be supported there and it is not surprising that the valley of the Niger should have been the centre of some of West Africa's most ancient and powerful kingdoms. Further east Lake Chad, lying on the fringes of the Sahara and fed by rivers rising in the Cameroun mountains, also modifies the climate and provides agricultural opportunities.

The Ethiopian highlands

On the eastern side of the continent the highlands of Ethiopia, lying within the triangular projection known as the Horn of Africa, constitute a special environment of their own. They consist largely of volcanic material which breaks down to give a rich soil of almost unlimited depth. It is this soil which washes down the Nile to provide the fertility of Egypt. Abundant rains fall every year and the climate of the cool uplands has been described as the closest to paradise on earth. No wonder the ancient Greeks regarded Ethiopia as the favourite earthly residence of the gods. Between this fertile highland area – a natural centre of civilisation – and the sea, is the dry and torrid plain of Somalia, suitable only for nomadic herdsmen and incapable of sustaining a large settled population.

East and Central Africa

Further south again the African continent consists of a vast plateau rising to its highest point in the Ruwenzori mountains, sometimes described as the spine of Africa. To the west of the Ruwenzori lies the great basin of the Congo and Kasai rivers system, much of it covered by forest which towards the south gives way to savannah and the Benguella and Katanga plateaus where the Zambesi river has its source. East of the Ruwenzori is the region of the Great Lakes, Victoria, Tanganyika, Malawi and many others that are smaller but still large and important. In spite of the presence of the Great Lakes much of this East and Central African plateau is hot and rather dry, covered with a poor tree scrub. There are important exceptions, however. The cool and fertile highlands of Kenya provide excellent farming country. The area between Lakes Victoria, Kyoga and Kivu, the so-called inter-lacustrine region which forms the heart of modern Uganda, benefits from abundant rains which make it a green and smiling land. Here was another natural centre for the development of African civilizations. The slopes of Mount Kilimanjaro and the Shire highlands of modern Malawi are other examples.

4

South Africa

The southernmost part of the continent constitutes a prolongation of the great African plateau, surrounded by a coastal strip of varying width, the result of age-old erosion of the plateau edge. Like most of the African plateau this is generally rather dry, open savannah country with grass or bush or thorn scrub. Its climate is strongly affected by its southerly latitude and the winter months of June and July can be bitterly cold. On the other hand the southern part of the continent is free from malaria and the tsetse fly which are plagues north of the Equator. It is ideal country for cattle keepers and mixed farmers but cannot support a dense agricultural population.

The peoples of Africa north of the Sahara

The peoples of this vast continent and the story of their development are as varied as the geography. The northern part of the continent, facing the Mediterranean Sea, and including the lower reaches and delta of the Nile, was the home of the ancient Egyptians and the Berbers in the Maghreb. They were basically similar in appearance and physique to the people of southern Europe and the structure of their languages suggests a link with Mesopotamia and Arabia also. Men of a similar stock probably formed the basic population of the Ethiopian highlands, though there and in the upper Nile valley they intermarried with negroes and hence came to be known by the name of 'Ethiopians', which means 'burnt face'. There is some evidence to suggest that people of the North-African southern-European type also occupied parts of East Africa in remote times, but this is much more uncertain.

Egypt before the nineteenth century

In the Nile valley, where the conditions for human settlement were particularly favourable, a dense population grew up in very ancient times and one of the most important civilisations of the ancient world developed. It was a civilisation strongly influenced by the natural conditions of the Nile valley and the dependence of man on the river and its floods. For the large population to support itself it was essential to make the best use of every drop of the flood waters and of the rich mud which they spread over the land. This could only be done successfully if irrigation and land-use up and down the valley were carefully controlled. Thus, from about 3000 BC, a very powerful state system grew up which exercised close control over the use of water and land and the crops derived from them. As these were the matters of fundamental importance to the Egyptian peasants the state virtually controlled all the most important aspects of their lives. One of the world's earliest known systems of writing, the hieroglyphic script, was developed, and an elaborate civil service of scribes grew to perform the complex tasks of administration. The king, or pharaoh, was, at least in theory, all-powerful and the owner of all the land in Egypt. It was believed that he was divine and that he and his ancestors in the spirit world influenced the fertility of the land. He was thus a central figure in an elaborate religious system with a complicated order of gods served by powerful priests. Though the standard of living of the ordinary peasant was always low, the king, the civil servants and the priests were able to live in great luxury and splendour. The mighty pyramids which have fascinated all subsequent generations were built as tombs for some of the kings, while others were buried in vast chambers cut out of the rock of mountain sides and decorated with paintings of rich and almost unbelievable beauty. Palaces too were built and splendid temples of great size. Arts and crafts of many different kinds were developed to a high pitch of perfection.

The Egyptian kingdom was not self-contained but traded widely with the outside world, using the enormous surpluses of wheat grown on the rich valley soil to profit from high prices resulting from famine in various parts of the Mediterranean world. Relations with the neighbouring and in some ways similar civilisation of Mesopotamia were always close, though often hostile. Syria and Palestine suffered much in biblical times from the competition of the two world powers of the day. For long Egypt exercised imperial authority over Syria but gradually its power declined and it was itself conquered, first by the Assyrians (663 BC) and then for a longer term by the Persians (525–332 BC). Thereafter Egypt was conquered by the Greeks (332 BC) and later by the Romans (30 BC). It formed one of the richest provinces of the Roman Empire and was converted, like most of the Empire, to Christianity. It was there that the idea of religious men withdrawing from the world to found monasteries for prayer and meditation was first developed and subsequently spread to Europe.

In AD 640 Egypt was conquered by the Arabs, who brought with them Islam, a religion and a way of life which has formed the basic framework of the life of the majority of Egyptians ever since. Egypt after the Arab conquest knew a variety of different rulers, including a long period from AD 1259–1517 under dynasties of foreign soldiers who were originally recruited as slaves and were known as the Mamelukes. In the sixteenth century the Mamelukes were conquered by the Ottoman Turks and Egypt became part of the Ottoman Empire. But under the Turkish administration the Mamelukes were allowed to rise again and by the end of the eighteenth century they were virtually independent of the Turkish sultan who was their nominal ruler.

A Mameluke

In spite of all these changes, certain factors have remained constant in Egyptian life from the time of the pharaohs to the present day: the absolute dependence on the Nile and the irrigation system, and arising from this, the high degree of dependence of the people on the administrative system; the powerful position of rulers and civil servants; and the large role played by the state in all development. These are not so much the results of particular ideologies and beliefs as of the inescapable facts of Egyptian life.

The civilisations of the upper Nile valley

Though Egypt traded widely with Mediterranean lands and competed with the Mesopotamian civilisations for control of the Middle East, it was no less interested in its African neighbours higher up the Nile in the northern parts of the modern Sudan. This part of Africa was inhabited from very early times by Negro peoples and Egypt was always a multi-racial state, or rather a state in which peoples of different race lived together without attaching much importance to racial differences. There are, it is true, pictures of pharaohs conquering the Negro peoples of the upper Nile and capturing them as slaves, but statues of important officers show that Negroes could rise to high positions in the state. As a result of Egyptian influence in the upper Nile valley, a civilisation grew up there based largely on the Egyptian pattern though modified by local traditions. Its rulers became very powerful and about 730 BC the great Nubian warrior Piankhy conquered Egypt and established a new dynasty generally known as the Ethiopian dynasty, on the throne of the pharaohs. After being defeated by an Assyrian attack, in 663 BC, however, the Nubians severed their connection with Egypt and established an independent kingdom on the upper Nile known as the kingdom of Kush. The first capital of the kingdom was at Napata. Later it was moved further up the Nile from Napata to Meroe and there the kings and queens of Kush continued to keep alive a form of the Egyptian civilisation – even building small scale pyramids – long after the old religion and way of life had died out in Egypt itself. Gradually the state was weakened, probably by the decline of agriculture caused by soil exhaustion, and by trade competition from the rising kingdom of Axum in Ethiopia. About AD 350 King Ezana of Axum stormed the capital and the kingdom came to an end.

This did not mean the end of civilisation and independent development for the upper Nile valley. Missionaries from Egypt, then under the Eastern Roman, or Byzantine, Empire, introduced Christianity into Nubia and a number of Christian kingdoms grew up where beautifully decorated churches and monasteries were built. These kingdoms too fell into decline and Muslim merchants and missionaries from Egypt converted many of the people to Islam. Then in the sixteenth century a brilliant leader, Amara Dunkas, in alliance with the Abdullab, the most important of the Arab sheikhs who had penetrated the upper Nile valley, conquered the whole area of the previously Christian kingdoms and united them in a Muslim Sultanate known as the Funj Kingdom with its capital at Sennar on the Blue

Nile. This kingdom survived until the nineteenth century, though it was by then in the last stages of decline.

The origins and development of the Ethiopian Empire

The history of Ethiopia is closely linked with that of the upper Nile valley on one side and of South Arabia, across the narrow straits of the Bab-el-Mandeb, on the other. Movements of population have probably taken place in both directions. Certainly, when powerful kingdoms grew up on the mountain plateau of modern Yemen it was only natural that they should take an interest in the fertile highlands, so similar to their own country, across the narrow seas. A series of South Arabian city-state colonies grew up in Ethiopia, taking with them the pagan religion of ancient Sabaea and the ancient South Arabian language and script. Eventually these separate cities were brought under the control of Axum, which laid the foundations of the Ethiopian Empire. In Axum a form of the South Arabian language was used, modified by local influences, to form a national language known as Geez. The holy books of Ethiopia are written in this language which is also used in Church services. Amharic, the modern official language, has grown out of it in the same way as French, Italian and Spanish have their roots in Latin.

As Axum extended its authority over the city-states of Ethiopia it became rich and powerful. Mighty temples were erected to the gods and colossal monuments were erected in their honour. Axum also became a naval power with a strong interest in the Red Sea trade, and at times it extended its authority over parts of South Arabia whence much of its culture originally came. These developments brought Ethiopia into contact with the outside world and made it one of the recognised world powers. Greek traders from the eastern parts of the Roman Empire thronged its court and Greek became a second official language in which some of the royal inscriptions were written.

Through these contacts Ethiopia was brought in touch with the religious changes taking place in the world. Many were converted to Judaism, which was spreading actively in South Arabia, and a Judaic community sprang up which still survives. In the reign of the same King Ezana (who destroyed the kingdom of Kush about AD 350) the kingdom as a whole was converted to Christianity, which has remained the national religion ever since. With the rise of Islam and the Arab conquest of Egypt the kingdom was isolated from the rest of the Christian world. It also suffered from internal upheavals; the old dynasty which claimed descent from Solomon and the Queen of Sheba went into eclipse for a time and the kingdom lost control of the vital coastlands occupied by the nomadic Somalis who adopted Islam as their religion. After this dark period the empire revived. The Solomonic dynasty was restored and by the beginning of the sixteenth century it was once more a powerful state engaged in reasserting its control over the Muslim states along the coast. Just when it seemed at the high tide of prosperity, however, a brilliant Somali leader, Mohammed Gran, relying on the religious fervour of his supporters and a troop of Turkish musketeers, turned the tide and came near to conquering the whole of Ethiopia. In despair the Ethiopian king turned to the Portuguese, who had already established contact with the kingdom, for help against his Muslim enemies. With their aid Mohammed Gran was killed and the Somalis defeated, but disagreements on religious matters between the Roman Catholics and the national Church of Ethiopia led to a number of upheavals and much bitterness. Ultimately the Catholics were expelled and the traditional Church re-established, but the monarchy had been weakened and it was faced with a new threat in the form of the slow but steady infiltration of the nomadic and warlike Gallas from the south-east. Princes and local chiefs struggled over succession to the throne and the empire almost ceased to exist as an effective state. But the long tradition of past history and the strength of the national Church kept the feeling of unity alive and made it possible for a series of powerful rulers in the nineteenth century to revive the kingdom and make it a state to be reckoned with in world affairs.

The Maghreb before 1900

The Maghreb has from very ancient times been the home of many different Berber tribes. Their way of life depended largely on geographical circumstances. Some who lived on the rich lands near the coast or in well-watered parts of the mountains were settled agriculturalists; others on the desert fringes or in the Sahara itself lived the life of nomadic pastoralists. The basic tribal pattern was only slightly modified when traders from Phoenicia on the Syrian coast established the city of Carthage about 750 BC. An empire was gradually built up along the coastal strip and more intensive methods of agriculture were introduced. Carthage had imperial interests in southern Spain and in Sicily, where it engaged in a long struggle with the Greek city-states. This ultimately brought it into conflict with the rising power of Rome, and after the failure of Hannibal's heroic but futile invasion of Italy (218–203 BC) the power of Carthage was destroyed, most of the Maghreb being taken into the Roman Empire. A long period of peace and prosperity followed. Agriculture was greatly improved, irrigation works established and desert land brought into cultivation. The Berber peoples increasingly took to settled life and many new cities were founded. To this day the ruins of mighty theatres and other monuments standing in what is now virtually desert land testify to the prosperity of the Roman period. The wealth of the Maghreb cities was not due only to their agriculture, for even at that time caravans were crossing the Sahara to West Africa and bringing back precious cargoes of gold and ivory.

Under the Roman Empire Christianity spread to the Maghreb, which produced one of the most revered of Christian scholars, St. Augustine of Hippo. But by this time the Roman Empire was already in the last stages of decay and excessive taxation and resulting over-farming were creating havoc on the Maghreb's agricultural system. As the Roman Empire in the west collapsed the Maghreb was over-run in AD 429 by the Germanic tribe known as the Vandals. Their kingdom in turn was destroyed in AD 534 by the forces of the Byzantine Empire, which under Justinian was attempting to recapture the lost western provinces. The Byzantine Empire, faced with mounting burdens of military expenditure, was oppressive and inefficient. It failed to keep the loyalty of the Berber peoples or to establish itself firmly in the country. In AD 670 Sidi Uqba began the long series of campaigns which culminated in the Arab conquest of the country. The decadent Byzantine administration offered little resistance but the Berbers held out desperately until AD 709. Thereafter they joined with their conquerors and participated in the Muslim conquests of Spain and Sicily.

The Arab conquest brought with it a major revolution through the introduction of Islam, which entirely replaced Christianity. Under the new religion the Maghreb went through a long series of political changes. Successive attempts were made to bring the whole area under unified political control together with Muslim Spain, and repeatedly they broke down, giving rise to kingdoms roughly corresponding to the present division into Morocco, Algeria and Tunisia. The city life of the Roman period continued to flourish and the Maghreb enjoyed a high level of cultural development in the early Muslim period.

The most important development between the Arab conquest and the nineteenth century, however, was the migration into the area of nomadic Bedouin Arab tribes generally known as the Beni Hillal and the Beni Sulaym. Their invasion began in the second half of the eleventh century. They infiltrated on to the cultivated land like a swarm of locusts and gradually spread westward from Tunisia to Morocco. The rulers often ignored or even encouraged this invasion for they saw in the newcomers valuable irregular troops who would be pleased to fight under any banner in return for land on which to settle. As the nomads spread out, their demands and the over-grazing of their animals tended to drive the settled cultivators off the land. Much agricultural land reverted to desert conditions. Towns diminished or were abandoned altogether and power shifted nearer to the coast where trade with the outside world still provided a measure of prosperity. All over the fertile lands of the Maghreb agriculture decayed and the intensive techniques of the past gave way to mixed farming of a very poor type. At the same time the coming of the Bedouin tribes brought considerable numbers of true Arabs into the Maghreb where previously they had been a tiny minority. Through intermarriage a high proportion of the Berbers were assimilated to the Arabs and the Arabic language became the normal everyday tongue for most of the population, except in mountainous areas such as the Atlas range in Morocco and the Kabylie mountains of Algeria, where the Berbers maintained their old language and culture together with a fierce spirit of independence.

As Muslim Spain receded before the progress of the Christian reconquest, the weakened Maghreb states suffered from repeated invasions from across the Straits of Gibraltar. In the fifteenth century Portuguese and Spanish strongholds were established on the coast though there was little attempt at outright conquest of the whole country. This Christian invasion in turn fired the spirit of national and religious resistance. As the states proved ineffective in fighting the infidels, religious organisations known as Brotherhoods sprang up to carry on the fight. In Algeria and Tunisia the Turks were invited to come to the aid of their fellow Muslims and in the sixteenth century seized control of these countries, which became incorporated in the Ottoman Empire.

In Morocco a new and vital dynasty, the Saadian, came to power and the Portuguese were drastically defeated at the Battle of the Three Kings in 1578. The victorious Moroccan ruler was killed in the course of the battle and his brother succeeded to the throne and the glory with the title of El Mansour (the victorious). He ruled from 1578-1610. He restored the power of the state in Morocco and then in 1591, hoping to increase his revenues in order to meet the expenses of his large army, he sent an expedition on a fantastic march across the Sahara to seize the Empire of Songhay, whence caravans brought gold to Morocco. The expedition succeeded in destroying the greatest of the Negro kingdoms of West Africa but it could not establish an effective administration to succeed it. El Mansour was temporarily enriched by the gold looted from Negro cities but in the long term the trade of his kingdom was damaged. After El Mansour's death, his sons fought for the crown and Morocco fell into chaos again until after 1660 when a new dynasty, the Alaouite, established itself. Under the energetic ruler Mulay Ismail (1672–1729), who based his power on a large army of Negro slaves from the Niger area, the kingdom once more knew unity and strong government, but after his death it split up again and, although the dynasty survived, by the beginning of the nineteenth century it effectively controlled only a part of the country.

In the rest of the Maghreb, Turkish administration declined, as it did in the whole Ottoman Empire. In Algeria the finances and prosperity of the state were heavily dependent on the profits of war at sea against the shipping of Christian powers. This not only led to a lack of attention to the administration and development of the hinterland, parts of which, like the Kabylie mountain area, were never brought under effective control, but also excited the hostile attention of European powers and the USA. By the nineteenth century all the Maghreb states were in a weak position for they had not been able to keep pace with the progress of western European countries. But where religion formed the basis of life, community of religion between the rulers and the people, even when the rulers were foreigners, assured them of a considerable measure of loyalty in face of any infidel power.

The peoples of Africa south of the Sahara

The Negro peoples who now occupy practically the whole of Africa south of the Sahara were once confined to a relatively small part of it. Their early place of origin and the course of their migrations have been much debated but no definite conclusions have been drawn. Nevertheless, it seems fairly certain that at one time Negro peoples were settled along the Sudanic belt to the south of the Sahara and for a considerable way into the Sahara itself at a time when it was more suitable for human habitation. South of this the whole of the rest of the continent was occupied by other races who are now known mainly by discoveries of their stone implements, cave paintings, and occasional skeletons. Throughout most of East, Central and Southern Africa the early inhabitants probably belonged to a race related to the Bushmen who still survive in parts of Southern Africa. They lived by hunting and gathering wild fruits and tubers. In part of East Africa skeletons and other remains suggest at one time the people there may have been similar to those of North Africa and the lower Nile valley, and in the Congo and parts of the West African forestlands the earliest inhabitants may have been related to the pygmies who still live in the Congo forests.

In course of time the Negroes of the eastern part of the Sudanic belt around the upper Nile valley tended to become different from the West African group. Their languages developed a very different pattern and their way of life became nomadic and pastoral, based on cattle. They probably also mixed to a considerable extent with the non-Negro peoples of the Nile valley. The Negroes of West Africa, where higher rainfall and the fertile lands of the inland delta of the Niger encouraged a sedentary way of life, became mainly agriculturalists, though there is a major exception in the case of the Fulani, who probably mixed extensively with the nomadic Tuareg of the desert. The two main sections of the Negro peoples were never entirely separate; migrations took place in both directions and some of the tribes around Lake Chad, for example, are thought to have come from further east.

The agricultural Negroes of West Africa were naturally able to develop much larger and more dense populations than those who relied exclusively on cattle-keeping. It is probable that they developed crops of their own from wild plants, and they also grew crops developed elsewhere. Then at a period in the remote past which is still unknown, they began to expand very rapidly. This may have been the result of the introduction of techniques for producing and using iron which made it possible to clear the bush more easily, and perhaps also of the introduction of new crops from Asia. Not only did they colonise the great forest areas of West Africa itself but one branch of them spread out of West Africa altogether and gradually spread over almost the whole of the continent south of the Sahara, giving rise to the great family of Bantu-speaking peoples.

These peoples have developed many different ways of life and hundreds of different languages, but they are called by a single name because, although the speakers of one language cannot understand the others, a study of the languages shows that they are related to one another and must have developed from a common origin. Recent research has shown that these Bantu languages are related to the languages of West Africa and probably developed out of one of them.

As the Bantu-speaking peoples advanced they gradually absorbed or expelled the previous inhabitants. In East Africa they came in contact with the cattle-keeping tribes known as the Nilotes and Southern Nilotes. The two groups, Bantu and Nilotes, have commonly been hostile to one another but they have also influenced each other. It may be that it was from contact with the Nilotes that some Bantu groups acquired the habit of cattle-keeping which they carried with them on their migrations to the south. The expansion of the Bantu over more than half the surface of Africa was a slow and gradual process taking hundreds of years. Though they began to enter Central Africa in the first few centuries AD Bantu colonisation of South Africa was not complete by the nineteenth century. The southern tip of the subcontinent and the area now known as South West Africa still provided a home for the earlier races which elsewhere had disappeared. Indeed the Bushmen and their relatives, the Hottentots, still form a significant element in the population of modern Botswana and South West Africa, and it is only recently that Bantu began to settle in significant numbers in the neighbourhood of Capetown.

For thousands of years the Negro peoples have been engaged in a tremendous enterprise which even to this day is not fully complete. They have had the task of opening up the vast African continent to settled agriculture. They are the true pioneers of Africa. When in addition it is remembered that millions of Africans were carried across the sea to the Americas and now form the vast majority of the population of the West Indies as well as a significant part of the population of both the American continents, the scale of their expansion can be realised. Inevitably this colossal colonising effort absorbed much of their energies.

The development of a complex material civilisation depends on the growth of large towns and the development of specialisation and division of labour. These in turn require a relatively dense population with a well-established agricultural system. Over much of Africa these conditions were lacking. Nature had still to be tamed or natural conditions precluded dense settlement. Furthermore, for geographical reasons, much of the continent was isolated from the contact with other peoples and cultures which is always the greatest stimulus to the development of new ideas and techniques. Thus over much of the continent the life of the average man has remained that of the simple peasant, tilling the land with the simplest of tools, living in a humble hut built of mud and thatched with grass or leaves, and recognising a political order no wider than that of his clan. But this is not the whole story. Wherever conditions were favourable Africans abundantly proved their ability for constructing complex political systems and mastering sophisticated techniques.

The kingdom of Kush

The upper Nile valley was one of these areas, where as we have seen (p. 8), the Negro kingdom of Kush, in spite of its isolation, preserved and modified the heritage of Egyptian civilisation for hundreds of years before being replaced by the Christian kingdoms of Nubia and later by the Funj Sultanate. Meroe, as the huge heaps of slag found around the site of the ancient city show, was a great centre of iron-working and may have been the main centre from which knowledge of the technique spread to other African peoples.

States of the western Sudan

The Sudanic belt of West Africa was particularly favourable to the development of complex civilisation. The fertility of the upper Niger area and modern Northern Nigeria encouraged the growth of a relatively dense agricultural population, well placed to trade local products and those of the forest belt for those of North Africa, using the caravan routes across the desert. In particular the presence of gold deposits in the western parts of the savannah and the adjacent forest was a powerful stimulus to trade. The powerful empire of Ghana, essentially a trading state, with its capital on the fringe of the Sahara, flourished from the eighth century AD until the latter half of the eleventh when it was attacked and destroyed by the Almoravids. The Almoravids arose as a movement of religious reform in Islam amongst the Tuareg of the western Sahara under the inspiration of a holy man who settled near the Senegal river. In addition to destroying the empire of Ghana they conquered most of the Maghreb and Spain.

The vacuum left by the collapse of ancient Ghana was filled in the thirteenth century AD by the rise of a new empire, the kingdom of Mali, based on the agriculture of the upper Niger valley but also actively engaged in the trans-Saharan trade. This kingdom became officially Muslim under the rule of its best-known king, Mansa Musa (1312–37) who made a pilgrimage to Mecca in 1324 and created a sensation in Cairo by his immense wealth and lavish gifts of gold. Under the Mali Empire West African towns like Timbuctu and Jenne became important centres of Islamic learning and scholarship and missionary activity. Internal disputes gradually weakened the Mali Empire and nomadic Tuareg from the desert and hostile neighbours from the south began to raid its provinces. When it finally crumbled in the fifteenth century its place was taken by the Songhai Empire, which had its base in what had once been the easternmost province of Mali. Songhai was the largest of the West African Sudanic kingdoms. It was a great Islamic centre and exercised a wide influence, particularly on the Hausa towns of modern Northern Nigeria which were growing into important centres of trade and civilisation. It was destroyed in the sixteenth century by the Spanish mercenaries of El Mansour, the king of Morocco, who sent his forces across the desert to capture the sources of the rich gold trade. The Moroccan army broke up the Songhai Empire but failed to provide a stable alternative government. New kingdoms like the Bambara states of Segu and Kaarta arose, but the collapse of the old order was a grievous blow for the cause of Islam in West Africa. The religion did not die out and a community of learned men still survived who kept alive the tradition of scholarship and contact with the holy places of Arabia, but they often found themselves living under pagan or near pagan rulers who did not respect Islamic law but feared the political power of the Muslim holy men.

To the east of Songhai and the Hausa city states, a powerful kingdom developed in Kanem, north-east of Lake Chad, which traded in slaves and ivory with Tripoli in modern Libya. The precise date of the kingdom's foundation is not known but it was possibly between AD 700 and 800. The conversion of one of the early rulers to Islam provoked a split in the ruling family, and long drawn out hostilities between the two sections led the royal family to flee south into Bornu in 1384. The Kanem-Bornu Kingdom, thanks to the energy of some of its rulers, for example Mai Idris Alooma (1571–1603), was able to conquer many of the earlier tribes of the Bornu area and incorporate them permanently into itself. At its high point it controlled the Fezzan, now a province of Libya, and in spite of the attacks of many enemies it was still powerful in the nineteenth century and survives as an important element in Northern Nigeria today. Further east still the states of Bagirmi, Wadai and Darfur stretched out to meet the Funj Sultanate of the Nile valley.

West African forest kingdoms

Though the Sudanic belt was particularly favourable for the development of complex societies it did not have a monopoly. The forest and its fringes in West Africa also saw the rise of powerful kingdoms. Amongst the most remarkable of these was the civilisation of the Yoruba peoples in what is now Western Nigeria. Its ancient centre was the town of Ife, with its magnificent artistic tradition of bronze casting and modelling in terra cotta, its stone carvings and monoliths and the potsherd floors of its tightly packed mud houses. Under its cultural influence a whole series of city-states grew up, some in the heart of the forest, others well to the north of it, each ruled by a king, who possessed some of the attributes of divinity, and a complex hierarchy of chiefs.

During the fourteenth century one of these city-states, Oyo, near the northern limits of Yoruba settlement, became an important military power and built up a supremacy over other towns which extended outside the limits of modern Nigeria to neighbouring Dahomey. One of the cities which experienced the influence of Ife was the town of Benin amongst the Edo people. It in turn became a powerful empire with a highly developed bronze casting tradition based on that of Ife, and exercised influence over a wide area. It was already a powerful state when Portuguese travellers arrived there in 1485 and is today the capital of the Mid-West state in the Nigerian Federation.

Another kingdom whose history is closely bound up with that of the Yoruba is Dahomey. It emerged as a powerful state in the eighteenth century when Agaja Trudo conquered the small city-states of the Aja people and brought them under unified control (1724–30). Dahomey developed a highly complex administrative system including a method of maintaining an accurate population census. It was dominated by Oyo throughout most of the eighteenth century, but strengthened itself through the slave trade with Europeans. In the nineteenth century it was able to assert its independence and engaged in a series of ferocious wars against the Yoruba.

Further west the powerful kingdom of Asante was founded in the late seventeenth century by Osei Tuto, who bound a number of small Akan states together in a federation under the paramountcy of the Asantehene. The association was given permanence by the religious reverence attached to the golden stool, the symbol of Asante unity, and by the nature of the military system. Originally created as a measure of self-defence, the Asante Empire soon became the dominant power in the area of modern Ghana. It was at its height in the early years of the nineteenth century.

In addition to these particularly powerful states there were many others which though less extensive showed a high degree of administrative complexity and sophistication: the Fante states of the coast of modern Ghana, the city-states of the Niger delta area, the rich commercial cities of Hausaland, the mysterious kingdom of the Kwororafa on the Benue, which suddenly expanded vigorously in the seventeenth century and then rapidly declined; and the kingdom of the Nupe with its complicated political system and its tradition of handicrafts.

Though the peoples with large-scale political structures have naturally tended to receive the greatest attention from the historians it should not be thought that the culture and skills of those whose political life was organised around clan villages was necessarily inferior. Peoples like the Ibo of modern Nigeria may not have built large kingdoms, but they produced bronzeworks of great beauty.

Kingdoms of the Congo

Further south, down the western coast of Africa, the land around the southern banks of the Congo river, where the forest gives way to savannah, was the centre of a complex and powerful kingdom which attracted the attention of the early Portuguese travellers. The Portuguese, who made contact with the kingdom in 1483, hoped to convert the king and people to Christianity and to build up the Congo Kingdom as a powerful Christian ally. Mbemba-a-Nzinga, who took the name Dom Affonso, the most famous of the Congo kings (1506–40), gave himself wholeheartedly to the project but the Portuguese expected to be reimbursed for their expenses in slaves, the only commodity the Congolese had to sell which could command a large market. Gradually the slave trade corrupted the fabric of the kingdom and the Portuguese connection became a curse rather than a blessing. By the eighteenth century the kingdom had almost ceased to exist as an effective political system, though its memory persists amongst the Bakongo people of modern Congo (Kinshasa), Congo (Brazzaville) and Angola. Further in to the interior of the Congo the Luba people developed a powerful state, possibly as early as AD 1500, which had a far-reaching influence and stimulated the development of other political systems. Amongst these was the powerful kingdom of the Lunda of Katanga under their king, the Mwata Yamvo. This state benefited from trade with the Portuguese. It was at its height in the eighteenth century when one of its armies under a general called Cazembe established a Lunda Kingdom on the Luapula river in modern Zambia. Also in the Congo area was the kingdom of Bakuba with its tradition of beautiful wood carving.

The East African trading cities

The East African coastline was visited by ships trading in the Indian Ocean from very remote times. An account written in the first century AD mentions that there was a large port, possibly on the Tanganyika coast, called Rhapta, where Arab merchants settled and intermarried with the African population. Later, Persian and Arab refugees from political persecution settled on the East African coast and a chain of towns grew up stretching from Mogadishu in modern Somalia to Sofala in Mozambique. The population of these towns was a mixture of Arab and Bantu. There the Swahili language was developed, a basically Bantu tongue with strong Arabic influences which now forms a common language in much of East Africa and is widely spoken in the Congo also. The East African coastal cities lived largely by trading in ivory and other African commodities. Sofala also exported considerable quantities of gold and iron which was considered to be of the highest quality for making sword blades. These goods were taken to India and China by Arab ships which in return imported Chinese porcelain and Indian and Chinese cloths. The Chinese themselves made two voyages to the East African coast, but the direct trade contact was not maintained. Diplomatic relations survived, however, and early in the fifteenth century the ruler of Malindi sent a giraffe as a present to the Chinese Emperor. In the towns the richer citizens enjoyed a high standard of living and were dressed in the most expensive cloths of the East. Kilwa boasted neat streets of stone houses and a large mosque. Some towns minted their own coins and Islamic scholarship was eagerly pursued. The arrival of the Portuguese in the fifteenth century brought the golden age of the East African cities to an end. The Portuguese, inspired by a mixture of greed and religious enthusiasm, brutally pillaged the cities and largely destroyed their trade. Thereafter they mouldered on, a shadow of their former glory, until the coming of the Omani ruler, Sayyid Sa'id, to Zanzibar in the nineteenth century infused new life into the old trading system.

Civilisations of East Africa

In the interior, the fertile area of the inter-lacustrine region was a natural centre of African civilisation. Legends speak of a mysterious people called the Bachwezi and an ancient kingdom of Kitwara. Whatever the truth of those legends may be, the discovery of ancient earthworks shows that powerful states existed there in remote times. In more recent periods the area saw the rise of a series of related kingdoms, Bunyoro, Ankole, Buganda, Toro, and Busoga.

Bunyoro, one of the oldest, was for long the most powerful, but during the eighteenth century the newer state of Buganda with its highly centralised administrative system and efficient military force began to get the upper hand. Further south in the mountainous areas around Lake Kivu there were the two powerful kingdoms of Rwanda and Urundi, each ruled by an aristocracy of cattle keepers, probably of Nilotic descent.

Civilisations of Central Africa

The area south of Lake Tanganyika and north of the Zambesi river (now occupied by the Republics of Zambia and Malawi and the Portuguese colony of Mozambique) is one of the great crossroads in African history.

The first Bantu probably arrived there soon after the beginning of the Christian era and thereafter successive groups of immigrants came into the country, steadily driving out or absorbing the earlier population of bushmen and pygmies. These first waves of Bantu settlement seem to have come from the north and the early Bantu settlers brought with them the art of cattle-keeping which they took on their further migrations across the Zambesi into Rhodesia and South Africa.

Long after these immigrants from the north another chain of migrants began to move into the area, this time from the west. The centre of this movement seems to have been the area occupied by the Luba and Lunda peoples on the Katanga plateau of the Congo, and its cause may have been the political upheavals in those two kingdoms which have been mentioned earlier. Some of the earliest of these immigrants from the west were the Yao and Macua and the Chewa and other related peoples who are known as the Malawi or Maravi. The present Republic of Malawi is named after them. They established a network of inter-related kingdoms in modern Malawi and the eastern part of modern Zambia. These kingdoms were in contact with the Portuguese from the sixteenth century. In the late seventeenth and eighteenth centuries still further migrations from the Luba-Lunda area took place. These included the Bisa and the Bemba who built up a powerful kingdom around Lake Bangweulu. The establishment of the Lunda kingdom of Kazembe on the Luapula River by one of the generals of the Lunda king, Mwata Yamvo, in the eighteenth century was one of the latest of these migrations. It is also probable that a migratory group from the Luba-Lunda area was responsible for building up the powerful kingdom of Lozi on the flood plain of the upper Zambesi.

These migratory groups from the west brought with them their custom of matrilineal descent and a predominantly agricultural culture. They largely overlaid the previous migrations from the north, though some peoples who belonged to the earlier group survived and maintained their cultural identity. It is because of the west to east migrations that there has come to be a great belt of matrilineal agricultural peoples known as the Central Bantu separating the patrilineal cattle-keeping peoples of East Africa from the patrilineal cattle-keepers of South Africa who probably originated from them.

South of the Zambesi in modern Rhodesia there arose one of the most extensive and interesting African kingdoms. This was the empire of Mwene Mutapa, which built elaborate stone buildings at Zimbabwe and many other sites. Its origin is lost in obscurity but it was certainly flourishing by AD 950 when the Arab traveller, al Musudi, visited East Africa. Its prosperity was based on the export of gold and other minerals from innumerable small diggings which were sold to Arab traders at Sofala. When the Portuguese seized Sofala from the Arabs they made contact with the empire and established markets at Sena and Tete on the Zambesi as well as at other points in the kingdom. Portuguese traders took advantage of quarrels in the ruling family to gain concessions of land for themselves and to bring the king under their control. The kingdom was weakened to the verge of collapse, but in the late seventeenth and early eighteenth centuries a new group, which had once been tributary to the Mwene Mutapa, made its appearance. This was the Rozwi under a dynasty of rules called Shangamire. They defeated the Portuguese and though they did not expel them altogether they confined their occupation to Sena and Tete and a few points on the coast. Under the Rozwi the old stone building culture flourished again and in the eighteenth century the buildings at Zimbabwe were enlarged to the impressive size of the ruins which now survive. At the beginning of the nine-

teenth century Mwene Mutapa under its new rulers appeared as strong
as ever.

External influences on Africa before 1800:
Islam and the Arabs

The most important external influence on Africa before the nineteenth century was that of the Arabs and Islam, and it may be worth
pausing for a moment to examine some of the most striking characteristics of a cultural system which has vitally influenced the life of a
very large part of the continent.

The Prophet Mohammed and the founding of the
Islamic community

The Holy Prophet Mohammed was born in AD 570 and brought up
in Mecca, a trading city on an important caravan route through
Arabia. He had visions in which he believed that he received direct
messages from God (Allah) through the Angel Gabriel. These
divine messages were written down without modification and make
up the Koran. This holy book is therefore for all Muslims the direct
word of God, recorded in the original Arabic words used in the
Revelation. It contains injunctions to believe in the unity of God
and the duty of prayer, but also many commands of a moral or even
legal nature. As Mohammed became well known and began to gather
a body of disciples around him he became unpopular in his native
city where it was believed that his attacks on idol-worship would
damage the trade derived from pilgrims who visited the pagan shrines
of the city. In AD 622 he and his followers fled on what is called the
Hijra to the neighbouring city of Medina and a separate religious
community was constituted under the authority of the Prophet.
In this community there was naturally no distinction between the
church and society, or between civil and religious laws. The whole
society was a religious body, its ruler was the Prophet of God, and
its whole life was dedicated to God. In 630 Mohammed and his
followers conquered Mecca and under his successors the Islamic
community engaged in a fantastic career of conquest and expansion.
But because of its early history the Muslim community has always
regarded itself in theory as a single religious body in which religious
belief and conformity to religious law is the qualification for member-

ship. Other religious bodies which believed in a single God and had written scriptures were recognised by the Prophet. He laid down that they should be well treated, protected and left free to practise their religion, but they could never become part of the Islamic community itself. They were not supposed to participate in military service in Islamic countries or to take part in affairs of state, but they paid a special tax, the Jizya, in return for protection.

The development of Islamic civilisation

Within the Muslim community itself there was no distinction in theory between religious and civil affairs. The words of the Koran, the practice of the Prophet and the way of life of the early community as handed down by tradition constituted a basic law, the Sharia, which every Muslim, whether ruler or commoner, was bound to respect. This law was administered by learned men known as Qadis. The Prophet himself and the Caliphs or deputies who succeeded him were both political and religious heads of the community they governed, and they led the people in prayer. There was never a formal hierarchy of priests similar to that of the Roman Catholics; any good Muslim could lead prayer in the mosques. In practice, however, this duty was generally the prerogative of learned men known as Imams who, together with the Qadis, made up the class of Ulama or men of learning, one of the most influential bodies in any Islamic society. As the Arab conquests gave them control of Persia, most of the lands of the Eastern Roman Empire, Egypt and North Africa, they became heirs to the greatest civilisation in the world of the time. For centuries they were far in advance of western Europe and preserved and expanded the wisdom they inherited from others. Philosophy, poetry, mathematics, medicine, architecture and many other arts were cultivated while education was developed to a high level in the Madrasas, as Muslim universities were called, with their magnificent libraries. For centuries scholars laboured on codifying the Sharia law and eventually four great schools, Hanbalite, Malikite, Shafiite, and Hanafite emerged. They differ slightly in interpretation but recognise one another as valid.

In spite of the vast area covered by the Arab conquests the Islamic community has never ceased to feel itself a single body, and this has been reinforced by the spread of Arabic as the universal language of learning and often of everyday speech throughout the Muslim world, by the custom of facing towards Mecca during prayers, and by the duty which every good Muslim feels of making a pilgrimage to the holy places if he can possibly afford it. Every year this brings Muslims from the most remote parts to Mecca and Medina, and powerfully emphasises the unity of the religious community.

The caliphate and the nature of the Islamic political system

At first in practice, and always in theory, the whole Islamic community had one head, the Caliph or deputy of the Prophet, but early in the history of Islam disagreement occurred about the qualifications for rulership. Ali, the son-in-law of the Prophet, became the fourth Caliph in 656, but he was challenged by Muawiya, who used the strength of the army in Syria to secure his overthrow and founded the Ummayad dynasty of Caliphs in 661. This led to a split between those who believed that the only person entitled to lead the Islamic community must be a member of the family of the Prophet and the direct descendant of Ali and Fatima, the Prophet's daughter (they are called Shiites), and those who felt that the choice of a leader depended on the will of the community (these are the Sunni). As the direct line of descendants from Ali was broken some Shiites developed the theory that the last true Caliph had disappeared and would come back to earth in the fullness of time as the saviour or Mahdi to be the head of the whole Muslim body and restore the faith to perfection. Generally the Sunni group were politically more successful than the Shiites, but Shiite dynasties arose from time to time in Africa as well as elsewhere. Shiism is still dominant in Persia, and in other parts of the world there are powerful Shiite groups like the Ismailiya which has many adherents in East Africa and the Ahmaddiyya, one of the most active Muslim missionary bodies in West Africa.

Although all Muslims believed that there ought to be one head of the whole community, political unity did not survive after AD 750. Quarrels over who should be the true Caliph led to the rise of separate Caliphates. The most important Caliphs, those in Baghdad, fell under the control of the commanders of their Turkish bodyguards who took the title of Sultan, reducing the Caliphs to mere figureheads.

The slave soldiery who ruled Egypt under the name of Mamelukes from 1259 to 1517, maintained a nominal Caliph in Cairo, but when Egypt fell to the forces of the Ottoman Turks in 1517 the authority of the Caliph was taken over by the Turkish Sultan. Nevertheless the belief in unity continued, and is inseparable from the religious beliefs of Islam. What is more, throughout the Muslim world a fairly uniform pattern of government emerged. Every community was governed by a single head who might be called Caliph if he believed that he was entitled to be the supreme head of all Muslims, otherwise Sultan if he was very powerful, or alternatively Emir. This word simply means commander and one of the titles of the Caliph is Emir al-Muminin (Commander of the Faithful). Under the head there was always a chief minister known as Wazir, and judges called Qadis who administered the Sharia. All rulers in theory recognised this as the highest law, but in practice they also applied a good deal of executive law, administered through the Wazirs rather than the Qadis, concerning matters not covered by the Sharia. Revolutions have been common in the Islamic world, but until very recent times they never took the form of trying to replace this type of government by some other system such as representative democracy, but simply of attempts to purify the system or to place someone who was believed to be the rightful ruler on the throne. As Shiite beliefs became widespread even in Sunni areas, claim to descent from the Prophet often formed the basis of claims of political authority. (Such people are called Sharifs or Sayyids.) From time to time also people have appeared in various parts of the Islamic world claiming to be the Mahdi and therefore rightful rulers of the whole Muslim world.

The Sufi brotherhoods

One of the most important forms of organisation in the Islamic world is that of the Sufi brotherhoods. Islam is very much a written religion with hard and fast doctrines and set duties. Some people found the mere conformity to the religious commands of their faith too cold and formal. They formed associations dedicated to the contemplation of God and the attempt to enter into a mystic sense of unity with him. Though they conformed to the requirements of prayer and other duties they laid more emphasis on the emotional side of religion, the love of God rather than formal obedience to his commands and correctness of belief. These brotherhoods appealed particularly to the less educated who could not read for themselves, and the brotherhoods became the most powerful missionary organisation in Islam. Their number is very large. Some run right through the Muslim world; others are local. Most of them have a strong sense of community and often revere their founders as saints. Inevitably the brotherhoods have often wielded political power and because of the closeness within their ranks they are often jealous or even hostile to one another and to all powers outside themselves. It sometimes happened that when people belonging to different tribes became converted to Islam they joined different brotherhoods and kept up their feuds.

The impact of Islam in Africa

The influence of Islam in Africa has been, and is, enormous. After the Arab conquest of Egypt in AD 640 that country became over-whelmingly Muslim, though a substantial Christian community survives. Arabic became the language of daily life as well as of learn-ing, and Islamic law set the pattern of existence. From Egypt Islam travelled up the Nile and became the religion of the Funj Sultanate in the northern part of the present Sudan. In the Maghreb also Islam became dominant after the Arab conquest, and from there it was carried along the caravan routes across the Sahara to establish itself in the states of the Sudanic belt. From there in turn it has been and still is being carried south into the forest lands. Today it is estimated that roughly 45 per cent of the population of Nigeria, which has far more people than any other West African state, is Muslim. In East Africa also Islam was brought by Arab traders and refugees to the coastal city-states. It established itself firmly there and spread inland along the caravan routes. In the nineteenth century Muslim communities had begun to arise as far inland as the inter-lacustrine region.

European influence on Africa before 1800

In comparison with the effects of the Arab invasions and the coming of Islam, European contacts were much less significant. Only at the southern end of the continent could they be said to have had results for the life of African peoples in any way like those of Islam.

The Portuguese

Apart from the northern coastline of Africa, which was always in contact with European states across the Mediterranean, European contact with Africa began with the voyages of the Portuguese in the fifteenth century. They were inspired by a mixture of economic, military and religious motives. The Portuguese wanted first to discover a route of their own to the gold of West Africa which did not pass through the hands of their traditional enemies, the Muslims of the Maghreb. Later they sought a direct sea route to India and its rich trade. They also hoped to find in Africa the legendary Christian king known as Prester John who they felt would prove an invaluable ally and enable them to attack the Muslims from the rear. They also sought to convert Africans to Christianity and to develop alliances with African kingdoms who would give them trade advantages and possibly military assistance. Their voyages brought them first to West Africa in 1482 when they established a fort on the coast of modern Ghana called Sao Jorge de Mina (now known as Elmina castle). There they traded for gold and succeeded in diverting part of the supplies from the northern route. They also made contact with the empire of Benin and colonised the islands São Tomé and Principe. Their attempts at evangelisation were far from successful, and increasingly they turned their attention to the slave trade.

Their policy of building up Christian allies in Africa was centred in the Congo, but as we have seen the plan was compromised by dependence on the slave trade and ended in collapse. In neighbouring Angola the Portuguese established a more permanent settlement after 1576. This was essentially a colony of slave traders who used native agents to maintain the supply of human beings to be loaded on the ships for transport across the sea to Brazil. Though the capital of the settlement, Luanda, was rich enough to be described in the eighteenth century as Lisbon in Africa, its prosperity rested on a very slender basis and the settlement had little direct effect on development inland apart from encouraging wars and supplying arms which ambitious rulers could use to strengthen and expand their kingdoms.

When they rounded the Cape and reached the East African coast the Portuguese found the flourishing Muslim trading cities. The Portuguese intrusion, however, had disastrous results on their prosperity and threw the old trading system into a long period of decline and decay. Only in Mozambique did the Portuguese acquire a permanent foothold. They were attracted by the gold trade of the Mwene Mutapa Empire and succeeded in establishing trading posts within the heart of the kingdom. By adapting themselves to African conditions the local Portuguese acquired a great deal of influence in the empire and virtually brought the king of Mwene Mutapa under their control. But their numbers were always very small indeed and their behaviour was often such as to make them very unpopular. With the rise of the Rozwi in the late seventeenth century their wide influence and landholdings disappeared and by the beginning of the nineteenth century Portuguese influence in Mozambique hardly extended beyond gunshot range from their forts.

In addition to establishing two small white communities in Angola and Mozambique the Portuguese contributed in two ways to African development. In the first place they were responsible for introducing a whole range of new crops which had their natural home in South America. These included cassava, maize, groundnuts and tobacco. Some of these, particularly cassava and maize, have been of tremendous importance as they have come to form the staple diet of large sections of the African population, partially replacing the indigenous millets and yams. The effect which this has had on the development of Africa can only be guessed at, but it must be enormous. The second way in which the Portuguese influenced Africa was through the introduction of the Atlantic slave trade.

The slave trade

There had always been a slave trade with the Arabs in parts of Africa, and in North Africa European slaves were bought and sold, but the trade across the Atlantic was to eclipse in scale anything of the kind that had happened before. At first the Portuguese were mainly interested in the gold trade but they always wanted slaves to sell in Portugal where there was a great shortage of labour. In time the number of African slaves in Portugal was estimated to form about 5 per cent of the population. But the slave trade only became really massive with the development of sugar planting on São Tomé and its later transference to Brazil and the West Indies. This created an almost unlimited demand for labour. The Portuguese, the Dutch, the Danes, the French and the British transported millions of Africans across the Atlantic. The Portuguese mainly traded from Angola though in the eighteenth century they revived their West African trade from the coast of modern Dahomey. The other nations traded mainly from West Africa and there the British succeeded in controlling the major portion.

The trans-Atlantic slave trade is one of the greatest crimes in all human history whether we think of the personal sufferings of the captives, their treatment on board ship, the degradation and humiliation of the life to which they were doomed or the misery, loss of life and brutalization which it brought to the African communities from which the slaves were taken. Undoubtedly this colossal business in human beings had terrible and widespread effects on the development of African societies, making warfare profitable, supplying the firearms which made it more deadly, encouraging militarism and a callous attitude to the value and dignity of human life.

Nevertheless it should not be imagined that the slave trade completely dominated the development of African societies. On the contrary, the period of the slave trade was one in which some of the most important and impressive African kingdoms developed or reached their high point and a study of their history shows that the slave trade in many cases played a relatively minor part in their lives. Throughout most of Africa south of the Sahara, therefore, pre-nineteenth-century European contacts were relatively superficial. The Europeans were confined to a few forts along the coast; the indirect effects of the slave trade may have been great but the direct impact of European culture was minimal.

The Cape Colony

An exception to this is found in South Africa where the Dutch East India Company established a small colony at the Cape of Good Hope to provide fresh vegetables for its ships travelling to India. In the healthy climate this tiny white community began to expand vigorously. As it did so it took away the land of the aboriginal Bushmen and Hottentots, fighting and largely destroying the Bushmen and turning the Hottentots into labourers on white farms. By the nineteenth century this community, still growing rapidly, was in contact with the advance guard of the Bantu who were pushing steadily southward.

The changed situation in the nineteenth century

Up to the nineteenth century the main direct influence on African societies was that of Islam, and over the greater part of the continent African peoples continued to evolve their own cultural systems without much interference or stimulus from outside the continent. During the nineteenth century, however, Africa underwent a dramatic period of revolutionary change which is still continuing. Part of this process was due to external factors. The Industrial Revolution was already under way in Britain, and Europe would soon be looking to Africa as a source of raw materials and as a market for the goods produced by the new factories. Europe was also acquiring technical means which would make it relatively easy to break down the physical barriers to penetration into Africa and an overwhelming military power sufficient to annihilate resistance. At the same time the social changes brought about by the Industrial Revolution aroused stirrings of conscience. A more vital attitude to religion sprang up, a hostility to the slave trade, and a desire to convert the heathen which went well with a situation in which it seemed more profitable to trade with Africans in Africa than to export them elsewhere, and in which Christian conversion seemed necessarily to imply the adoption of European tastes and a demand for European goods. Thus through traders and dedicated missionaries Europe began to exert an influence by actually changing African societies in the light of Christian ideas. This inevitably brought with it political consequences. European political authority gradually extended itself until under the influence of almost hysterical competition between the European powers it culminated in the Scramble for Africa which brought the vast preponderance of the continent under the control of European states.

Internal movements in nineteenth-century Africa

It must not be thought, however, that the revolutionary changes in African history were all the result of external influence. By the beginning of the nineteenth century internal stresses within the continent were preparing the way for two massive movements. In West Africa the inevitable tensions between Muslims and Pagan rulers that resulted from the situation caused by the fall of Songhay were coming to a head and preparing the way for a whole series of religious movements known as the West African jihads.

In South Africa population pressure in Zululand had already set in motion a process which was to culminate in the dramatic rise of the Zulu as a military power and a vast series of wars and migrations which vitally affected the whole history of South and Central Africa.

Content and divisions of the two volumes

The Partition of Africa between European powers forms a natural division in the history of Africa since the beginning of the nineteenth century. Subsequent developments took place within the new borders imposed by colonialism which often bore little logical relationship to older divisions between tribes and peoples. From this point on the story is of the struggle of African peoples to master the techniques of their white rulers, of their regaining their independence and the developments which have followed and created the picture of Africa as it is today.

It is with this revolutionary period in African history that this book is concerned. The first volume will deal with the changes leading up to Partition, and the second with developments from then till the present. Our purpose is to describe the development of the African peoples themselves and to deal with external influences from the point of view of their effects on Africa rather than as a subject in their own right. For this purpose it is necessary to look closely at the histories of particular peoples rather than just at continent-wide developments, and we have found it necessary to study the continent region by region. The development of the continent will throughout be treated in accordance with these regions, except for the case of the process of Partition itself which is most easily looked at from a continental point of view. The regions have been chosen on historical grounds. Africa north of the Sahara forms a natural unit of study and with this is connected the history of the Nile valley and neighbouring Ethiopia. West Africa, again, is a convenient unit from the geographical and historical points of view. In talking of the great block of Africa from the Congo to East Africa as another division we had in mind the effects of Arab penetration from the East African coast to the Congo in the nineteenth century. Finally Southern and Central Africa, including South Africa, Rhodesia, Zambia, Malawi and Mozambique, have links which make it convenient to group them together. It should not be thought, however, that these regions are absolute, or that they have any other purpose than as a convenience to avoid the difficulty of trying to talk about everything at once. There are no sharp divisions between the peoples of the continent and the history of every African people is connected with that of its neighbours in a great network which covers the continent without a break. It would be perfectly possible to use different divisions from those we have chosen; any such divisions are arbitrary and useful only as an aid to explanation.

Part **one**

Northern Africa

1 Egypt from the Napoleonic Invasion to the British Occupation

Egypt, an Arab nation

As was pointed out in the Introduction, Egypt had lived under a series of foreign rulers ever since the defeat and conquest of the last dynasty of pharaohs in 341 BC. Of these foreign rulers the Arabs who conquered the country from the Eastern Roman (Byzantine) Empire in AD 642 made the most profound impact on its life. From the Arab conquest began the process which led to the adoption of Islam as the religion of the overwhelming majority of the population. As Islam is not just a matter of personal beliefs but a comprehensive way of life, the adoption of the religion has influenced every aspect of the peoples' existence. The administrative and legal systems, family life, education and the attitude of the people to life and to other peoples have all been profoundly influenced by Islam. This, together with the fact that Arabic became the language of the people, almost completely replacing the native Egyptian tongue, and the considerable admixture of Arab blood, accounts for the situation in which Egypt to this day regards itself as an Arab state with ties to the Middle East as well as Africa. Islam is still such a powerful force in the country that there has recently been a danger that the Muslim Brotherhood, a fanatically religious organisation, would assassinate the President in order to establish a system of government based on their religious beliefs.

The Copts

Although Egypt after the Arab conquest became, and has remained, an Islamic society there always survived a substantial community of Christians who are known as the Copts. These Christians, who are still a large community today, occupied an ambiguous position in Egyptian society. Under Muslim law they were entitled to protection but could not be full members of the state. They often held important posts in the service of the state but they were distrusted and disliked by their Muslim fellow subjects.

The Mamelukes 1249-1517

After the Arab conquest Egypt was at first part of the vast empire established by the early Caliphs, but with the break up of the political unity of Islam it fell under a number of different dynasties in succession. In 1249 the slave bodyguard of the ruler (who belonged to a dynasty known as Ayyubid) seized power. This was the beginning of a long period in which Egypt was governed by a military class of ex-slaves of foreign origin. These slave rulers were recruited from Turkey and South Russia and were known as Mamelukes. They gave Egypt one of the most glorious periods in its history and the magnificent buildings erected under the Mamelukes are still among the wonders of modern Cairo. But the Mamelukes weakened their power and wasted the resources of the country in internal struggles for power. They divided up the land of Egypt between themselves and forced the peasants to pay heavy taxes. They failed to keep up with progress in the rest of the world and in 1517 they were utterly defeated by the forces of the Ottoman Sultan of Turkey.

Egypt under the Ottoman Empire

Thereafter Egypt became a part of the Ottoman Sultanate. At first the new rulers introduced many welcome improvements. Regular centralised administration was established, taxes were lightened, irrigation canals were cleared and improved and the country became prosperous again. But in time the Ottoman Sultanate fell into decline. The sultan's administration became weak and corrupt, and the generals and other officers in the provinces were left to do much as they pleased. In these circumstances the Ottoman officials in Egypt began recruiting their own slave bodyguards and the Mameluke system was revived in a new form. By the eighteenth century Ottoman authority had so declined that the sultans had virtually no influence in the country which was still officially part of their empire. The real rulers of the land were the Mamelukes headed by officers known as beys. Only the bitter rivalries between the beys, which gave the Ottoman ruler the chance to play one faction off against another,

36

prevented the Mameluke Beys from establishing complete independence. Inside Egypt one Mameluke band fought against another to make its leader the most powerful figure in the country. Bloody battles were fought in the streets, the shops of merchants were looted and the peasants, or fellahin as they are called, were unmercifully overtaxed to support the fighting bands of their overlords.

In these grim circumstances the peasants began to neglect the cultivation of the land, the irrigation system deteriorated, merchants were unable to make improvements in commerce or industry, and the once prosperous country became steadily poorer, falling far behind the developments that were taking place in western Europe. The Mamelukes themselves were so absorbed in the continual struggle for power that they did not even keep abreast of changes in military methods and continued to cling to long outdated methods of warfare on horseback. To complete the miseries of Egypt the land was subject to repeated epidemics of plague and the population dwindled from about eight and a half million in the fourteenth century to about three million at the beginning of the nineteenth century.

Napoleon Bonaparte

Napoleon invades Egypt

In 1798 the course of Egyptian history was suddenly and violently altered when Napoleon with his French forces landed on Egyptian soil. His reasons for making this move were complex. Amongst

the ideas of the French Revolution, of which he considered himself
the leader, was the belief that there should be a universal law for all
humanity, and that the whole human race should be liberated to
enjoy the ideals of Liberty, Equality and Fraternity as well as other
aspects of the French revolutionary system. Although a soldier,
Napoleon had a real interest in, and respect for, the ancient Egyptian
civilisation, and his army included a large team of scholars and experts
to study the monuments of the land he was about to conquer. His
deeper reasons were less unselfish. As he told his government in
France, his main objects were to ensure the exploitation of the riches
of the country for the benefit of France and to use it as a stepping
stone for the conquest of the British Empire in India.

The Battle of the Pyramids

When Napoleon's forces reached Egypt power was in the hands of
two notoriously quarrelsome beys, Murad Bey and Ibrahim Bey.
The mass of the people, long used to being passive spectators as
one group of foreigners after another seized their country and worn
out by the oppressions of their Mameluke overlords, could hardly
be expected to rally to the defence of their masters, even against an
infidel invader. The Mamelukes themselves were militarily years
out of date and in no position to offer serious resistance to the French
army. Their magnificently clad horses and riders fell in heaps before
the accurate musket and cannon fire of the French at the Battle of the
Pyramids (1798), and Napoleon made himself the master of Egypt.

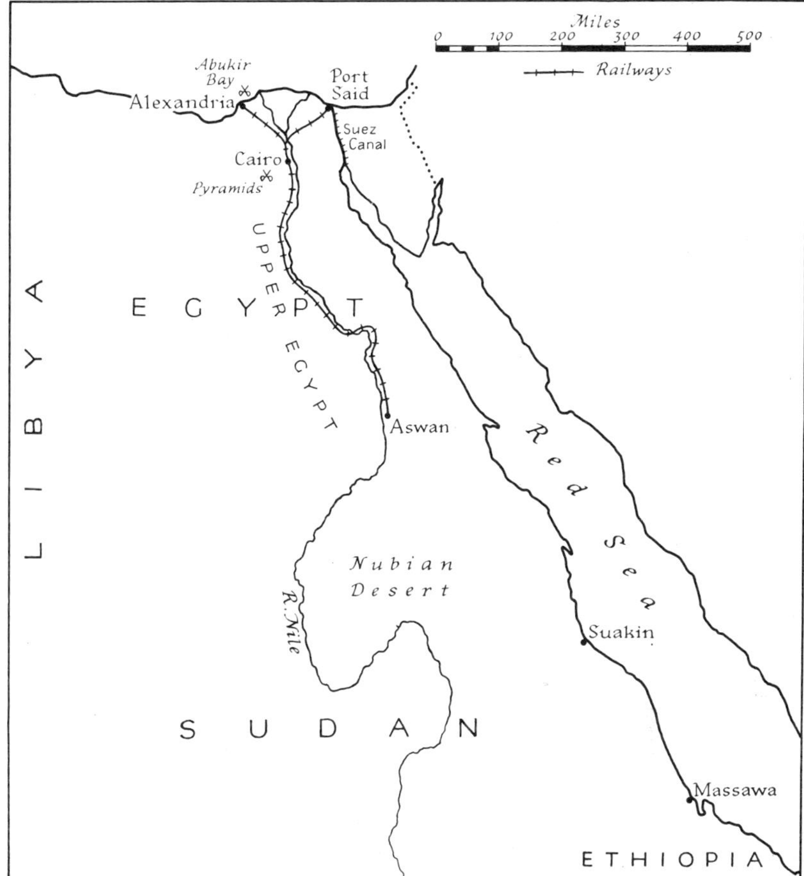

2 Egypt in the nineteenth century

Consequences of Napoleon's invasion

The Napoleonic conquest of Egypt, even though it lasted for no more than three years, had important consequences for the history of Egypt and the entire Arab world. Ever since the ending of the Crusades (towards the end of the thirteenth century) the heart of the Islamic world in Egypt and the Middle East had been free from serious attack from Christian Europe. During the later Ottoman period the whole area had become increasingly backward and out of date in contrast with Europe. But because of belief in the superiority of the

Islamic religion this was not obvious to the peoples of those areas, who had continued to drift complacently downhill. The unexpected conquest of Egypt, the most powerful province of the Ottoman Empire, by Christian forces suddenly made the real situation painfully clear. Thereafter the whole Islamic world began to be agitated by reforming movements of one kind and another. Some aimed at the adoption of European ideas and their reconciliation with Islam, others at sweeping away corruption and a return to the purity of the original faith. All were aimed at wiping out the shame of the weak position of Muslims in relation to Christian Europe and restoring the power and prestige of Islam. This movement was felt throughout the whole Ottoman Empire and as far as Afghanistan and Northern India. In Africa it influenced not only Egypt itself but the Eastern Sudan, Somalia, Libya and the Sudanic belt of West Africa. It was the beginning of a revolution in thought and attitudes as well as in techniques and political systems which is still in progress in much of the Islamic world today.

In Egypt the short period of French rule brought many important developments. In the attempt to win the support of the Egyptian masses Napoleon proclaimed that he had come to Egypt to deliver the Egyptians from their Mameluke oppressors, whose greed and injustice had ruined the once prosperous land. He would give Egyptians freedom, respect Islam and help all Muslims, including the Ottoman Turks, to fight against Christian infidels. He ended his proclamation by saying: 'Let every qadi, imam and sheik in Egypt proclaim these truths from his mosque. Glory to the Sultan, glory to the brave French army, curses on the Mamelukes and happiness to Egypt.' The Egyptian populace could not be expected to accept these sentiments wholeheartedly from the mouth of an infidel conqueror. However much they had disliked the Mamelukes, their deep religious beliefs made them hate Christian invaders even more. Violent riots broke out in Cairo which were severely suppressed. Nevertheless, Napoleon still attempted to take Egyptians into partnership in the administration of their country by setting up local and district councils on which native Egyptians – as opposed to alien Mamelukes – were represented. He also established a central council called the Diwan to advise him on matters of state. Two newspapers were founded, one of them in the Arabic language. This was the first Arabic newspaper in the Nile valley, and was an important development, considering the role which newspapers subsequently played in the growth of Egyptian nationalism and its struggle against British rule. Another significant innovation of the French period was the founding of the Institut de l'Égypte (Egyptian Institute) to study the rich past of the country. It played an important part in the development of the study of ancient Egypt, now known as Egyptology, and in reminding Egyptians of their cultural heritage. The same idea can be seen in many countries of modern Africa where Institutes of African Studies have been established.

The British force Napoleon to leave Egypt

The French occupation of Egypt was seen in Britain as a direct threat to the British possessions in India and it became the object of British policy first to prevent Napoleon from carrying out his plans to use his conquest as a base for an attack on India, and secondly to force him to withdraw from Egypt altogether. British forces sent to the Syrian fortress of Acre prevented Napoleon from advancing through the Middle East on his planned invasion of India from the North and Nelson destroyed the power of the French navy in the Mediterranean by defeating the French fleet at Aboukir Bay in August 1798. This meant that the army in Egypt could easily be cut off from its supplies and the French were forced to leave the country in 1801. This struggle between the British and the French was only the first step in a long process which resulted in the British occupation of Egypt. The basis of the struggle was a conflict of strategic interests. Britain could never feel that her position in India was safe if another powerful European country which might at some time become hostile, had a dominant influence in Egypt.

The Battle of the Nile

Mohammed Ali

The rise of Mohammed Ali

When the French departed, Egypt returned to a state of chaos. The Mameluke Beys resumed their rivalry, the British gave their support first to one and then another, and the Ottoman Sultan sent forces to the country in the attempt to make his rule effective. This confused situation provided the opportunity for a remarkable man to come to the fore and make himself the real ruler of the country. His name was Mohammed Ali. An Albanian born in 1769, he had taken to the career of soldier of fortune in the sultan's army. Though fully trained in the principles of the Ottoman regime under which he lived, he clearly saw the need for the Muslim world to adopt and apply the methods and techniques of western Europe. It was to be his role to wake Egypt from its slumbers and to attempt to bring it in one great leap into the modern world. Though many of his plans resulted in disastrous failure, and though some of the policies which he initiated resulted, when they were later carried on by less able men, in Egypt coming under foreign rule, there are few who would deny him the title of founder of modern Egypt.

Mohammed Ali first showed his political genius in triumphing over the numerous factions struggling for power in Egypt. At first he played the two main Mameluke factions – Bardisi and Elfi – off against one another. Then he threw his weight behind the official Ottoman governor (pasha), Kirshid, against both Mameluke groups. Then as Kirshid became unpopular both in Cairo and Constantinople Mohammed Ali led the people of Cairo against him. Kirshid was

deposed and his successor lasted for six months. Having weakened
all the powerful factions that were struggling for power Mohammed
Ali then seized the leadership of the country for himself, taking care
to win the Sultan's approval for his action. By 1805 he was effectively
in control of the country and in 1806 he was officially confirmed in the
position of wali (governor) by the Sultan.

Mohammed Ali's policies

Once in power he consistently pursued a number of closely related
policies. Firstly he sought to strengthen his own position in Egypt,
to destroy all possible rivals and to ensure that his power would be
handed down hereditarily to his descendants. This inevitably involved the policy of establishing the independence of Egypt from the
Ottoman Sultanate because as long as the country was in theory just
a province of the Ottoman Empire he was legally no more than an
Ottoman official, liable to dismissal at any time and with no guarantee
that his children would be allowed to succeed him. This in turn
meant that he must strive to make Egypt a rival to Turkey as the
centre of the Muslim world and was related to the most famous
and deeply cherished of Mohammed Ali's policies, namely the attempt
to turn backward and poverty-stricken Egypt into a fully-fledged
modern state.

Destruction of the Mamelukes and social reforms

One of his first and most significant acts was to stamp out the Mamelukes and put a final end to a system which had lasted since AD 1249.
In 1807 the Mameluke Beys rose in an unsuccessful revolt against
the new master of Egypt and were suppressed with the aid of Ali's
Albanian soldiery. In 1811 he invited a large part of the surviving
Mamelukes to a great banquet in Cairo. Then when his guests had
assembled he gave the order and they were all put to death. This
crushing blow was followed by an all-out attempt to hunt down and
destroy the remaining Mamelukes in the provinces. Only a small
number escaped to take refuge in the lands of the Funj Sultanate
higher up the Nile valley. Having destroyed the Mamelukes, Mohammed Ali abolished the system of land ownership under which they
had exploited the peasantry and declared the land returned to the
tillers of the soil.

Military reforms: the creation of a national army

The elimination of the Mamelukes meant that Mohammed Ali must base his military power on other means. To rely exclusively on his Albanian troops would be too dangerous, for they were soldiers of fortune in a foreign land. Having put him in power they might easily turn against him and remove him. He was thus led to take the momentous step of recruiting native born Egyptians into the armed forces and laying the foundations of a modern national army. This was a step of tremendous importance for the future for it meant that the native Egyptians, who for centuries had been unarmed and helpless under successive foreign rulers, would be in a position to decide their own destiny. It is not too much to say that the creation of a truly Egyptian army meant the beginning of effective Egyptian nationalism. This was first seen in the nineteenth century in the career of Arabi Pasha, and it can be most clearly seen today in the light of the career of Abdul Gamal Nasser. At the time, however, the move was not at all popular. For more than a thousand years the Egyptian fellahin had taken no part in the military defence of their country. Army life was something alien and dreaded. What is more the Egyptians recruited to the army were taken only into the lowest ranks; the officers remained Albanians or Turks. Thus the peasants had to be forced most unwillingly into the armed forces and Mohammed Ali was anxious to find alternative sources of military manpower.

Mohammed Ali's new army (Nizam Jadid) was an innovation not only because it was made up mainly of native Egyptians, but also because he deliberately set out to equip and train it in the most modern fashion. A French military instructor, Captain Seres, was appointed to take charge of the training programme and the latest military equipment was imported from Europe. To the astonishment of the world, which tended to regard the Egyptians as incapable of fighting, Mohammed's army distinguished itself in a number of difficult and laborious campaigns.

Land forces were not Mohammed Ali's only concern. He clearly realised the importance of sea power and with speed and determination set about building up a modern navy.

Attempts to modernise the Egyptian economy

To support these new and expensive forces and pay for the campaigns on which he used them, Mohammed Ali required a greatly increased revenue and he devoted himself with as much energy to the modernisation of the Egyptian economy as he did to the improvement of the armed forces. By far the most important of his innovations in this field was the development of cotton-growing as a major agricultural activity. Seeing the economic value of the crop he introduced a strain of cotton grown in the upper Nile valley but previously little grown, if at all, in Egypt itself. A tremendous campaign was launched to persuade the peasants to plant the new crop which became, and still remains, the main basis of the Egyptian economy. In addition Mohammed Ali undertook many measures to improve the position of agriculture generally. He cleared old canals and dug new ones to extend the area of cultivable land. In upper Egypt large new areas were brought into cultivation and by 1844 he had introduced not less than 38,000 waterwheels to supplement the traditional method of canal irrigation.

With his keen interest in European techniques Mohammed Ali saw that agricultural improvements alone would not be enough to turn Egypt into a fully modern state. He devoted a great deal of energy to the establishment of industries and spent twelve million pounds on factories for the manufacture of military equipment and cotton cloths, for making sugar and distilling rum. Unfortunately Egypt at the time did not have enough people with the business and technical skills and experience to make these ventures a success. Most of Mohammed Ali's industrial schemes failed and became a financial burden on the state. Nevertheless they show that he had seen what all African states recognise today, namely that industrialisation is essential to raise the living standards of the people and build a prosperous and powerful state.

In order to carry out his programme of modernising Egypt it was essential that Egyptians should be trained to understand the science and technology of western Europe. One of Mohammed Ali's most important contributions to the future of Egypt was that he sent a number of young Egyptians abroad for education, mainly to France. When these young men came home they took part in a real cultural revolution. The eyes of educated Egyptians were opened to the ideas of western Europe and many great works of European writing were translated into Arabic. Some of these young men were to be the pioneers of modern Egyptian nationalism.

In the administration of the country Mohammed Ali also made important reforms which gave the native Egyptians some say in the running of their country. Some Egyptians were employed in the civil service, though usually under better educated Turks, and

Citadel Mosque, Cairo

Egyptians were appointed as village-heads, district-heads and tax-collectors.

In spite of his modernising and Europeanising schemes Mohammed Ali was well aware of the strength of tradition and took care not to offend the religious beliefs of his subjects too deeply. He himself built one of the most magnificent mosques in Egypt on the top of the citadel in Cairo. The Islamic judges (Qadis) and Muftis were also kept in office to dispense justice in accordance with Muslim law. Realising that Egypt was becoming cosmopolitan, however, he established two courts for foreigners. These courts were dominated by merchants, not by Muslims. The one at Alexandria had nine members; four of them were Arabs and there was one Frenchman, a Jew, a Greek and two Middle Eastern Christians. Mohammed Ali was liberal in religious matters and allowed freedom of worship to the Copts and other Christians and to the Jews.

Mohammed Ali's foreign policy

Foreign policy was probably Mohammed Ali's greatest interest. Unless he could win a great degree of independence for Egypt from the Ottoman Empire he could in theory be deposed at any time by the Sultan, and all his plans might be undone. He therefore tried to strengthen Egypt's position as an Islamic power and to win more independence from the Sultan. At first he set out to achieve his aims by co-operating with the Sultan. The Ottoman Sultan on the other hand was afraid of the growing power of his overmighty subject and hoped to weaken him by getting him involved in difficult and expensive campaigns.

In 1812 the Sultan asked Mohammed Ali to undertake the suppression of a rebellion by the fanatical Wahhabi sect in central Arabia. Egyptian forces were sent to Arabia and in spite of the extreme difficulties of fighting in that mountainous and desert area they succeeded in defeating the Wahhabis and establishing Mohammed Ali as the dominant power in the neighbourhood of the Holy Cities of Islam.

The next task for which the Sultan asked Egyptian aid was to help suppress the Greeks, who had risen against the Ottoman Empire in a war of independence. Mohammed Ali's forces, led by his son Ibrahim, almost turned the tide of the war, but the British and French navies came to the aid of the Greeks and destroyed the new Egyptian navy at the battle of Navarino in 1827.

Mohammed Ali's military schemes were not all outside Africa. He set out to extend his power up the Nile valley, where the ancient Egyptians had had their gold mines. He also hoped to recruit large numbers of Negro slaves to strengthen his army and to obtain timber from the tropical areas of the Upper Nile for his navy. In 1820 his armies invaded the area which is now the Republic of the Sudan. That area was then under the Funj Sultanate (see Introduction) but the Funj Kingdom was in the last stages of decline. A number of different claimants to the throne were struggling for power, many tribes had asserted their independence from any central government, and the position was made worse by the squabbles and intrigues of the Mameluke refugees who had fled into the area at the time of Mohammed Ali's destruction of the Mamelukes in Egypt. The people of the Sudan were therefore not able to offer a united resistance and Mohammed Ali was able to establish his authority. He introduced a number of important reforms in the Sudan which will be discussed in the next chapter. He found that the gold of the Nubian desert had been largely exhausted in ancient times but he did succeed in forcing large numbers of Negroes from the Sudan into his army.

Occupation of Syria and conflict with the Ottoman Sultan

Mohammed Ali had undertaken his campaigns in support of the Sultan as a way of winning greater autonomy for Egypt but the Sultan was unwilling to grant this and the Egyptian ruler then tried to strengthen his position by taking possession of the Turkish province of Syria. His son, Ibrahim, began the campaign in 1832 and the Egyptian forces easily gained the upper hand. He was hailed by the Syrians as a deliverer from the corrupt and oppressive rule of the Ottoman Turks and there seemed to be nothing to prevent him attacking. But this campaign involved Mohammed Ali in the politics of the major European powers. The Ottoman Empire had been declining for a long time and Russia was hoping that when it collapsed its territories would be divided between the European powers in such a way that Russia would get control of the Bosphorus and access to the Mediterranean. She did not wish to see a more powerful ruler take the place of the Sultan as he might revive the Ottoman state and deny Russia the chance of gaining her ambition. As the Sultan's armies had been defeated and there seemed a possibility that Mohammed Ali might advance on Constantinople the Sultan appealed for Russian aid. In the Treaty of Unkiar-Skelessi of 1833 Russia promised to give military support to the Sultan in case of need in return for access to the Bosphorus. This treaty was much disliked by Britain; for in the interests of safeguarding her trade routes, Britain had always tried to bolster up the Ottoman Empire to keep Russia from gaining too much influence in Constantinople. Britain was therefore anxious to prevent the Sultan from making use of the Russian offer and hoped to win the Turks away from a pro-

Russian policy. For this reason Britain was anxious to prevent Mohammed Ali from putting the Sultan in a position where he had to ask for Russian military assistance under the terms of the treaty. Faced with this international situation Mohammed Ali stopped his forces and fell back on trying to get his way by negotiation.

In spite of the weak position of the Ottoman Empire, however, the Sultan refused to give him what he wanted. In 1839 fighting began again and Mohammed Ali's forces easily defeated the Turks and began to advance rapidly towards Constantinople. His forces reached as far as Konieh and the way seemed open to the Ottoman capital. This move created great alarm amongst the European powers, with the exception of France which was particularly friendly to Mohammed Ali and hoped to gain trading advantages.

European intervention

In 1840 the European powers, with the exception of France, signed a treaty in London in which they agreed to limit Mohammed Ali's territorial ambitions. They agreed to maintain the sovereignty of the Ottoman Sultan over Egypt but they also agreed that Mohammed Ali should be recognised as the hereditary governor (pasha) of the Ottoman Sultan in Egypt and life governor of Acre in Syria. France refused to sign the treaty and continued supporting Mohammed Ali. The British navy then began bombarding Syrian ports and landing troops to cut off Mohammed Ali's advance forces from their base. He had the wisdom to see that he could not hope to fight against the combined forces of the major European powers and therefore agreed to accept the London treaty.

Achievements of Mohammed Ali

Mohammed Ali thus failed to achieve his ambition of winning complete independence from the Ottoman Empire. But at least he ensured that his descendants would succeed him in the rulership of Egypt and he had taken the country a long way on the road to complete independence. Like his foreign policy his internal schemes in Egypt were also a mixture of success and failure. His industrial plans were unsuccessful and the heavy expenses involved in maintaining his armed forces and using them on major campaigns meant that the Egyptian peasants had to be very heavily taxed. This did a great deal to undermine the value of his agricultural reforms. Peasants began to refuse to plant the new crops as the taxes were so high that they received very little profit. Some of them abandoned the land altogether. Mohammed Ali then began to grant land to individuals on a large scale. This was done to bring land which had fallen into neglect back into cultivation, but it brought into existence a class of wealthy landlords to replace the Mamelukes whom he had earlier destroyed. Mohammed Ali's own family was naturally prominent in this class and acquired enormous estates. This landlord class was later to gain a great deal of political influence until it was swept away by the reforms of Gamal Nasser in recent years.

It should be remembered that the mass of the Egyptian peasants had lived for more than a thousand years under oppressive foreign rulers. Poverty-stricken, uneducated and over-taxed they were little interested in government. They were intensely conservative, and ill-disposed towards any improvement in their age-old methods. It was simply not possible to change all this in the course of a single lifetime.

Nevertheless Mohammed Ali's achievements are amazing. He had put Egypt on the way to modernisation and independence. He had established her as a major cotton producer. He had built a national army and showed that Egyptian soldiers could be the equal of any in the world. He had given Egyptians some place in the government of their country and laid the foundations for the growth of a western-educated class. Under him Egypt had suddenly appeared on the world stage as a power to be reckoned with, and he had done all this without taking any loans from the European powers which might have committed him to them.

Abbas I

Mohammed Ali died in 1849 and it was the tragedy of Egypt that none of his successors had his ability. Abbas I who ruled from 1849 to 1853, was almost his exact opposite. He was deeply conservative, and lacked Mohammed Ali's understanding of the modern world. Under his rule the factories were abandoned, schools were shut and many European advisers dismissed. This did mean, however, that state expenses were reduced. This large cut in state expenses in turn lightened the burden of the fellahin, for Abbas found it possible to lower their taxes. Moreover Abbas endeared himself to the fellahin by treating them kindly.

Said and the Suez Canal agreement

Abbas I was succeeded in 1853 by Said. He had received a French education, was highly westernised, and loved to surround himself with European friends. He fully shared Mohammed Ali's desire to modernise Egypt but he lacked his shrewd sense of political realism. In his reign Egypt became a happy hunting ground for the promoters of various schemes of improvement and for the agents of European bankers who were only too eager to advance the money on conditions favourable to themselves. The greatest of these schemes was the project for building a canal at Suez to link the Mediterranean and the Red Sea. This idea had been put forward some time before, but it became a practical reality when the Frenchman de Lesseps persuaded Said to give his support on terms very unfavourable to Egypt. Under the agreement Egypt was to provide the labour for the construction of the canal as well as a substantial proportion of the other costs. Egypt was also to give up to the International Company of Suez a stretch of territory through which a sweet water canal was to be cut for irrigation. At the same time the control of the Company and the bulk of the profits were to remain with the French shareholders. It was a clear case of swindling. In order to fulfil his part of the bargain as well as to finance other expenses Said resorted to European bankers who gave him huge loans in return for heavy interest. By the time Said died in 1863 Egypt had borrowed £14 million from foreign bankers.

Ismail Pasha and his extravagance

Said was succeeded in 1863 by Ismail Pasha, the man who is often held responsible for allowing Egypt to fall under British rule. His character is difficult to judge. To British imperialists like Lord Cromer and Sir Alfred Milner, Ismail was a weak, cunning and selfish pleasure-seeker who borrowed money from Europeans and later turned against them and ungratefully refused to pay his debts. An American writer, Crabites, however, described him as a shrewd, progressive and enlightened ruler with the best interests of Egypt at heart and a victim of the swindling tricks of unscrupulous Europeans. Neither of these views is entirely right or entirely wrong.

Ismail's main failing was that while he sought to carry out a policy very similar to that of Mohammed Ali he lacked the cleverness and sense of proportion to carry it out successfully. He tried to do every-

The procession of ships at the opening of the Suez Canal, 1869

thing too quickly and on too big a scale for the economy of the country. He was too easily tricked by the moneylenders and their agents who flocked around him. In the attempt to modernise Egypt overnight he built over 8,000 miles of irrigation canals, almost 1,000 miles of railway, 5,000 miles of telegraph lines, 450 bridges, 4,500 elementary schools and a modern port at Alexandria. Enormous sums were also spent on personal and prestige affairs. He spent a million pounds on entertaining guests at the formal opening of the Suez Canal in 1869. He built luxurious hotels and patronised art on a lavish scale. Like Mohammed Ali he sought to extend his power in Africa. He employed European explorers to search for the sources of the Nile, and he despatched costly expeditions to Ethiopia which met with complete defeat. To carry out his schemes he employed ever-increasing numbers of Europeans who rose in numbers from 5,000 in 1836 to 100,000 in 1875.

Towards self-government

One project in which he was fairly successful was in winning further concessions from the Ottoman Sultan of Turkey. Unlike Mohammed Ali, his grandfather, he did not use force but bribes of silver and gold with which he persuaded the Sultan to increase the independence of

Egypt. In 1863 the Sultan conferred the administration of Egypt on Ismail and his heirs and gave the important Red Sea ports of Suakin and Massawa to Egypt. Then in 1867 the Sultan gave Ismail the title of Khedive and the right to enter into administrative and commercial conventions as well as to make laws and regulations for internal government. The measure of self-government which Egypt had gained was internationally recognised in 1874 at the Conference of Berne, when Egypt was admitted to the General Postal Union and became one of the original signatories of the Berne Convention.

Ismail's character was a strange mixture. He was strongly attracted to European culture but still deeply attached to the traditional Islamic way of life, and he could never work out how to combine the best of both. Thus he remained a traditional Muslim landlord while at the same time he tried to abolish the system of slavery which was the basis of that type of land-ownership. To impress Europeans that he was a modernist he introduced a constitution that laid the foundations for a parliamentary system but at the same time he went on behaving as an autocrat whose authority should not be questioned.

British purchase of Suez Canal shares

As a result of his grand schemes and lavish spending Ismail accumulated enormous debts for Egypt and as he was careless in financial matters he was easily cheated. By 1879 Egypt had acquired debts of £100 million. Of this the country had only received £65 million, the rest going to swindlers. As the debts grew Ismail inevitably reached the situation where he was unable even to pay the interest on outstanding loans. It was this situation which made him sell Egypt's shares in the Suez Canal to Britain.

Ever since the Napoleonic invasion of Egypt, Britain had been aware of the danger that if the country were dominated by a hostile European power it could be used as a stepping-stone for an attack on India. At first Britain did not want to get politically involved in the country but merely wished to prevent French influence getting too strong. When the project for the Suez Canal was launched Britain expected it to fail and took no part, but when it proved a success the British government saw that Egypt had become very much more important to her than before, as the shortest way to India was through the Canal. The British Prime Minister, Disraeli, seized on the chance offered by Ismail's financial difficulties to buy Egypt's shares in the Canal for the sum of £4 million which was only a fraction of the amount Egypt had spent on the project. Disraeli's purchase of the Canal shares was not simply a clever business deal. It was a deliberate attempt to establish a foothold in Egypt and control of the vital Canal which was becoming the lifeline of the British Empire. Disraeli told the British Parliament on 21 February 1876 that his motives in buying the shares were political and imperialist. He said: 'I have never recommended and I do not recommend this purchase as a financial investment . . . I do not recommend this purchase as a financial speculation . . . I have always and do now recommend it to the country as a political transaction, and one which I believe is calculated to strengthen the empire.' Disraeli's motives in buying the Canal shares can be compared in some ways with the imperialist motives of the Royal Niger Company in Nigeria or the British South Africa Company in Rhodesia. Once Britain had come to feel that Egypt was vital to the survival of the British Empire it was clear that she would stop at nothing to prevent the country falling under the influence of any other power. The weakness of Ismail and Tewfik, his son and successor, were convenient excuses for further intervention. The days of Egypt's independence were numbered.

International control of Egyptian finances

From 1876 onwards Egypt's independence began to disappear. As the Khedive was unable to pay his debts, Britain and France, the countries with the largest stake in the country, began to exert increasing pressure to ensure that debts to their citizens were paid. During 1876 the British government sent Stephen Cave, the Paymaster-General to investigate Egypt's financial situation. Then in 1878 Britain and France, acting together, forced the Khedive to place Egyptian finances under joint Anglo-French control on the grounds that Egypt could not be relied upon to fulfil her obligations to the European moneylenders. The scheme of joint control was a convenient device whereby Britain and France could both secure their essential interests in the country without coming into conflict with each other. As Lord Salisbury, who was British Foreign Secretary for a long time, explained: 'When you have got a neighbour and faithful ally who is bent on meddling in a country in which you are deeply interested – you have three courses open to you. You may renounce – or monopolise – or share. Renouncing would have been to place the French across our road to India. Monopolising would have been very near the risk of war. So we resolved to share.'

Arabi Pasha

(right) Ismail Pasha

Nationalist reaction and the rebellion of Arabi Pasha

With joint Anglo-French control over the Egyptian finances, Egypt virtually lost independence and this provoked a powerful reaction, which brought the system of joint control to an end and led to outright British occupation. Educated Egyptians began nationalist agitation through the Press and the General Assembly, demanding that Ismail and his son, Tewfik, together with a number of corrupt Turkish office holders be removed from office. They denounced British and French interference with the affairs of the country and insisted that if allowed to control their country's financial affairs, they could fulfil Egypt's international obligations. The British and French, however, did not trust the nationalists and were not prepared to surrender control of the Egyptian finances. They were also anxious to preserve the power of the Khedive so that they could continue to control the country through him.

As the nationalist agitation grew it spread to the army and a man emerged who was to become the leader and inspirer of the whole movement. His name was Arabi Pasha and he was one of the few senior officers of pure Egyptian descent. He had joined the army at seventeen and like many other true Egyptians in the armed forces he suffered a great deal at the hands of Turkish officers. He thus fully shared the growing hatred of the mass of the fellahin for the privileged class of wealthy Turks, relatives of the Khedival family, court favourites and a few wealthy landlords. Arabi Pasha was an embodiment of the growing spirit of nationalism, with its demand of Egypt for the Egyptians and its hatred of both external European interference in the country and of the dominance of a small, largely Turkish class in Egypt itself. He was so popular that Egyptians nick-named him 'The Only One'.

Arabi Pasha was far-sighted enough to see that in order that Egyptian independence could be re-established, thorough reform must be undertaken before abolition of the monarchy and the introduction of a republican constitution. His movement was very nearly successful and Lord Cromer, who became British ruler of Egypt from 1883 to 1906, confessed: 'Had he been left alone there can be no doubt that he would have been successful. His want of success was due to British influence.'

British occupation of Egypt

As the nationalist movement grew the Khedive's position became weaker and weaker. It was obvious that unless something were done the system of joint British-French control of Egyptian finances would collapse, and Arabi Pasha and the nationalists would emerge as the effective rulers of the country. Both European governments were under pressure from those of their own citizens with financial interests in Egypt, and Britain was anxious to ensure that whatever happened the French should not be allowed to act first and establish a position which would endanger the route to India. The excuse for armed intervention came in June 1882 when nationalist riots broke out in Alexandria and about fifty Europeans were killed. Britain decided that a show of force was necessary if the collapse of European authority in the country was to be prevented. The French were asked to take part but they refused to take immediate action before their National Assembly had given its consent. Thus the British fleet alone mounted the show of force. On 10 July the warships bombarded Alexandria and when this did not put an end to the nationalist movements, troops were landed. The British Parliament lost no time in voting money for military occupation. On 13 September the British forces under Sir Garnet Wolseley, who was already famous for his victory over the Asante in 1874, met Arabi Pasha's forces. The Egyptian army could not stand up against the well-trained and well-armed British forces. Arabi was defeated and three days later the British occupied Cairo. Egypt became for all practical purposes a part of the British Empire until 1922.

2 The Sudan and Ethiopia in the nineteenth century

As we have seen, the life of Egypt is, and always has been, dependent on the river Nile. This great river has two main sources. The White Nile starts from Lake Victoria and flows through the modern Sudan. The Blue Nile rises in the Ethiopian uplands and flows westward to meet the White Nile at Khartoum, the capital of the Sudan Republic. The two rivers then unite their waters and flow on northwards through the desert to reach the sea at the Nile Delta. Both branches of the Nile are of great importance to Egypt. The White Nile maintains the flow of water down the Nile valley throughout the year and provides most of the water that is now used for irrigation in the summer months. The Blue Nile is responsible for the annual floods which until recent times provided the most important means of irrigation. The Blue Nile also brings down from Ethiopia the rich silt which is left behind when the flood waters dry up and which produces the great fertility of the Egyptian soil. Egypt, the Sudan and Ethiopia are thus linked together geographically and have a joint interest in the use of the Nile waters.

In addition to the geographic link the three areas have longstanding historical relations. The ancient kingdom of Kush in the Sudan arose under the influence of Egyptian civilization and then for a brief period kings of Kush ruled in Egypt itself. Much later Kush suffered from the rivalry of the kingdom of Axum in Ethiopia, and about AD 350 it was destroyed by the Emperor Ezana, the first Christian ruler of Axum. Christianity was introduced into the northern part of the modern Sudan from Egypt and by the sixth century AD two Christian kingdoms, Maqurra and Alwa, had come into existence. In Ethiopia Christianity was introduced by Greek traders, but the Ethiopian Church affiliated itself to the Church in Egypt and received its Patriarchs from Alexandria.

After the Arab conquest, Egypt was gradually converted to Islam and inevitably the new religion tended to spread up the Nile along the routes of trade which linked Egypt with the upper Nile area. By the fourteenth century as the result of the infiltration of Islam and the immigration of Arab tribes moving up the Nile, Maqurra had ceased to be a Christian kingdom. The kingdom of Alwa, which was further south, continued to survive for another century.

The Funj Sultanate in the Sudan

In 1504 the remains of the kingdom of Alwa were destroyed by the conqueror Amara Dunkas, who built in its place an Islamic kingdom, the Funj Sultanate, with its capital at Sennar. This state survived until 1821 and was known as the Black Sultanate. Its founders, the Funj, were Negroes though their origin is not precisely known. Some writers believe that they were Shilluks, a people who are still important in the Sudan.

At the height of its power the Funj Sultanate controlled a very large area, from the neighbourhood of its capital at Sennar to as far north as the first cataract of the Nile. It did not, however, include the Dinka, Azande and other tribes of the southern area of the modern Sudan.

Within the large territory of the Funj Sultanate many areas enjoyed considerable independence. This was particularly true of the Arab tribes along the Nile valley north of the confluence of the Blue and White Nile, who were ruled in the name of the Funj Sultan by an Arab viceroy called the Abdullab. It was also true of many tribes in the southern part of the kingdom, who kept their own chiefs and merely accepted the paramountcy of the Funj ruler. This type of kingdom was naturally very fragile and could only be held together if the power of the sultans remained strong. This power depended on a well-trained cavalry force and an infantry force made up of slaves who were captured in the Nuba mountains. The strength of the Funj kingdom was shaken when the Shaiqiya tribe which lived around the great bend of the Nile rebelled against the Sultan's viceroy and succeeded in asserting its independence. This revolt damaged the trade of the Funj Sultanate and in compensation the sultans attempted to expand into Kordofan. This led to too much power being given to the army commander Abu Likeilik and he marched on Sennar and deposed the Sultan. Thereafter the sons and grandsons of Abu Likeilik fought one another for power, each of them supporting one or other member of the Funj royal family as puppet sultan. In these conditions of civil war many tribes broke away from the kingdom and its authority became confined to a very small area. After 1811 the position was further worsened by the arrival of squabbling bands of Mameluke refugees from Egypt.

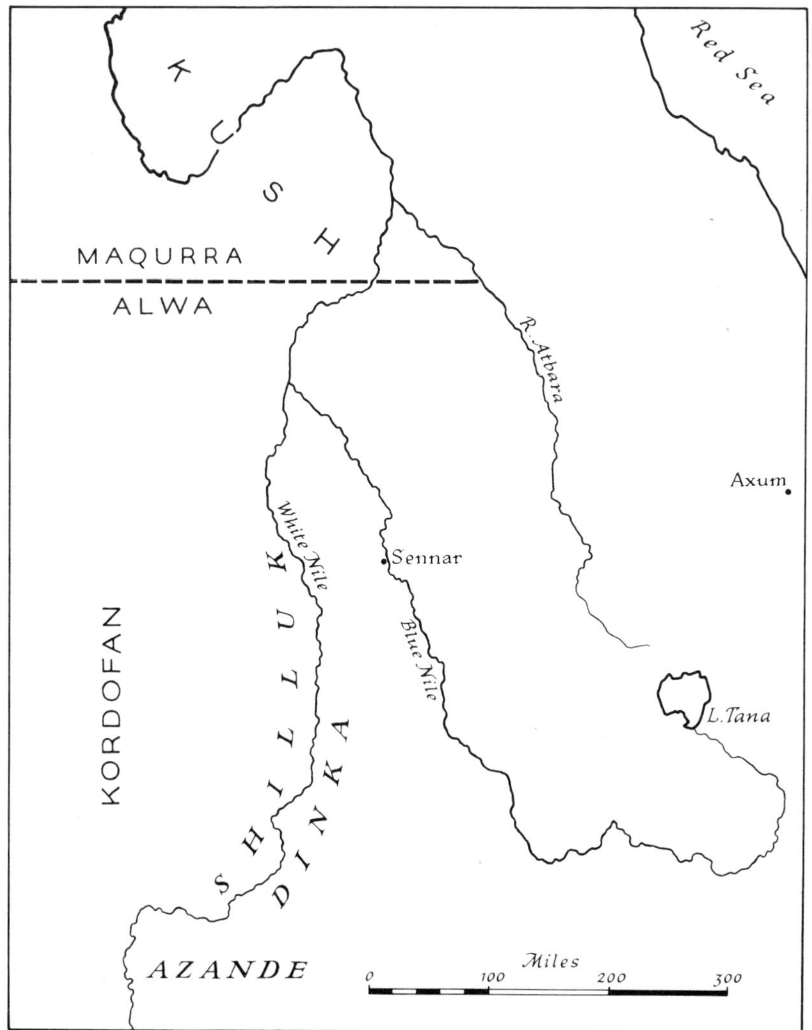

3 The area of the Funj Sultanate and the Nile confluence

Turko-Egyptian conquest of the Sudan

It was this weak and confused territory that was invaded in 1820 by
the army of Mohammed Ali under the command of his third son,
Kamil Pasha. The Funj Sultanate was in no position to make an
effective stand and the 4,000 troops under Kamil Pasha met with
little severe resistance except from the Shaiqiya tribe. Mohammed
Ali's objects in conquering the Sudan were to find the gold mines
of the ancient Egyptians, and to acquire sources of timber for his
fleet and manpower for his army. The first proved a complete dis-
appointment and the second of relatively little value but Mohammed
Ali did succeed in forcibly recruiting large numbers of Sudanese
Negroes into his army. In addition he and his successors introduced
into the Sudan much of their modernising programme.

Turko-Egyptian administration 1820–81

Between 1820 and 1881 the Sudan was administered by Turko-
Egyptian governor-generals known as likimdars. The area was divided
into a number of provinces administered by provincial administrators called mudirs and the provinces were in turn divided into
districts called qisms, each administered by an officer called qism
naziri. Finally each of the qisms was divided into still smaller units
called khatts ruled by khatt hakimi. The Turko-Egyptian government
was maintained by a large army of 10,000 infantry recruited from
the Sudanese Negroes and known as the Jihadiyya, and about 9,000
cavalry largely recruited from the Shaiqiya.

Mohammed Ali's conquest of the Sudan naturally led to a greatly
increased flow of trade between that country and Egypt. Egyptian
cultivators were also sent into the area to teach new farming methods
and introduce new crops. Cotton-growing was started on a substantial
scale and now provides the Sudan's major export crop. New lands
were brought under irrigation and plantations of indigo and sugar
were established. Improvements in communications were also made
in the Turko-Egyptian period. A telegraph system was introduced
which by 1866 linked Wadi Halfa to upper Egypt. In 1874 this was
extended to Khartoum. Another line was built linking the Sudan to
the Red Sea and another extended westward through El Obeid to
the borders of Darfur. Nile steamers speeded up communications
and helped the administration. The foundation of Khartoum, capital
of the modern Sudan, was also an achievement of the Turko-Egyptian

administration. In 1825 it was a mere village near the confluence of the Blue and White Niles but by 1833 it had expanded so much that it was made the administrative capital of the country. By 1837 its population was estimated at 20,000.

The Turko-Egyptian government expanded its area of authority far beyond the limits of the Funj Sultanate. The pagan Negro tribes of the southern Sudan were conquered and for the first time brought under common government with the Muslim peoples of the north. The rulers of Egypt employed many European administrators and experts in the territory in their efforts at modernisation and they engaged European explorers to investigate the hinterland with a view to further extensions of territory. One of these, Baker, discovered the sources of the Blue Nile and confirmed that the White Nile did rise in Lake Victoria. Another European employee of the Turko-Egyptian regime, a German called Emin Pasha, reached as far as the northern part of modern Uganda with a number of Egyptian soldiers, and the Turko-Egyptian regime might have been extended into the heart of East Africa if it had not been for the outbreak of revolt in the Sudan itself.

Unpopularity of the Turko-Egyptian government

Though modern Sudanese patriots like to dwell on the seamy side of the Turko-Egyptian regime, there can be no doubt that it conferred many benefits on the peoples of the Sudan. Nevertheless, it was far from popular. In the first place, like most conquerors, Mohammed Ali and his successors were concerned first and foremost to exploit the Sudan for their own benefit rather than in the interests of the Sudanese. In the attempt to profit from the area they imposed heavy taxes which were much resented. This was particularly so in the reign of Khedive Ismail (1863–79) who tried to increase his revenue from the Sudan as much as possible to help meet his ever-mounting debts to Europeans. The administrators who were sent to the Sudan disliked being sent there. They tried to get away as soon as they could. Between 1821 and 1885 there were no less than twenty-three likimdars serving for an average period of two years. Only one of them, named Kurshid, served for the substantial period of thirteen years. During their stay many of the administrators at all levels engaged in corrupt practices in the hope of making quick money. The administration was strongest in the reign of Mohammed Ali himself and afterwards fell into a sad state of decline. The Khedive

Ismail managed to restore efficiency to some extent but after 1876 he became so preoccupied with his European debts that he could only think of the Sudan as a source of revenue. In addition to their mal-administration the Turkish administrators belonged to the Hanafite

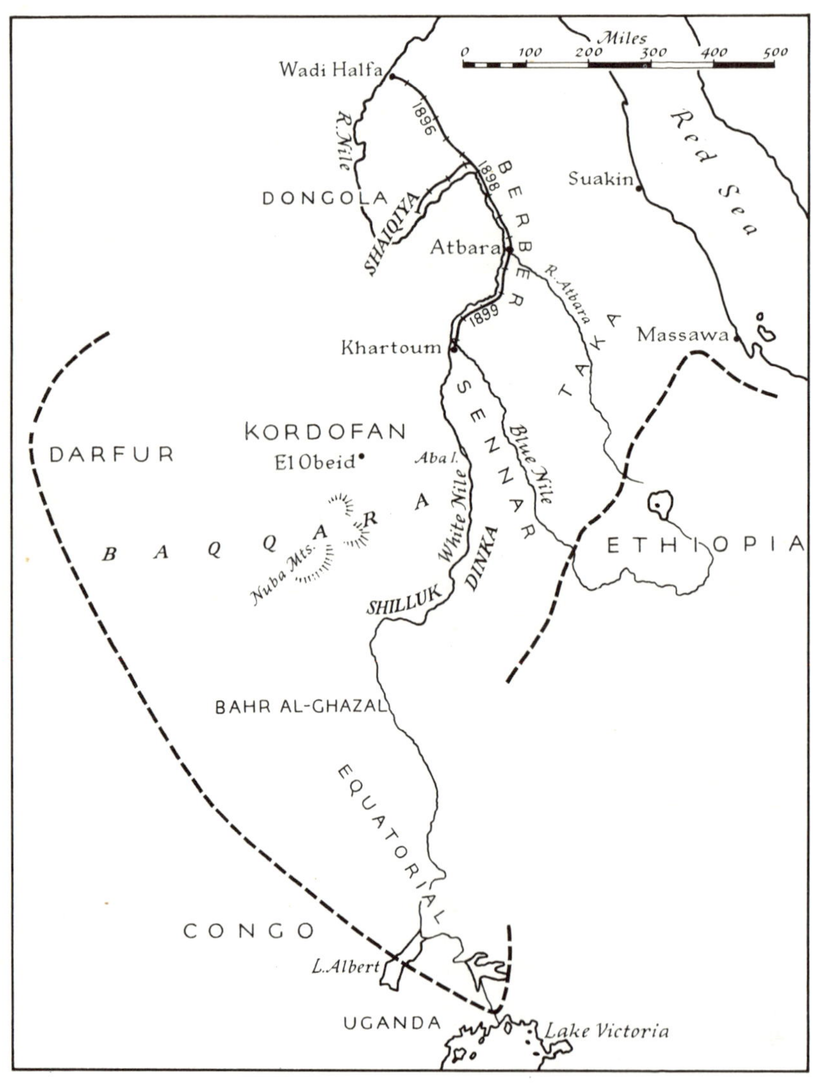

4 Sudan under Egyptian rule

school of Muslim law, the most lax of all the Islamic codes. Many of them were open wine-drinkers, and this was particularly shocking to the Sudanese, who belonged to the strict Malikite school. The religious feelings of the Sudanese were also disturbed by the employment of European Christians in important positions and the belief grew that the country was to be handed over to Europeans. The position was not helped when in 1877 Ismail Pasha appointed an Englishman, Charles George Gordon, as governor-general. Gordon's active opposition to the slave trade and the steps he took to punish slave traders disturbed the traditional economy of the Sudan and aroused bitter opposition. The fact that he employed increasing numbers of Europeans in administrative posts under him further increased the bitterness.

Muhammad Ahmad, the Mahdi

Muhammad Ahmad, the Mahdi

Almost immediately after the 1820 conquest there were revolts against the taxes imposed by the new masters. There were uprisings in Darfur against the new administration in 1838 and 1878, and in the Bahr el-Ghazal in 1877 and 1878. These sporadic outbursts of discontent were suppressed but events took a new turn with the emergence of a new political and religious leader, Muhammad Ahmad. He was born in 1844 in Dongola Province to a family of boat-builders. As a young man he received an education in Islamic law and theology at the feet of a famous learned man, Sheik Tayib. He was an eager scholar and himself became a faqih, that is a man learned in Islamic laws. He became a member of the Sammaniya brotherhood and opened a lodge on Aba island, south of Khartoum. Like other religious reformers in the Islamic world at the time – such as the Fulani reformer Uthman dan Fodio in West Africa – Muhammad Ahmad dreamt of a return to the ideal Islamic government that was believed to have existed in the days of the first four Muslim Caliphs. He hoped to see the whole Islamic world reunited under a righteous ruler who would govern in strict accordance with the sacred teaching of the Koran. He also preached against the luxury and corruption of the times and called for a return to the purity and asceticism of the ideal Islamic life. He saw the Turks as ungodly and corrupt and condemned the Sudanese Sheikhs for their lax and luxurious way of life and their acceptance of offices under the Turko-Egyptian regime. He began to see himself as the heaven-sent deliverer destined to rule the entire Muslim community and restore it to godliness and purity. In 1881 his followers proclaimed him as the *Mahdi* (the Guided One).

Collapse of the Turko-Egyptian regime and triumph of the Mahdi

The proclamation of Muhammad Ahmad as the Mahdi alarmed the Turko-Egyptian administration and he was summoned to Khartoum. He refused to come and an expedition sent against him was defeated. The news spread rapidly among the masses that Allah had fought on the side of the Mahdi and that he had defeated his enemies without military effort. Support for the new leader grew rapidly and soon became too much for the Turko-Egyptian forces. The Mahdi conducted his campaign on Islamic lines modelled on the life of Mohammed. He began by performing a hijra (or flight from the ungodly) like Mohammed's flight from Mecca to Medina. This flight took him to Kordofan in the west where most of his supporters were to be found at first. There the numbers of his followers, who were called Ansar, increased rapidly. In Kordofan and Darfur he won several military successes and then began to extend his power eastwards. By 1883 he was not only ruling over Kordofan and Darfur but was also master of areas around the Blue Nile. The eastern part of his conquests was governed in his name by Osman Digna.

The Turko-Egyptian administration was in a particularly weak position for, as we have seen, the British had occupied Egypt in

1882 to support the authority of the Khedive and ensure the payment of Egypt's international debts. In 1883 the British decided to support their puppet regime in Egypt in its attempt to restore Turko-Egyptian control of the Sudan. A mainly Egyptian army led by an English commander, Hicks Pasha, was sent to capture the Mahdi in Kordofan. The invaders were decisively defeated and the Sudanese, who interpreted the victory as another miracle and a sign that Muhammad Ahmad really was the Mahdi, hesitated no longer in rallying to his side. Lord Cromer, the British Consul-General in Egypt, was in a difficult position. The Khedive, whose government the British occupation was officially intended to support, was naturally anxious to regain control of the Sudan, but Gladstone, the British Prime Minister, was opposed to what he regarded as unnecessary extensions of British responsibility and had often spoken of the rights of the Sudanese to struggle for their independence. The British cabinet was divided, and there were some who felt that as Egypt was dependent on the Nile, British strategic interests in Egypt demanded that she should control the upper Nile valley.

General Gordon

An official decision was taken to evacuate the Sudan and leave it to the Mahdi, but those who disliked this decision managed to ensure that the man sent to carry out the evacuation should be the eccentric General Gordon, a man who could be relied upon to disobey his official instructions. When Gordon reached Khartoum he refused to proceed with the evacuation and announced his intention to smash

Khartoum in the nineteenth century

the Mahdi. His forces were far too small, however, to face the massive following of Muhammad Ahmad and he found himself cut off and besieged in Khartoum. Gladstone, who was furious at Gordon's behaviour, refused for a long time to do anything to rescue him. Finally, however, a relief expedition was organised under General Wolsely and fought its way to Khartoum. By the time it arrived the town had fallen to the Mahdists and Gordon was dead. The relief column therefore retreated, leaving the Mahdi in complete control of the Sudan, (1885).

Muhammad Ahmad did not live to enjoy the fruits of his victory for long. He died soon after his troops had occupied Khartoum. During his short reign he had tried conscientiously to put into practice his ideals of Islamic government. He collected only taxes that were laid down in the Koran and based his administration of justice on the Sharia. He tried to purify society and administered severe punishments for theft, adultery, drunkenness, smoking and bringing of false accusations. He succeeded in enforcing the law requiring women to wear veils, though he was unable to suppress some traditional Sudanese practices of which he disapproved, such as the wearing of amulets, elaborate wedding ceremonies and mourning customs at funerals. During his reign he minted gold and silver coins. To help him in his campaigns the Mahdi appointed three deputies or Khalifas named Abdullahi, Ali and Muhammad Sharif. The title is the same

as that used by the political successors of Mohammed, the early
Caliphs who ruled the whole Islamic world. The three Khalifas
were army commanders during the life of the Mahdi and on his
death soon after the capture of Khartoum one of them, Abdullahi,
succeeded to the supreme position in the Sudan.

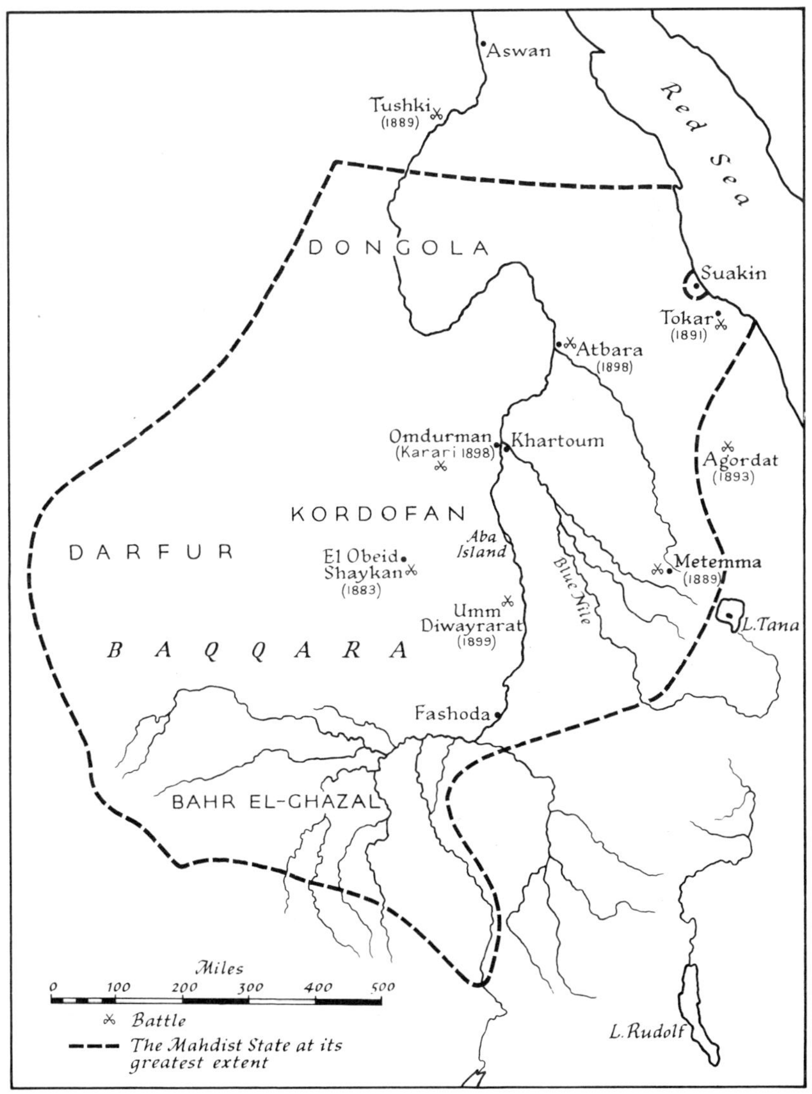

5 The Mahdist State

The Sudan under the Khalifa 1885–98

The rule of the Khalifa has been described in the past by European writers, some of whom were anxious to justify the subsequent British conquest and others who had suffered as prisoners of the Khalifa, as one of unrelieved brutality and barbarism. Recent researches have shown, however, that it was in fact a remarkably successful system. The death of the Mahdi created a crisis for his followers. As the Mahdi was supposed to be immortal his death led many to doubt whether he was really the Mahdi at all. Abdullahi also found it difficult to make the other two Khalifas accept his position as the supreme head of state, and members of the Mahdi's own family felt that they should hold the highest offices in the land.

The Mahdist movement was one of religious as well as political reform. Muhammad Ahmad, by virtue of his claim to be the Mahdi, denounced all the traditional law schools of the Islamic world and prepared his own code; though he had himself been a member of a Sufi brotherhood he also denounced all the Sufi Orders. These moves were naturally unpopular among the more conservative learned men and the leaders of the powerful Sufi groups in the country. The reforms were much more difficult to maintain when the Mahdi himself was dead. The movement had grown up very quickly under the inspiration of the Mahdi's personality and brought many tribes together in common opposition to the Turko-Egyptian rule. Once the hated foreign government had been overthrown and the Mahdi was gone, traditional tribal hostilities were soon renewed.

Abdullahi thus had to struggle against many difficulties. In 1888 and 1892 he was faced by revolts led by members of the Mahdi's family. A more serious source of trouble, however, was the attempt of some of the tribes to establish their independence from central government control. Abdullahi's own tribe, the Baggara, a cattle-keeping people near Darfur, were among the most obstinate. Expeditions had to be sent against them in the first three years of the Khalifa's reign. In 1889 he sent one of his relatives, Uthman Adam, to administer them and when even this did not put an end to the troubles he forced a number of members of the tribe to leave Darfur and settled them in the Omdurman district.

In addition to internal problems there were also questions of foreign policy. Although the British government had at first decided on a policy of non-intervention in the Sudan the Egyptian rulers had never abandoned hope of recovering the territory. A large section of the Egyptian army was stationed near Aswan, not far from the frontier, and this forced the Khalifa to maintain a large army in preparedness for an attack. In 1889 he took the initiative and himself invaded Egypt but he was repulsed.

On the eastern frontier of the Sudan lay the Christian empire of Ethiopia. As a religious leader the Khalifa was duty bound to make war against the infidels and a jihad was declared against Ethiopia. Sudanese forces invaded Ethiopia in 1889 but were severely defeated at the battle of Metemma, where the Ethiopian Emperor John was killed. This did not mean the end of the struggle, however, and tension continued when Menelik came to the throne of Ethiopia and began a policy of vigorous expansion. In this he had the tacit support of Britain, France and Italy, with whom he had treaty relationships. Menelik was regarded with particular hostility by the Khalifa as he openly claimed Fashoda and Khartoum as part of his empire. Between 1892 and 1897 Menelik made overtures to the Khalifa suggesting that they unite their forces to resist the designs of European imperialists but no permanent alliance between the Christian empire and the head of an Islamic reforming movement was possible.

By about 1892 Abdullahi had succeeded in solving most of the country's internal problems. The capital was established at Omdurman on the other bank of the Nile from Khartoum and a metropolitan area grew up around Aba island which the Khalifa ruled directly. The rest of the state was divided into provinces governed by amils who in accordance with the practice of the early Caliphate were both governors and tax collectors. It was the Khalifa's policy to appoint amils who were not necessarily members of the tribes over whom they ruled. The attempt to purify society in accordance with Islamic beliefs, which had been such a marked feature of the Mahdi's policy, was continued, and a high moral tone was maintained in the administration, where corruption was severely punished. Taxes were much lighter and more honestly collected than in the Turko-Egyptian period and the people paid them much more willingly. The necessity for the state to maintain a large army meant that most of the revenue was spent on defence and relatively little was done in the way of economic improvements. The army was provided with firearms, some of which had been captured from the defeated Egyptian army but most of which were made in Omdurman. The men came largely from the Nuba mountains where Mohammed Ali had previously recruited soldiers for his Egyptian forces. They were brave fighters and remained loyal to the state to the end.

Tribal disturbances were eventually brought under control. The Baggara, which gave most trouble of all, was finally converted into a group of the Khalifa's most ardent followers; a number of its leading men were taken to Omdurman and given high positions in the government. The Khalifa had succeeded in establishing a theocratic system which might have proved satisfactory to the Sudanese people if it had been left alone by the European powers.

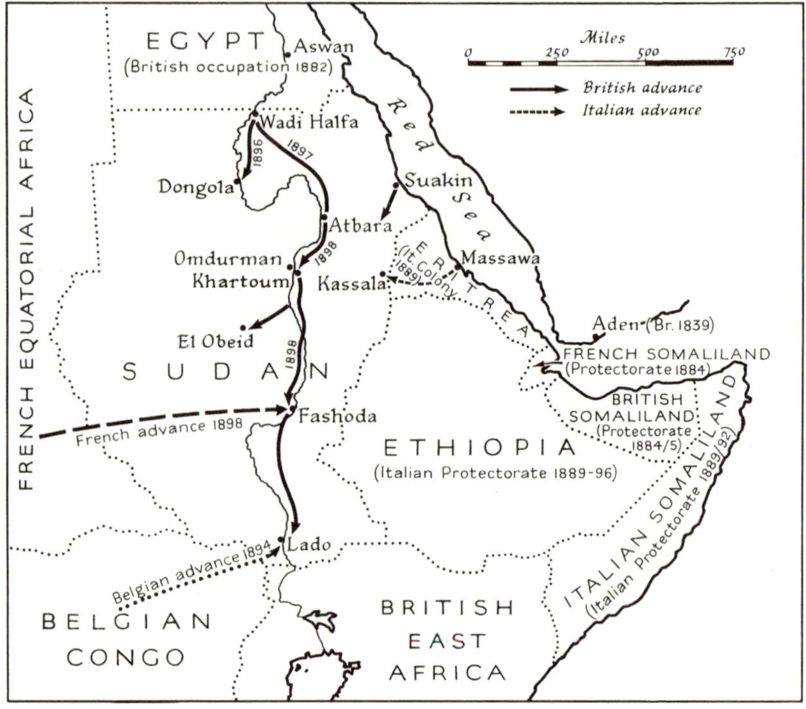

6 The European advance on the Sudan

The British conquest of the Sudan 1898

In the last decade of the nineteenth century the imperialist designs of several European powers were moving towards the upper Nile. The Germans were heading towards it from Tanganyika, the British from Uganda and Kenya. The Belgian king, Leopold II, was extending his possessions in that direction from the Congo Basin. The Italians were looking inland from the Red Sea coast and the French were thinking of seizing a great stretch of territory right across Africa from their possessions in Equatorial Africa and Senegal to the Red Sea. In South Africa, Cecil Rhodes was dreaming of a great chain of British territories from the Cape to Cairo, linked together by a transcontinental railway and telegraph system.

As already stated, Britain was concerned first and foremost with the strategic position of Egypt and realised that she could not hold her position there if a strong and possibly hostile power controlled the upper Nile valley. The British government therefore did its best to keep other powers out of the area and bought off the threat from Belgium, Italy and Germany by agreeing to recognise the sovereignty of those nations where they already had interests, at the price of their agreeing to leave the Upper Nile valley alone. The French, however, refused to be bought off. They had always regarded Britain's occupation of Egypt as a treacherous act and hoped to undermine the British position there. Accordingly the French prepared a grand programme for a march on the Nile. They planned to send expeditions from the French Congo and North Africa. In 1896 the French explorer, Major J. B. Marchand, set out from the Upper Congo and achieved the difficult task of reaching Fashoda on the Nile, a frontier town of the Sudan. Britain became thoroughly alarmed, and the government decided that it could no longer leave the Sudan as a tempting bait for another European power. Plans for an invasion of the Sudan were hurriedly prepared, a railway line was built and troops armed with the most modern weapons marched under the command of General H. H. Kitchener into the country. In 1898 Kitchener faced Marchand at Fashoda and forced him to withdraw, thus provoking the 'Fashoda incident' which nearly led to war between Britain and France. But before this happened Sudan's independence had already been destroyed by Kitchener's army. The Khalifa's forces were substantial and very courageous though they lacked the fire power of the British troops. Unfortunately for them they advanced too far instead of falling back on a position where the nature of the land would have given them the best chance of resisting the British attack. In their forward position they found it very difficult to maintain enough supplies and they did not have the weapons to attack the British camp successfully. Thus their morale declined and their numbers grew less so that when the British felt strong enough to push ahead they were able to pass the most difficult point on their advance without serious opposition. The most severe battle of the war was fought near Omdurman but in the open country the bravery of the Khalifa's followers was of no avail against the deadly fire of

General Kitchener

the British troops. They were defeated with great loss of life and the British occupied the Sudan. Lord Kitchener, the head of the British expedition, proclaimed that the reconquest of the Sudan was being undertaken on behalf of the Khedive of Egypt and the administration which was established in the country was known officially as the Anglo-Egyptian Condominium. But it was the British who had the real power and they administered the country until its attainment of independence in 1956.

The Battle of Omdurman

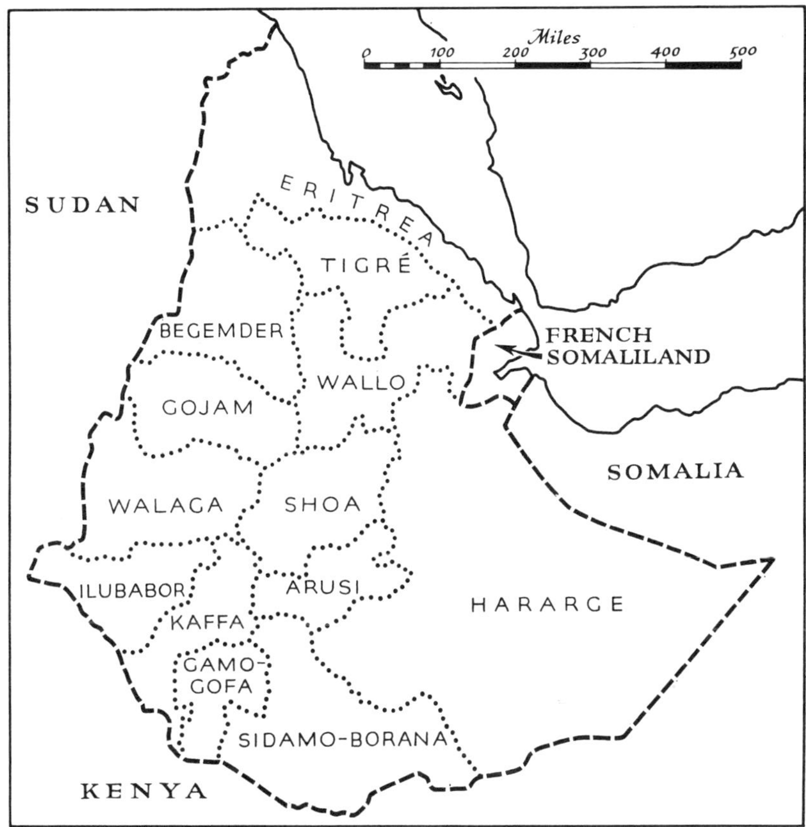

7 The provinces of Ethiopia

The Ethiopian Empire at the beginning of the nineteenth century

Ethiopia, as we have seen in the Introduction, is the centre of one of Africa's most ancient civilisations. From the beginnings of the empire of Axum more than two thousand years ago until today the Ethiopian highlands have had a continuous history. From about AD 350 when the Emperor Ezana adopted Christianity, the Christian religion had been the official state religion, and throughout the history of the empire the Church has played a vital role as the guardian of Ethiopia's culture, just as the authority of the emperor, who is believed to be descended from King Solomon of the Holy Scriptures, has been a symbol of unity and political identity. Geography has played a double

73

part in Ethiopian history. On the one hand, the great height of its flat-topped mountains, ranging from 5,000 to 12,000 feet, with great valleys and gorges, and the semi-desert lowlands which surround them, have made Ethiopia a land very difficult for a foreign aggressor to attack. These natural features have isolated the Ethiopians from other peoples and made it possible for them to continue developing their own unique culture. On the other hand the mountainous country and the difficulties of communications have placed obstacles in the way of the development of a strong and highly centralised kingdom. There has always been a tendency for rulers of provinces (or rases as they are called) to take advantage of any weakness of the central government to establish themselves as virtually independent kings.

At the beginning of the nineteenth century the kingdom was in a very weak state. Ever since the invasion of Ethiopia by the Somalis under Mohammed Gran in the sixteenth century the position of the emperors had been growing weaker. The Muslim invasion led to the emperor inviting Portuguese aid. With this help the Somalis were defeated but the coming of the Portuguese brought religious controversy into the country. The conversion of one of the emperors to the Roman Catholic faith and the civil wars which followed before the traditional church was restored, weakened the emperor's position. Worse still, they distracted attention from a more serious problem, the gradual movement onto the plateau of the cattle-keeping Galla. In the end the Galla overran almost half the area traditionally belonging to the Ethiopian Empire and their raiding activities made travel difficult even in the areas they did not occupy. In these circumstances the provincial rases broke away completely from the central government and fought each other in endless little wars for the almost worthless dignity of the imperial crown. Nevertheless in spite of the sad state to which the country was reduced the traditional civilisation did not collapse entirely. The Church still survived and succeeded in preserving the values of traditional Ethiopian culture. The Galla began to settle down and adopt much of the Ethiopian way of life. Some of them became Christians, others became Muslims. Finally, even though the emperors had lost almost all their power and there were often several persons claiming the title at the same time, the tradition that there should be an emperor who was the rightful ruler of all Ethiopia still survived. It was in these circumstances that three great rulers arose who succeeded in restoring the power of the monarchy, reuniting Ethiopia and making it a powerful state once more.

Emperor Theodore II of Ethiopia

Emperor Theodore

The first of the three great Ethiopian rulers of the nineteenth century was the son of the governor of the small frontier province of Kwara. His childhood was very poor but he grew up a brave and adventurous lad and began his climb to power by building up a band of followers who helped him in plundering trading caravans. Eventually his following became so powerful that he was in a position to intervene in the struggle for power that was going on between the great rases. The two main contenders for the imperial title at the time were the rases of the two large provinces of Gondar and Shoa. He defeated them both and forced the Abuna or Patriarch of the Ethiopian Church to crown him as emperor in 1855. He took the name Theodore as his imperial name and soon showed that he intended to make his imperial position a reality in a manner that had not been attempted for more than a hundred years. For this purpose he maintained a very large and well-paid army which he used to put down the numerous rebellions which broke out from time to time. He attempted to destroy the independent power of the rases completely and to turn them into salaried officers to be appointed and dismissed at will. He also tried to improve the taxation system, to regulate the power of the Church, to suppress the slave trade, and to enforce monogamy.

In foreign affairs Theodore had sweeping ambitions. He dreamed of conquering the Sudan, Egypt and Jerusalem and wiping Islam from the face of the earth. In particular he was determined that Ethiopia should be given the respect she deserved from the great powers. Theodore easily saw the advantages of modernisation, particularly in the field of weapons, and many Europeans were attracted to his court. Two of them, Bell and Plowden, became his trusted advisers and encouraged his programme of reforms. Others were not such worthwhile persons, and contributed to turning the Emperor's mind against the Europeans.

As Theodore's reign continued he ran into increasing difficulties. He tried to do too much too fast. His attempts at centralisation naturally aroused bitter opposition from the provincial rases, and this opposition was increased by resentment at the heavy taxes needed to maintain his inflated army. As a result Theodore became more and more unpopular and steadily lost control over growing areas of the country. This in turn produced a sense of bitter frustration which affected his personality until by the end of his reign he had become almost insane.

The crisis which ended in the fall and death of Theodore began when he addressed a letter to Queen Victoria proposing the opening of an Ethiopian embassy in London. Unfortunately the letter was given no serious attention and no reply was sent. Theodore took this as a calculated insult from a ruler whose subjects he had always befriended. In his rage he threw the British Consul, Cameron, into prison. When the British sent an agent to demand Cameron's release, with a message condemning the Emperor's action as uncivilised, he threw the agent and sixty other Europeans into jail also. The British government then felt in honour bound to rescue its subjects and in 1867 an expedition under Napier was sent out for the purpose. The British expedition found great difficulties in surmounting the geographical obstacles in the way of an invasion of Ethiopia but they met with no serious military opposition. By this time the great majority of the Ethiopian people were in opposition to their ruler and as the British made it clear that they did not intend to occupy the country permanently but merely to rescue their own subjects the rases were inclined to encourage them. Indeed the progress of the British force was made much easier by the fact that for much of their journey one of the rases provided them with free food for men and animals. Theodore was deserted by all but a small fraction of his once massive army. He decided to make a stand at his capital of Magdala and on 10 April 1868 the remnants of his followers were easily defeated by the British troops. The unfortunate emperor shot himself rather than fall into the enemies' hands.

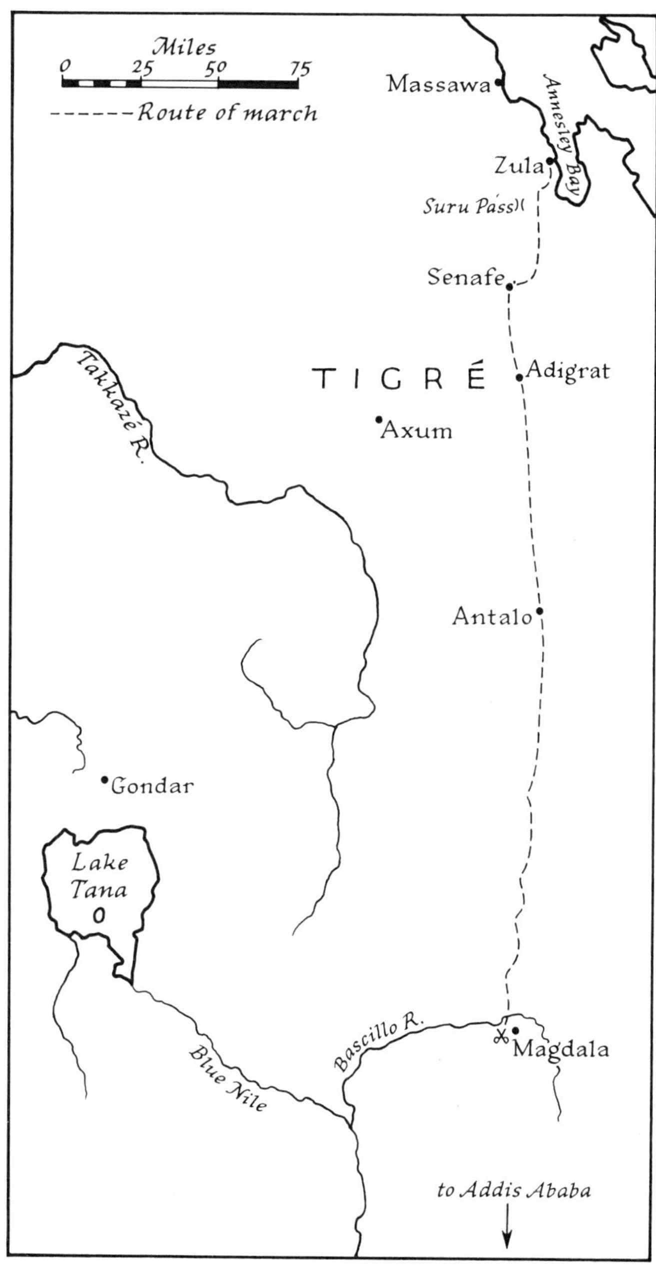

8 Napier's march from Zula to Magdala

After the successful achievement of their purpose the British left the country again, taking the released prisoners with them. The British expedition to Ethiopia created a quite false impression about the strength of the country. It looked as if the kingdom had been very easily defeated when in actual fact the only fighting had been between the British and the small remnant of Theodore's bodyguard. The mass of the people had been neutral or actively supporting the invaders. To conquer Ethiopia in face of a real national resistance would be quite a different matter.

Theodore's reign could thus be said to have ended in failure but from the point of view of Ethiopian history this was not really so. Even though he became so unpopular that he was deserted by the majority of his subjects, and even though his schemes for centralisation of government were unsuccessful he had restored the position and prestige of the monarchy. Henceforward no one doubted the power of whoever occupied the imperial throne. Indeed the throne became a precious jewel which the rases coveted and struggled among themselves to win.

Emperor John IV

The reign of Emperor John IV

The death of Theodore left three great rivals for the imperial throne. They were Gobaze the ras of Amhara, the ras of Tigre and Menelik the ras of Shoa. Gobaze proved the strongest at first and was crowned as emperor in 1868. He ruled for four years only, and his reign was

78

uneventful. The end of his reign in 1872 left the two great rases of
Tigre and Shoa face to face. Of the two, the ras of Tigre proved the
most successful and was crowned as the Emperor John IV. Menelik
remained largely independent, however, and it was not until 1878 that
John was able to force him to renounce the imperial title of Negus
Negast (King of Kings) which he had claimed ever since the death of
Theodore. John was a skilful diplomat and with wise statesmanship
he did not attempt to crush Menelik completely. Instead, in return for
recognition of the emperor's paramountcy, Menelik was given a free
hand to extend his territorial possessions in the southern part of the
empire over provinces which had long been overrun by the Galla. In
1882 the relationship between the two great men was further strengthened by a marriage alliance between two of their children, coupled
with an agreement that the succession should pass to Menelik after
John's death.

The energies of the Emperor John were largely absorbed by the
necessity to defend the empire against a succession of aggressors.
The threat came first from Egypt. Amongst the grandiose plans of
Ismail Pasha was the idea of building a great empire in Africa, and
included in this was the design to invade and occupy the Christian
Empire of Ethiopia. The Turko-Egyptian government had a base on
the Red Sea coast at Massawa which had originally been seized by
the Turks in the sixteenth century. With the aid of European advisers
and the most up to date weapons two attempts were made to invade
Ethiopia, in 1875 and 1876. In spite of the superiority of weapons
in the hands of the Egyptian forces and the presence of expert European military advisers, both these invasions were decisively defeated.
Large quantities of arms and equipment were captured by the
Ethiopians. The defeat of the second Egyptian expedition, the Egyptian financial crisis and the outbreak of the Mahdist revolt in the
Sudan, meant the end of the threat to Ethiopia from Egypt.

But the withdrawal of the Egyptians from the scene was followed
by the appearance of an even more serious danger. The French had
acquired the Red Sea port of Obok as early as 1862 and this was
destined to become the nucleus of French Somaliland. The Italians
acquired a coaling station in the Bay of Assab in 1869 and thereafter
began to take an increasing interest in Somaliland and the interior.
With the collapse of the Egyptian schemes the Italians began to
emerge as the chief contenders for control over the Ethiopian kingdom. They established themselves on the coast of the area now
known as Eritrea in 1885 and began to push inland in the direction
of the Ethiopian province of Tigre. At the same time the Italians did

their best to weaken the kingdom by playing Menelik against John. Menelik took the arms and money they offered him as he had previously accepted aid from the Egyptians, but he gave no real help to the invaders. In 1887 Italian forces clashed with Ethiopians at Dogali. The Italians were defeated and forced to fall back on Massawa, but it was clear that it would not be long before they tried again.

The dangers which John IV had to face did not come only from the direction of the Red Sea. The fanatically religious government of the Khalifa in the Sudan declared a jihad against its Christian neighbour and the Sudanese forces overran a large part of Ethiopia before they were decisively defeated by the Ethiopians at the Battle of Metemma in 1889. In this battle the Emperor John lost his life and Ethiopia was left without a ruler at a critical time.

Emperor Menelik II

Emperor Menelik II and the Italians

Throughout the reign of the Emperor John IV, Menelik the ras of Shoa continued to take every opportunity to strengthen his position. He allowed first the Egyptians and then the Italians to believe that they might be able to use him in their attempts to gain control of the country, and by this means he acquired large quantities of up to date fire arms which he used to extend his conquests over the Galla areas. He had, however, no intention of being used as a tool to establish foreign rule over the empire to which he hoped to succeed, and in spite of the aid he received he did nothing to help the invaders.

With the death of John the question of succession arose. Under the agreement which had been made between John and Menelik, Menelik was entitled to the succession but John had a son, Mangasha, who hoped to establish his claim to the throne. The Italians, who had been intriguing with Menelik for some time, believed that he would be a useful puppet ruler and at first gave him their support. He realised that Ethiopia's chances of survival depended on the possession of modern armaments and found it convenient to allow the Italians to continue believing that he would be a willing tool for their ambitions. Thus Menelik and the Italians entered into the Treaty of Ucciali in 1889 under which the Ethiopian emperor received huge supplies of arms and ammunition.

The clause in the treaty for which Italy had been prepared to pay so heavily was one which stated that Ethiopia consented to use Italy as her intermediary in foreign affairs. This could be interpreted to mean that Ethiopia was no longer an independent state but under Italian protection. The Italian government exploited this and informed the European powers that she had established a protectorate over the Ethiopian kingdom. Thus the kingdom of Ethiopia disappeared from maps produced in Europe and was replaced by Italian East Africa. In preparing to accept the Treaty of Ucciali, however, Menelik had taken care to see that there should be nothing in it which could be interpreted as a surrender of independence to the Italians. Two versions of the treaty had been drawn up, one in Italian and one in Amharic, and the wording of the two versions was subtly different in an important way. It was only the Italian version which said that the emperor consented to use the services of the Italians in foreign affairs; the Amharic version merely said that he might do so. Menelik wisely signed the Amharic version only. Thus when he heard of the way in which Italy was exploiting the treaty he was in a position to respond. In 1891 he sent a circular letter to the European powers pointing out that Ethiopia had not surrendered any part of her independence. In the same letter Menelik claimed very wide frontiers for the Ethiopian Empire, including Khartoum and Lake Rudolf, and stated that he did not intend to sit idly by while distant powers came to partition Africa.

By the time Italy realised that she had herself been cheated by the Ethiopian monarch she had hoped to cheat it was already too late. She fell back on giving support to Mangasha who was still holding out in Tigre but it soon became clear that he would be no more willing than Menelik himself to buy a throne at the price of placing his country under foreign domination. Thus Italy was faced with the fact that she could only hope to establish her claims by a direct attack on a ruler who she herself had armed and strengthened. Plans were therefore made for an invasion of Ethiopia. The example of the British expedition led the Italians to believe that the conquest of Ethiopia would be a relatively easy task for a modern European army. They forgot that they had themselves supplied the emperor with arms at least as good as those they intended to use against him. They gravely underestimated the numbers of men that he could assemble for battle, and above all they failed to realise that while the Napier expedition had only had to fight against a small bodyguard, their invasion would be opposed by the whole mass of the people. Indeed as the menace of an Italian invasion grew nearer Menelik whipped up the sense of national patriotism. *Rases* who had hitherto been dissidents gave him their support and even Mangasha rallied to the national cause. The Italian army which invaded Ethiopia in 1896 was thus inferior in numbers and no better armed than the defenders of Ethiopia. Its commanders had very little conception of the gravity of the task before them and were deceived for some time by false rumours, deliberately put about, that the emperor had died suddenly of snakebite. They allowed themselves to be brought to battle on most unfavourable ground at Adowa by the whole Ethiopian

The Battle of Adowa;
a drawing based on a picture in Haile Selassie University, Addis Ababa

army under the personal command of the emperor. The result was an overwhelming Ethiopian victory. The Italians were completely and disastrously defeated. Most of their armaments fell into Ethiopian hands and large numbers of their troops were taken prisoner. Italy was forced to abandon her claims and recognise Ethiopian independence in return for the release of her subjects. This humiliation, the greatest ever suffered by a European power in Africa, continued to rankle in Italian hearts and one of the reasons behind Mussolini's invasion of Ethiopia in 1936 was the desire to wipe out the memory of this disgrace.

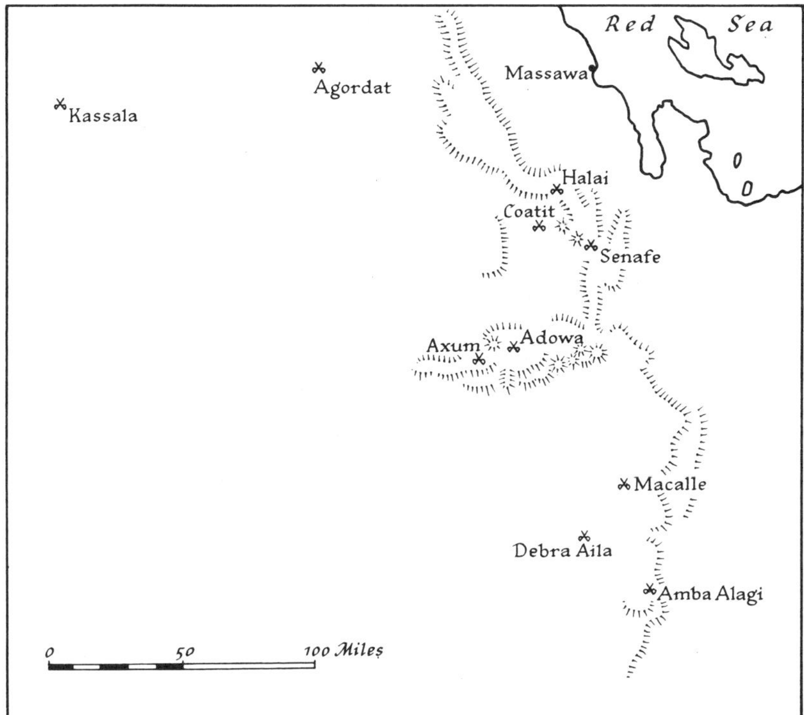

9 The Italian campaign in Ethiopia

The victory of Adowa established Ethiopia's independence beyond question and Menelik was free to continue his policy of consolidating and extending his rule. In a series of campaigns led by Hapta Giorgis, Tessama and Ras Makonnen the frontiers of the empire were pushed outwards and during his reign Menelik is said to have more than doubled the territory under effective Ethiopian control.

With the dramatic defeat of Italian claims Ethiopia appeared once more on European maps and the European powers hastened to establish diplomatic relations with the Ethiopian court. In the year following the Battle of Adowa Britain, Russia and Turkey opened embassies in Ethiopia. When Britain was about to engage in the conquest of the Sudan she was very anxious to ensure that Menelik did not give aid to the Khalifa which might make the reconquest more difficult, or even impossible. Britain accordingly sent the Rodd mission to Ethiopia, which in return for the promise not to give aid to the Khalifa or allow arms to pass through Ethiopia to the Sudanese, recognised all Menelik's conquests and gave him a further 15,000 square miles in the settlement of the Somali frontier. Finally in 1906 Britain, France and Italy signed a Tripartite Treaty formally recognising the independence and territorial integrity of Ethiopia.

Thus at the end of the nineteenth century, whilst the Sudan lost the independence she had won from Egypt in 1885, Ethiopia had her independence strengthened and recognised by the colonial powers.

3 The Maghreb and European intervention

The land

The north-western part of Africa, where the modern states of Morocco, Algeria, Tunisia and Libya are found today, is often referred to by the Arabic name, Maghreb. Most of the area faces the Mediterranean and Morocco has a coastline facing the Atlantic also. The sea winds bring rain which falls on the areas near the Mediterranean coast and this makes the coastal strip a relatively fertile area, known as the Tell. South of the Tell, which varies in width in different places, there are the mountains of the Atlas range and its extensions which run right through Morocco and Algeria and into part of Tunisia. Behind the mountains there lies the vast expanse of the Sahara. In some places, where there are no mountains, the fertile land gives place directly to the desert. The mountains receive considerable quantities of rain, especially on the side facing the sea, and in the mountain valleys there has always been intensive cultivation and a considerable population. In the desert settled life is only possible in scattered oases and along river beds which run down from the mountains to lose themselves in the Sahara. On the desert fringes, however, there has always existed a considerable nomadic population, living from their camels and other livestock. The Maghreb lies on a crossroads between the seaborne trade routes of the Mediterranean and the camel caravan routes across the Sahara.

Foreign invasions

The area has known a succession of foreign conquerors. The first were the Phoenicians from the coast of Syria and the Lebanon who established a powerful commercial empire around their great city of Carthage. After 146 BC much of the Maghreb was incorporated in the Roman Empire. Between 647 and 700 it was conquered by the

Arabs and has ever after remained an area where Islam is the religion of the great majority. The original population of the area consisted of numerous tribes of a people generally known as the Berbers. They are closely related to the peoples of the northern part of the Nile valley and to the peoples of southern Europe. Some of them migrated deep into the desert and penetrated as far as the northern areas of West Africa. (These people who are nomads and who wear large veils around their faces are generally known as the Tuaregs.) After the Arab conquest the Arabic language began to spread and there was a great deal of intermarriage, particularly after the eleventh century when a number of nomadic Arab tribes migrated into the area. Most of the population today is Arabic-speaking and they regard themselves as Arabs even though they are of mainly Berber descent. In the mountains, however, it was more difficult for the immigrant Arab groups to penetrate and considerable communities survive who still speak the ancient Berber language.

The Maghreb has always been a difficult area in which to develop strong governments. Tribal divisions have always been a source of difficulty but the problem is made much worse by the nature of the geography. The Tell is relatively easy to control and is the area in which most governments in the Maghreb have been based. It was always the area of highest population where the large cities were to be found. Until the invention of modern means of transport and communications the mountains and the desert were almost impossible for a government to control. The tribes of these areas would always take every opportunity to rebel against the central government and to attack their richer neighbours in the more fertile areas.

Successive governments in the Maghreb countries tended to go through the same process. When they were strong they would try to keep the mountain and desert people under control but these peoples would always await the chance to reassert their independence. Once a government became weak the desert and mountain peoples would break away and tribal quarrels would arise even in the coastal areas. Sometimes the desert people conquered the coastal areas and built up states there. When the Maghreb states were weak they offered an invitation to invasion from European countries across the Mediterranean and this happened in the fifteenth and early sixteenth centuries when Spain and Portugal seized a number of points on the Mediterranean coast and the Atlantic coast of Morocco. This Christian invasion led to a reaction from the Muslim population. In Morocco two strong dynasties arose which drove the Europeans out of most of their positions though the Spanish still retained (as they do until this day) a tiny area in north Morocco. In the rest of the Maghreb the Ottoman Turks were invited to help the Muslims against the infidel Christians. They succeeded in driving the Europeans out of most of the area but in return they made themselves masters of the country which became a part of the Ottoman Empire.

The Turkish Maghreb

The whole of the Maghreb, apart from Morocco, became part of the Ottoman Empire and was divided into the provinces of Algeria, Tunisia and Libya. The Turks who occupied the area regarded themselves as engaged in a jihad or holy war against the Christians, and this war was fought very largely by sea. The Turkish warships from ports in the Maghreb attacked and captured European ships in the Mediterranean. They also raided the coasts of Spain and Portugal and at the height of their power they even established a base in the Irish Channel. The merchandise they captured, and the numerous prisoners who were sold as slaves, made Algiers a rich and thriving town. All the Turkish provinces in the Maghreb were affected by the decline of the effective power of the Ottoman Sultanate. In all of them the local military and naval leaders made themselves the masters of the situation and became virtually independent of the Turkish Sultan, just as the Mamelukes did in Egypt. But development of the state was different in different areas.

In Algeria the main source of income of the ruling Turks was from the capture of Christian ships and the sale of captured goods and slaves. The rulers made little attempt at a direct administration of the hinterland. Local government was left almost entirely in the hands of local Arab and Berber chiefs. The Turkish government kept them from rebelling by using one tribe against another, in accordance with the policy of divide and rule. In Algiers, the capital, there were repeated upheavals and coups as the leaders of different military factions struggled for the position of Dey, the title held by the head of state.

In Tunisia, the opportunities to engage in profitable naval warfare were rather less than in Algeria, and there the governing group were much more concerned with the improvement and administration of the interior. There were many struggles for power until 1705 when Hussein Ibn Ali Agha, a Turkish soldier whose homeland was the island of Crete, seized power and succeeded in establishing his dynasty as hereditary rulers, with the title of Bey. Tunisia was thus to all intents and purposes an independent monarchy and the ruling class had a much closer relationship with the mass of the people than was the case in Algeria.

In Libya attacks on Christian shipping were frequently made from the port of Tripoli, but not on a scale sufficient to rival Algiers. In this territory also Turkish authority declined until it was overthrown in 1711 by Osman Karamanli, the offspring of a Turkish-Libyan marriage, who founded the Karamanli dynasty. The descendants of Osman remained in power in Libya until 1835.

European influence in the Maghreb before 1830

Before the beginning of the nineteenth century there were a number of attempts by European powers to destroy the bases of the Turkish warships (corsairs) which took such a heavy toll of shipping in the Mediterranean. None of these resulted in permanent European conquest. A number of European powers found it convenient to

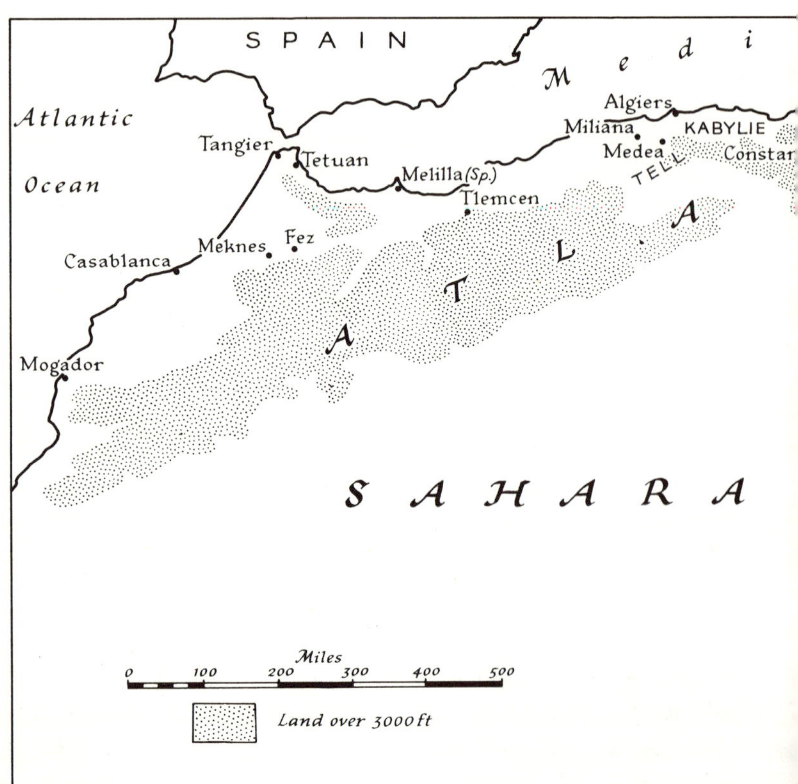

establish diplomatic relations with the Maghreb countries and sometimes to pay them tribute in return for trading privileges and guarantees of safety for their ships. By the nineteenth century, however, the situation had changed considerably. The Maghreb had not kept up with the tremendous industrial and economic progress of European countries and America. European navies had been improved and armed with weapons far more powerful than anything at the disposal of the Maghreb rulers. European powers also began to combine in hostility to what they regarded as the piratical practices of the Maghreb states. The rulers of the Maghreb themselves became increasingly aware of the backward and weak state of their countries and in their anxiety to modernise their lands they fell increasingly under European influence.

As early as 1804 the United States attempted to remove the ruler of Libya, Yusuf Karamanli, from the throne, in favour of a puppet named Hamed. Then Warrington, who was the British Consul in Libya from 1814–35, succeeded in establishing a dominant position

10 The Maghreb in the nineteenth century

for himself in the country. In 1816 he introduced vaccination into Libya and he was also responsible for suggesting ways in which the agriculture of the country might be made more productive. In order to extend British influence into the interior he proposed to the British government that a vice-consul should be established at the oasis town of Murzuk in the Fezzan, an important staging post on the caravan route from Tripoli to Bornu in West Africa.

By 1825 the European countries which did not have independent representation in Libya entrusted the responsibility to Warrington. Between 1815 and 1827 he used his good offices to settle disputes between Libya and Denmark, Sardinia, Tuscany and Sweden. Thus Warrington was virtually Secretary of State for Foreign Affairs to the Libyan kingdom and he exercised a great deal of influence in internal matters as well. In 1832 he plotted with a group of rebels against Yusuf, in the hope that a successful rebellion 'would establish British influence for the next half century'.

The French occupation of Algeria

The year 1830 marks a turning point in the history of the Maghreb for it marked the beginning of outright European conquest. Once this process had begun in Algeria the independence of the other Maghreb states became increasingly precarious until they too fell under European rule. Relations between France and Algeria had always been close as France, from its port of Marseilles, was one of the major Mediterranean trading powers. Profitable trading arrangements were built up during the eighteenth century in which France secured wheat and olives from Algeria in return for European goods. During the Napoleonic wars Algeria was one of the main sources of supply of provisions to maintain the French armies in Egypt and Italy. After the fall of Napoleon the regime of the French king Louis XVIII considered the Algerian trade of sufficient importance to enter into new commercial treaties with the country.

Trouble arose as a result of financial transactions between two wealthy Jews and a number of Frenchmen with the Algerian authorities. Towards the end of the eighteenth century two wealthy Jewish financiers, Bacri and Busnach, attempted to establish a virtual monopoly of Algeria's export trade. The Dey became involved in their financial transactions and ran up huge debts with the financiers in circumstances which led him to believe that he had been badly cheated. When he refused to pay, the financiers sought the help of the French administration. After investigation the commission set up by the French to look into the matter reduced the debt claimed from the Dey from 24,000,000 to 7,000,000 francs. Nevertheless there was a feeling that the state of the Algerian administration was a hindrance to the profitable development of French trade.

The appointment of Deval as French Consul in 1819 led to a rapid deterioration of Franco-Algerian relations. He had a bad reputation for crooked dealings and it was believed that he was hand in glove with the Jewish moneylenders. Hussein, the Dey of Algeria, asked for the Consul to be removed on several occasions, but the French government refused and took no account of the Dey's charges against Deval. The climax came on 29 April 1827. On that day the French Consul had a meeting with the Dey in which Hussein became so annoyed that he hit Deval with his fly-whisk. This trivial incident would normally have been allowed to pass, but the French monarchy was very unpopular at the time and King Charles X felt that a military success was what was needed to restore the prestige of his regime. Thus the incident of the fly-whisk was treated as an insult to the French nation and plans were made to redeem French honour by a military expedition against the Dey. The French Press and much of the assembly (parliament) were opposed to the North African adventure but there were commercial interests in France which supported it, because of the financial possibilities they saw in increased trade with Algeria. There were also some who dreamed of a great French empire in North Africa.

In 1830 the French forces invaded Algeria in what was intended at first to be a short campaign. France justified her action to the outside world by arguing that her main purpose was to suppress the Algerian pirates. The Dey's forces were speedily overwhelmed and the French proclaimed, as Napoleon had done in Egypt, that they were not fighting against the Algerian peoples but had come to liberate them from Turkish oppression. But however much the Algerians may have disliked their Turkish overlords, they were united with them in the common Islamic faith. As Christians, the French represented the traditional infidel enemy against whom the Maghreb peoples had been fighting since the Portuguese-Spanish conquests of the fifteenth and sixteenth century. No amount of promises of social and economic improvement could reconcile the Algerians to their country being occupied by the hated unbelievers. Religious and nationalist feeling united to produce a massive national resistance of a type unknown since the days when the Berbers of the Maghreb had fought against their Arab conquerors in the original Arab conquest.

Abdel Kader

Abdel Kader and resistance to the French occupation

This national war of resistance was led by a remarkable man named Abdel Kader. He was a man of great learning in the traditional Islamic subjects. He had a profound knowledge of Islamic law and the traditions of the Prophet and his companions. He had also studied history, philosophy, astronomy, geography, and the works of the great philosophers of ancient Greece, Plato and Aristotle. Unlike Mohammed Ali in Egypt, whom he knew and admired, Abdel Kader was a native born Algerian and had little personal political ambition. Until his people pressed him to take the lead against the infidel invaders his intention had been to lead the life of an ascetic. With the ardent support of the mass of the people and aided by the geography of the country, which made the movement of troops difficult, Abdel Kader was able to hold out successfully in the mountains. His people fought desperately, largely with arms made in Algeria itself, as well as a few imported from Tunisia and Morocco. So successful were the tactics of surprise attacks and withdrawal into the mountain fastnesses which Abdel Kader used against the French that by 1834 they were prepared to make peace with him. In that year the Desmichaels Treaty was signed and in 1837 another treaty, the Treaty of Tafna was drawn up. Under these treaties the French conceded to Abdel Kader the control of the greater part of Algeria and contented themselves with the narrow fertile coastal strip.

In the areas which he governed Abdel Kader made strict obedience to Islam the keynote of his rule. He appointed learned Qadis to administer law in accordance with the Malikite code. He collected only those taxes specifically mentioned in the Koran. He took a stern attitude to drinking and vice and set his face against luxuries of all kinds. He took a keen interest in the spread of Islamic education and established numerous schools in the territory under his control. He led his forces personally in their struggles with the French. For more than ten years his leadership succeeded in holding together many traditionally warring tribes in a common endeavour.

The French occupation becomes permanent

The long struggle with Abdel Kader profoundly changed the nature of the French occupation. The original intention had been a speedy campaign to avenge the insult to French honour and to establish French influence in the country, followed by withdrawal. But the bitter and prolonged resistance which the French met caused them to alter their approach. The more they invested in the lives of soldiers and money the more difficult it became for them to think of giving up the country. What is more, as the deep and abiding hostility of the Algerians to their Christian conquerors became apparent, the French began to feel that they could never hope to hold the country unless they introduced substantial numbers of their own citizens there. Thus they fell back on an idea taken from the history of the ancient Roman Empire of establishing their own citizens on farms as colonists. The Algerians were punished for their resistance by being deprived of much of their best farming land which was given out to French colons, as they were called.

As the French established themselves ever more firmly on the coastal lands, they felt it essential to destroy the power of Abdel Kader. The existence of his Islamic society as an independent state in the neighbourhood of the French held territory was a constant incitement to rebellion. Thus in spite of their treaties the French began to plot his downfall. They did this by finding means of dividing his followers. Throughout the Maghreb the Muslim societies known as Brotherhoods were very strong. They were usually jealous of one another and disliked being under the control of anyone except their own leaders. The French therefore found it possible to win over the support of one of the most powerful of the Brotherhoods, known as the Tijanniya, and turn it against the rule of Abdel Kader. In addition some of Abdel Kader's followers deserted him because they found his puritanical government too strict for their liking, while others lost confidence in him because they felt he did not go far enough in his opposition to the Christians and should never have entered into any kind of treaty with them at all. Finally the French were able to bring sufficient pressure on Morocco and Tunisia to stop them sending arms to Abdel Kader's followers. In 1847 the French were in a position to bring the independence of Abdel Kader to an end. Overwhelmed by his better armed enemies and deserted by many of his followers, he was forced to surrender and was made a prisoner in France for many years. He is revered by Algerians today as a pioneer of the national resistance struggle.

The removal of Abdel Kader from the scene did not mean the collapse of the spirit of resistance. The mountainous Kabylie area, the homeland of a Berber-speaking population, was not occupied until 1857. By 1869 the French had lost about 150,000 soldiers and a similar number of colonists in their struggle to establish their rule in Algeria. Then in 1873 violent rebellion broke out again in the Kabylie mountains. This was crushed with much bloodshed and was the last attempt during the nineteenth century of the Algerian peoples to win back their independence.

Development of French policy in Algeria

As the long and bitter struggle dragged on in Algeria the French took increasingly ferocious measures to break the spirit of the people and ensure their own position. Apart from the large number of people who were killed in actual fighting, the French adopted savage measures against the mass of the population. Villages were burned down, crops were destroyed and the peasants driven from their lands. The nature of the struggle can be seen in the words of the French General Bugeaud, who in speaking to a group of French colonists in Algeria in 1846 said: 'We have burnt a great deal and destroyed a great deal. It may be that I shall be called a barbarian, but as I have the conviction that I have done something useful for my country, I consider myself as above the reproaches of the press.'
Combined with this policy of repression against the Algerian population the French encouraged more and more colons to settle on the lands seized from the Algerian peasants. In 1839 there were 25,000 European settlers in Algeria, by 1849 they had grown to 109,000. In 1871 the number was 245,000, and by 1912 they were nearly 800,000. The colons were introduced largely as a means of consolidating the French grip on the country. It was also realised that the more fertile areas of Algeria were ideal for farming of the southern European type and could produce heavy crops of wheat, olives and grapes for wine-making. The growing European population, it was hoped, would give France a valuable source of basic commodities and a large market for her manufactured goods. The French were so anxious to increase the number of colons that they were prepared to grant land and French citizenship to almost any European who was prepared to settle in Algeria. Large numbers of Italians, Spaniards and Maltese migrated to Algeria to swell the colon population.
As the colon community in Algeria developed, it naturally tried,

like other settler groups in other parts of Africa had elsewhere, to protect and even increase its privileged position in relation to the indigenous people. To justify their privileges the colons claimed that the Algerians were unprogressive farmers incapable of making improvements and that their bad farming methods were preventing mankind at large from enjoying the benefits of Algeria's natural resources. Only the colons, they argued, were capable of calling forth the riches of the Algerian soil.

French policy in Algeria was also aimed at replacing the traditional culture of the people with French culture. The reason for this was partly that the French believed their own civilisation was the best in the world and partly because they thought that if the Algerians absorbed French culture they would be loyal to France. Thus the Muslim law which was regarded as sacred by the mass of the population was replaced by the French code. The traditional Muslim judges, known as Qadis, were removed and replaced by the French machinery of justice. This policy could not be entirely successful and the Muslim law was allowed to come back for the settlement of personal matters affecting indigenous Algerians but the French system remained the law of the land for most things above the private level.

This policy of turning the Algerians into Frenchmen meant that in theory they should be allowed in time to enjoy all the rights and privileges of French citizenship, including the right to a share of political power. These principles were accepted in theory, but in practice they were never applied. The reason for this was the large body of colons. They were given considerable political power in Algeria and they also had powerful political friends in France itself. Many of them were Frenchmen with relatives in their home country, and they were also supported by commercial groups who benefited from their trade. The colons were naturally anxious to hold on to their privileged position and they saw that if large numbers of Algerians were given full citizenship and political rights the special position of the colons would speedily disappear. Thus they tried to portray the Algerians as backward and incapable of being educated and to put every kind of barrier in the way of their gaining citizenship rights. By means of their political position in Algeria itself and by their representatives in the French National Assembly, together with the influence of their political friends in France, they were able to block any attempt to extend citizenship rights to the mass of the Algerian population even when the French government was anxious to do so.

Tunisia

The French conquest of Algeria was the beginning of the end of the independence of the Maghreb states but it did not lead to an immediate attack on other areas for two reasons. In the first place the grim struggle which the French had to undertake to establish their control over Algeria did not encourage them to attempt the conquest of another Muslim North African area. Thereafter they preferred to practice the technique of gradual infiltration, using the traditional rulers as instruments of their policy, rather than outright conquest and the introduction of direct French government. In the second place the great European powers were jealous of each other and each did its best to prevent any of the others gaining an advantage. As a result of these intrigues European occupation of the remainder of the Maghreb was delayed for many years.

When the French first attacked Algeria the Bey of Tunis thought he could profit from the situation. He was pleased that the power of his enemy, the Dey of Algiers, was being weakened, and he hoped to take advantage of the situation to seize the eastern part of Algeria, the area around the town of Constantine, and incorporate it in his own kingdom. The French also held out the hope that if they were successful in their conquest they might make him the ruler of all Algeria. The Bey therefore gladly entered into a treaty with France giving certain privileges to French citizens. Later, however, as the struggle of the French with the Muslims in Algeria continued, public opinion in Tunisia favoured Abdel Kader and supplies of arms were brought to him from Tunisia. This made the French bring all their pressure to bear to stop this arms supply.

The influence of France in Tunisia displeased the British government, which tried to find a means of preventing the French from occupying the country. The British did not want to occupy the country themselves and so they tried to persuade the Ottoman Sultan of Turkey to reassert his rule over the land, which had been a dead letter ever since the seizure of power by Hussein Bey in 1705. The result of this was to make the Bey turn even more towards the French as his only protection against the Turks.

The reign of Ahmed Bey

In 1835 an energetic ruler known as Ahmed Bey came to the throne in Tunisia. Like Mohammed Ali in Egypt, he realised the need to modernise his country if it was to survive. In particular he tried to modernise the armed forces. In 1840 he founded a military academy where officers were trained by experts from a number of European countries. He also built a naval base and shipyard at Porto Farina, where twelve ships were built for his navy. For these schemes, and for the sake of preserving his independence from the Sultan of Turkey, he remained on very close terms with the French. Under their influence he agreed to the abolition of slavery in 1842. He also undertook a state visit to Paris and in return for the hospitality shown to him he agreed to remove the restrictions on Jews in Tunisia and to allow the establishment of Roman Catholic schools. In spite of his pro-French attitude, however, he was careful to preserve his independence and to avoid falling into the debt of European powers. By careful management of his finances, he increased the money in the treasury; when he died in 1855 he left his successor assets amounting to about 120,000,000 francs.

Mohammed es Sadek, Bey of Tunis

Mohammed es Sadek and the growth of European influence

His successor, Mohammed es Sadek, was a very different man. He also saw the need to modernise the country but he had not the ability to carry it out. He lacked financial wisdom and was easily cheated by European moneylenders, and he was lavish in his personal expenses. Large sums were expended on the purchase of beautiful

Turkish slave girls for his pleasure. During his reign European influence in the country steadily increased. In 1859 the French were given the monopoly of telegraph services in Tunisia and the British were given the right to build a railway from Tunis to Goletta. Under European influence the Bey decided to introduce some important reforms. Religious equality was to be introduced and the disadvantages which non-Muslims had previously suffered were to be removed. In 1861 the Bey proposed to introduce a European type of constitution. There was to be a representative assembly and the Bey was to act only on the advice of his ministers. The financial administration was to be improved, and government expenditure was to be kept within a budget which would be presented to and discussed by the representative assembly. There were also to be legal reforms and the introduction of an appeal court. These proposals pleased the younger elements of the country, who were acquiring western education, but they were never put into practice. As a result a party grew up called the Destour or Constitution Party, which pressed for the introduction of this 1861 constitution. It is a breakaway branch of this party known as the Neo-Destour which forms the government of Tunisia today.

The threat to Tunisia's independence became greater as the Bey fell deeper and deeper into debt to European moneylenders. In 1863 he borrowed £1,400,000 from Messrs Oppenheim and Erlanger of Paris. The terms of the loan were so unfavourable that the Bey only received one-seventh of the total sum in cash. To repay this and subsequent loans, which were given to him at very heavy interest, he had to increase the rate of taxation on his subjects. A new tax known as the majba was introduced but it was so unpopular that a rebellion broke out, headed by a leader called Ali ibn Ghadhahim, who came to be known as the 'Bey of the people'. The struggle to suppress this uprising plunged the Bey still further into debt and by 1869 the financial condition of the country had become so desperate that an international commission consisting of English, Italian and French interests was set up to see to the fulfilment of Tunisia's international financial obligations. It was obviously only a matter of time before Tunisian independence disappeared altogether. This was delayed while the European powers quarrelled over who should have the right to the country.

The three countries with the largest interests involved were France, Britain and Italy. The Bey, who saw the French as the greatest danger to the independence of his country, tried to ward them off by placing himself under the suzerainty of the Ottoman Sultan in

Constantinople. In 1871 an imperial decree, or firman, was issued, affirming that Tunisia was part of the Ottoman Empire. The Bey, Muhammed es Sadek, was recognised as governor (Vizir) with the right of hereditary succession and Tunisia was bound to give military support to the Sultan in case of war. In addition to acquiring this protective umbrella the Bey also began to guard against the further extension of French interests in his country. An ambitious scheme advanced by M. Ferdinand de Lesseps whereby French engineers would flood a large area of Tunisia, turning it into an inland sea and thus improving the rainfall and creating possibilities of greatly extended agriculture, was refused. In 1880 the Bey also refused to grant harbour concessions to the French at his port of Goletta. These checks naturally irritated the French and increased their desire to be masters of the country, but they were powerless to act in the face of British and Italian opposition.

In 1878 the German Chancellor, Bismarck, summoned the Congress of Berlin to settle problems arising out of the decline of the Turkish Empire. Bismarck was anxious to encourage the French to expand their colonial empire in Africa. He hoped that this would distract French attention from the idea of a war against Germany to recapture Alsace and Lorraine, which Germany had seized from France in 1870. At the conference an agreement was reached in which the British agreed to allow the French a free hand in Tunisia in return for French recognition of the British occupation of the Mediterranean island of Cyprus.

The only remaining obstacle to French imperialist designs on Tunisia was Italy. By 1880 the number of Italians in Tunisia was considerably greater than that of the French. There was a growing agitation in Italy for a revival of Roman North Africa and the Bey's government leaned more towards Italy as a counter-weight against France. An Italian company succeeded in winning control over the Tunis to Goletta railway from the French, and in 1881 the Bey's brother made a visit to Sicily and met the Italian King.

The French occupation of Tunisia

Faced with this threat to their position the French decided on direct intervention. For hundreds of years the tribes on the borders of Algeria and Tunisia had been accustomed to raiding one another. These raids were suitable pretexts for war, and when a group known as the Krumirs made a minor raid from Tunisia into Algeria in

March 1881 the French seized the opportunity to invade the Tunisian kingdom. There was virtually no resistance. The Bey was forced to agree to the Treaty of Bardo, under which the French assumed control of Tunisia's foreign affairs, and two years later the Treaty of Marsa gave the French control of internal affairs also.

The French occupation of Tunisia took a different form from that of Algeria. There was no prolonged fighting and the French did not destroy the whole structure of the Tunisian kingdom. In international law they had acquired their rights in the country from the Bey's agreement in the Treaties of Bardo and Marsa. Thus Tunisia became a French protectorate rather than a colony like Algeria. For this reason the French had to administer Tunisia on rather different lines from Algeria. A good deal of the traditional system of government was retained and the policy of trying to run the country on purely French lines was not adopted. The French entrenched themselves economically and a number of French settlers were allowed to occupy land but this was on a much smaller scale than in Algeria. Thus it was possible in the next century for the Tunisians to regain their independence with much less struggle and much less bitterness than in the case of Algeria.

Morocco

Morocco in the nineteenth century was ruled by a dynasty which had come to power in the seventeenth century. They claimed the title of Sharifs, that is, descendants of the Prophet. The greatest figure in this dynasty was Moulay Ismail who ruled in the seventeenth and eighteenth centuries. He tried to overcome the forces of division in his country by building up a very strong central army made up of Negro slaves from the area of the upper Niger. After his death, however, his sons and their descendants struggled for power, using sections of the army for their own purposes until the army lost its value and eventually disappeared. By the nineteenth century the hope of building a strong, united Morocco had virtually collapsed. Though members of the dynasty were still on the throne they could control only a part of the country. The numerous different groups in the mountainous and desert parts of the land resumed their traditional hostilities with one another, and to maintain his authority the Moroccan ruler could rely only on the unstable loyalty of the Arab tribes, who in return for their support demanded privileges of exemption from taxes and high government appointments.

Moulay Suleiman

Moulay Suleiman, who ascended the throne in 1792, was engaged throughout his reign in an almost continuous struggle against rebellions in every part of his realm. In 1820 his army was defeated by rebels in the very heart of the kingdom, between the two major towns of Meknes and Fez. It was in such chaotic conditions that Abdel Rahman ascended the throne in 1822. The weakness of the country was an open invitation to foreign intervention. Britain had economic and strategic interests in the area. Germany and Belgium became increasingly active in the economic life of the country during the nineteenth century. Spain, which had always managed to hold on to small areas of coastline which it had seized in the fifteenth century, sought to expand into the interior. France was determined to make Morocco part of her North African Empire.

When the French first occupied Algeria, Abdel Rahman in Morocco, like the Bey of Tunisia, saw the invasion as an opportunity to extend his frontiers. The people of Tlemcen asked for his aid and in reply he established his authority over their area in western Algeria. He appointed his representatives (khalifas) to Tlemcen, Miliana and Medea. As the French invasion of Algeria turned into an occupation, and the long struggle between the French and Abdel Kader took place, the ruler of Morocco was forced by public opinion to support Abdel Kader in his struggle with the Christians. The French therefore declared war on Morocco in 1844. Mogador and Tangier were bombarded and the Moroccan forces defeated at the Battle of Isly in 1845. The Moroccan ruler had to make peace and stop supporting Abdel Kader.

The weak state of Morocco provided an opportunity for the Spanish to expand their holdings on Moroccan soil. In 1859 there was a dispute about the Spanish fortification of Melilla, and Spanish forces invaded the Moroccan kingdom. They met with little opposition, and after capturing the important town of Tetuan were about to advance into the heart of Morocco when they were prevented by British intervention. Peace was made, but humiliating conditions were imposed. The Spaniards gained an extension of the area they held around Mellila, and Morocco had to pay a penalty of £4 million.

Moulay Hassan

Thus Morocco was already in grave danger of losing its independence when a new ruler, Moulay Hassan, ascended the throne in

1873. He proved himself an energetic ruler, who, while being a devout Muslim, realised the need to modernise his country if it were to retain its independence. Like his great ancestor, Moulay Ismail, Moulay Hassan saw the need for a strong army to overcome the dividing forces in the country. He thus attempted to develop a modern army as well as introducing a number of industries into the country. Throughout his reign he was almost constantly engaged in campaigns against rebels in different parts of his kingdom, and he came closer than any other king since Moulay Ismail in the seventeenth century to bringing the whole country under effective control. He possessed a high capacity for administration, but even his energies and abilities were not sufficient to overcome the difficulties of establishing central-ised government throughout such a mountainous and diversified country.

Moulay Hassan's foreign policy was aimed at gaining the advan-tages of European trade and contact while at the same time preserving his country's independence. He saw that British and French interests in his country were in conflict and tried to use the British as a shield against the French. During his lifetime his policy proved very success-ful. Morocco provided a substantial market for British manufactured goods, British interests obtained a monopoly of the trade in Moroccan merino wool and also exploited Moroccan iron and phosphates. Thus Britain had an interest in preventing the French from taking over the country and became the champion of Moroccan independence and territorial integrity. Moulay Hassan's policy of using one Euro-pean power against another could only give temporary security. Britain and France had many common interests which were more important to them than a dispute over Morocco. Both powers were competing for empire in many parts of Africa and there was always the possibility that they would agree to an exchange under which Britain would stop resisting the French in Morocco in return for French concessions elsewhere. In 1904 this came about when in the agreement known as the Anglo-French Agreement, Britain stopped upholding Moroccan independence and gave formal approval to French imperial ambitions there.

By this time there was a new ruler on the Moroccan throne. Moulay Hassan died in 1894 and was succeeded by Abdel Aziz. The new King was only sixteen years of age, inexperienced and easily misled. He fell under the influence of European advisers, particularly two Englishmen. One was Walter Harris, correspondent of *The Times* in Morocco, and the other Harry Maclean. The King's associ-ation with these infidels as advisers, and his lax attitude to the rules of the Islamic faith, inevitably weakened his position amongst his subjects. His greatest weakness, however, was his fondness for European goods of all kinds on which he spent huge sums to the delight of British manufacturers.

The French occupation of Morocco

By 1903 Abdel Aziz's lavish spending had almost emptied the treasury and he resorted to borrowing like Ismail of Egypt and Mohammed es Sadek of Tunisia. In 1903 Abdel Aziz took a loan of £800,000 from French, British and Spanish moneylenders. The French were naturally anxious to encourage the King to get himself heavily in debt, and in 1904 they persuaded him to take a loan of 62,500,000 francs, of which 12,500,000 francs were taken as commission. In the meantime imperialist-minded bankers, financiers and business-men in France had formed the Comité du Maroc in 1900 which urged the government to take over the country to protect their financial interests. While engaged in this financial penetration of Morocco the French also took steps to weaken the ruler's authority and to produce a breakdown of law and order which would justify their

11 The European advance into the Maghreb

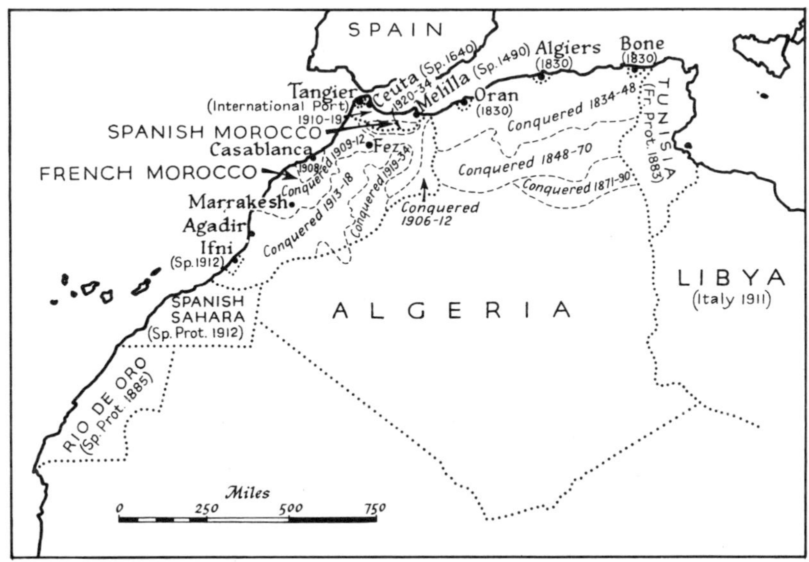

intervention. They thus gave aid to Bou Hamara, a pretender who proclaimed himself king, and to Raisuli, a sharif, who acted as a brigand chief and made himself the virtually independent ruler of the Tangier district.

Sensing that the French were closing in on him Abdel Aziz attempted to get the support of Germany against them. In 1906 the international conference which was held at Algeciras in Morocco paid lip service to Moroccan independence, but Germany was not prepared to take effective steps to resist French ambition in the country and in 1911 Germany agreed to give France a free hand in Morocco in return for concessions elsewhere. But by that time the French occupation of Morocco had already begun. In 1907 riots against Christians and Jews broke out in Casablanca. The French argued that the Sultan's government was no longer able to maintain law and order and protect European lives and property. French troops marched into the country. In 1912 the occupation was legalised and Morocco proclaimed as a French protectorate. The French administration in Morocco was more similar to that of Tunisia than Algeria. The traditional structure of the Moroccan kingdom was largely preserved and though there was considerable French immigration the Moroccans still retained the use of most of their land.

Libya

Libya, the poorest and weakest of the Maghreb states, was the last to suffer European occupation. In the early years of the nineteenth century as we have seen, Libya, which consisted of a loose grouping of Cyrenaica, Tripoli and the Fezzan, under rulers of the Karamanli family, had begun to fall under European influence, especially that of the British Consul, Warrington. After the French occupation of Algeria in 1830 French attention was directed to Libya. A treaty was forced on the ruler Yusuf Karamanli under which he was to apologise to the French Consul, Rousseau, for past humiliations. Trade monopolies were abolished, enslaving of Christians was to stop, all exactions from French citizens were to cease, the Libyan navy was not to be further strengthened, and Yusuf was to make a large payment for the losses of French subjects in Libya. The French and British then gave their support to rival heirs who struggled for succession to the throne. The French backed the legal heir, Ali Pasha, while Warrington lived amongst the rebels and gave them his support. This confused situation provided an opportunity for the

Ottoman Sultan to restore his long lost authority in the country. A Turkish force under Mustapha Nedgib was sent to Tripoli on the pretext of restoring law and order. It landed without meeting any opposition and the general proceeded to arrest all members of the ruling family. He then declared the Karamanli dynasty abolished and installed himself as governor of the Pashalik.

The newly re-established Ottoman government was confined to the coastal areas. The government at Constantinople was afraid to allow its representatives in Tripoli to grow too strong in case they should seize their independence as the Karamanlis had done before. The walis (governors) were frequently changed and between 1835 and 1911, the year of the Italian invasion of Libya, there were no less than thirty-three walis. These frequent changes obviously undermined the efficiency of the administration. What is more, the Ottoman government did not have the military forces necessary to maintain order throughout the country.

The Senussiya

In these circumstances the administration of the interior of the country was undertaken by a Muslim Brotherhood known as the Senussiya. The founder of this organisation, Sayyid Muhammad bin 'Ali al-Sanusi, was born in Algeria about 1787 into a distinguished family of Sharifs. Well informed in Muslim theology, the law and interpretation of the Koran, he travelled to Morocco where he was associated with the Moroccan Brotherhood called the Tijaniya. In the 1820s he left Morocco for Mecca, probably to avoid opposition from the Moroccan authorities, who were alarmed at the political consequences of his propaganda in support of pan-Islam. He went through Tripoli and Benghazi and gathered around him a number of disciples (Ikhwan) mostly of Algerian origin. A number of them followed him when he moved on to Egypt. It is likely that what he saw of the cultural and political revival of Egypt under Mohammed Ali influenced him. From Egypt he went on to the Holy cities of Mecca and Medina in Arabia where he studied for some time. While there he began to preach of the need to return to the practice of Islam as it had been in the time of the Prophet, and in 1837 he founded his own Brotherhood near Mecca. Four years later he came back to North Africa, and in 1843 he established the Mother Lodge of his Order at al-Baida on the Central Cyrenaican plateau. In 1856 he established his headquarters at Jaghbub, 160 kilometers from the coast and there he was succeeded in 1859 by his eldest son, al-Sayyid Muhammad al-Mahdi. In the same year the capital of the Brotherhood was moved to Kufra still further from the coast.

The Senussiya came to be accepted by the Turks as their agency for administering the interior. It performed many of the functions of government, including education, justice and the maintenance of security. The traditionally warring tribes of the interior of Libya came to accept the special holiness (baraka) which the head of the brotherhood was thought to possess. As many of his disciples came from outside Libya, their role as impartial arbitrators between one tribe and another came to be appreciated. A good impression of the law and order that prevailed in the interior can be gained from these remarks by an Egyptian Oxford graduate, who gained his information from Libyan Bedouin tribesmen: 'There can be no doubt that the influence of the Senussi brotherhood upon the lives of the people of the region is good. The ikhwan of the Senussi are not only teachers of the people both in the field of religion and of general knowledge, but judges and intermediaries both between tribe and tribe . . . The importance of these aspects of the Senussi rule in maintaining the tranquility and well-being of the people of the Libyan desert can scarcely be overestimated.'* Economically the brotherhood became the guardian of the Trans-Saharan caravan routes connecting Libya with Bornu, the Hausa states and Wadai.

The Italian invasion

Italy had long been dreaming of recreating the Roman Empire in North Africa. Foiled by the French in Tunisia she at last managed to get a foothold in Libya. Since 1838 she had been casting longing eyes at the territory, and in 1911 she seized three of the main towns in the country with the object of securing the territory as her share in the eventual break up of the Ottoman Empire. Turkey, whose energies were fully engaged by the nationalist revolts of the Balkan peoples against the Sultan, was in no position to defend Libya against the Italians and it was left to the Senussiya who kept up the resistance from 1911 to 1917.

---

* A. Boahen, *Britain, the Sahara, and the Western Sudan 1788–1861*, Oxford 1964, pp. 110–111, quotes A. M. Hassanein Bey, *The Last Oases*, (1925).

106

Part **two**

West Africa

Publisher's Note
Chapter 4 in this section was edited by the publishers with a view to reducing the length and cost of the book. Unfortunately, due to difficulties in postal communication during the Nigerian crisis, it was not possible to find a formula for these cuts acceptable to Dr. Afigbo. The publishers have, therefore, to accept responsibility for the final form of this chapter and to express regret to Dr. Afigbo for any stylistic or historical shortcomings arising from the editing.

4 West Africa to 1800

The habit of dividing history into periods, though a convenient and widespread practice amongst historians, has often been condemned as artificial and misleading. It needs to be emphasised here that West African history was not one thing before 1800 and entirely another thing after that date.

Trans-Saharan trade routes

For well over sixteen centuries after Christ, the dominant factor in West African history was the trans-Saharan caravan trade, in which the initiative lay outside West Africa, or, to be more exact, in the Maghreb and North Africa. Recent evidence from archaeology and geology has established beyond reasonable doubt that in the very distant past the region of the present Sahara desert, which now looks like a formidable divide between West Africa and North Africa, carried a richer vegetation and enjoyed a better supply of rivers and rain. It was therefore more thickly populated by mixed groups of Caucasoids and Negroes, some of whom lived from seasonal agriculture and others of whom grazed large herds of cattle. As the Sahara began to dry up the Caucasoids retreated northwards and the Negroes southwards. Continued contact was possible, however, because here and there in the Sahara there survived green patches, known as oases, carrying enough water and vegetation to support human existence. Contact in the forms of trade and war led to established routes from one oasis to the other, and thus linked the fertile belts which lay to the north and south of the Sahara.

Until the fifteenth century these routes across the Sahara remained West Africa's most sure and certain link with the outside world, while until even later the trade and ideas which penetrated the region through them constituted the most dynamic forces in its history. Because of its location and peculiar characteristics, the Sudan of West Africa benefited more from this link than the Guinea lands and so assumed historical leadership of West Africa. The Sudan, with its vegetation of grass and orchard bush, is a more open country than Guinea, with its vegetation of thick evergreen bush; thus travel was easier. This advantage of the Sudan over Guinea was emphasised through the use by the Sudanese of beasts of burden, especially with the introduction of the horse as a riding animal. This ease of travel favoured conquerors and traders, as well as the rise of empires and of commercial centres enjoying international renown.

The Sudan also had the advantage of being able to support a wider variety of occupations than Guinea; it was able to combine occupations borrowed from the desert to the north of it, and the tropical rain forest to the south. Along the main river banks the Sudanese practised artificial irrigation agriculture, as did the Negroes of the Saharan oases and of the Sahildid. With this, in certain areas, they combined rainy season agriculture supplemented by husbandry, which was more characteristic of the forest zone. Certain classes of Sudanese peoples, especially the cattle Fulani, practised nomadic pastoralism, and in addition there was long distance trade. From this rich variety of occupations the Sudan was able to support a sizeable population and maintain the soldiers and politicians required for large scale political organisation.

Because of its location, the Sudan was able to play a key role in the international trade that went to North Africa. This trade was between the products of the Mediterranean and Europe on the one hand, and of the forest zone of West Africa – gold, kola nuts, ivory and slaves – on the other. The Sudan had a few gold-bearing areas, in the valley of the Senegal and the Niger, and produced animal skins, but the actual role of the Sudanese in the trade was to collect the products of their forest neighbours to the south for exchange with the dates, salt and manufactured articles brought from the desert, North Africa and Europe by the North African caravans. In a sense, therefore, the historical pre-eminence of the Sudanese in West Africa was for centuries rooted in their economic exploitation of their neighbours to the south. The impression which the outside world had of the Sudanese wealth was so exaggerated that, even up to the nineteenth century, European travellers expected to find Timbuctu a fabulously wealthy city and were disappointed to find it a decadent town with only drab mud huts and mosques. But, however exaggerated the wealth of the Sudan was in European and Asiatic imagination, there is no doubt that the trade made the Sudan, until about the eighteenth century, a much richer land than Guinea.

Islam

International trade brought the Sudan in particular, and West Africa in general, face to face for the first time with one of the world's universalist religions. From time immemorial all West Africans had followed the religion of their fathers which some, for lack of a better term, call Paganism. Then from AD 632 Islam gained a foothold in Egypt and from there set out to conquer the rest of North Africa. The ancient North African urbanised cities were relatively easy to conquer, but the Berbers of the desert put up a stout resistance. Rather than submit, some of them started to migrate, the Lemtuna tribe taking the lead in this. But the Arabs and Islam followed them on; refugees and their pursuers followed the beaten track of the ancient trade routes across the Sahara. By the eighth century the Sanhaja had got to Mauretania; by that same century a Muslim state of Southern Algeria, Tahert, was already trading with Awdaghast, a Sanhaja city. From the latter place Islam penetrated further south into the Sudan proper, the ruling dynasty of Takrur being the first Negro dynasty to embrace the new religion.

This new factor which entered West Africa through the trade routes eventually proved a more permanent and dynamic historical force than the trade which brought it. At first however, its role in shaping events appeared subordinate to that of trade. Only in the nineteenth century did Islam become the chief determinant of political change in the Sudan.

In other spheres of life Islam also represented a factor of change. The pilgrimage which it encouraged brought the élite of the Sudan into contact with the most advanced ideas of the time and so kept them up to date and progressive. Idris Aloma of Bornu (1511–1603), for instance, learnt of the use of firearms in the course of his pilgrimage, introduced their use into the Bornu army and thus won himself a place in history as a military reformer and conqueror. Islam also introduced into the Western Sudan the mode of dressing now considered traditional in the Sudan belt, and, more important, the Arabic script.

This latter event is perhaps, from the historian's point of view, the most important innovation by Islam in West Africa, for it made the keeping of written records possible.

Development of European trade

Earlier in this chapter, it was indicated that the role of the trans-Saharan trade as an important historical force was not limited to the Sudan. Directly and indirectly it determined the political and economic development in the forest. European merchants, especially from Italy, the Iberian peninsula and France, were early participators in the trans-Saharan trade, but only indirectly. The merchant princes and kingdoms of the Maghreb succeeded in creating for themselves middlemen's monopoly of this trade. To preserve, and benefit from, this position they prevented their European customers and rivals from going into the interior with them to participate directly in the Sudanese trade. One or two Europeans succeeded in breaking through the middlemen's cordon and penetrated the interior along these routes. A merchant from Toulouse, Anselme d'Isalguier, is said to have got as far as, and lived in, Gao between 1405 and 1413, while a Genoese merchant was able to get to Touat in 1447. But such cases as these remained exceptional. By and large, what Europeans knew about the interior came to them second hand. Fed on stories of fabled cities of gold and the like they grew all the more anxious to participate directly in this trade. It was this desire that was partly responsible for the European bid, starting in the fifteenth century and led by the Portuguese, to reach West Africa by sea. The Europeans hoped that when they got to West Africa they would be able to divert this trade towards the south to their incalculable advantage. In a sense, therefore, the trans-Saharan trade gave rise to the impulses which created the trans-Atlantic trade which first competed with it and then stifled it.

But the European exploration of the West African coast derived not only from the economic motive. There was also a missionary motive. From about the eighth century, when the Muslims gained control of the Mediterranean and seriously embarked on the conquest of southern Europe, especially the Iberian peninsula, Christian Europe had been involved in a seemingly endless conflict with Islam. From the internal crusade for the liberation of Portugal and Spain the struggle had developed into the crusade against Islam in the Holy Land during which Christian Europe for a while actually seized the initiative. By the fifteenth century the crusading ideal had died in the rest of Europe but not in Portugal and Spain, the two countries who had suffered most from the Muslims. As part of their offensive against Islam the Portuguese now had the ambition of side-stepping the Muslims of North Africa to reach the (pagan)

Negroes of West Africa, whom they hoped to convert to Christianity. Along with this ambition went the even vaguer hope of making contact with Prester John, a legendary Christian potentate whom they hoped would come to the aid of the Christians.

Spurred on by economic ambitions as well as these vague dreams, the Portuguese in about 1417 launched their plans to reach West Africa. With the able management of Prince Henry the Navigator they achieved startling success in a short time, considering the navigational difficulties they encountered and dealt with. They reached Cape Verde in 1444, the Bight of Benin in 1475 and the Congo in 1482.

On getting to West Africa the Portuguese set out to put their discoveries to their advantage. Contacts for trade were made in the regions of Senegal, Gambia, Ghana and Benin, and adventurers were sent inland to find the gold mines that supplied the trans-Saharan trade. Hand-in-hand with the trade went missionary effort. In the key islands off the shores of the Windward Coast and the Gulf of Guinea, Portuguese colonies were planted to serve as centres for the exploitation of the continental trade. In this trade at first emphasis was on natural produce, such as gold, ivory, and pepper. But early in the history of Portuguese contact with West Africa there was also a small volume of trade in slaves who were sent to Portugal. The first of the unfortunate Africans who were shipped to Portugal were not actually captured as slaves. They were to be trained for missionary work in West Africa. But then it was discovered they were useful as farm hands in the underpopulated areas of Portugal and so trade grew in volume.

With the Spanish colonisation of America, and the discovery that Africans were better able than the native Indians to work the Spanish mines and plantations, the trade progressively acquired a new importance until by about 1650 slaves became West Africa's main export.

The first effective challenge to the Portuguese came only in the 1590's from the Dutch. In 1642 and 1647 the Danes and the Swedes respectively entered the race for West African trade, while the English and the French intensified their participation in the trade from the 1650s. The Prussians were the last on the scene, entering as they did in 1682. In any case by the middle of the sixteenth century the trans-Atlantic trade with Europe had become an established concern. Like the trans-Saharan trade in the Sudan, this international trade with Europe proved an important historical force in the West African forest.

The influence of European trade on West African states

The forest lands of Ghana inhabited by the Akan-speaking peoples were rich in gold and kola, two of the principal items of the northern trade. From here trade routes radiated northwards via Begho to Jenne and Hausaland. In consequence of this northward trade the earliest Akan state, Bono-Tekyiman, rose on the forest fringe some time after AD 1450, and perhaps the foundation of a number of petty principalities was laid in the forest zone proper and along the coast. Then, about 1470, the Portuguese got to the coast of Ghana and in 1482 built the castle of Elmina to establish effective exploitation of the trade of the region. With the establishment of this trade there developed more intense rivalry amongst these petty kingdoms for its control than there had ever been for the more remote northern trade. Up to about 1650 among the more successful of the older states were Denkyira, Fante, Akyem and Akwamu. Then about 1670 the Asante kingdom was founded with its capital at Kumasi. While fully exploiting the northern trade it sought also to control the coastal trade. In this process it swallowed up Denkyira in 1701, Akyem in 1742, and then got ready to engulf Fante.

In modern southern Nigeria west of the Niger an identical event led to the rise of Oyo. Benin's case was a little different since it was already a flourishing state by the time the European trade was established. Its rise would seem to owe much to its trade with Yorubaland which connected it with the northern trade. Edo oral traditions link the rise of Benin's historic dynasty with Yorubaland. In Yorubaland a number of principalities would seem to have arisen between AD 1000 and 1500. Of these Oyo, the most strategically located to participate in these two international trades, became pre-eminent. Being on the northern fringe of the forest it had commercial links with Hausaland, while in the south-western direction its cavalry could operate as far south as Porto Novo. In the region of modern Dahomey the earliest states, Allada and Whydah, arose along the coast after 1550 and must have done so largely in response to the Atlantic trade. Abomey, the youngest of the Aja states, rose after 1620 and in direct response to the challenges of the coastal trade. The rise and expansion of this last Aja state resulted directly from the attempt of the Fon of Abomey to organise themselves for defence against the Oyo, Allada and Whydah, who constantly raided them to supply the trans-Atlantic slave trade.

The regions of Guinea to the east of the Niger and to the west of

An Oba of Benin. The Benin dynasty is one of the oldest in West Africa
and maintained its royal traditions intact for over five hundred years
until conquered by a British expedition in 1897

Ghana were isolated from the direct impact of the northern trade.
Political developments here were inspired solely by the Atlantic
trade. Along the eastern Nigerian coast the House system arose
among the Ijo and the Efik to meet the challenge of the Atlantic
trade. On the windward coast small principalities and chieftaincies,
but no empires, emerged to organise and exploit the European trade.
It would appear, therefore, that except in those areas which participated in the northern and more ancient traffic, the Atlantic trade
was not able by itself to inspire large scale political organisation.
Even in Dahomey there was a trade route linking Whydah and
Abomey with the Sudan.

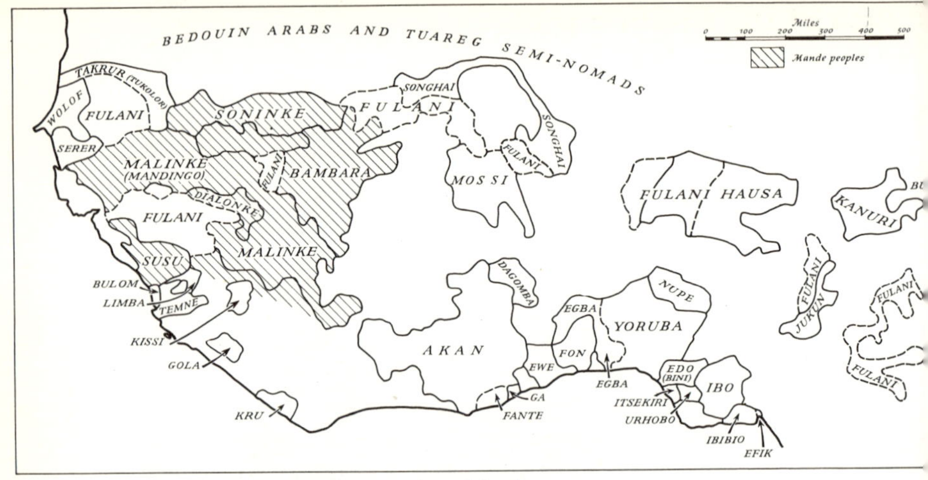

12 West African peoples mentioned in the text

13 States, towns and physical features of West Africa in the early nineteenth century

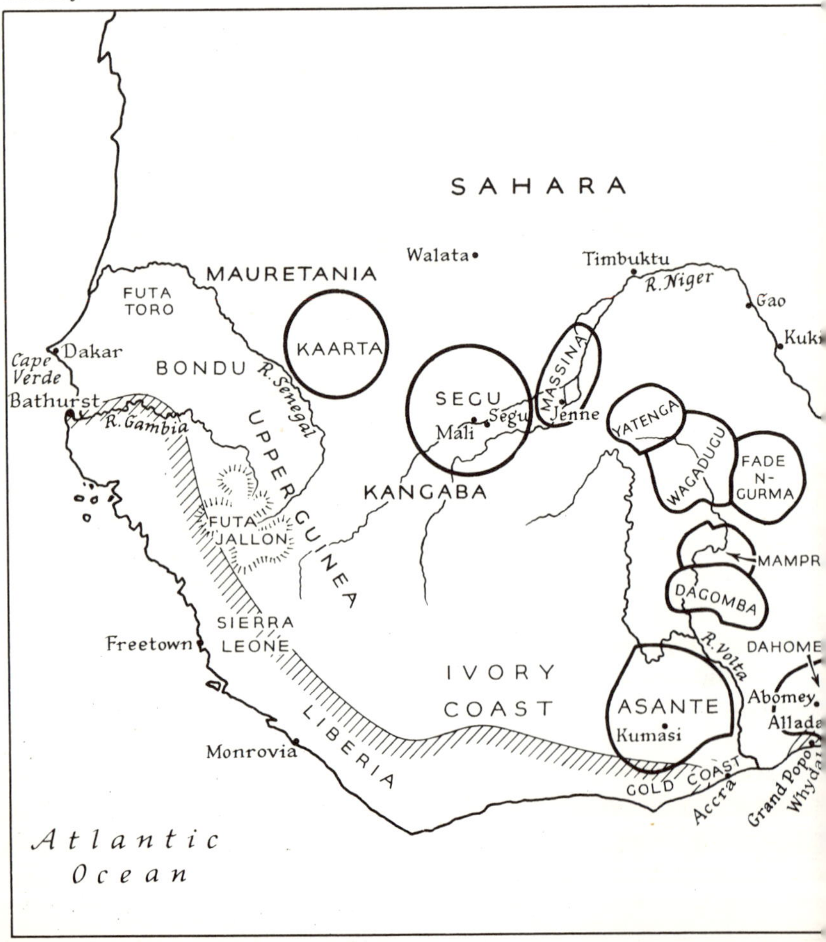

Rise of the Atlantic trade

On the economic side, the Atlantic trade ended the isolation of Guinea as well as the period when it lay in the economic backwaters of West Africa. But, contrary to Portuguese expectation, this trade was not able, until the twentieth century, to stifle completely the northern traffic and focus attention on Guinea alone. The trans-Saharan routes were still important by the nineteenth century, so important in fact that, as will be shown, Europe at times seriously thought of using North Africa (in particular Tripoli) as the gateway to the West African interior. The Atlantic trade, unlike the northern trade, was not an unmixed blessing for those who participated in it. From about 1650 the slave trade was its lifeblood. This trade was not only morally bad for the Africans and Europeans alike, it also caused a heavy, and for West Africa unprofitable, transfer of population from Guinea to the New World. The total loss to West Africa in human beings in the course of the trade has been variously estimated

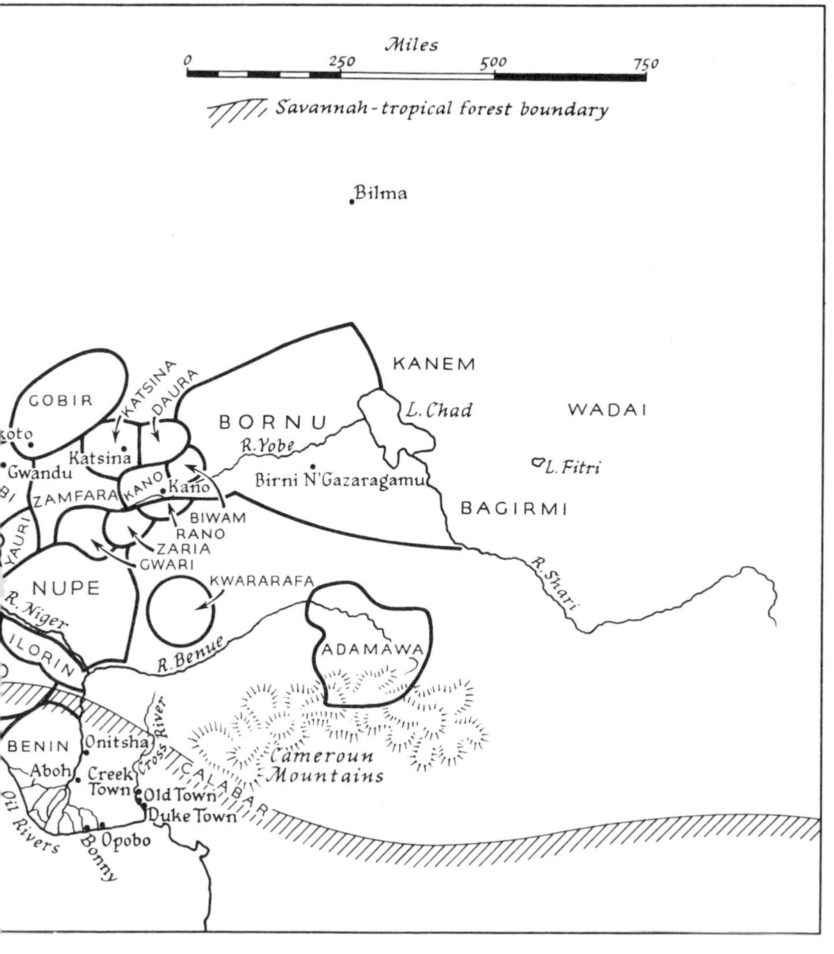

at between thirty and forty million souls. As most of these were the most vigorous sections of the population, their enforced emigration was a severe loss to the land of their birth. It was partly because of this and partly because of the insecurity and destruction caused by the forcible recruitment of the slaves that many productive indigenous industries declined with the triumph of the trade.

Like its northern counterpart, the Atlantic trade brought with it to Guinea another universalist religion, Christianity, which was subsequently to contribute immensely in shaping the destiny of West Africans. Up to the nineteenth century, however, it was of even less account than Islam. Portuguese missionary efforts in the windward coast, at Benin and Warri, achieved nothing, partly owing to lack of well-trained missionaries and partly owing to the stifling influence of the slave trade.

In West Africa, therefore, before 1800 the factors that determined much of the history of the indigenous peoples were international trade, and alien universalist religion. With varying emphasis they remained the same in the period covered in this book. European commerce and Christianity led first to the exploration of West Africa and then to its colonisation by France, England, Germany and Portugal. West African nationalism and the achievement of independence were the results of African reaction to this new form of economic exploitation. But even before these forces had unfolded themselves, Islam had inspired a series of attempts at empire-building in the Sudan. The subsidiary effects of this, allied with the militant advance of European economic exploitation, led to the fall of the Guinea states which had survived into the nineteenth century. In the following chapters these new developments of the nineteenth and twentieth centuries will be dealt with. They should be seen in perspective as the further unfolding of forces already present in West Africa by 1800.

But there was some difference. Whereas it was the northern trade that dominated life in West Africa before 1800, after that date the Atlantic trade gradually took over the leadership and eventually completely destroyed the northern trade. Whereas Islam and Christianity in the main played a subsidiary role to the economic factor before 1800, after that date they assumed an importance of their own. Christianity in particular became more central than previously in the political, social and moral evolution of West Africa. And finally whereas international trade, especially the European trade, did not threaten the independence of West Africans before 1800, after that date it became more and more evident that for some time, at least, the two things could not exist side by side.

5 The growth and changing nature of European influence (c. 1800 - 61)

For nearly three centuries European interest in West Africa had two dominant features. In the first place it was commercial. In the second place it was limited to the coast, despite the fact that the climate of the West African interior was healthier than that of the malaria infested coast along which Europeans conducted their trading business for over three centuries. In West Africa the Europeans remained at the coast for so long because of the nature of the trade in which they were primarily interested. The slave trade did not need European intervention inland to keep going the steady flow of captives.

In the fifteenth century the Portuguese, who had hopes of discovering the gold mines that supplied the northern trade, had tried to penetrate the interior. On the Senegal, for instance, they had gone as far inland as the Felou falls, while on the Gambia they had reached the Geba river. In 1485 they went into Benin. But these early voyages inland proved uniformly unrewarding. Unlike South America, with its rich mines of Peru, the West African interior had no dazzling attractions for the Europeans, at least until the nineteenth century.

It has often been contended that it was indigenous opposition that kept the Europeans off. It would seem, however, that if the latter had seriously wanted to penetrate the interior they could have done so in spite of local African obstruction. The African communities of Guinea were certainly better organised and better armed in the nineteenth century than they were in the sixteenth and seventeenth centuries, when the Europeans had the monopoly of the musket and the cannon. Yet African opposition in the nineteenth century could not keep off the Europeans.

Until about 1800 therefore the European nations did not seriously consider the conquest and colonisation of West Africa for economic exploitation. The Portuguese colonised the Canary Islands, Madeira, Santiago, São Thomé and some other off-shore islands but these

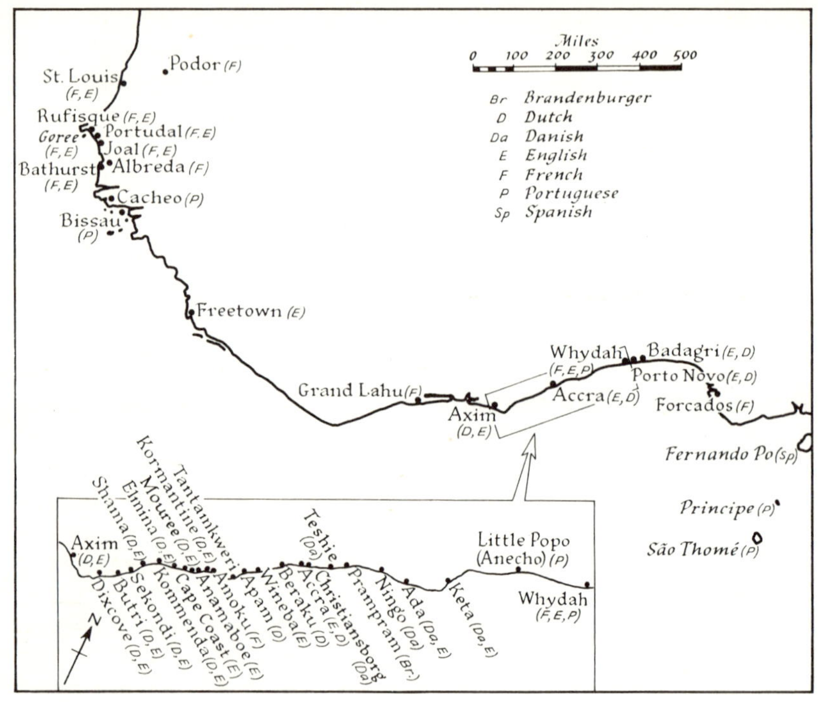

14 European forts and trading posts

were used as centres from which to tap the continental trade. São
Thomé was in addition a plantation colony which by the middle of
the sixteenth century was an important source of sugar for Europe.
The French between 1687 and 1702, and the English in 1763 had
sought to plant colonies in the Senegal and Gambia areas respectively.
All these efforts were tentative and not vigorously pressed. In consequence, in spite of three centuries of European presence, trade along
the West African coast was an affair between equals. The Africans
remained their own masters, and lived their own lives according to
their own standards and traditions. Even when they copied European
ways they did so at their own wish. They were in fact responsible for
seeing that law and order were maintained on the coast in order to
protect trade. On the coast of modern Ghana they were able to enforce the payment of rents by the Europeans for the pieces of land
on which the latter's forts stood. And in spite of these forts the
Europeans found themselves devoid of any real political power or
influence. From time to time they managed to exploit rivalries

120

amongst African chiefs, and used bribes to establish some influence,
but by and large it was the Africans who were politically supreme.
In 1786 the commandants of the forts of Tantumkweri, Sekondi and
Mouree were kidnapped, stripped and flogged for insulting Africans,

The Danish fort at Christiansborg (Osu) before the nineteenth century

while in 1812 the commandant of Winneba was killed, but the Europeans lacked the power to avenge this drastic treatment.

On the coast of Dahomey the Yevogan dictated to Europeans and
Africans alike the regulations guiding trade and had the means of
securing obedience to his will. There, as on the coast of the Oil
River (the name by which the creeks of the Niger Delta were known)
and elsewhere, Europeans had to pay harbour and trade duties before
being allowed to engage in the coastal trade. A detailed study of the
relationship which existed about 1800 between Africans and Europeans
along the coast shows that the latter were neither feared nor liked
but tolerated by the former. They were tolerated because Africans
realised that Europeans were useful in providing goods which could
not be manufactured locally and which, from being luxuries, had
become necessities.

But in the course of the nineteenth century this relationship was
undermined and superseded by a new master-servant relationship.
At heart European interest remained economic. But revolutionary

121

changes which took place in European society caused a shift of emphasis from trade in human beings to trade in natural produce. This shift in emphasis dictated a new strategy which included political domination. For some time however, the full implications of this change were obscured by apparently harmless interests in the abolition of the slave trade, the exploration of the interior and the propagation of Christianity. It is with these three movements that we shall now deal.

The campaign against the slave trade

The reasons behind the abolition of the slave trade were many and various, but the most important of them was economic. To some extent the slave trade destroyed itself. By the middle of the eighteenth century surplus capital, part of which came from the slave trade, had helped to bring about the industrial revolution in Britain. In the other parts of Europe the same changes were about to take place. Fundamental to the industrial revolution was the application of science to industry which made it easier and quicker to turn raw materials into manufactured goods. The economic implications of this were far-reaching. More raw materials were needed to keep the machines fully and profitably employed and it was discovered that of these raw materials West Africa could supply vegetable oils, rubber, indigo, cotton, ivory, timber and the like.

Hand-in-hand with the quest for raw materials went a quest for new and expanding markets to absorb the products of the industries. With regard to this it was again discovered that West Africa had great promise.

The old relationship between Europe and West Africa based on the slave trade was seen to be unsuitable in the new circumstances. The slave trade not only carried away from West Africa men and women who could help in raising the new crops needed by British industries and in providing an ever-expanding market, but also the raids and wars associated with it were believed to create such chaos and in-security as would hamper agriculture and peaceful trade. In the light of these new needs the slave trade appeared outdated and had to be abolished.

There was also another side to the economic factor. About this period there arose in Europe a group of economic thinkers who propagated and popularised the idea that free trade, free competition and free labour are more profitable than rigidly regulated trade and forced labour. Slavery was forced labour and so, according to these thinkers, was unproductive and wasteful. The slave could not give his best because he was made to work against his will. Furthermore, he was generally not a skilled worker. Here again, the slave trade was shown to be an anachronism.

But it was not the economic arguments alone that gave birth to the campaign against the slave trade. In fact it was not the rational economists and the new trading interests which launched and carried through the movement. The importance of these new interests lay rather in the fact that, without their support, the spearheads of the abolitionist movement would have achieved little. For, at the same time as the economic developments sketched above were taking place, a group of men generally known as humanitarians began to campaign against the slave trade and other forms of oppression in many parts of Europe and America. These men opposed the slave trade and gave their lives to its abolition not on economic grounds but because it caused too much human suffering. It was these men who never tired of collecting for publication stories of atrocities committed in the process of the trade. In their effort they were supported by churchmen who at about the same time developed a keen interest in the propagation of Christianity amongst Africans and Asiatics. Members of this group, known as the Evangelicals, opposed the slave trade mainly on religious grounds. They argued that slavery was evil because it contravened a law of God, according to which all men should be brothers and equal under the Fatherhood of God.

The British anti-slavery movement

It was these economic, humanitarian and evangelical arguments which, in the second half of the eighteenth century, combined to give rise to the British anti-slavery movement. The detailed story of the struggles and campaigns of the movement belongs properly to British domestic history. Only the outlines will be given here. The foremost leaders of the movement were Granville Sharp, Thomas Clarkson and William Wilberforce, the last being the representative and spokesman of the movement in the British Parliament for many years. Apart from these, however, there were other participants in the crusade whose roles have not yet been properly assessed or even widely recognised. Among this later group was a former Ibo slave, Olauda Equiano, also known as Gustavus Vasa the African. Equiano

Olaudah Equiano, the ex-slave
who became prominent in the British anti-slavery movement

(Ekwoanya?), who was born either at Essaka in the Abo Division of the Mid-West Region of Nigeria or at Isieke in the Orlu Division of Eastern Nigeria, was kidnapped and sold into slavery early in the eighteenth century. After a most startling life of adventure and travel which took him to America, the West Indies, Europe and Turkey he purchased his freedom and settled in England. With the rise of the anti-slavery movement he plunged himself wholeheartedly into it. He organised public lectures at various centres in England in which he ventilated the evils of the slave trade and told the English public what rich material reward they could reap if they suppressed the slave trade and developed the natural resources of Africa. He embodied these ideas in his autobiography which he published in 1789. This book contained one of the earliest enunciations of the idea that only legitimate commerce, agriculture and Christianity could effectively destroy the slave trade.

The anti-slavers achieved their first success in 1772 when Granville

Sharp brought a case about a runaway slave to an English court. In dealing with the case Chief Justice Mansfield declared that English law did not recognise slavery and that as soon as a slave set foot on English soil he became free. This decision had an important consequence for West Africa which will be dealt with later in this chapter. From this time the campaign grew in volume and intensity. After a long and hard struggle in and outside the British Parliament by Sharp and others a law was passed in 1807 which made the trade illegal for British subjects. After this the scene of the campaign shifted from Britain, where it had been carried out by means of public lectures, parliamentary lobbies and highly coloured pamphlets and newspaper articles, to West Africa, where these methods were replaced by naval force, diplomatic persuasions and pressures, legitimate commerce and missionary propaganda. All these methods, with the possible exception of the last, were inter-related, and the campaign in West Africa must be seen as a piece. Its outlines are bold and clear.

International agreements

Until the later 1830s Britain concentrated her effort on getting other European nations and America to give up trading in slaves. She sought to achieve this by the use of diplomacy, and in addition a detachment of the Royal Navy was stationed permanently in West Africa for the purpose of seizing slave ships (often called the West African, or the Preventive, Squadron). The two instruments of diplomacy and naval force were complementary. The British Foreign Office negotiated treaties banning the trade with nations which had not yet done so, while the Royal Navy enforced the terms of these treaties. In theory all those nations which either outlawed the slave trade completely or restricted the area in which it could be carried on by their nationals were expected to co-operate with Britain in capturing and bringing to justice those who continued the trade; but in practice it was only Britain that was both able and willing to assign a reasonable naval force to this patrol.

Since Britain was not at war with the other nations of western Europe and America, her gunboats could not capture their slaving ships on the high seas without breaking international law. Hence the Foreign Office took pains to negotiate treaties with the chief slave-trading nations which would give British warships the scope to do their duties without fear of creating international crises. Thus

Britain got France and Brazil to ban the trade for their nationals in 1818 and 1825 respectively; while Portugal in 1818 and Spain in 1825 were persuaded to restrict their slave-trading activities in Africa to areas south of the Equator. In 1817 Britain also negotiated Reciprocal Search Treaties with Spain and Portugal, under which her warships could stop and search any ship flying the flag of either of these two countries which was suspected of carrying slaves. Spain and Portugal enjoyed similar rights with regard to ships flying the British flag. If a ship was found to be carrying slaves it was seized and taken either to Sierra Leone or to some port in America where special courts known as Courts of Mixed Commission were established to deal with such activities. These were courts whose membership comprised judges from countries which had agreed by treaty to co-operate in this matter. In 1831 France signed a similar treaty.

The Equipment Treaties

Soon it was found that the Reciprocal Search Treaties did not give sufficient scope to the British Preventive Squadron to deal with slavers, because they contained the provision that only ships *actually* carrying slaves could be seized. But many ships were seen which, though not carrying slaves at the time, were certainly slaving ships since they carried equipment for the purpose. To make the naval patrol more effective the Foreign Office bent its energies to negotiating treaties which covered this loop-hole. This was the origin of the so-called Equipment Treaties which Britain negotiated with France in 1833, with Spain in 1835, and with Portugal in 1842, under which ships could be caught and condemned if they carried equipment used by slaving ships.

This method of fighting the slave trade by persuading or forcing European and American nations to give it up did not prove very effective, as many of the nations were not prepared to co-operate with Britain. This was partly because they suspected that the British zeal was not entirely the result of humanitarian intentions but was also serving an economic interest. Some of the nations were jealous of British naval power and feared that Britain would misuse rights granted her under the Reciprocal Search and the Equipment Treaties. The United States, for instance, refused to sign any of these treaties.

There were other reasons which helped to make the campaign ineffective. There were not enough gunboats. As mentioned above, Britain alone maintained a naval force of any consequence in West

British anti-slavers attack a slave settlement

Africa, yet up to 1832 the British West African Squadron never had more than seven ships at a time; often it had less, and sometimes it had only two. Since these few ships had to watch the entire coast between Cape Verde and the Equator it is not surprising that many slave ships escaped and that in this period more slaves were carried from West Africa annually than in any year before. It has in fact been suggested that not more than twenty-five per cent of the slavers were caught. Moreover not all the ships used in this strenuous watch were suitable. Some of them were old and rotten, while the class of ships known as frigates were not only too large and too slow but had the extra handicap that their masts were easily seen from long distances by slave ships, which naturally made good their escape. Also the ships engaged in slaving were built to suit the difficult times and were generally very fast.

The African view

There was only one place, Sierra Leone, on the West African coast, where captured slavers could be sent for trial. This meant that even if a ship was caught at the southernmost end of West Africa, it had to be taken on a journey of nearly 2,000 miles before it could reach the nearest place where it could be tried. What was worse, the members of the courts of Mixed Commission did not always co-operate. The non-British members carried their national jealousies to the sittings of the Court, and their intrigues not only caused delays but often led to the acquittal of guilty ships.

The ineffectiveness of the methods used to stop the trade was to some extent the result of African opposition. It was not easy for West Africans to abandon overnight a trade which had lasted for so long that they had come to regard it as part of the normal way of life. The slave trade was accepted as part of their economic, social and even ritual life. The coastal peoples in particular had become so entirely dependent on the trade, had invested so much capital in it, that they could not abandon it without serious economic loss. Throughout West Africa the trade had come to be the normal means of getting rid of thieves, bankrupt debtors, witches and other un-desirables; it was also the means of procuring the men and women who were used in satisfying some of the demands, for instance human sacrifice, of ritual life. In Dahomey it was the basis of economic life. The royal plantations depended on it and part of the army received its training in military tactics during the annual slave raids. Throughout West Africa slaves were also economically useful in the sense that they were used as currency, and by acting as carriers played a great part as a means of transport in an area that had no wheeled carriage. At the time of the abolition it was not easy to think of a ready economic substitute for the slave trade. The British talked of ivory, vegetable oil, timber, indigo and so on, but profitable trade in these needed time to develop. One coastal chief, when persuaded to sell ivory in place of slaves, pointed out that slaves were easier to catch than the elephants from which ivory came.

African traders wondered what right the British had to dictate to them about their trading practices. Many simply refused to consider abolition, because the slave trade had become traditional in their society. In 1863 King Glele of Dahomey told Commodore E. Wilmot of the West African Squadron that slave trading was the custom of his ancestors. As a king, it was held, he could not break with custom without incurring some divine punishment. Much later, in the 1890s, the Aro of Eastern Nigeria told a British political officer that they would not give up slave dealing because it was the custom of their fathers.

African objections to abolition were strengthened by the activities of the Portuguese, Spaniards, Cubans, Brazilians and others. While the British told West Africans to abhor the slave trade and to patronise the oil trade, others persuaded them to do the opposite. This was very confusing. Africans took the conflicting attitudes of the different European powers to mean that Britain was at war with the other nations of Europe and America, and as the quarrel did not concern them, African middlemen did not see why they should ruin their business by siding with Britain. Some of the coastal middlemen were able for a long time to ignore the menace of the British gunboats because of the nature of the coast along which they lived. On the coast of Nigeria, for instance, there is such a maze of creeks and water channels that, while gunboats watched one port closely, traders could ship their slaves through another which was quite unknown to the British. When, for instance, the British boats watched Bonny too closely Bonny men transferred their slaving business to Brass.

West African treaties

In the late 1830s, therefore, Britain was forced to re-examine and modify this method of fighting the slave trade. As a result the campaign was extended to the West African interior. First Britain signed slave trade treaties with a number of West African chiefs. Under this kind of treaty the African chief undertook to abolish the slave trade in his territory and to encourage trade in palm oil and the other products of the forest. In return he received annual subsidies from Britain for a fixed term of years. Britain reserved the right to say when the treaty was broken and to mete out punishment in consequence. Two chiefs of the Cameroons entered into this type of treaty with Britain in 1840 and 1842, the Calabar villages of Creek Town and Duke Town in 1843, Bonny in 1848. The Bond, which bound Fante chiefs to abolish 'barbarous' customs, seems to come under the category of slave trade treaty (though this treaty will be discussed in detail later). Treaty-making as a means of fighting the slave trade was not limited to the coast. It became in fact a permanent feature of European strategy in West Africa throughout the nineteenth century.

By the 1840s the practice had penetrated the interior. The British civilising mission of 1841, for instance, concluded such a treaty with a prince as far inland as the Ata of Igala. One interesting revelation of these treaties is that the Africans who opposed the abolition were not necessarily morally bankrupt. On the contrary they were hard-headed businessmen whose concern was that there should be good business. Bonny's treaty with Britain came so late for a coastal state because over and over again Britain would not live up to the terms of the contract. Since this occasioned financial loss for Bonny she too over and over again ignored the treaty and revived the slave trade. Another illuminating example was the attitude of King Obi Ossai of Abo in 1841. This king did not need much persuasion to sign the treaty. His first request was that British men and ships should visit Abo in large numbers to buy Abo's natural produce. These treaties gave Britain the excuse to intervene in the affairs of many West African states, even in matters which lay beyond the scope of the treaty. As another way of dealing with the slave trade, British missionaries and legitimate traders decided to push into the interior, establish their posts there and cut the root of the slave trade by persuading Africans to embrace Christianity, legitimate commerce and agriculture. The details of this development will be given later.

The founding of Sierra Leone

Both in the short and long run the campaign against the slave trade had far-reaching consequences and significance for West Africa, Europe and America. The earliest and most tangible of the results was demographic. The enforced exodus of Negroes from West Africa was checked. What was more, an attempt was made to reverse the migration through shipping former slaves from Europe and America back to West Africa. This did not happen to many, but it led to the foundation of first Sierra Leone and then Liberia. How this came about needs to be told in some detail, in view of the places which Sierra Leone and Liberia occupy in West African intellectual and political history.

For long it had been the practice of British planters in the West Indies who were going home to England either on leave or on retirement to take along with them their Negro domestic slaves. In this way by 1772 there were about 14,000 such slaves in Britain. When therefore Chief Justice Mansfield gave his celebrated decision in 1772 on the place of the slave and slavery under the English law and constitution all these men became free. Their owners, who were not happy with Mansfield's judgment, turned them out. Since these ex-slaves had not been previously prepared for emancipation they could not all fend for themselves effectively, with the result that many of them resorted to begging and thus became a nuisance in English society. Soon their state aroused the pity of the humanitarians who in 1786 formed the Committee for Relieving the Black Poor to organise the giving of alms to these destitute men. The Committee soon found that the numbers of those needing its help grew daily, and was forced to think of another way of tackling the problem. As early as 1783 Granville Sharp had thought of settling the 'Black Poor' somewhere along the coast of West Africa. Now his scheme was taken up seriously. Dr. Henry Smeathman, who had once visited Sierra Leone, recommended it as suitable for such a settlement. As the Committee prepared for the venture the British government undertook to contribute towards the cost of the project at the rate of fourteen pounds for each settler. In February 1787 the first party, about 411 in number, left the British Isles for West Africa, and arrived in Sierra Leone some time in May.

It proved very difficult to establish the settlement on a firm basis. To start with, the party got to Sierra Leone in the wet season, that is at a time when it was too late to start the planting of crops or the building of houses. Without good shelter and care, disease soon spread, and by March 1788 only about 130 of the 411 original settlers were alive. The others had died from fever. What was worse, the two coastal chiefs who had sold the settlers the land they occupied had done so without consulting their paramount ruler, Miambana, King of the Temne. The infant settlement now faced the rage of this King. The other European traders on the coast, especially members of the Royal African Company, were also hostile. Though Granville Sharp sent a new party of settlers with fresh supplies in May 1788, the future of the settlement remained gloomy.

Granville Sharp and his friends, who now realised that a new arrangement was needed if the colony was to survive, formed a company, first known as St. George's Bay Company, to take over the affairs of Sierra Leone. By forming such a commercial company, Sharp and his friends hoped to persuade wealthy businessmen to invest in the project. To some extent they were successful. On receiving a charter from the British government the company was renamed the Sierra Leone Company. Somehow the affairs of the colony began to improve. In 1792 about 12,000 former Negro slaves, known as Nova Scotians, arrived to swell the population of the settlement. These men had sided with the British against the Americans in the American War of Independence. After the war the British settled them in Nova Scotia where they found life very difficult and as a result applied for transfer to Sierra Leone. In 1800 the Maroons, a batch of ex-slaves who had been involved in a slave revolt in Jamaica in 1796 and had been sent to Nova Scotia, also arrived in Sierra Leone.

In spite of this growth in population the Sierra Leone Company failed to prosper and found the work of defending and administering the colony beyond its resources. Revenue was restricted because the company did not engage in the slave trade, which was the only lucrative business at that time. Legitimate trade in which alone it was interested was only being pioneered, and was as yet unpopular with Africans and Europeans alike. The company therefore appealed to the British government to take over responsibility for the settlement. In 1807 Britain abolished the slave trade and committed herself to the difficult task of preventing other nations from continuing it. As she needed a naval base in West Africa from which to carry out the campaign, Sierra Leone, with its good natural harbour, was the obvious choice. As a result on 1 January 1808 Sierra Leone became the first British crown colony in West Africa. The same year a Vice-Admiralty Court was established in Freetown for the purpose of trying slave traders whose ships were seized by the Preventive Squadron. When later Britain persuaded Spain, Portugal and France to abolish the trade, a Court of Mixed Commission was established in Freetown to try ships of these nations caught carrying on the prohibited trade. Sierra Leone benefited immensely from all this. Her population was greatly augmented since the slave cargoes of many of the arrested ships were liberated and settled there. In order to ensure that Sierra Leone's economy benefited from this rapid growth of population a Liberated Africans Department was established to do the work of settling the new arrivals either by apprenticing them to trade or by grouping them in villages to pursue agriculture.

American settlement of Liberia

The successful issue of the Sierra Leone venture was to some extent
responsible for the American experiment in settling free Negroes
on the portion of the West African coast now known as Liberia. In
the early decades of the nineteenth century the United States faced
problems which were in some ways similar to those which Britain
faced as a result of Mansfield's famous judgment, but which were in
some ways more acute. There were in the United States in 1800 about
200,000 free Negroes. Some of these were people freed by masters
who in course of time had become convinced that slavery was evil
and contrary to the law of God, some were those who by their own
hard work had purchased their freedom, some were those freed on
the death of their masters, others were simply run-aways. Many of
the free Negroes became small businessmen and were able to find
honourable means of living; others lived by less honourable ways,

15 Sierra Leone and Liberia

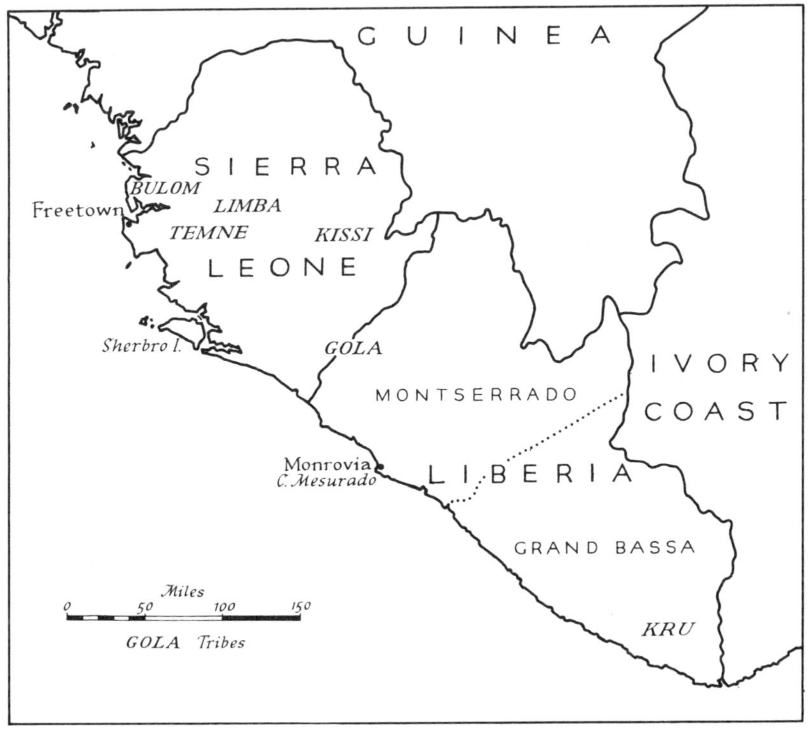

including theft, not so much because they were lazy but because they could find no employment.

The existence of this large and growing community of free Negroes presented a serious problem to the United States. It was thought, for example by Thomas Jefferson, that the best solution lay in colonising the Negroes somewhere, preferably outside the United States. This view was shared by the large section of the community which still owned slaves, and argued that free Negroes were a nuisance in society because they endangered the institution of slavery. Especially in the Southern States, laws were passed designed either to make it impossible for more Negroes to become free or to force those already free to return to slavery. The Northern States, most of which had emancipated their slaves, feared that the free Negroes in the South would flock into their territories, and so passed laws to prevent this.

About this time there arose in the United States a movement which was both humanitarian and evangelical, and which aimed at helping the poor and oppressed and at applying Christian principles to social life. The members of this movement, out of sympathy, came to favour the idea of transporting the free Negroes back to Africa. This step, they hoped, would save the Negro the humiliation and degradation he suffered in America, while enabling him to be the instrument by which 'civilisation' and Christianity would spread to 'darkest' parts of Africa.

The American Colonisation Society

It was these different groups of people who in 1816 formed the American Society for Colonising the free People of Color of the United States, more popularly known as the American Colonisation Society. In 1818 this society sent Samuel J. Mills and Ebenezer Burgess to Sierra Leone to survey the possibilities of carrying out its intentions. These men picked on Sherbro Island about 30 miles south of Sierra Leone. It was here that the first party of 88 landed in 1820. It was soon found that the site was very unhealthy for within a short space of time 22 of the settlers died. The remaining 66 ran to Sierra Leone in panic. When the second batch of settlers arrived in 1821 they took local advice and moved lower down the coast to Cape Mesurado where they secured a piece of land from the local chiefs and founded a settlement in 1822. A few months after this another batch of 55 settlers arrived under Jehud Ashmun, who was to prove himself the real founder of Liberia. One General Harper now suggested the name Liberia (Land of the Free) for the settlement, and Monrovia, after President Monroe of the United States, as the name of the capital city.

When the settlers first arrived the local chiefs, not knowing that they had come to settle permanently, welcomed them enthusiastically. When these chiefs discovered their mistake they became hostile and sought to wipe out the settlement, partly because it interfered with their slave dealing activities and partly because the settlers adopted an irritating and superior attitude towards the established people. The Spaniards and Cubans urged them on, and even helped to provide them with the arms and ammunition with which to attack the colony. The stability and progress of the colony was also threatened by the fact that many settlers refused to undertake agriculture. They preferred trade which yielded quick profits and these profits they spent on foreign goods. The economy of the country was thus unstable.

Though Liberia was many years younger than Sierra Leone its political development was more rapid. This was largely because the United States government was not prepared to carry the burden of administering Liberia and so did not interfere, while the American Colonisation Society, which was responsible for the welfare of the settlement, was also liberal. The officials of the colony were white men up to 1841, after which Negroes took over. In 1828 the elective principle was introduced. In 1830 the *Liberia Herald* was published and it remained for twenty-five years the only newspaper in West Africa. In 1838 Liberia was divided into two counties, Montserrado and Grand Bassa, each of which had a national council of ten elected members who, with two officials called the Agent and the Vice-Agent, formed its governing authority.

Liberian independence

All this while, the authorities of Sierra Leone remained hostile to Liberia and their hostility was one of the factors which forced the infant settlement to declare its independence rather prematurely. By 1830 Liberia laid claim to about 300 miles of the coast, most portions of which were hardly populated. But European traders and the authorities of Sierra Leone who made fun of the idea of a Negro government refused to recognise Liberia's claims to the whole of the area, or her right to levy harbour and customs duties at any point of it. Liberia's attempt in 1845 to collect customs dues from an English trader, Captain Davidson of Sierra Leone, only provided an occasion for humiliation, for the Sierra Leone government sent Commander Jones of the West African Squadron to seize from a Liberian port a vessel belonging to a Liberian subject. The United States government was not prepared to take up the case of Liberia with Britain, or with any other power. The American Colonisation Society was powerless to assist and so advised Liberia to declare her independence in order to secure recognition as a sovereign nation. In June 1847 the Liberian authorities summoned a constitutional convention and on 26 July of the same year proclaimed Liberia a sovereign republic with a constitution modelled on that of the United States.

The suppression of the slave trade also brought about an economic revolution in West Africa, a revolution which not all the former participants in the coastal trade – European and African – could survive. The slave traders who had invested heavily in the business by way of equipment suffered heavily. True, these men were already familiar with the techniques and tricks of business in West Africa, and some of them also had accumulated capital, but the transition from slave running to legitimate commerce was painful and profits at first were low and uncertain. The change-over estranged former friends. The arrangements for the trade throughout the period of the slave trade recognised and respected the position of the middlemen. But the rise of legitimate trade demanded a new arrangement which would enable the Europeans to penetrate the interior. The Europeans wanted to go inland partly to increase their profit margin and partly to establish collecting centres for produce which were more efficient than those existing along the coast. In the event a war ensued between the middlemen and the European merchants. By the time the conflict died down the middlemen had lost their pre-1800 privileged position. For those communities along the coast this loss of economic position also meant loss of political stability. The history of the trading states of the Oil Rivers in the second half of the nineteenth century provides the best illustration of the truth of the above analysis. There the House system which had arisen to serve the needs of the slave trade largely went down with that trade.

European penetration of West Africa

During the last two decades of the eighteenth century European interest in West Africa shifted from the coast to the interior. Explorers sent out by private European organisations and governments made determined attempts to penetrate and explore inland. The earliest attempts in this direction were dictated more by scientific than by commercial interests. The eighteenth century witnessed the exploration of the interior of many continents and countries. For instance Southern Asia, the basin of the Amazon and the interior of Australia were all explored in this period. In view of this progress being made in the exploration of other parts of the globe, some scientifically minded men in Europe felt that their prevailing ignorance of the interior of Africa was a challenge. They wanted to know more about Africa's river systems, especially about the course of the Niger, about Africa's botany and natural history, about its peoples and their ways of life.

But there was also an economic motive for the enterprise even from the beginning, and as the business of exploration progressed this motive acquired greater importance and even came to overshadow all others. One of the results of the Industrial Revolution, as already noted, was Europe's pressing need both for new markets and for raw materials. For Britain in particular, who took the lead in exploring the African interior, this need became more pressing after the loss of America in 1783. In fact it was only five years after this event that the African Association, which at first led the movement for exploration, was founded.

The third important factor partly responsible for this growing interest in the interior of Africa was the movement for the aboliton of the slave trade. This did not influence the promoters of African exploration until after the second decade of the nineteenth century. Before that time Britain, as already shown, had thought that her plan to abolish the slave trade could be achieved through naval patrols off the coast of West Africa and diplomatic negotiations in the courts of European nations and America. But experience later showed that this hope was misplaced. It was only then that a number of far-seeing men, the first of whom was James McQueen, started to argue that the only way to abolish the trade effectively was to persuade Africans to turn from it to agriculture and legitimate commerce. Since it was believed that Africans could not do this by themselves, it was urged that European traders, agriculturalists and missionaries should penetrate the interior and teach the people how to earn a living by exploiting the natural produce of their country. For many years McQueen was a lone voice crying in the wilderness. Though he advocated this policy in the book *A Geographical and Commercial View of Northern and Central Africa,* published in 1821, it was not until 1841 that the first really organised attempt was made to carry out the programme.

British attempts at penetration

The exploration of the West African interior was the affair of the few private individuals who formed the African Association before it became a government-sponsored enterprise. The Association was formed on 9 June 1788 and with that the European drive to penetrate the interior of West Africa could be said to have begun in earnest. Between 1788 and 1805 the Association sponsored all the British exploratory missions into the interior. There were six of these. Then the British government stepped in and took the lead. The African Association had taken time to publicise the successes of its agents and to advertise the possibilities for profitable trade in the Western Sudan which these agents had found. This propaganda captivated the commercial and industrial classes who were becoming progressively influential in British politics and public life. If the mouth of the Niger, for instance, was discovered, it was argued that British commerce would have a highway into the Western Sudan. Also about 1800 it came to be known that the French were showing serious interest in the region of the Senegal. This caused some concern; if England did not act fast enough the French would reap the benefits of the labours of the African Association. In the light of these new developments it became clear that the work of African exploration was too weighty an issue to be left in the hands of private men who had no authority to act on behalf of the nation.

The problem of exploring West Africa was tackled from two main directions, from the West Coast and from North Africa, especially Tripoli. The first and second attempts were made from Cairo and Tripoli respectively. When penetration from here seemed to hold no promise whatever, both explorers having died before they reached the Sahara, Britain decided to use the southern approach through the coast. In a sense this seemed the natural route of approach. British business here was already about three centuries old and there was no single barrier as great as the Sahara to be encountered from the south. What was more, British business along the coast was already immense and it would not be difficult to organise trade after initial exploration, since what was already established could be extended. However, it soon became clear that the southern approach could easily turn out to be the graveyard of British explorers. The leaders of the three expeditions sent out between 1805 and 1816 died, and this loss of life led Britain to the conclusion that the West Coast was not the best base from which to explore the Sudan.

Once again attention turned to Tripoli in the north, which now showed promises of providing the long-sought-for gateway to the Sudan. For one thing, Tripoli stood at the narrowest crossing of the Sahara. Secondly, Tripoli now had an able and energetic ruler, Yusuf Karamanli, who had established peace in the interior. Furthermore, this prince was on good terms with Shaikh al Kanemi of Bornu and Sultan Bello of Sokoto, the two men who controlled the southern half of the route from Tripoli to the Sudan. Karamanli could thus guarantee safe conduct to all travellers crossing the Sahara with his consent. Though the attempt to use this route in 1819 failed, the leader of the expedition having died at Murzuk, the next attempt in 1821 was a success. The explorers reached the Sudan, and of the three members only one died. But the expedition which followed this failed, the leader, Major Gordon Laing, dying in circumstances which caused estrangement between Britain and Tripoli. In consequence, attention shifted to the Niger waterway, whose mouth had been discovered in 1830, but this route soon proved as treacherous. Two expeditions which sought to use it in 1832 and 1841 suffered severe losses of human life.

Britain once more turned her attention to the northern route which had meanwhile come under the control of friendly Turkey. The preparations she made for return to this route gave the impression that, if things went well, the route would be in use for a long time. For instance she established a Vice-Consulate at Murzuk in 1840, and another at Ghadames in 1847, which soon became centres for spreading British influence and acquainting the people with British goods. Then in 1854 the Central African Mission was sent to open up a secure way of communication with the interior of West Africa across the Sahara. But this expedition, which held out so much hope and promise, sealed the fate of the northern route. Two-thirds of its members died, while a supplementary expedition sent to help it lost four of its five members. There were also other factors which helped to resolve the choice between the northern and southern approaches in favour of the latter. Dr. William Balfour Baikie, leading a government expedition up the Niger in 1854, showed that the dangers posed by malaria on the southern route could be effectively met by using quinine as a prophylactic. Furthermore, as the southern route became more frequented, more European goods got to the Central Sudanese empires – Nupe, the Hausa cities and Bornu – from the south. This meant that much of the trade which hitherto travelled between Hausaland and North Africa via the Sahara was diverted to the south. The rivalry between the northern and southern approaches was to some extent another side to the old rivalry between

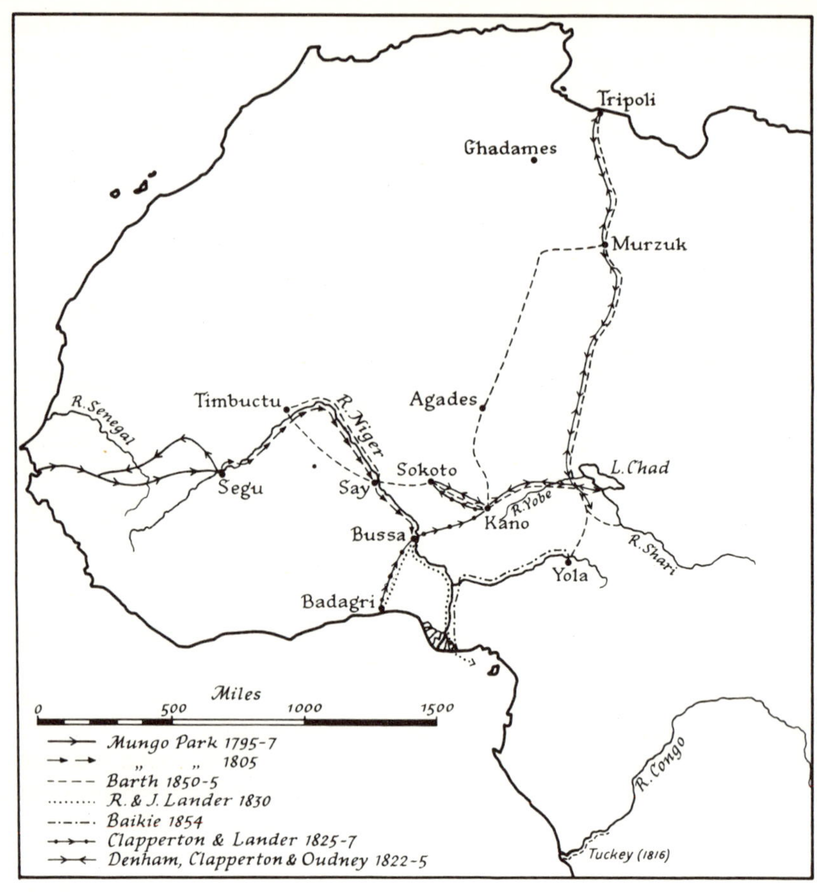

16 European exploration of West Africa

the trans-Saharan trade and the Atlantic commerce. By resolving it in favour of the southern approach the British achieved what the Portuguese had aspired to long ago but failed to achieve.

The list of West Africa's explorers and would-be explorers is long and impressive. It is headed by John Ledyard who sought to penetrate through Cairo but died before he could leave the ancient city. He was followed by Simon Lucas who made the first attempt to use the route through Tripoli but had to abandon the idea owing to the disturbed political situation in southern Tripoli. The third on the list was Major Houghton who, starting from Gambia, explored the region of modern Senegal and Mali and then disappeared without

140

trace. More famous are Dr. Mungo Park, Walter Oudney, Hugh Clapperton, Major Dixon Denham, Major Gordon Laing, Richard and John Lander, James Richardson, Dr. Heinrich Barth and Dr. Overweg.

Mungo Park

Mungo Park

The first major success in the exploration of West Africa was achieved with Mungo Park's first journey which was sponsored by the African Association. He was charged with the duty of finding the course and if possible the termination of the Niger, about which there was great ignorance in Europe at the time. One theory about the Niger, for instance, maintained that this great river rose in the east, flowed to the west and entered the Atlantic as three rivers. It was also hoped that Mungo Park might get to Timbuctu, about which Europe had heard so much but knew nothing.

Leaving England in May 1795 Mungo Park entered West Africa through the Gambia and reached the Niger at Segu in July 1796. His plans to move further down the river could not be implemented, partly because a state of war existed between the Bambara states of Segu and Kaarta, partly because his resources were running short, and partly because the rainy season was getting more severe. He therefore went back to England in 1796 with reports of his travel which excited so much public interest that in 1805 the British government sent him back to Africa. Park got to Segu from where he set

A Kanembo spearman from an engraving by
Major Dixon Denham. This is typical of the
kind of detailed drawing that nineteenth
century European explorers made on their
travels, before the invention of photography

out down the Niger and to his death. Later reports revealed that he
perished at the Bussa rapids. Park's travels were a landmark in the
history of West African exploration in the sense that he was the
first European in centuries to set eyes on the Niger and thus establish
beyond any dispute that the river existed. His testimony that the
Niger flowed west to east disposed of the earlier belief that it flowed
in the reverse direction. But it also created a new complication.
Some armchair geographers speculated, on the basis of this, that the
Niger joined the Nile somewhere, or disappeared into an inland sea
in the desert.

The Landers

The other great landmark in West African exploration was the discovery of the estuary of the Niger by Richard Lander. Richard
Lander had been introduced to the field of West African exploration
by Captain Hugh Clapperton, who had been a member of the expedition also comprising Walter Oudney and Dixon Denham which

142

for the first time, in 1821, showed that the northern gateway through
Tripoli was a possible route into the Sudan. When sent back to Africa
to follow up the results of this expedition Clapperton took Richard
Lander as his personal servant. This expedition had not only failed
but had also seen the death of Clapperton. Richard Lander got back
to Europe only to be sent back by the British government to complete his master's half-finished assignment. Taking his brother John
with him, Richard Lander first got to Bussa by land and then, travelling down the Niger, emerged into the Atlantic through the river
Nun in the Oil Rivers. The Landers thus solved the puzzling geographical problem of the course and termination of the Niger.

Heinrich Barth

The benefits of exploration

The significance of these journeys was mainly twofold. The first was
scientific. Europe came to know more about the geography and topo-
graphy of the interior of West Africa than she did before 1800. For
instance, the sources of West Africa's main rivers as well as the
estuary of the Niger were discovered. The explorers brought back
much useful and detailed information on the peoples of the region they
visited, on their commerce and civilisation as well as on the flora and
fauna of the interior. The explorers' narratives, especially Barth's
five volume *Travels and Discoveries in North and Central Africa*,
constitute a rich source of information on the geography, history,
languages and peoples of the Western Sudan.

143

The second importance of these journeys was economic. The explorers painted an attractive picture of the opportunities which existed in the Sudan for profitable business. To the mercantile interests in Britain this was perhaps more important than the scientific information brought home by the explorers. Thus each major advance in the exploration of the interior was followed up with grandiose schemes and plans for the introduction of British commerce. The best illustration of this point was the reaction of the British business class to the discovery of the mouth of the Niger by the Landers. They considered it, and rightly, as opening a highway for British commerce into the interior and immediately set about exploiting it. A Scottish merchant, MacGregor Laird, led the formation of the African Inland Commercial Company, which declared that its purpose was to penetrate the interior and establish a commercial depot at the confluence of the Niger and Benue, as a centre for collecting the produce of the Sudan. The first expedition of the company left in July 1832 under Richard Lander, but the project failed hopelessly. Many of the members, including Lander, died from malaria. The African Inland Commercial Company wound up in 1834. For about six years after that only individuals like John Beecroft and Jamieson attempted to trade up the Niger, but they did not actually go beyond the Oil Rivers. This was not the end of organised attempts at the commercial exploitation of the discoveries of the explorers. In fact the drive received further justification from humanitarian impulses.

By the 1830s it had become abundantly clear that diplomacy and naval blockade were not enough as measures against the slave trade. What was more, the bid to reach the Sudan through the northern gateway had brought the British face to face with the internal slave trade from the Sudan to North Africa. In consequence of this the humanitarians, now led by Thomas Fowell Buxton the author of *The African Slave Trade and Its Remedy*, 1839, started pressing for the implementation of the programme which McQueen had put forward in the early 1820s. In 1841 an expedition directed towards the attainment of these two purposes – the commercial exploitation of the interior and the supplanting of the slave trade with legitimate commerce backed by agriculture and Christianity – was organised on a large scale by the British government and sent up the Niger. This also turned out to be a failure. About 49 of the Britons who took part in it died within three months and the expedition had to be abandoned.

But the attempt continued. The British were not to be cheated of the profits of their labours by a capricious climate. The next organised attempt to tap the resources of the Niger was made in 1854.

Dr. W. B. Baikie

In that year a government expedition under Dr. William Balfour Baikie was sent up the Niger. This expedition eventually became famous for two achievements. Firstly, through the use of quinine as a prophylactic, Baikie was able to prevent the loss of even a single life among the members of his party. This expedition thus turned out to be the first up the Niger during which nobody died. Secondly, the *Pleiad*, the ship in which the expedition was made, navigated the Niger without great difficulty. This showed that the technical problems connected with navigating the Niger were being satisfactorily met.

In 1857 the British government entered into a five year contract with Laird under which it agreed to pay him an annual subsidy in return for his maintaining steamer service on the Niger. Between 1857 and 1859 Laird and his agents established trading stations at Abo, Onitsha and Lokoja on the Niger. From now on European enterprise and influence started to penetrate the various sections of our region of study.

Baikie's ship, the *Pleiad*.

145

French attempts

Though they certainly dominated it, it was not the British alone who were active at this time in the business of exploring the West African interior and exploiting its resources. France, Britain's great rival in West Africa from the eighteenth century, not only played some part in the exploration, but was also concerned with tapping the resources of the interior from the Senegal, the other important waterway of West Africa. In the field of West African discovery their two most distinguished travellers were G. Mollien and Réné Caillie. The former discovered the sources of the Gambia, the Rio Grande and the Senegal in 1818, while the latter was, perhaps, the first European to reach Timbuctu and return alive to relate his experiences to the world. In many British circles, however, it was believed that Caillie did not enter Timbuctu but had merely stolen the journals of the English explorer, Major Gordon Laing, who reached Timbuctu but later died in the Sahara.

With regard to exploiting the resources of the interior the French concentrated their activities on the Senegal, where their interests had been dominant since 1659 when an agent of the Compagnie Nomande established the city now known as St. Louis. A little later, in 1672, a French admiral drove the Dutch from Goree, while another chartered company, the Compagnie Sénegal, occupied such coastal towns as Rufisque and Joal. In 1818 the French returned to the posts on the Senegal from which they had been expelled by the British in the course of the Revolutionary and Napoleonic wars. As part of the attempt of the restored Bourbons to strengthen the economy of France they conceived a grand programme of establishing on the Senegal large plantations of tropical crops like groundnuts, cotton and indigo. To this end they appointed Colonel Schmaltz as governor. The experiment, however, proved a failure owing to hostile climate, lack of labour, poor soil and indigenous opposition.

Still the attempt continued. The French obtained land from the Walo kingdom in return for an annual subsidy. On this land they established experimental farms and gardens under the charge of experts specially sent out from France. But this again ran into trouble. The Traza branch of the Moors, who inhabited the right bank of the Senegal, claimed that the Walo had no right to the land they leased to the French and so ravaged the plantations and drove off the planters. Also the problem of labour remained unsolved. At one time the French government thought of an arrangement with the Spanish government under which the latter would send labour from the Canary Islands. But this plan was soon dropped and about 140 coloured prisoners were sent down from Martinique (a French island in the West Indies) to work on the farms. Indigenous Senegalese prisoners were also made to work there. Still the labour was not enough. Attempts to raise free labour failed. Meanwhile the Traza continued to ravage the farms. The French attempt to punish them only led to the further destruction of the farms. Disillusioned, the French abandoned the dream of flourishing tropical plantations on the lines of the Dutch Indies and turned to commerce.

Nor did this flourish. For many years the only profitable trade was that in guns. French penetration of the interior was made hazardous by the Traza who through a system of alliances with the Negro peoples ringed the French colony with hostile neighbours. The rise of al-Hajj Umar in the 1840s made the penetration of the interior even more difficult. Moreover there was the fear that Umar would soon issue a call to all Muslims to take up arms against the infidels. This, it was felt, would make the French position even more untenable. Governor Bouet-Willaumez (1844) advocated the use of force to solve the problem of interior penetration, but since the French treasury had no money for this the home government did not support him. French presence on the Senegal remained precarious and economically unrewarding until the appointment of Louis Faideherbe as governor in 1854.

Louis Faideherbe turned out to be a very able soldier and administrator as well as a clear-headed diplomat. His first period of governorship of the colony transformed its history and brightened its prospects. On his arrival he started a number of public works, and founded the Ecole des Otages for the training of interpreters and French emissaries into the interior. By means of military demonstrations on the river he firmly established French prestige. In 1855 he brought the Walo kingdom under direct French control, while in 1858 he defeated the Traza and forced them to cease their molestation of French traders in the interior. To open up the overland route connecting Dakar and St. Louis he intervened in the politics of the state of Cayor and deposed the Damel in 1861. To defend the colony and offer effective protection to French traders he built forts at Medina, Joal and Kaolack.

Towards al-Hajj Umar he adopted a wise policy. He was not, like many of his contemporaries, full of blind prejudice against Muslims, perhaps owing to his wider experience with Muslims in Algeria. Therefore he was not prepared to blame Umar for every indiscretion committed by his over-zealous supporters and admirers on the Senegal, who at times acted without his direction. All the same he was not opposed to showing Umar that French enmity could be dangerous. Thus when his garrison at Fort Medina was attacked by Umar's forces he first relieved it by force before talking of negotiation. Faideherbe knew he had not the forces to pursue a policy of confrontation against Umar and so did not seek to follow up his victory. He was also lucky that at the time Umar's eyes were fixed on Segu and Macina. In 1860 the two reached a peaceful settlement delimiting their frontiers. Faideherbe left Senegal in 1861, the most successful administrator the colony had so far had. He came back a second time, but with less dramatic results. Thanks to his achievements Senegal became the base for French advance into West Africa.

African reaction

What, one is bound to ask, was the reaction of Africans to this growing European invasion of their fatherland? What the common people thought about this we may not know, but the vested interests in traditional African society were plainly hostile. A few examples can easily be given. During his second expedition Mungo Park got into Segu with an odd assortment of goods. He displayed these in a small shop and sold them at great profit. In doing this he aroused the hostility of the Mandingo traders from Jenne and of the Moors who had hitherto monopolised all the trade here. They decided to make things difficult for Park, and even tried to bribe the authorities to kill him.

The same attitude was typical of the middlemen traders in the Oil Rivers. Part of the difficulties which wrecked the 1832 expedition of the African Inland Commercial Company was the opposition of these men. They wanted to protect their position by preventing direct European trade in the interior, and the Liverpool Merchants who had long been established on the coast joined the African middlemen in opposition to their fellow Europeans. They feared that if the trade shifted to the interior they would sustain heavy losses in consequence of their having already spent much money in equipping themselves for the coastal trade.

African rulers were generally enlightened and friendly in their attitude to the explorers. Park's journals record the hospitality and readiness to help displayed by the chiefs of the territories through which he passed. The King of Segu, for instance, was deeply impressed by Park's arguments on the advantages of establishing direct trade with Europe. In spite of the hostility of the traders in his territory he was prepared to give Park an escort. Clapperton's relations with Sultan Bello of Sokoto and al Kanemi of Bornu on his first mission also tell the same story. But the chiefs, concerned with the safety and peace of their territories, were also suspicious and on their guard against the intruders. The attitude of Sultan Bello was a case in point. When Clapperton on his first journey talked of the advantages of European traders coming to trade directly within the caliphate, Bello warned him against 'big capitalists'. On his second mission Clapperton came at an inauspicious time, when relations between the Sokoto and Bornu Empires had worsened. Without knowing of this changed relationship Clapperton included in his gifts for al Kanemi guns and pistols. Bello confiscated these weapons on seeing them and forbade Clapperton and Lander to go to Bornu. Bello's first duty was to protect the caliphate which he inherited from his father Uthman dan Fodio.

The coming of the Christian missions

At the beginning, European interest in West Africa was not only commercial, it also had a missionary motive. This was particularly true of the Portuguese who in the fifteenth and sixteenth centuries attempted to introduce Catholic Christianity into the Senegambian region, Sierra Leone, Benin and Warri. However this missionary aspect of European interest was soon blighted by the slave trade. With the onset of this traffic in human beings, slave traders not only maintained that Africans were such inferior beings that their miserable position in life would not be bettered by admission into the Christian fold, but also opposed any attempt by missionaries to convert Africans along the West Coast. Although in 1800 there were European priests in many of the coastal forts, they were there to cater for the souls of the European agents, and to carry out a meaningless baptism of African slaves before shipment. In places like Benin and Warri what remained of the earlier attempts at planting Christianity were memories preserved in oral traditions, the motif of the cross which had been adopted by indigenous artists, and ruined temples.

In the nineteenth century the attempt to Christianise West Africans was revived, first by Protestant missions and then by Roman Catholics. The Evangelical Movement which had supported the abolition of slavery also took steps to introduce the Christian message to the non-Christians of Asia and Africa. The first missionary society to arise out of this movement was the Baptist Missionary Society, founded in 1792 by William Carey. Others followed: the London Missionary Society (1795), the Glasgow Missionary Society (1796), the Church Missionary Society (1799), the British and Foreign Bible Society (1804), and the General Missionary Society of the Methodists (1818). The movement was not limited to Britain. Societies were being founded at the same time in America and Europe. In the United States the American Board of Commissioners for Foreign Missions was founded in 1810, the General Missionary Convention of the Baptist Denomination in 1814. On the European continent the Netherlands Missionary Society was founded in 1797 and the Basel Missionary Society in 1815. Catholic Missionary Societies came much later. Among the earliest was the branch of the Society for the Propagation of the Faith founded in Lyons (France) in 1822. Fifteen years later the missionary society of the Holy Ghost Fathers was founded in Paris, then came the Society of African Missions founded by Father de Bressilac in 1856.

Before the end of the eighteenth century British missionary societies, led by the Baptists, began work in West Africa, starting with Sierra Leone; but by 1800 none of these missions had a solid outpost in West Africa. The real beginning of the new missionary effort in West Africa can be taken to be 1806 when the Church Missionary Society (C.M.S.) was established in Sierra Leone. From then on mission stations grew apace along the coast. By 1853 the C.M.S. had other stations at Abeokuta (1844), Lagos (1851), and Ibadan (1853); the Wesleyan Methodist Missionary Society at Sierra Leone (1811), in the Fante states (1833) and at Abeokuta (1844); the Basel Missionary Society among the Fante (1827); the Church of Scotland Mission at Calabar (1846) and the Bremen Society among the Ewe of Ghana (1847). The American missions, also led by the Baptists, concentrated on Liberia.

For many decades and for a variety of reasons missionary enterprise in most of West Africa was limited to the coast. Until the discovery made in the 1850s that quinine could be used in preventing malaria, the missionaries, like other European visitors to the coast of West Africa, died in large numbers, with the result that there was a perpetual shortage of the qualified men needed for expansion inland. The tendency therefore was to concentrate on the coast. Also, African rulers and elders in the interior, unlike their counterparts along the coast, proved very hostile to the new religion. It was only after they had been brought under European rule that they were forced to allow missionaries a free hand in their territories.

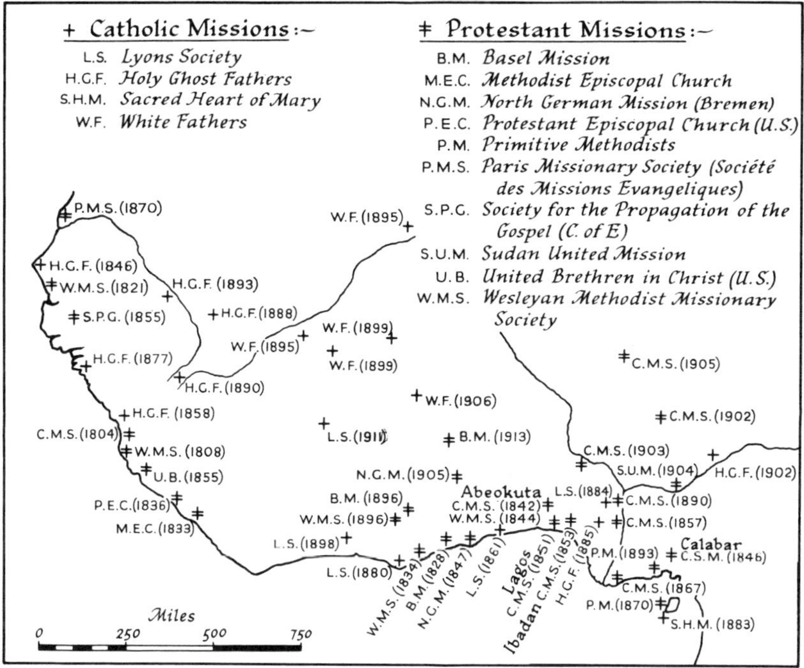

17 The spread of missionary activities in West Africa

In Sierra Leone the missionaries had more than enough to do as a result of the continued addition to the population of the colony of thousands of liberated slaves who needed conversion and education. In Liberia the hostility, open or veiled, between the Americanised settlers and their indigenous neighbours in the interior was an obstacle to the spread of the influence of the missions beyond the boundaries of the republic. On the coast of Ghana the incessant war between the Ashanti and the British made it unsafe for missionaries to venture inland, though it must be mentioned that Thomas Birch Freeman, who was half-Negro and half-European, opened a Wesleyan outpost at Kumasi in 1839. The reputation of Dahomey for barbarism and blood-thirstiness, whether merited or not, warned missionary intruders off her interior for a long time.

In the Yoruba country, where by 1853 the C.M.S. had gone as far as Ibadan, about a hundred miles from Lagos, the situation was different. The rivalry among the states which emerged after the collapse of Oyo in 1830 made many Yoruba states willing to accept any group of Europeans, traders or missionaries, as each state hoped to strengthen itself through alliance with Europeans who brought the guns it needed for war. The Egba found the C.M.S. missionaries who settled amongst them a great asset in their wars with Dahomey. Otherwise indigenous opposition to missionary activity was the rule in the interior. As a result the great age of missionary expansion did not come until the establishment of colonial rule, with which event Africans ceased to be masters of their own fates.

Since the nineteenth century was spent by most missionary bodies in gaining toe-holds on the West African coast, missionary impact on West Africa did not manifest itself in any pronounced form until the twentieth century. But from the beginning there was clear indication that socially, morally and politically missionary propaganda was going to inaugurate many changes. These lines of change can be briefly indicated here.

Conversion to Christianity necessarily involved weaning Africans away from traditional religions as well as from traditional social values which were based on that religion. From their past experience the missionaries believed that to make their work permanent they needed to change most aspects of African traditional life. Thus they preached not only against the slave trade and slavery, against human sacrifices and twin destruction, but also against such practices and institutions as polygamy, the taking of titles, body tattooing, secret societies, traditional dances and modes of dress. In return they extolled the adoption by Africans of European ways of life, for instance of European modes of dressing and the habit of tea drinking.

The missionaries chief instrument of effecting change was the spread of western European education. They felt that to achieve their ambition in West Africa they needed to raise an indigenous class of people who would be able to carry on the work of evangelisation if for any reason Europeans should withdraw. And in any case, because of the ravages of the West African climate and of malaria on the Europeans, Africans were required who were used to West African conditions. To fit into the missionary shoe the Africans had to know how to write, and how to read, interpret and teach the Bible. To achieve this, western literary and technical education had to be introduced into West Africa. In pursuit of this programme the missionaries became the greatest champions of education in West Africa, especially in the areas which later became British territories. In Sierra Leone, for instance, by 1861 the C.M.S. already had twenty-one elementary schools. During the following four years it founded a secondary school for boys and another for girls. The Fourah Bay College, now the University College of Sierra Leone, was founded by the same missionary body in 1829. The other missionary bodies were not as energetic as the C.M.S. in this period, but they all contributed towards the establishment of educational institutions in West Africa. Also, since the missions were confined to the coast until much later, the impact of their education was felt most in Lagos, Accra, Freetown, Bathurst and like places.

The missionaries also initiated the scientific and systematic study of West African languages and gave most of them a written form. The missionaries needed a thorough knowledge of the languages of West African peoples in order to approach them directly instead of through interpreters, and also in order to translate the Bible or sections of it into vernacular languages for the use of the people. The missionary study of West African languages was born in Sierra Leone between 1830 and 1832 when the C.M.S. Missionary, Rev. J. T. Raban, began a study of Yoruba with a view to effectively reaching the increasing Yoruba population of the colony. When the civilising Mission of 1841 was being projected the study of Nigerian languages was intensified under Rev. J. F. Schon in order to raise interpreters. From these small beginnings the study of indigenous West African languages had made rapid progress by 1862. By that year many Primers, Dictionaries and Grammars of indigenous languages had been produced by the missionaries. Rev. S. W. Koelle produced in 1854 a *Grammar of the Bornu or Kanuri Language* and *African Narrative Literature in Kanuri;* Schon published a *Hausa Primer* in 1857 and his *Grammar of the Hausa Language* in 1862. In the latter year also Rev. Hugh Goldie of the Presbyterian Mission produced his *Principles of Efik Grammar and Specimens of the Language.* In the years that followed the missionaries not only deepened and broadened their achievements in the fields indicated above, but also extended their services to providing such social amenities as hospitals and maternity homes.

The educated élite

As a result of this spread of education there arose in West Africa a new class of people generally called the western educated élite. They came to occupy leading positions in West Africa because they could read and write, and had learnt many of the ideas and techniques which were responsible for the progress of Europe in the nineteenth century. These people dressed in a new way, thought in a new way, and led their people when it came to dealing with white men. The missionaries and other Europeans expected them to spread western civilisation, western commerce and Christianity among their people. For many years members of this class believed that they and the missionaries and European traders were all pursuing the same goals in West Africa, that is promoting progress and spreading civilisation. It soon became evident, however, that many Europeans who came to West Africa were concerned more with their own gain than with serving West Africans. It shocked Africans to discover that there were even missionaries who were sometimes ready to help those who wanted to deprive West Africans of their independence. With this discovery relations between the educated Africans and Europeans soon turned into mutual hostility.

The beginning of this quarrel could be seen in the politics of Sierra Leone in the 1850s. Sierra Leone, like Liberia, produced many members of this new élite; in fact it was from there that many of them spread to Ghana and Nigeria. In Lagos in the 1860s nearly all the members of this class came from Sierra Leone. Most of them were freed Yoruba slaves who, after their stay in Sierra Leone, started, from about 1839 onwards, to go back to the land of their birth. In the 1850s the educated class in Sierra Leone were disappointed by British unwillingness to introduce democratic government into the colony, though the British themselves enjoyed democracy at home. These educated Sierra Leoneans became all the more discontented when they compared what was happening in the colony with what was happening in Liberia, where the people governed themselves. They therefore started to attack the Crown colony system of government which was imposed on them. In 1853 they formed the Sierra Leone Committee of Correspondence to ask for more political rights and for a change in the existing situation. Here we can see that, from the beginning of the quarrel between the new élite and the Europeans, the former adopted the method of grouping themselves together which in later years led to the growth of the highly organised political parties which helped to bring an end to European rule in West Africa.

6 Revolutions and Wars

The first eight decades of the nineteenth century brought great and often violent changes to many areas of West Africa. In the Sudan the period saw the forcible establishment of new states by men who claimed to be inspired by the desire to ensure that relations between man and man, as well as between man and state, were guided by Islamic codes of law, justice and morality. In Guinea it witnessed the disintegration of one of the greatest empires of the forest region, as well as attempts at military expansion by two of the remaining three. It is with these great happenings and how they helped to shape the history of many West African peoples that this chapter deals.

The jihads of the western Sudan

The jihads, which were among the most noteworthy events in nineteenth century West African history, were brought about by factors which were so many, so varied and so complex that historians are not yet agreed on their true nature. However, they may be seen as resulting from tensions which had existed in Sudanic society for some time before the nineteenth century.

In the first place there was a conflict in most Sudanic communities between Islam and the traditional religions of the peoples. Though by 1800 Islam was many centuries old amongst most Sudanic peoples, it had not succeeded in displacing the traditional cults. This was an explosive situation, for Islam, like Christianity, did not recognise the validity of any other religion. In orthodox Islamic doctrine the only way to the good life in this world and to salvation in after life was provided by the teachings of the Prophet Mohammed. Furthermore Islam commanded that all faithful believers had a duty to persuade, and if need be to force, all non-Muslims to embrace the

156   Interior of the Great Mosque at Jenne

faith. The parallel existence of Islam and the traditional religions in the Sudan was thus very unsatisfactory and challenging to orthodox Muslims.

Moreover Islam was not just a religion to be practised privately by individuals; it was also a way of life and so had its own codes of law, justice and morality, which it held should guide all properly ordered societies and states. At the opening of our period of study the ways of life pursued in many Sudanic states and societies were a contradiction of this ideal. Some of the states, like Segu and Kaarta, were ruled by Pagans. Other states like the Hausa Bakwai were nominally Muslim in the sense that their dynasties were Muslim, but did not enforce the code of laws known as the Malikite code which most orthodox Muslims in the Sudan expected them to follow. Since there were Muslim communities in most of the Sudanic states it meant that orthodox Muslims were made to live under conditions which did not satisfy their religious consciences. What was more painful to such Muslims was that these Pagan or nominally Muslim states often forced them to pay tributes and to undertake other obligations which were either not commanded by the Koran or were forbidden by it.

From the above general sketch it becomes clear that if some determined Muslim reformers were to come into existence at any time in the Sudan there would be open conflict between them and those who did not want the existing state of society to change. This was precisely what happened in the nineteenth century.

There were also political reasons for the jihads. Generally the Muslim clerical class were better educated than their Pagan or nominally Muslim neighbours and rulers, with the result that they believed they knew more about the world in which they lived than their illiterate neighbours. As educated men they were often employed as secretaries and advisers by rulers; they also had a high reputation as makers of powerful charms which could protect their wearers from evil-minded people and spirits, or ensure victory in war. These Muslim clerics enjoyed a great deal of influence in the communities in which they lived. This was another source of trouble between them and the non-Muslim or nominally Muslim groups in the Sudan. The clerics felt superior to their neighbours and rulers who depended so much on their services, and also became politically ambitious after having tasted power as advisers and secretaries. The rulers on their side not only became jealous of the influence which their advisers accumulated but also grew suspicious of their political intentions.

Fulani Muslims

These tensions started coming to a head from about 1725 when the reforming Muslim clerics began pressing their points of view. Most of these men came from among the Fulani, especially from the town Fulani who were often fanatical Muslims. The Fulani led in these movements not only because they were good Muslims, but also because they had economic grievances against the Sudanic peoples, who saw them as strangers and discriminated against them in matters of land ownership and rights of trade. Because they were scattered throughout the Sudan the movement spread over the whole region. Some other Sudanese peoples, such as certain branches of the Songhay and Mande-speaking peoples who had been associated with Islam for a long time, also took part in the jihad. Though the participants in the revolution thus differed in their ethnic origin, they were united in the fact that they had a common ideology (Islam) and were generally from sections of the people who could be described as politically underprivileged.

Open conflict between the Muslim reformers and the Pagan or lukewarm Muslim dynasties of the Sudan began in the eighteenth century in the western half of the Western Sudan. In 1725 some Islamic reformers led by a Fulani called Alfa Ibrahim bi Nuhu successfully rose against the pagan rulers of Futa Jalon and established there an imamate, that is a state under an imam, a religious leader who claimed to rule in the name of Allah. A little later a similar move occurred in Futa Toro, a state west of Futa Jalon and on the southern bank of the river Senegal. There the reformers, led by a man called Suleiman Bal, declared a jihad against the pagan rulers of the state in 1769. In 1776 the latter were overthrown and a state along the lines of Futa Jalon was established by the victorious reformers. Later still another imamate was founded at Bondu in the region between Futa Jalon and Futa Toro.

Uthman dan Fodio

But the most important of these jihads were fought in the nineteenth century, and of these the most successful and the one with the most enduring results was that fought in Hausaland under the leadership of Uthman dan Fodio.

Uthman dan Fodio, a Fulani of the Toronkowa clan, was born in December 1754 in Kwonni in the leading Hausa state of Gobir. At the early age of seven he was taught to read and copy the Koran by his father who was himself a scholar and teacher of some note. After this, like other young Muslim students, he started wandering from place to place in search of distinguished teachers under whom he could further his education. In the process he passed through the hands of many shaikhs who introduced him to the rich intellectual heritage of Islam. Abdul-Rahman ibn Hammada taught him syntax and grammar; Uthman Binduri imparted to him his zeal for right living and action; while a third cleric, Jibril, also infected him with his zeal for radical religious, social and political reform. Jibril had got so exasperated with what he considered social injustice and irreligion in the Hausa states that he had at one time planned a jihad but had been thwarted.

By the time he was twenty Uthman dan Fodio had finished his studies and settled down to teach (1774–5). With his centre at Degel, he travelled far and wide in Hausaland teaching the Islamic religion and pleading for social reform. His preaching journeys took him especially to Kebbi and Zamfara. By the time he completed these travels he had become so famous that he decided to settle at Degel while those in need of instruction flocked to him. It did not take long before the King of Gobir, Bawa, recognised the political danger in Uthman dan Fodio's activities and sought to control him. But it was with Bawa's successor, Nafata, that the clash between the reformer and established authority came into the open. In a bid to counter Uthman's influence, Nafata issued decrees which laid down that only those born as Muslims could practise the Muslim religion and that all those who had been converted to Islam as a result of the recent propaganda of Uthman should return to the faith of their fathers. Some of the decrees denied any cleric except Uthman dan Fodio the right to preach, and forbade such Islamic practices as the wearing of turbans by men or of veils by women. This conflict deepened when Yunfa, a former pupil of Uthman dan Fodio, succeeded Nafata as king of Gobir. The final break came when Uthman released a group of Muslims who were about to be sold into slavery, for according to the Koran Muslims should not be slaves. This action of Uthman angered Yunfa, who gave orders that his former teacher should be seized for trial. Before this could be done Uthman dan Fodio and his followers fled to Gudu on 21 February 1804, and from there declared a jihad against Gobir. At the same time Uthman Dan Fodio was proclaimed Amir al-Muminin (Leader of the Faithful) by his followers.

Yunfa was quickly defeated by Uthman's brother, Abdullah.

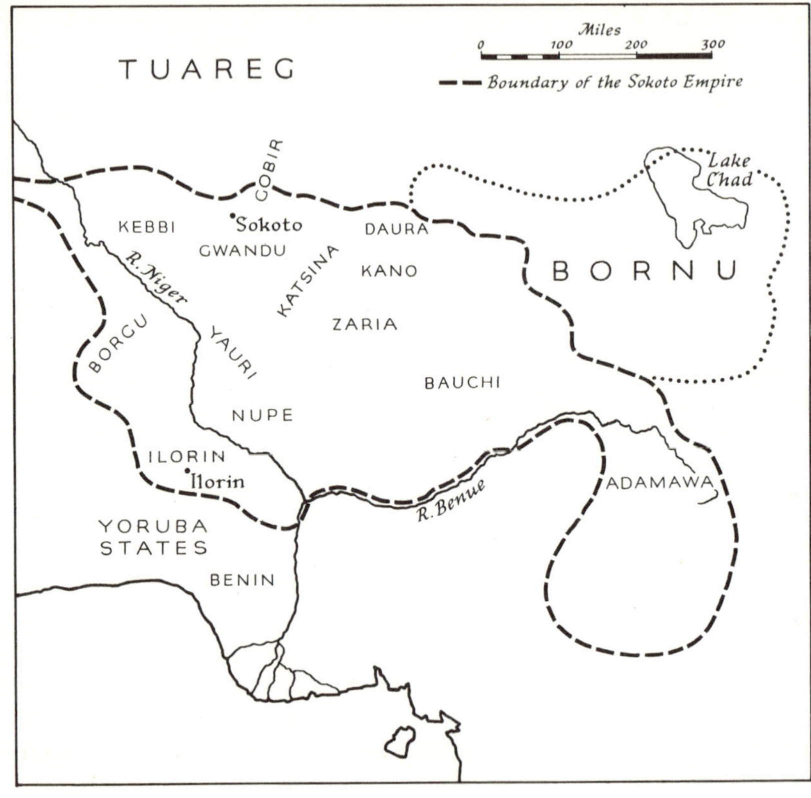

18 The Fulani Jihad

Fearing that the Fulani would support Uthman, other Hausa states attacked the Fulani in their areas. This step made matters worse, since it forced the cattle and town Fulani to unite against their Hausa oppressors. The jihad thus spread beyond Gobir and covered all Hausaland. One after the other the Hausa states fell into the hands of Uthman and his followers. By 1810 most of Hausaland had come under the control of the Fulani who formed them into an empire (Khalifate) under a Khalif with his capital at Sokoto, which was founded in 1808 to mark the dawn of the new era.

After seeing the jihad through its early years Uthman dan Fodio retired from active politics to resume his life of contemplation and scholarship which the wars had interrupted. Before doing so he divided his empire in two with capitals at Sokoto and Gwandu. The Sokoto part he gave to his son Muhammad Bello who was later to

160

succeed him as Sarkin Musulmi (Leader of the Faithful); Gwandu
went to his brother Abdullah.

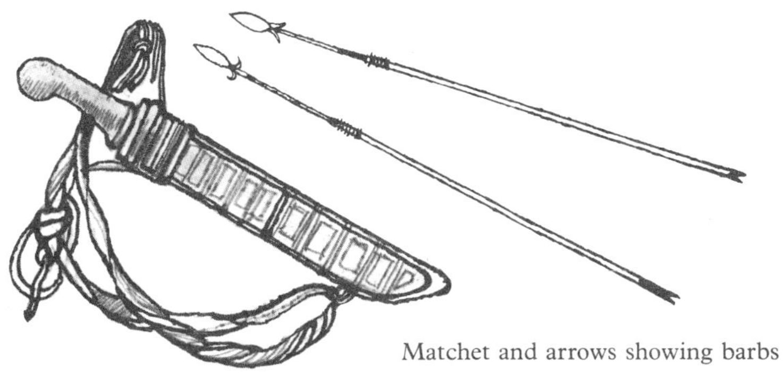

Matchet and arrows showing barbs

Reasons for the success of the jihad

Why, one might ask, did the Fulani rebels find it so easy to overthrow the old Hausa aristocracy? The reasons were many but the
main one was the inability of the different Hausa states to unite in a
common effort against Uthman dan Fodio and his followers. The
states had risen as rivals and they remained rivals to the end. Neither
the invasions of the Songhai in the early sixteenth century, nor of
the Bornu from the fifteenth century nor of the Jukon of Kwararafa
in the seventeenth and eighteenth centuries, nor the unceasing raids
of the Tuaregs of the desert over the centuries, had succeeded in in-
ducing the Hausa states to co-operate. Instead they gloried in their
independence and often went to war against one another. Thus, when
Yunfa appealed to the other states for help, he received no response.
The mutual jealousy and suspicion among the Hausa rulers gave the
Fulani the opportunity to attack and defeat each in turn.

Another reason was that it was not the Fulani alone nor Muslims
alone who resented the rule of the old Hausa aristocracy. Different
sections of the central Sudanese society at this time felt discontented
for different reasons. Some resented over-taxation, while others
resented the moral and religious laxity of their rulers. All these
discontented elements saw Uthman dan Fodio's uprising as a chance
to build a better and happier world, and joined him. Some of them
were later to find that Fulani rule was no less irksome than Hausa

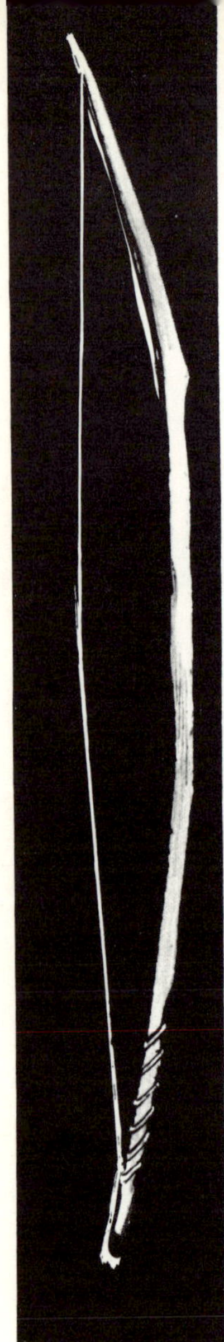

Bow

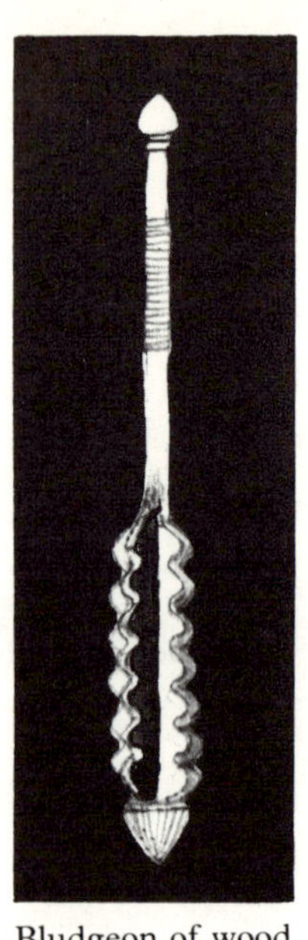

Bludgeon of wood

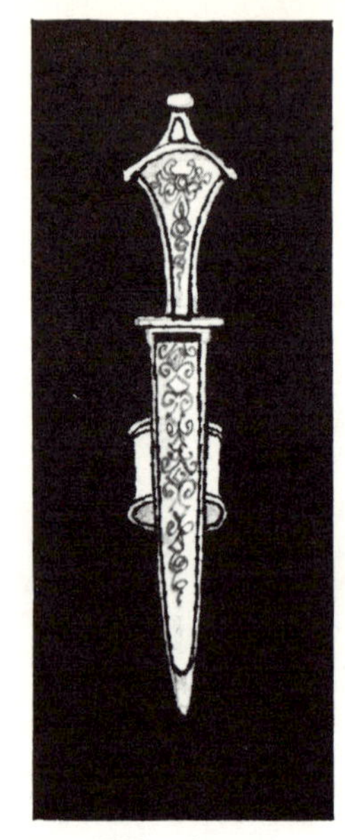

Wrist dagger

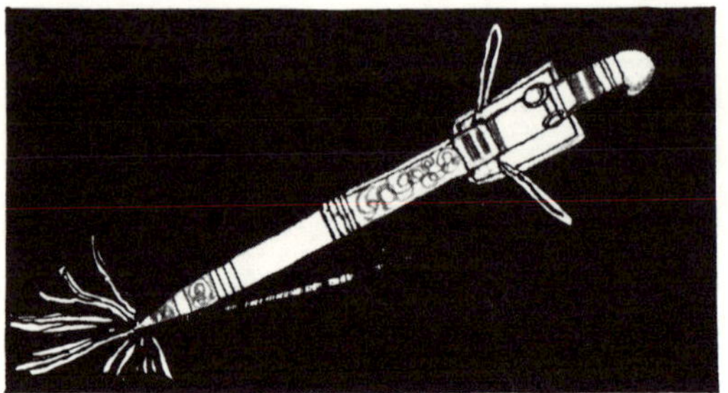

Common native sword

Knife with sheath

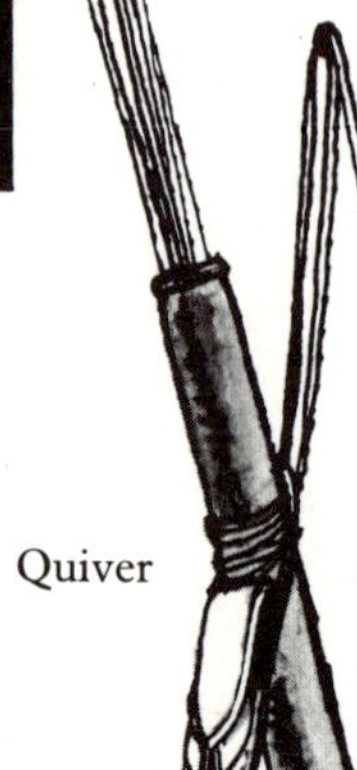

Quiver   and arrows

162

rule, but not before they had helped to destroy the Hausa city states. There were some who supported the Fulani because they saw the ensuing confusion as an opportunity for loot and rape. At the time of the conflict, therefore, the Hausa kings lacked enough supporters to overwhelm the Fulani.

What was more, Uthman dan Fodio and his followers, convinced of the purity and righteousness of their own cause, fought with a zeal and enthusiasm which the bewildered Hausa rulers could not match. Finally, from a strategic point of view, the wide dispersal of the Fulani in previous centuries worked to their advantage. The Hausa rulers had to deal not with foreign invaders but with organised groups within their gates.

Repercussions of the jihad

The echoes of Uthman dan Fodio's jihad were not restricted to the Hausa states; on the contrary they were heard with varying intensity and results in three other neighbouring states and beyond. In 1808 a section of the Fulani in the Bornu Empire rose in sympathy with Uthman against the Sefawa; as a result that ancient but decadent dynasty lost its western provinces, which became emirates under Fulani lieutenants of Uthman within the Sokoto Khalifate. The Sefawa dynasty and Empire were only saved from complete ruin by a remarkable Islamic scholar and soldier from Kanem who was popularly known as Muhammad al-Kanami. It was not al-Kanami's military genius alone that saved the Bornu Empire. He was also a reforming Muslim, and his puritanical reforms in Bornu made the religious propaganda of the Sokoto jihadists sound hollow in the ears of the Kanuri. He also wrote books, in which he accused Uthman and his followers of self-seeking and hypocrisy and defended the stand of Bornu. But, although the Fulani failed to capture the whole of Bornu, their jihad affected that empire seriously. The jihad not only deprived it of its Hausa satellites and of some of its western provinces, but was also responsible for the rise of al-Kanami and his children to positions of political importance. The latter development was to end in the total eclipse of the Sefawa. After saving the

Opposite A selection of Northern Nigerian weapons. It should be remembered that the majority of the soldiers fighting in the jihads had no firearms. Much skill and care was thus taken with the manufacture of traditional weapons, as can be seen from these drawings

Bornu Empire, al-Kanami came to enjoy a great deal of political authority and influence in Bornu as the commander-in-chief of the military forces and as a great religious leader. What was left for the Sefawas was simply the title of *Mai* (ruler). al-Kanami died in 1835, to be succeeded by his son Umar who in 1849 completed the political revolution which his father had started by dethroning and killing the last of the Sefawas and stepping into his shoes as the undisputed ruler of Bornu.

The jihad of Uthman dan Fodio also affected the fates of the Pagan states of Nupe and Oyo lying to the south. We shall deal with Oyo and the jihad later. In Nupe there were Fulani Muslims who, like their counterparts elsewhere, wanted to benefit from the revolution started by their kith and kin in the Hausa states. Fortunately for them at this time the Nupe state was in the throes of a disputed succession. The Fulani supported first this and then that contestant and after they had weakened the old dynasty sufficiently, quietly installed themselves as rulers and brought Nupe under Gwandu.

Hamad in Macina

The second of the three great jihads of the nineteenth century in the western Sudan took place in Macina, which lies west of Hausaland. Here it was led by a reforming Fulani Muslim called Shaikh Hamad (Ahmad, Ahmadu, Hamadu). This man had taken an active part in Uthman dan Fodio's jihad in its early stages. Fired with the spirit of this movement he returned west to Jenne from where he was soon expelled for subversion. From there he fled north to Sebera where he established a school and rallied men around him. In addition to his routine teaching, Hamad tried to persuade his fellow Muslims that in the present corrupt state of society the only course open to a faithful Muslim was the jihad. He did not however meet with much success until the writings of Uthman dan Fodio on his own jihad reached the region, and those who doubted whether Hamad was correct in his view read these works and were convinced. Meanwhile Hamad had sent to Uthman dan Fodio for a flag, which was the accepted symbol that a jihad had Uthman's blessing; but before this could arrive Hamad and his followers had fallen out with the Bambara ruler of Segu, who was their overlord, and had declared a jihad and defeated the armies sent after them.

Feeling confident of his ability to stand on his own, Hamad rejected the flag when it eventually arrived. From Sebera he conquered

Macina, Jenne and Timbuctu and the neighbouring areas. He pitched his capital at Hamdullahi, from where he organised his theocracy. The empire of Hamad of Macina was perhaps better organised than that of Uthman dan Fodio though much smaller in size. After his death in 1848 Shaikh Hamad was succeeded by his son Ahmadu Seku who was able to maintain his inheritance intact. When Ahmadu Seku died in 1852 he was succeeded by his son Ahmadu Ahmadu. It was under the latter that this Caliphate came into conflict with another which had arisen further to the west, and was destroyed by it in 1862.

Al-Hajj Umar

This other caliphate grew out of a similar movement led by another Muslim reformer known as al-Hajj Umar who, in all probability, was a Fulani, though some scholars have described him as Tukolor. Umar, born either in 1794 or 1797, was a great soldier as well as a scholar of considerable ability. Like Uthman dan Fodio he started his studies under his father, Saidu Tall, who was in his own right a learned man. After graduating from his father, Umar travelled widely in the Sudan in search of learned scholars under whom he would finish his studies. This took him to Mauritania, Futa Toro (his home) and Futa Jalon. In the latter place he met the Tijani scholar Shaikh Abdul-Karim al-Naqil who initiated him into the Tijaniyya religious brotherhood. In 1826 he undertook the pilgrimage to Mecca where he met Sidi Muhammad al-Ghali who gave him further instructions in Tijani lore. At Mecca Umar came into contact with the revolutionary ideas which agitated the Islamic world at this time. He travelled extensively in the east, visiting Egypt where he met the Shaikhs of al Azhar university in Cairo. After leaving the east Umar passed through Bornu where he met the reformer al–Kanami, and Sokoto where he spent twelve years in close touch with the court of Muhammad Bello. He married two Sokoto women, one of them a sister of Muhammad Bello.

In 1838 Umar left Sokoto for Macina soaked in the revolutionary ideas of his time and world. His stay at Macina was short since his relations with Shaikh Ahmad were strained. From there he renewed his wanderings, going to Segu and Futa Jalon preaching reform, making friends as well as enemies. Finally he withdrew to Dinguiray with his followers to lay deep plans for the jihad which he eventually launched in 1851. His plan would seem to have been to create a

Ahmad, the son of al-Hajj Umar. A picture of al-Hajj Umar himself
is unobtainable but he must have worn similar clothing and perhaps
bore some family resemblance

khalifate on the Senegal but he was thwarted by the French who drove
him from Medina which he had invaded in 1857. He then decided
to strike eastwards against the Bambara states and by 1861 had
conquered Segu and Kaarta. In capturing Segu Umar alienated
Ahmadu Ahmadu of Macina, who regarded Segu as falling within
his sphere of influence. The Macina authorities had in fact sent
forces to aid Segu against al-Hajj Umar. The latter, regarding this
as justifying war, invaded Macina and captured it in 1862, killing
Ahmadu Ahmadu in the process. For the next two years Umar
found himself entrapped in Macina trying to suppress local rebellions.
He in fact lost his life in one of his many campaigns there in 1864.

At his death, Umar's far-flung empire had no administrative
system to hold it together. Ahmad Seku, his son and successor as
Khalif, inherited administrative problems which he never succeeded

166

in solving. Unfortunately he could not inherit his father's great influence and prestige, which had helped to keep the conquests together and his followers under control. As soon as Umar's death was announced the empire broke up into three virtually independent states. One part was under Ahmad himself who ruled from Segu, the others were respectively ruled from Hamdullahi and Mioro by Umar's brother, al-Tijani, and slave, Mustafa. Mustafa and al-Tijani, while they acknowledged Ahmad Seku as Khalif, remained practically independent. In addition to these problems there was the threat posed by the French based on the Senegal, who had developed an appetite for the whole of the Sudan and looked upon Ahmad's empire as a mere obstacle to their advance.

Umar's jihad differed from the other jihads of the western Sudan in two ways. Firstly it was centrally organised. Its military campaigns were carried out from the centre according to previously laid plans, while Uthman dan Fodio's jihad, for instance, had depended on un-coordinated risings by his Fulani brethren who sympathised with his cause. Secondly this jihad depended on the use of fire-arms to a greater extent than any of the preceding ones. It was to obtain these arms that Umar encouraged trade even with European unbelievers.

Effects of the jihads

In spite of the ease and rapidity with which some of these khalifates disappeared, the jihads of the nineteenth century in the western Sudan made a great impact on the lives of the peoples in the region. On the political plane they brought appreciable sections of the western Sudan under large empires, a feature that recalled the glorious days of Ghana, Mali and Songhai. Uthman dan Fodio's jihad brought about 180,000 square miles of territory under the allegiance of the Khalif at Sokoto. The jihad of Shaikh Hamad of Macina created a state of about 56,000 square miles, while that of al-Hajj Umar created an empire 150,000 square miles in area. To a great extent within these states, at least within the states of Uthman dan Fodio and Shaikh Hamad, this meant the re-establishment of order and good government over a wide area, leading to the expansion of trade.

The Macina Khalifate was the most centralised of these states. The Sokoto Khalifate, though a loose confederation of practically autonomous states acknowledging allegiance to the Sarkin Musulmi at Sokoto, was also able to ensure a certain measure of law and order. The explorers of West Africa who entered the central Sudan and lived to tell their story were full of admiration for the peace which reigned within the khalifate. But with al-Hajj Umar's empire, the story was different. Umar died before he had organised an administrative system. His son and successor had not sufficient energy and drive to provide one. In consequence, unregulated and apparently purposeless wars and raids rendered life here nasty, brutish and short. To some extent the French were regarded as deliverers from an intolerable state of affairs.

On the religious side these jihads led to extensive conversions of Pagans to Islam, while strengthening the faith of those nominally attached to Islam. In northern Nigeria for instance, places like Bauchi and Adamawa were for the first time brought within the influence of Islam. Further west the wars and rule of Shaikh Hamad of Macina brought about extensive and permanent conversions. In the empire of al-Hajj Umar things were different. Extensive conversions were achieved or enforced at the point of the sword. But when that sword was withdrawn there were equally large-scale reversions to the traditional religion, especially among the Bambara. Although the jihads on the whole strengthened Islam, they also weakened it in some areas, especially within Umar's Khalifate. Umar made no distinction between outright non-Muslims and Muslims who did not belong to the Tijaniyya brotherhood. His Tijani exclusiveness and arrogance alienated many Muslims, especially those who belonged to the older Qadiriyya brotherhood. This explains why they did not support him, and in fact were sympathetic to the French. Even in the central Sudan the two Islamic states there, Sokoto and Bornu, remained irreconcilable. Co-operation between them was impossible even in the face of foreign aggression.

Socially the jihads were revolutionary. The old aristocracies of the states against which the jihads were fought were overthrown, and in their place rose new groups who hitherto had been among the unprivileged in society. In particular the Fulani underdogs of previous centuries became the arrogant and overbearing aristocrats of the future.

On the cultural plane the jihads were important mainly in the ferment of intellectual activity they encouraged and created. The jihadists felt called upon to produce written justifications of their actions, especially of their attacks on supposedly fellow Muslims. Uthman dan Fodio and his son Muhammad Bello were particularly productive in this field. So was al-Hajj Umar, but not on the scale of the former two. In other spheres of culture the movement does not seem to have been very significant. In the central Sudan, for instance, the Hausa, who suffered political defeat at the hands of the Fulani, culturally conquered the latter. Even in political and administrative fields, the Fulani merely took over Hausa institutions. In language too most of the Fulani lost their language and adopted Hausa.

By and large, however, the jihads caused much dislocation, much confusion and much suffering, especially among the non-Muslims who were raided to swell the volume of the trans-Saharan slave trade. The distinction in Islam between the 'abode of war' and the 'abode of Islam' provided philosophical and religious justification for raids against non-Muslims which had no higher purpose than to satisfy the greed for gain. This was at least so in northern Nigeria where raids against non-Muslims stopped only with the imposition of British rule in the early part of the twentieth century.

19 The empires of al-Hajj Umar, Samori Toure and Hamad

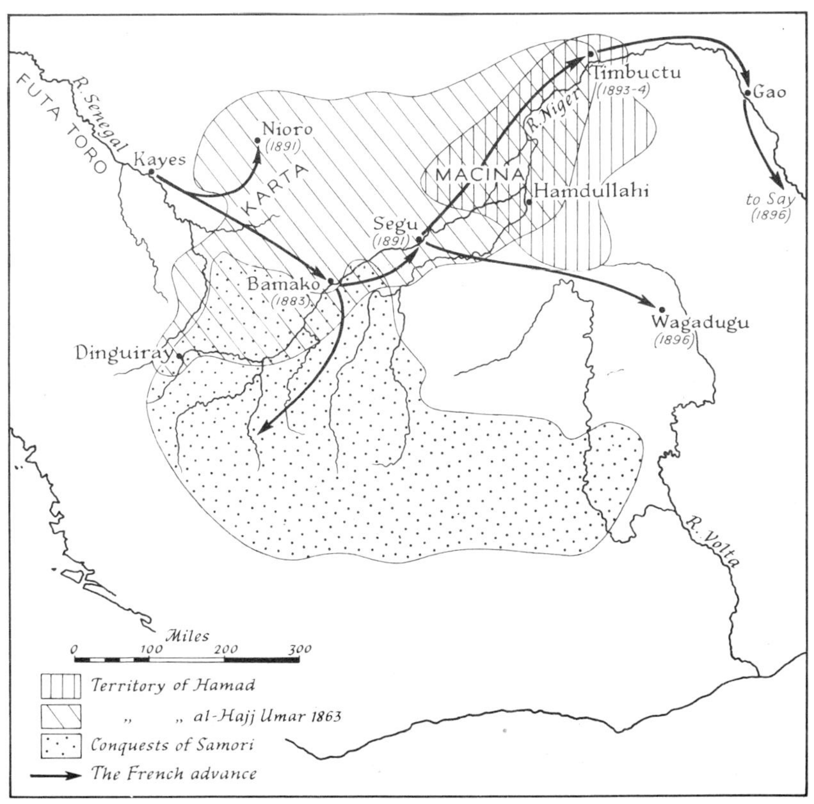

A drawing from a contemporary print of Samori's arsenal.
When Samori's supply of firearms from the coast was cut off
he was compelled to manufacture and repair his own arms

Samori Toure

A similar state of dislocation existed in the upper Niger region and
it was to some extent this which enabled Samori Toure, the son of a
Malinke farmer, to establish an empire for himself from the 1850s
onwards. Samori, who was born about 1830, became a trader, until
in 1852 he joined the army of Sori Birama, King of Bisandugu.

It was immediately obvious that Samori was a brilliant soldier,
and it soon became his ambition to create a force strong enough to
establish an empire and impose peace throughout Malinke-land.
Thus, after a few years in the army of Sori Birama, Samori felt strong
enough to establish himself independently, and his abilities as a
leader attracted many to serve under him; those who were less willing
to join him he persuaded, by force or diplomacy, to rally to his side.

170

Sanankoro became the main town of his new army and from the end of the 1860s and through the 1870s, Samori's armies campaigned regularly. By 1879 he controlled an area from Sierra Leone in the west to Ivory Coast in the east, and from a point near Bamako in the north, to the Liberian frontiers in the south. His capital was at Bisandugu.

The system Samori gradually built up to administer this empire was to split it into provinces; the three central provinces were directly controlled by Samori and his ministers, while outlying areas were governed by an appointed military official, who shared his authority with a qadi (judge) who was also the local head of the religious community. This direct control was carried down to the level of the village, groups of which formed a district within each province.

But Samori depended on the army to acquire, and then to hold, his empire. His power rested in the loyalty of the army and not, as for example with al-Hajj Umar, on his authority as a religious leader. The ranks of this army were filled mainly with captives, who were trained as rifle-carrying infantrymen, and were known as sofa. These men formed a standing army directly loyal to Samori, while in times of need a conscripted reserve was also available, as well as a volunteer militia of those who owned horses. Samori's flexibility in using his forces – as raiding parties, as protection for caravans or towns, or to lay siege to fortified enemies – lies at the heart of his genius as a soldier. In addition the army was supported by a highly-organised administration which ensured that supplies of all sorts were readily available. Apart from food, Samori established groups of metalworkers known as forgerons to manufacture rifle parts, cartridge cases and other military requirements.

Up to the year 1882 Samori's armies continued to expand his empire. Then, while they were laying siege to the village of Keniera (near Siguiri in modern Guinea), there came the first clash with the French. This was ultimately to result in the defeat and capture of Samori, and the destruction of his empire, but his military genius enabled him to resist the French for a long time, so that it was not until 1898 that he was finally overwhelmed.

Samori's career has been the subject of controversy. He has been regarded by some as a national leader fighting to maintain his empire in the face of a colonising power, and by others as a ruthless and cruel tyrant who brought suffering to very many people, for example by his involvement in slave trading.

Another empire builder, cast somewhat in the Samori mould was Rabeh ibn Fadl Allah, who started his career in what is now the Sudan, where he had served a slave dealer called Zubair Pasha. Like Samori, Rabeh broke away from his former master, and set up a strong and well-organised army of his own, with which he invaded the Chad region around 1891. Rabeh invaded and conquered Bornu but, before he could consolidate his conquests round Chad, he was challenged by the French at Bagirmi. He was defeated by them and killed in 1900, after which his empire collapsed. It had been held together only by his own ability as a soldier and, although he tried to associate himself with the Mahdist movement in the Sudan, religious zeal was not a notable part of his career.

The collapse of the Oyo Empire

The Yoruba Empire of Oyo, founded about the fifteenth century, reached the height of its power about the middle of the seventeenth century and then disintegrated in the nineteenth century. Its collapse can be traced to constitutional and administrative breakdown going back to the mid-eighteenth century. The strength and peace of the Oyo Empire depended on the readiness and ability of the Alafin and the Oyo Mesi (State Council) to keep each other in check. Some time in the eighteenth century the balance between the two was upset by an ambitious Bashorun called Gaha, a politician of great ability, influence and fame who used his traditional position as chief king-maker to bring a succession of Alafins and his fellow members of the Oyo Mesi under his absolute control. In this way he made himself the virtual ruler of the empire. Though his tyranny was later ended in 1774 by Alafin Abiodun, who destroyed him and his entire family, the events associated with the years of his ascendancy left a lasting imprint on the fortunes of the empire.

In the years before Gaha's career some of the chief officials of the Oyo Empire were usually slaves of the Alafin's household. This was particularly the case with certain offices at the metropolis. Since these slaves were usually eunuchs they had no children and so never raised families which could be in rivalry with the royal lineage. The slave officials knew that they owed their position to the Alafin and so obeyed him implicitly. But in order to raise the forces with which to defeat Gaha the Alafins had been compelled to give important offices of state to some powerful Yoruba families of free status who did not owe all they possessed to the Alafin. Thus the chief officials of the empire became less dependent on the Alafin, with the result that the central authority became weakened by a continuous struggle for power. As the Alafin and his advisers and lieutenants were pre-occupied with the constitutional crisis at the centre, the provinces of the empire were less effectively governed. The provincial residents (the Ajele) did as they liked and became corrupt and oppressive, while the local population of the provinces became restive and independent and rebelled at the earliest opportunity. For instance the Egba took the opportunity of the conflict between Abiodun and Gaha in 1775–80 to rebel against the oppression of the Ajele and to throw over the yoke of Oyo. All subsequent attempts to bring the Egba back to Oyo rule failed. The trouble between Gaha and the Alafins had led to the neglect of the army, which therefore decayed.

The Oyo Empire thus entered the nineteenth century afflicted with a serious constitutional and administrative crisis which rendered it incapable of effectively facing external threats to its existence. But in 1804 Uthman dan Fodio had launched his great jihad, and the triumphant Fulani advance towards the south which followed threatened the northern provinces of the Oyo Empire. To meet this threat the Alafin appointed Afonja, a descendant of the Yoruba royal line, Are-Ona-Kakanfo, with headquarters at Ilorin and the duty of defending the empire against the Fulani. But Afonja treacher-ously proceeded to use his office to strengthen himself against the central government. The Alafin therefore decided to destroy him in the traditional way by setting him an impossible task which he had to accomplish or commit suicide. But Afonja not only refused to tackle the task or to commit suicide, but also rose in revolt against his king in 1817. At once all the discontented people, of whom there were many in the empire, joined him. Unfortunately for the Oyo Empire the hands of the Alafin were weakened by a struggle with the Oyo Mesi at this time. What was more important, Afonja further strengthened himself by allying with the Fulani and in doing so opened the gate into the Oyo Empire for the Fulani jihadists. First the Fulani helped Afonja to establish the independence of Ilorin, and then they overthrew and killed him in order to become the rulers of Ilorin, which now became an emirate under Gwandu. The extension of the jihad into Ilorin was the immediate cause of the collapse of Oyo. It touched off a chain of events which kept Yoruba-land disturbed by wars and rumours of wars for the rest of the nineteenth century.

These events greatly affected the outcome of the Owu war which broke out in 1820. The people of Owu had quarrelled with the Ife and the Ijebu over trade matters, as a result of which the Ife and the Ijebu began a combined attack on Owu in 1820. About this time the war between Oyo and Ilorin was causing the inhabitants of northern Yoruba towns to flee to the south for safety. These displaced men thronged the highways and the paths, seeking for means of livelihood and spreading panic and unrest as they went. When they got to Owu they joined the Ife and the Ijebu, thus helping to bring about the fall of the invested town. The fall of Owu did not mean the end of the disturbance in Yorubaland, since the army that destroyed Owu contained many homeless refugees, who had become accustomed to live by plunder and who were not ready to demobilise and settle down. This army therefore continued southwards from Owu until it got to the place now occupied by Ibadan, where it destroyed Egba towns and villages, thus forcing out the Egba who had to start a new settlement at Abeokuta. About the same time the war between the Fulani of Ilorin and the Oyo Empire grew in volume and intensity. In 1830 the Alafin made a great effort with the aid of the Bariba of Borgu to recover Ilorin. The attempt not only failed hopelessly but led to the destruction of Oyo, the capital of the empire, by the Fulani. The Alafin and his court fled in panic into the forest town of Ago-Oja to the south, where a new capital was built and named after the old. This is the present Oyo, which lies about thirty miles north of Ibadan. The old Oyo Empire had thus completely collapsed. The aftermath was a series of wars waged by a number of states which sought to occupy the position of pre-eminence which Oyo had hitherto enjoyed in Yorubaland.

The Yoruba wars

Though Atiba, the first Alafin to rule in new Oyo, tried to revive the time-honoured traditions of the empire and to maintain the prestige and dignity of the royal court, Oyo ceased to play an important part in Yoruba politics after 1830. The Alafin was forced to recognise that Oyo was no longer a military power, and that the defence of Yorubaland against the outsider had passed to the towns which were either founded or grew in importance as a result of the confusion following the Fulani invasion. The best he could do was to confer traditional imperial honours and titles on the leading chiefs of these rising towns in the hope of using them for his purposes.

There were four principal Yoruba states involved in the struggle for ascendancy. The first was Ijaye which was situated between Oyo and Ibadan, and which was dominated by Kurunmi, one of the ablest Yoruba generals of the day. Ijaye was responsible for defending the western provinces of Yorubaland against Dahomey which now threatened to conquer the Yoruba. In order to keep Ijaye within the imperial system Atiba conferred on Kurunmi the title of Are-Ona-Kakanfo.

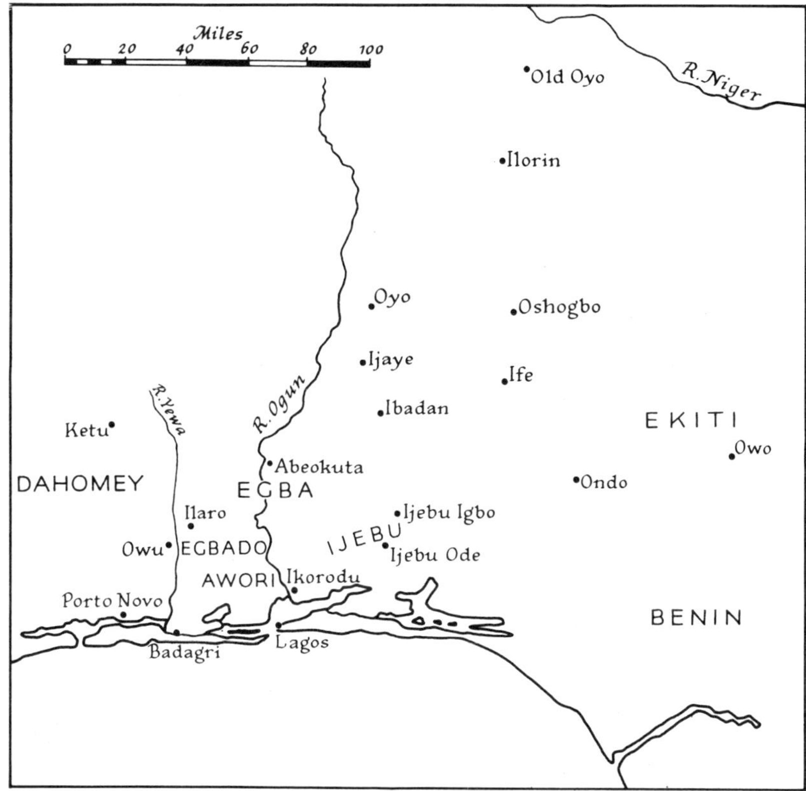

20 Yorubaland at the time of the wars

Then there was Ibadan which began as a war camp but soon became one of the leading powers in Yorubaland. Here Oluyole was supreme. To control him Atiba made him Basorun. Ibadan had the duty of defending the northern and north-eastern provinces against the Fulani.

The Egba with their new capital at Abeokuta were also in the struggle for supremacy in Yorubaland. They were not interested in the reconquest of the provinces which the Fulani had seized, but only wanted to defend themselves first against Ijebu and Ibadan and then against Dahomey and Ibadan. For this they wanted an outlet to the coast from where they could get the necessary European weapons.

Lastly there were the Ijebu. These shrewd businessmen were keenly interested in the confusion in the interior, since it offered them immense opportunities for profitable business. Success in these wars depended greatly on the availability of guns and powder, which came from the coast through Ijebu. The wars also produced a large crop of slaves which passed through the hands of the Ijebu to the Europeans on the coast. The Ijebu therefore were determined to preserve their monopoly of the trade between the port of Lagos and Benin. They were thus hostile to the Egba who were trying to get a port on the coast. But when later Ibadan threatened to swallow up all the rest of the Yoruba states the Ijebu were frightened and allied with the Egba to frustrate this ambition.

The struggle between these states grew very intense after the Battle of Oshogbo (1840), where the Ibadan defeated the Fulani and put a check to Fulani advance towards the south. The history of this struggle falls into two clearly marked phases. The first phase was dominated by the struggle between Ibadan and Ijaye in which the latter enjoyed the support of the Egba. The rivalry between Ibadan and Ijaye led first to the Battle of Batedo (1844) which neither party won; and then to the more famous Ijaye War (1860–2) in which Ijaye was destroyed.

The disturbances associated with this war lingered on until 1878 as an engagement between the victorious Ibadan and the Egba. One important development in this period was the fact that the British became involved in the conflict. The British had seized Lagos in 1861, not only as a means of stopping the slave trade but also in order to benefit from the trade of Yorubaland. Their hopes were disappointed as the wars in the interior disturbed the flow of trade, and they therefore became interested in the restoration of peace. In 1865 they sent soldiers to expel the Egba, who were besieging Ikorodu and so harming the trade of Lagos. In this way the British entered the war on the side of Ibadan.

British intervention

The second phase of the rivalry covered the years 1878 to 1892–3. Ibadan emerged from the conflict of 1840 to 1878 as the strongest single state in Yorubaland, and seemed likely sooner or later to assume the position of leadership which Oyo had occupied before the nineteenth century. The other Yoruba states were alarmed and formed a series of military alliances and coalitions against her. The leaders of the coalitions were the Ekiti, a people who had never come under the rule of Oyo and now wanted to recover the independence which they had lost in 1858 when Ibadan conquered them. For them, therefore, this was a war of independence. The Egba and the Ijebu were by now the traditional enemies of Ibadan and wanted to break her up. The Fulani of Ilorin sought to gain from the confusion in Yorubaland and entered the war against Ibadan.

By 1886 all the sides in the conflict had exhausted themselves without any side gaining a clear victory. From this time negotiations to end the war started. But no progress was made until in 1892, when the British allies of Ibadan defeated the Ijebu and forced all rival groups to end the war, which they were no longer able to continue effectively or end on their own. In 1893 the Lagos government also forced the Ibadan and the Ilorin to end their struggle. Peace now returned to Yorubaland.

The collapse of the Oyo Empire at the hands of the Fulani thus had grave consequences for the Yoruba people. First, it brought about a massive shift in population. As the Fulani advanced from Ilorin the Yoruba fled from the more open lands of the north to the thickly forested lands of the south in search of shelter. Secondly it brought the full impact of the slave trade to Yorubaland. Before the events of the nineteenth century most of the slaves from the West Coast came from the Niger Delta ports, Dahomey, the area of modern Ghana, and the region to the west of it. The influence of the Alafin was somehow able to limit the extent to which the Yoruba caught and sold each other, with the result that most of the slaves sold by the Yoruba came from the markets to the north of Yorubaland. When the Fulani conquest of Ilorin closed the northern markets to the Yoruba the slave demands of Ijebu and other coastal groups had to be met by increased raiding in Yoruba country. The interstate rivalry which followed the fall of Oyo supplied these needs. Thus, though the desire for slaves did not cause the wars, the fact that the wars produced slaves provided an extra reason for prolonging them unduly. The wars were lucrative business. Thirdly, the wars created the opportunity for British intervention in Yorubaland. Since the Yoruba were divided amongst themselves the British found it easy to have their way. While appearing to be bringing peace to the Yoruba people the British actually deprived them of their independence.

The Dahomean invasions of Yorubaland

From about 1840 to the end of the nineteenth century the kingdom of Dahomey made a number of military incursions into Yorubaland. These invasions have sometimes been treated as part of the internal history of Yorubaland, and in particular as a phase in the Yoruba wars of the nineteenth century. Here, however, they will be examined as part of the history of the Dahomean state from which the invasions originated.

There were two main reasons behind the invasions. The first was political. Ever since Dahomey rose to greatness in the first half of the eighteenth century it had been a dependency of Oyo. Various attempts by its kings to become independent of Oyo had only brought severe punishments at the hands of the Oyo army. Oyo overlordship at times meant for Dahomeans subordination to irritating laws and regulations. For instance the Alafin of Oyo regarded the Dahomean army as part of his military forces which should be placed at his service as he wanted. Also the Alafin from time to time passed regulations forbidding the kings of Dahomey to use certain materials for clothing because those materials were considered as only fit to be used by the Alafin himself. Though the Oyo were never really able to enforce obedience to these rules, they were humiliating to Dahomean national prestige. Then Dahomey had to pay tributes to the Alafin throughout the eighteenth century. It was thus certain that any king of Dahomey who could would end this subservience to Oyo, which the proud Dahomeans found uncongenial. Also it must be remembered that at the beginning of the nineteenth century Dahomey was still an energetic state full of imperial ambitions. It thus had a mission not only to win its independence of Oyo, but if possible to expand at the expense of that empire.

The second reason behind the invasions was economic. From about the 1740s the Dahomean economy rested mainly on slavery. Some of the slaves were sold to Europeans on the coast, from whom the kings of Dahomey got the manufactured goods needed by their people, especially the arms and ammunition which were required for the army. Of those slaves who were not sold overseas some were used in working the extensive royal plantations while others served as the unfortunate victims of the human sacrifices for which the kings of Dahomey were notorious. It was to provide the slave needs of the state that the Dahomean army was constantly in action to the west and north of the kingdom. By the beginning of the nineteenth century these traditional raiding grounds had been seriously depopulated. Dahomey thus had to turn to the country to the east and south-east, that is to a section of the Yoruba country. This change was made possible by the break-up of the great Oyo Empire which had hitherto frightened Dahomey off Yorubaland.

In the nineteenth century the economic motive for expansion in the direction of Yoruba country was reinforced. In 1807 Britain abolished the slave trade for her subjects and started a campaign to abolish the trade throughout the world. By the end of the first half of the nineteenth century the volume of the slave trade across the Atlantic was being drastically reduced. For Dahomey this meant economic ruin. It became essential to find a substitute for slaves as an export. This meant that Dahomey had to find new tracts of fertile territory in which to grow the products which the Europeans now required. The region to the west and north was dry and infertile. It was the area to the east and south-east, the Yoruba country, that once again answered Dahomey's needs. Thus whether it was slaves or land that Dahomey needed, she had to look to Yorubaland. Nothing could have prevented the clash between the Dahomeans and the Yoruba in the nineteenth century.

For Dahomey the conditions appeared favourable: 1817 was the year of Afonja's revolt at Ilorin which opened a gate into Yorubaland for the Fulani; 1820 was the year of the Owu war which started a civil war in Yorubaland which lasted for eighty years. On the other hand Dahomey was as strong as ever. In 1818 Gezo, a very energetic and ambitious man, came to the Dahomean throne. When he saw that the time was ripe he declared Dahomey independent of Oyo. This claim was not contested and it looked as if nothing would prevent Dahomey from overrunning the country to the east and south-east, occupied by the Egbado and Awori Yoruba.

The Egba stand

This situation was complicated by other factors. As a result of the confusion arising from the Owu war the Egba had been expelled from their ancestral home around Ibadan and forced to found the new town of Abeokuta. The nature of politics in Yorubaland at this time made the Egba develop ambitions in the direction of Egbado and Awori. To be able to defend themselves against their enemies, the Egba needed a port on the coast through which they could obtain the guns which were changing the nature of warfare in Yorubaland. Since they could not hope to control Lagos, which was held by the Ijebu,

King Behanzin, the last nineteenth century king of Dahomey

their enemies at the time, they hoped to gain control of Badagry. To do this they needed to control the roads leading from Badagry to Abeokuta. This in turn meant they had to control the Egbado and Awori country. In this way the Egba came to stand in the way of Dahomey.

It was these rival interests that soon brought the Egba and Dahomey into conflict. Dahomey opened the aggression by sending forces to help Egbado and Awori towns which·the Egba were trying to seize. The Egba bitterly resented this Dahomean intervention and retaliated in 1844 by ambushing a Dahomean army which was going to attack the Egbado town of Ilaro. In the scuffle that followed the Dahomeans suffered more than the Egba. King Gezo narrowly escaped capture but lost his royal umbrella, stool and war charms. It was in that year that Gezo made up his mind to destroy Abeokuta as a punishment for the insult. To prepare the way he destroyed Oke Odan in 1848. The Egba retaliated two years later by sacking Igbeji which was under Dahomey. The following year (1851) Gezo undertook his long expected, full scale invasion of Abeokuta only to be beaten off with severe losses. He was not able to return to the attack before his death in 1858. But his son and successor, Glele, regarded the destruction of Abeokuta as his life's assignment and refused to complete the ceremonies connected with his coronation until he had achieved this ambition. But events proved him no luckier than his father for when he attacked Abeokuta in 1864 he suffered a severe defeat. After this attempt Dahomey did not again try to seize Abeokuta by storm, but resorted to isolated raids and forays against the Egba. Glele, however, met with better luck in his attack on Ketu, a Yoruba kingdom, which he devastated in 1883 and took by seige in 1886.

Abeokuta's victory over Dahomey was to some extent the result of British aid. The Lagos government in particular supplied the Egba with guns and powder and sent trained soldiers to educate the Egba on how to repair their defences and how to fire some of the new guns they supplied. The C.M.S. missionaries who at this time were settled at Abeokuta identified themselves with Egba interests. In their writings they presented the Dahomeans as devils against whom the British should help the harmless Egba to defend themselves. This propaganda proved very effective as a means of evoking British help.

The Anglo-Asante wars

As already shown in an earlier chapter the rise of the Atlantic trade had precipitated intense rivalry among the numerous Akan principalities for its control. By 1800 Asante, the youngest of these, had emerged the undisputed power in Akan land except that it had still to absorb the Fante and Ga states of the coast.

But, contrary to what one would expect from the trend of the past, the history of nineteenth century Akan land is not the story of the triumphant achievement of the Asante ambition and the universal reign of Asante peace throughout Akan land. On the contrary it is a monotonous story of a series of wars fought between the Asante and the British. One interesting aspect of these wars is that neither the British nor the Asante really desired them. Both parties wanted to trade peacefully with each other, yet they constantly found themselves at war with each other. The main causes of these wars and their results for those involved will be briefly sketched here.

In accounting for these wars, a distinction must be made between those fought before 1880 and the wars which came after that date. No doubt the wars which came after 1880 derived to some extent from the embittered relations between the British and Asante arising from

the earlier conflicts and from the unfulfilled terms of past treaties.
But all the same a survey of events in Africa after 1880 would show
that the Anglo-Asante wars of post-1880 would have come whether
or not the British and the Asante had fought each other earlier on.
By 1880 the scramble for Africa was on, and everywhere on the continent colony-hungry European nations were assailing and destroying
African states. Since it was unlikely that the proud Asante would have
submitted meekly to British annexation of their territory, the two
powers were bound to come to armed conflict.

What, then, were the causes of the earlier wars? On the side of the
Asante there were two factors which drove them into war with the
British. The first was political and derived mainly from the nature of
the Asante constitution. The Asante Union or Confederacy was a
great military power, but never a highly centralised state. Adminis-
tratively speaking it consisted of three concentric rings of divisions
under varying degrees of control. At the centre was the state or province of Kumasi which was the capital of the Asantehene who ruled it
directly in his capacity as Kumasihene, that is as the original king of
Kumasi before the union. Here the power of the Asantehene was
extensive and effective. After Kumasi came the other states of Ofinso,
Nsuta, Dwaben and Kokofu which with Kumasi had originally
brought the Asante Union into existence. Each of these states had its
own king who before the union was equal to the Kumasihene. He ruled
his state with his own council of chiefs, but recognised the Asantehene
as his overlord. Within this circle the supreme authority was the
Asante state council or Asante Kotoko of which all the chiefs of the
above states were members. In this council if the Asantehene was not
merely the first among equals, neither was he a dictator. The council
dealt with all important matters of war and peace; it was the supreme
court of the realm before which even the Asantehene could be tried.
It was also responsible for crowning and removing the Asantehene.
The great bond of union within this wider circle was the fact that all
these states descended, or believed that they descended, from the
Oyoko matrilineal clan; also all of them recognised the Golden Stool
as embodying the spirit of their nation.

Outside this circle was one more, occupied by the conquered provinces of the Union such as the states of Akyem, Akwamu, Akwapim,
Denkyira, Wassa and Ga in the south; and Dagomba and Gonja
in the north. This circle had an ever-changing radius, shrinking
when any of these states rebelled, and expanding when new conquests
were made. The provinces in this group were not effectively inte-
grated into the Asante Union. Their kings had no seats in the Asante

Kotoko and though they might be under the supervision of Residents appointed by the Asante, they practically ran their affairs without reference to Kumasi. The Residents were often absentees.

Being under so loose a control, and not having forgotten their ancient independence and greatness, while also living near their kith and kin who were still independent of Asante and who often encouraged them to rebel, these states were constantly in revolt. This was a situation that forced the Asante state to be constantly at war in order to punish rebellious chiefs and provinces, and to conquer those neighbouring groups who were still independent and who instigated rebellion against the Asantehene. In the nineteenth century the Fante states of the coast were notorious for aiding and abetting rebellions within the Asante kingdom. Partly for this reason it became necessary for the Asantehene to bring the Fante under his control.

The other factors which helped to determine Asante policy towards the Fante and the British was economic. Asante was an inland power and wanted to gain free access to the coastal forts in order to trade directly with the Europeans. In particular the Asante wanted to ensure a steady supply of arms and ammunition which they needed for their wars. By 1800 Asante had gained access to the forts of Appollonia and Accra, but still wanted direct business with the Europeans at the forts of Anamaboe, Karmantine, Cape Coast and Mouree. It was in these places that the Asante came into conflict with the Fante. The latter had built up a strong and prosperous position as middlemen in the trade between Europeans on the coast and their fellow Africans in the interior, and since they did not want to lose this lucrative position, they insisted that the Asante should continue getting the European goods they wanted through them. To this end they tried to prevent the Asante from getting to the forts. If the Fante succeeded in doing this the Asante would then buy imported European goods in the interior markets at prices fixed by the Fante. For the Asante to prosper economically the Asantehene had to incorporate the Fante into his empire.

Since the British on the coast were all traders, one would have expected them to co-operate with the Asante to promote trade. For instance the British could have helped the Asantehene to assert his authority in his empire in order to maintain peace in the interior, which would help to promote trade. But this the British would not do. Rightly or wrongly they believed that the Asante Empire was a savage state, and after the abolition of the slave trade came to regard the Asante as incorrigible slave dealers. For humanitarian reasons the British therefore adopted the policy of giving protection to rebels against the authority of the Asantehene. The result was that the British intervened in the internal affairs of Asante against the authority of the Asantehene and his council.

Also one would have expected the British to welcome direct trade contact with the Asante and try to promote it, especially as it was common knowledge that the Asante wanted the goods which the British brought to the coast. The British therefore might have been expected either to have allowed the Asante to conquer the Fante, or to have controlled the Fante themselves in order to deal directly with the Asante. But they saw the Asante Empire as a tyranny and would not allow their Fante friends to be made part of it. More importantly they were afraid that if the Asante held the entire coast of modern Ghana the Asantehene would control the Europeans as strictly as the king of Dahomey did along his own coast, and this might have meant high tolls and less profit for them. The existing situation along the coast, in which the Fante were disunited and weak, suited the British because it allowed them to have their way by playing one Fante chief against his neighbour. Up to the 1870s the British did not seek to gain control themselves; they were not interested in acquiring colonies along the West African coast since colonies were considered expensive to maintain.

For all these reasons the British and the Asante found themselves repeatedly at war. The story of the origin of the first Anglo-Asante war is sufficient to show how most of these wars came about without either side wanting to fight the other. In 1807 two Assin chiefs rebelled against the Asantehene. The rebellion was easily put down but the chiefs managed to escape to the Fante for protection. The Asantehene asked the Fante to surrender the refugees but the Fante would not. If the Asantehene had allowed them to keep the refugees his authority would have been greatly endangered, because all other rebels could easily run to the Fante to escape punishment. When the Fante refused to surrender the rebels the Asantehene had to invade the coast. In the battle which followed the Fante were easily defeated. But once again the two chiefs in question managed to escape capture and fled to the British fort of Anamaboe for protection. Though the British did not want a war with the Asante they would not surrender the fugitives because they did not believe they would receive a fair trial. Nor would they allow the Asante to continue their slaughter of the Fante since it might end in the Asante controlling the coast and imposing their will on the Europeans. The British therefore came to the defence of the Fante and the refugee chiefs. The result was the first of the Anglo-Asante wars.

184

Within the century the British and the Asante fought about ten wars, in 1807, 1811, 1814–6, 1823–4, 1826, 1863, 1869, 1873–4, 1896 and 1901. In all these it was only on three occasions, in 1873–4, 1896 and 1901, that the British invaded Asante. On the remaining occasions it was the Asante who invaded the coastal districts. This does not mean that the Asante were aggressive. On the contrary they were essentially a peace-loving people who did not resort to arms unless diplomacy and negotiation failed. In fact many of their invasions of the coast came after weeks or even months of fruitless attempts to achieve peaceful settlements of outstanding quarrels.

21 Asante and the coastal states

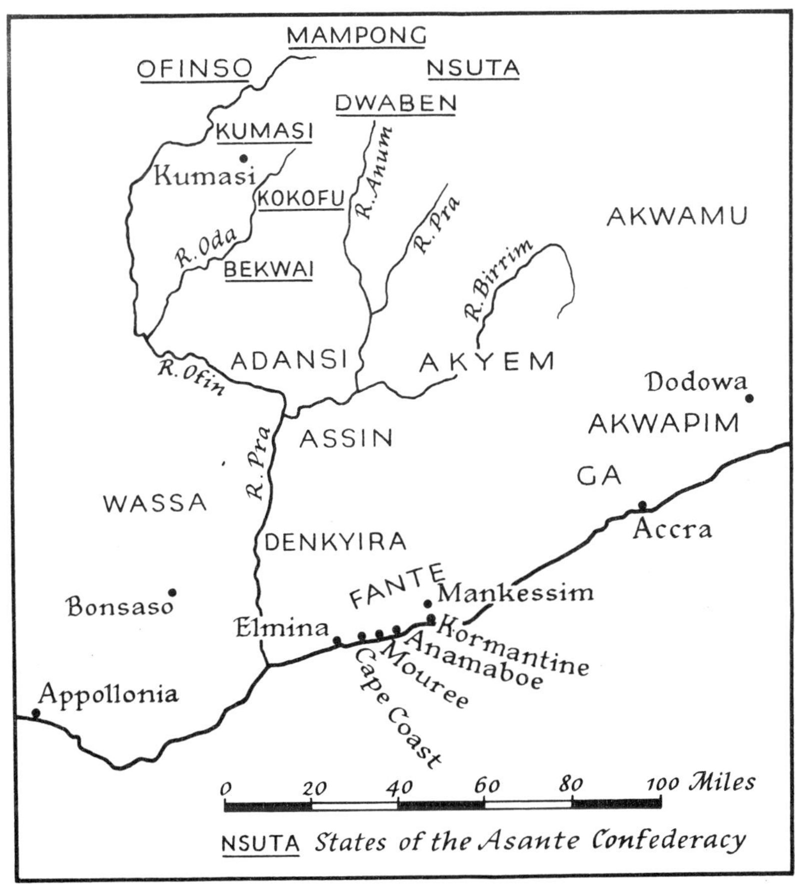

British administration on the coast

The Anglo-Asante wars started because the British would neither control the Fante nor allow the Asante to do so. When they ended the British had annexed not only the Fante but the Asante as well. The process by which this came about is interesting. At the beginning of the wars the affairs of the British forts were in the hands of merchants. After the third Asante war of 1814–6 it was felt that there would be no peace on the coast as long as merchants, who were preoccupied with ways of maximising gain and minimising loss, were in charge of British interests on the coast. The company of merchants was therefore dissolved in 1821, when all the British possessions on the West Coast were taken over by the crown and placed under the Governor of Sierra Leone. In 1822 Sir Charles MacCarthy, the Governor at that time, visited his Gold Coast provinces to see Britain's Fante friends. In the process he treated the Asante shabbily, thus precipitating the war of 1824 in which he lost his life. Two years later the British managed to avenge the death of MacCarthy by defeating the Asante at Dodowa. The British government then reconsidered the whole question and having found that it was not easy to maintain the peace decided to abandon the forts. But the merchants on the coast persuaded it to hand the forts over to a committee of three London merchants, who formed themselves into a company in 1828 and appointed a governor, Captain George Maclean, to administer the affairs of the forts with the aid of a council of merchants resident on the coast.

Maclean arrived on the coast in 1830 and the following year signed a treaty which maintained peace between the British and the Asante for over thirty years. He raised a small body of men whom he used as policemen and soldiers as the occasion demanded, and with this was able to make sure that the Fante did not provoke the Asante. He maintained peace along the coast by patiently listening to and settling all disputes that might lead to trouble. Though this administration was cheap and effective, complaints against it soon arose. Some traders who did not like Maclean accused him of not fighting slavery on the Gold Coast, others accused him of misusing his powers. A Select Committee of the House of Commons appointed to look into the matter found that Maclean was not guilty of the charges made against him, but recommended that since his administration of the Fante was illegal, it should be legalised.

Once again the British government took back the forts and placed them under a Lieutenant Governor who was responsible to the

Governor of Sierra Leone. Maclean, who was made the chief justice in the new administration, negotiated a series of treaties with the Fante chiefs in 1844–5 which gave the British the loophole through which to intervene in Fante affairs and help the chiefs in settling cases of murder and robbery. These treaties are known in history as 'The Bond' and did not in any way hand over Fante territory to the British.

The British now tried to face the problem of raising money locally to cover the cost of administration. After an attempt to levy taxation had aroused so much opposition that it had to be abandoned, the British sought to raise money by imposing customs duties. But if they imposed duties on goods passing through their forts, then traders would divert their activities to Dutch forts. The British therefore sought a way of buying off the Dutch, the Danish having been bought off earlier in 1850.

Before this could be arranged the British and the Asante blundered into war again in 1863. The British had once more refused to surrender an Asante refugee. For the second time the British government started wondering whether it had acted wisely in assuming responsibility for the affairs of the Gold Coast, for the whole business was costing too many men and too much money. Since at the same time Britain was finding it difficult to administer her other possessions along the West Coast, a select Committee of the British Parliament was appointed in 1865 to investigate the whole question. The Committee recommended that the British government should, if possible, stop getting involved in West African politics, except perhaps in the affairs of Sierra Leone.

The news spread quickly along the coast that the British were about to withdraw. If this happened the Fante would have to face the Asante alone. The Fante then decided to make their own defence arrangements. In 1869 about thirteen of their chiefs came together and formed the Fante Confederacy. With the aid of some educated Africans these chiefs in 1871 drew up a constitution at Mankessim under which they would govern themselves and raise forces to defend their territory against the Asante. The British, who had said they were about to go, turned round and said the drawing up of the constitution was a rebellion against their authority. The leaders of the movement were arrested and thrown into prison and the scheme collapsed.

As these things were happening the British succeeded in buying out the Dutch from the Gold Coast. This meant that the people of Elmina, who had been the allies of the Asante, were handed over to their British enemies. The result was an Asante invasion of the coast

in 1873. The British replied by sending a force under Sir Garnet
Wolseley, which marched to Kumasi and destroyed it. Then the
British turned round, and without consulting the people, declared
Fante Territory their colony. This was how the Fante lost their
independence thirty-two years before the Asante.

The end of Asante independence

The British sack of Kumasi in 1874 was a great blow to the Asante
Empire from which it never recovered. Many of the chiefs of the
northern and southern provinces seized the opportunity to declare
their independence. The British did nothing to discourage the rebellions; in fact they encouraged the rebellious provinces by promising
some of them protection. At the same time the power of the central
government declined as a result of disputes between the Asantehene
and his council. One Asantehene was de-stooled in 1874 for breaking
an ancient tradition. After some struggle a successor was enthroned,
only to be removed in 1883 for not being in favour of war to reconquer
the southern states which had broken away. Then there followed a
period of confusion during which the member states of the empire
could not agree on a successor. In 1888, however, Agyeman Prempe
was elected as Asantehene.

The Asantehene-elect succeeded to a difficult inheritance. After
so many wars, with their interruptions of trade and dislocation of
normal life, the Asante kingdom was not only impoverished, but
also depopulated as people fled southwards to the coast either to
escape punishment for crimes or to pursue their business in peace.
Also, on his accession Agyeman Prempe was faced with rebellion
from several provinces – Kokofu, Nsuta and Mampong. Two events
of the early years of the reign clearly indicate to what depths the
fortunes of the empire had sunk. First the Asantehene sent a personal message to the governor of the colony for a loan of £320 towards
the cost of his enstoolment though when this was made public he
denied it to save his face. Then in 1890 the Asante war machine
was reduced to such impotence that the Asantehene asked for troops
from the colony to help him quell rebellions against his authority.
While Agyeman Prempe was turning and twisting helplessly to keep
the empire together, the British came to the conclusion that the only
effective way to maintain peace in the interior was to bring the Asante
Union and its dependencies under their control. How this was done
is very revealing and should be described at some length.

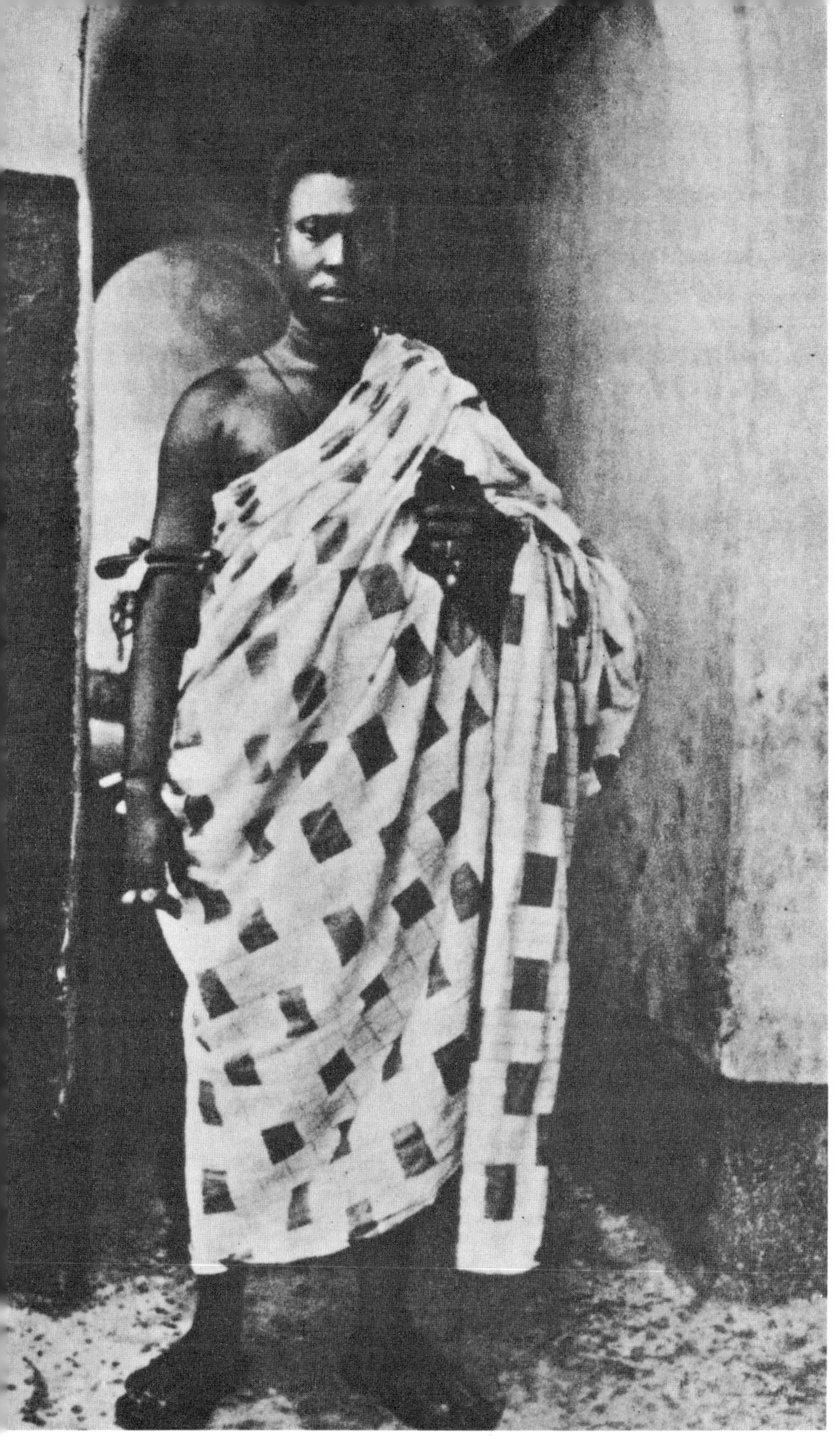

Asantehene Agyeman Prempe I

In 1891 the Governor of the colony, Brandford Griffith, sent his Acting Travelling Commissioner, Mr. H. M. Hull, to Asante with a letter inviting the Asantehene to place his kingdom under British protection; but this Prempe refused. In 1894, the year of Prempe's enstoolment, the British again asked the Asante to accept the stationing of a British Resident at Kumasi, repeating the demand of 1891. In 1895 Joseph Chamberlain became Colonial Secretary and pressure on Asante increased. The Asantehene in despair sent an embassy to London to get a guarantee from the British government that Asante independence would be respected, but this embassy was disgraced and ridiculed. Even while the embassy was still away the British sent an ultimatum to the Asantehene asking him to explain his failure to fulfil all the terms of the Treaty of Formena, imposed on the Asante Union in 1874. Prempe wanted to hear the result of his embassy before replying. The British regarded this as a refusal of the ultimatum. The forces in the colony were put on a war footing. In 1896 they occupied Kumasi without resistance. Behind this occupation lay the fact that the French were advancing from west to east in the Sudan, and seizing territories as they went. It was therefore feared that if the British did not act fast enough the French or even the Germans would seize Asante.

There was an anti-climax to this event. The Asante had decided not to resist the British in 1896 because they hoped for a peaceful settlement. But they had been disillusioned. The British seized Prempe and his principal chiefs and courtiers and exiled them. The Asantehene's court was looted, a Resident was stationed at Kumasi, and then the British proceeded to encourage the disintegration of the Asante Union by treating each province as an independent state. This hurt the pride of the Asante. Therefore when in 1900 the Governor of the colony, Sir Frederick Hodgson, asked for the Golden Stool of Asante to sit on, a privilege not even possessed by the Asantehenes, the Asante rose against the British. The uprising was put down after nine months of dogged resistance by the Asante. In 1901 the Asante state was annexed to the British crown.

These wars thus ended in the loss of their independence by the Fante and the Asante. The dream of a union of all the Akan under the leadership of Asante vanished. On the side of the British, the wars drew them deeper and deeper into the politics of what was then the Gold Coast and is now Ghana. In consequence by the time of the Scramble they already had a strong excuse for the conquest of what remained of Akan land.

Part three

Southern and Central Africa

7 Southern and Central Africa at the beginning of the nineteenth century

The geographical features

Southern Africa is not marked off by any clear line of demarcation from the rest of the continent but is simply a continuation of the great African plateau. Around the edge of the plateau there runs a coastal strip separated from the interior highland by an escarpment which is particularly marked on the eastern coast of South Africa where it is known as the Drakensberg. The whole area lies well within the southern hemisphere and has its winter from June to August and its summer from November to February. The severity of the winter is naturally more marked in the extreme south. In South Africa frosts are normal and snow not unknown. Nearer the Zambesi it is much milder.

The whole area has a basic climatic pattern of dry winters, and summer rains brought from the Indian Ocean. In South Africa these rains fall first on the eastern coastal escarpment and then die away gradually leaving the most westerly part of the continent extremely dry and arid. This is the area of the Kalahari desert. In the Cape territory itself the general pattern is disturbed by mountains known as the Cape series and a winter-rainfall climate of the Mediterranean type is experienced. Behind the Cape mountains lies a very dry area of semi-desert known as the Karoo.

The Khoisan peoples in South Africa

Southern Africa was the last area to be settled by the expanding Bantu peoples and to this day there are still pockets in which the earlier peoples survive. These were the Bushmen and the closely related Hottentots. Both belong to a race with a tawny yellow skin colour and short stature. They both speak languages which contain clicking sounds, unknown in any other human tongues except those of people who have borrowed them through contact. For these reasons, they are often referred to collectively as the Khoisan peoples. Their religious beliefs and practices are also very similar but in other respects the original culture of Bushmen and Hottentots was very different.

The Bushmen

The Bushmen were the earliest group and belonged to a people who at one time occupied a great part of the continent. They practised no agriculture and kept no cattle but lived entirely on the wild animals that the men killed with their poisoned arrows, and the wild roots and tubers that the women dug up with their digging sticks. They had no permanent houses but lived in temporary shelters made of branches or in caves which they decorated with beautiful pictures of hunting scenes and animals. Their way of life made it impossible to provide food for a large number of people in a small area and they lived in fairly small groups known as hunting bands. These might contain a hundred or more members, usually all related by blood or marriage. They had no particular chief; the older men took whatever decisions were necessary after discussion. The Bushmen were very attached to their simple but free way of life and were not easily persuaded to abandon it, even for a much richer existence. Each hunting band was jealous of its hunting territory. Though the group was always moving in search of animals each band had a definite area within which its members moved. They would resist to the death any intrusion on their hunting grounds.

At one time the Bushmen may have occupied most of east and central Africa as well as southern Africa but by the nineteenth century they had long lost most of their original homeland to other races. They remained numerous mainly in South-West Africa, the Kalahari and Angola, though small groups still remained in the northern parts of present Cape Province, southern Orange Free State and Transvaal, and the Lesotho mountains.

The Hottentots

The Hottentots differed from the Bushmen in their way of life. They were cattle keepers, and their lives centred around their flocks and herds. But they too were always on the move and lived in flimsy

194

HOTTENTOT KRAAL.

House building in a Hottentot settlement, a contemporary engraving

shelters which were sometimes carried on the backs of oxen. Though each group had its own home area they were less strongly attached to their territory than the Bushmen and were also more easily persuaded to change their habits for material rewards. They were organised in tribes, each made up of a number of related clans. The head of the senior clan was the tribal chief, but these chiefs had little power. Decisions were taken by consultation among all the clan heads and when there were disagreements tribes often split up. One or more of the clans would simple break away and in time grow into another large tribe. This type of split was often caused by tribes growing too big to keep their cattle together. The Hottentots were less widespread than the Bushmen. They mainly occupied South-West Africa, the coastal areas around the Cape of Good Hope, and the eastern coastal strip as far north as modern Transkei. By the nineteenth century they had been driven from much of their original home, but they still occupied much of South-West Africa, and groups of them were found around the Orange and lower Vaal rivers.

The Bantu-speaking peoples

At the beginning of the nineteenth century, as today, by far the largest proportion of the peoples of southern and central Africa belonged to the Bantu-speaking group (see Introduction). They had been established as far south as modern Rhodesia as early as AD 200 and had probably begun to enter the area south of the Limpopo river as early as the twelfth or thirteenth century. In South Africa, however, the process of settlement was still not complete as late as the nineteenth century. The Bantu had advanced furthest on the east coast. There by the eighteenth century they had reached the Fish River and begun to settle in the land between it and the Sundays river which is known as the Zuurveld. It was in this area that they first came into contact with the white settlers who were advancing from the Cape. In the central part of South Africa the Bantu were still north of the Orange river by the nineteenth century, and in South-West Africa they were still confined to the area north of modern Windhoek.

The southern Bantu : important subdivisions of the group

The Bantu-speaking peoples of South Africa, Rhodesia and the southern parts of Mozambique belong to a great group known as the

196

southern Bantu. They were mixed farmers who kept cattle but also cultivated the land. It is possible that their ancestors may have come from the far north where they would have been in contact with the cattle keeping Nilotes. The southern Bantu fall into several different language groups, each of which contains many tribes. In South Africa the most important groups are the Nguni-speaking group who live along the eastern coastal strip from Zululand to the Zuurveld. This group has adopted more of the click sounds from the languages of the Bushmen and Hottentots than any other Bantu people. The Sotho people occupied most of the central plateau of South Africa as far as the Kalahari desert. The languages of the many. different tribes of this group have close similarities though those of the most westerly tribes are rather different; they are called Tswana. West of

22 Peoples of southern Africa

the Kalahari two Bantu groups lived in the northern areas of South West Africa: the more southerly were the Herero, whose way of life was rather similar to the Hottentots for they relied only on cattle and did not practise agriculture; and further north were the Ambo, who lived by mixed farming like other southern Bantu.

In southern Mozambique the main population belongs to a group called Thonga, who are thought to be related to the Nguni-speaking group of South Africa although they do not use the click sounds. In Rhodesia there were many different tribes belonging to the group who are now called Shona. They really consisted of two main groups, the Kalanga and the Rozwi.

The central Bantu

North of the southern Bantu there lived another great group of peoples known as the central Bantu. They are different from the southern Bantu because, while all southern Bantu tribes trace descent from father to son and regard a child as belonging to his father's clan, the central Bantu trace descent through the mother and regard a child as belonging to his mother's people. In their social systems the person a man respects most is not his father but his mother's brother, and the person to whom he leaves his property is not his own but his sister's son. Many central Bantu tribes did not keep cattle but relied only on farming.

Social and political organisation of
the Bantu-speaking people

The Bantu lived in larger groups than the Bushmen or Hottentots and their tribes might contain several thousand members. They moved much less frequently than either of the other peoples though they sometimes shifted their homes to find new land and grazing for their cattle. Their homes were much more substantial. Some were round huts of mud decorated with designs drawn in coloured clay and thatched with grass or leaves, their floors carefully smeared with cow dung to give a smooth surface without dust; some were beehive-shaped structures of woven grass. Usually the family possessed a few simple stools, some mats and cooking pots, and cloaks made of animal skins against the winter cold. Among cattle keeping tribes the cattle enclosure was the centre of every settlement and grain

198

was carefully stored to last until the next harvest. Though the material standard of living of the Bantu-speaking people was generally very simple their social organisation was complex. They had a strong belief in law, and a respect for traditional ways, and they had complicated rules governing the conduct of individuals. Many of these were connected with their family systems which were very strong and linked large numbers of persons. They also believed that the spirits of their ancestors took a close interest in, and exerted an influence on, everyday life. This strengthened their devotion to their traditions and customs. The young men of the southern Bantu had to go through prolonged and severe initiation ceremonies before they were admitted to manhood and allowed to marry. During the ceremonies the customs of the tribes and the proper behaviour of a man were deeply imprinted on their minds.

Warfare between tribes was frequent and was often caused by quarrels over farming land or the theft of cattle, but these wars did not usually result in great loss of life. They were governed by rules which were known to all and generally respected. The greatest cause of bitterness and loss of life among the Bantu of southern Africa was fear of witchcraft. Many diseases of which the cause was unknown were believed to be caused by the ill-will of witches and when someone, particularly an important person, fell mysteriously sick the witch-doctor would be consulted and the individual he named as responsible would be put to a cruel death. Among the central Bantu, persons accused of witchcraft or other crimes were given a poison called mravi; it was believed that if they were innocent they would vomit it but if they were guilty it would kill them. These practices led to much loss of life and gave opportunities for wicked people to take a terrible revenge on their enemies by having them accused of witchcraft. Generally speaking the Bantu of southern Africa were peaceful, law-abiding peoples, with few material goods apart from cattle. They were dignified and courteous in accordance with their rules of etiquette and kind to strangers if they respected their customs.

Though there were considerable differences between different tribes, the southern Bantu tribes were governed on basically similar principles. At the head of each tribe was a hereditary chief who was the supreme head of the community. Under him districts of the tribal territory were ruled by subordinate chiefs who were often important members of the royal family. The chief was assisted by officials often called indunas and amongst these there was a senior induna who acted as deputy chief. Holders of these offices had a great deal of power and were therefore usually chosen from families with no claim to the throne. Although the chief was very powerful he did not rule as an autocrat. The subordinate chiefs were also important and might rebel or break away if the chief behaved in an unpopular way.

Chiefs were careful to discuss their plans with important members of the tribe before taking decisions. In day-to-day matters they had a small circle of close personal advisers, but before taking major decisions they would summon the subordinate chiefs to a large conference. Amongst the Sotho-speaking tribes public assemblies were also held in which anyone could make suggestions or criticise the chief. The government of subordinate chiefs was very similar to that of supreme chiefs, only on a smaller scale. They had their own indunas and councillors and they sat in judgment over cases which occurred in their own districts, but in these a right of appeal to the court of the supreme chief always existed.

One of the characteristics of the southern Bantu tribal system, especially in South Africa itself, was the tendency for tribes to divide into two or more at frequent intervals. Such divisions usually arose from disputes over succession, but sometimes happened if a chief became unpopular or annoyed some of his subordinate chiefs. They would then break away with their own followers and set themselves up as independent rulers. This process was continually taking place as the Bantu moved into and settled new land.

Although the southern Bantu tribal organisation seemed to encourage the splitting of tribes it could also work in the opposite direction. If instead of being surrounded by open and unsettled land offering an easy opportunity to break away, a tribe attacked its neighbour, the victor could join the two tribes under his own rule simply by recognising the defeated chief as a new district sub-chief. In this way extensive supertribal empires could be built up without altering the basic system of government. This happened at a very early date in the area of modern Rhodesia and southern Mozambique. A tribal empire grew up there under rulers of the Kalanga group which extended its authority over some non-Kalanga tribes.

The Mwene Mutapa Empire and the Portuguese

This Mwene Mutapa Empire traded gold and other metals with the Arabs at Sofala, and later with the Portuguese. We do not know in detail how the empire was organised, but according to Portuguese accounts it had many provinces and districts which were governed by chiefs who enjoyed considerable independence. They even fought minor wars with one another though all recognised the supremacy of the ruler, who was known as the Mwene Mutapa. Stone buildings were erected at Zimbabwe and other sites in this kingdom. The Portuguese managed to gain influence in the kingdom by taking part in succession disputes and the power of the kings crumbled away. In the seventeenth century the Rozwi broke away from the Empire. Under their chiefs, who were called Shangamire, they began to conquer the Kalanga and drive out the Portuguese. Eventually they reconquered almost the whole of the empire and though the Portuguese were allowed to remain in their main trading posts and trade with the new rulers they lost their influence in the interior. It was in the Rozwi period that the largest buildings were built at Zimbabwe.

Amongst the central Bantu there were many different types of government. Many tribes did not feel the need for government systems wider than the organisation of the local village. This was the case with the Yao and Macua of northern Mozambique. The Tumbuka, Henga and Tonga of the northern shores of Lake Malawi were also organised in this small-scale way. Other groups built tribal empires along somewhat similar principles to those of the southern Bantu, though each kingdom had its own peculiar and often highly complicated system of government. Amongst these larger states there was the Lozi kingdom of the Barotse Province of modern Zambia and the powerful state of the Bemba with its king, the Chitimukulu, which had its centre near Lake Bangweulu in modern Zambia. Both these kingdoms are believed to have been founded by immigrants from the area of Katanga in the modern Congo. In addition, during the eighteenth century a general called Cazembe of the Lunda King, Mwata Yamvo, in the Katanga area penetrated to the Luapula valley and set up a powerful kingdom. In the same century an adventurous elephant hunter from Tanganyika visited the Tumbuka people near the head of Lake Malawi and succeeded in uniting many villages into the Kamanga Kingdom which was ruled by his successors with the title of Chikura-mayembe. The great Maravi group of peoples who live in modern Malawi and the eastern parts of Zambia are believed like most of the central Bantu peoples to have had their origin in the area of the modern Congo. In the seventeenth century they built up a widespread empire ruled by a chief called Kalonga who had his capital near the Shire river in modern Malawi. This empire broke up within a century of being formed but a relative of the Kalonga named Undi broke away from his overlord and moved westward to establish his capital in modern Mozambique near the eastern border of modern Zambia. There he built up a second Malawi empire covering a very wide area.

This empire still existed at the beginning of the nineteenth century but it was not very strongly organised.

Foreign influence in Southern and Central Africa

Foreign influences on southern and central Africa began with the Arabs from their base at Sofala. They were replaced after the fifteenth century by the Portuguese who in addition to their island fortress of Mozambique had trading stations at Sena and Tete on the Zambesi, Sofala' Quilimane and Inhambane on the coast. They also made fairly regular trading voyages to Delagoa Bay and established a fort there called Espirito Santo. In Mozambique a distinct African Portuguese community grew up, largely consisting of persons of part African or Indian descent. Though the Portuguese in Mozambique were never more than a few hundreds in number they acquired a great deal of power. In consideration for services to the Mwene Mutapa they were given chieftaincies in his kingdom and the people living in these areas became their retainers. To keep their Portuguese identity they offered these territories to the king of Portugal and so came to hold them as feudal dependencies of the Portuguese crown. The Portuguese owners of these prazos (as they were called) taxed the inhabitants and kept private bodyguards of armed slaves whom they provided with guns. These bodyguards they employed on their trading ventures in search of gold in the interior. In cases of grave conflict they also used the ordinary inhabitants of the prazos as their soldiers, equipped with spears and bows and arrows. The Portuguese thus came to command very considerable armies which they used to fight private wars with one another as well as to take part in internal troubles in the Mwene Mutapa kingdom and thus win further concessions. With the rise of the Rozwi in the seventeenth century the Portuguese lost many of their prazos but they still retained some around their main settlements. Their most important influence on the history of southern Africa lay in the introduction of maize which gradually spread and replaced millet as the main crop.

The establishment of the Cape Colony

In 1652 a European settlement was established by the Dutch East India Company at the Cape of Good Hope. The Colony was very

23 Mozambique

An early painting showing the landing of Jan Van Riebeeck and the first Dutch settlers at the Cape of Good Hope, 1652

small at first and was intended merely as a refreshment station for the company's ships on their way to India. To begin with it consisted only of the company's servants, but it was soon decided to allow a few of these to settle as free citizens with farms of their own. They would then have the incentive of personal profit to farm diligently and efficiently. The first of these settlers, nine in number, were established on small farms in 1657. Gradually their numbers increased and then under the governorship of Simon van der Stel (1679–1700) a deliberate policy of increasing the population was undertaken to strengthen it against possible attacks by France. More Dutchmen came and a party of French Huguenots, Protestant refugees from religious persecution in France, was also settled in the Colony. They were equal to about one third of the European population and many modern white South African families are their descendants. The French refugees introduced efficient farming techniques but they lost their language and were absorbed into the predominantly Dutch population.

Expansion of the white settlement at the Cape

In the healthy climate this little community continued to grow rapidly in numbers and soon began to spread over a vast territory. The majority of the whites were farmers and this meant that as their population increased they would need more land. At first they concentrated on growing vegetables, wheat and wine on fairly small areas and the Colony expanded slowly. The costs of production were high, the land was not as fertile as Europe and suffered from uncertain weather conditions, and the market for agricultural produce at the Cape was very small. Farmers depended on selling to the company itself and to passing ships. Attempts to find export markets for Cape produce failed to come up to expectations and matters were made worse by the corrupt practices of company officials. The notorious Willem Adriaan van der Stel, in particular, used the company's servants to help him operate a private farm which gave himself and his friends almost a monopoly in supplying provisions to the Company.

In these circumstances only the rich could farm successfully and poorer men found themselves falling ever deeper into debt. Thus while some became rich and comfortable and built substantial houses beautifully decorated with gables in the Dutch style, others were forced to look for another means of livelihood. In comparison with growing wheat and wine at the Cape the life of a cattle trader or cattle rancher in the interior offered fairly easy profits with little initial expense. There was always a sale for meat and animal skins. Cattle could be led to market and did not need expensive transport. Unlike perishable agricultural produce they could be kept for another occasion when prices were not high enough. What is more young men in the interior could lead a very inexpensive life with none of the costs of city existence. They could feed themselves and their families to a considerable extent by shooting wild animals, and they could hope to persuade or force Hottentots to work for them as herdsmen for very little wages. The life was hard and without much material comfort but it provided a great sense of freedom. The Dutch settlers came to regard it as the happy life.

In spite of all prohibitions to the contrary, settlers began to drift away from the Cape, first trading with the Hottentots for cattle, later taking up farming themselves and often forcing the Hottentots to abandon their lands. Cattle keeping required very large areas of land in the dry and often drought-stricken South African conditions; to be successful a cattle farmer in the interior needed at least four

A farmhouse in the Dutch style at the Cape

square miles. Once considerable numbers of settlers took to cattle farming, therefore, the Colony was bound to expand at tremendous speed and in spite of its very small white population and large area there was always a shortage of land. The Dutch East India Company disapproved of this expansion, but it needed the meat provided by the cattle farmers, and it lacked the resources and was too inefficient and corrupt to prevent or control it. The main stream of expansion flowed up the east coast where the rains were heavier, and there in the eighteenth century settlers began to enter the area called the Zuurveld, near the Fish river, which the Bantu belonging to the Nguni-speaking group were also just beginning to settle.

The growth of race prejudice in the Cape Colony

When the Colony was first founded there was no intention on the part of the company to encourage racial discrimination. To show approval for inter-racial mixture the surgeon of the original tiny settlement was given promotion and a wedding feast in the commander's house when he married a Hottentot girl called Eva. Simon van der Stel, the greatest of the early governors, was the son of an Indian woman. The situation began to change after 1716 when the company decided to allow the free importation of slaves. Negroes were brought from West Africa, Delagoa Bay and Madagascar, and a few Malays came from Indonesia to form the origin of the present Cape Malay community. As manual work became the monopoly of slaves or Hottentots the whites began to develop the attitude that they were naturally superior and entitled to rule over the inferior people.

This attitude was fostered still more on the cattle farms of the interior where the whites felt themselves extremely isolated, sur-rounded by large numbers of slaves and Hottentot servants who might easily turn against them. They believed the only way to protect them-selves was to support one another at all times against the non-European peoples and keep them very firmly down. Thus the attitude of white superiority and non-white inferiority was strengthened by fear and established a deep hold on the minds of the settlers. The Calvinist form of religion which the Dutch settlers brought with them supported these attitudes for it taught that all men were divided from birth into the chosen and the damned. Thus although the officials of the church did not accept it, the ordinary farmer came to believe that the whites were the chosen race and non-whites the condemned heathens, and that the distinction between the races was in accordance with the will of God.

Reaction of the Khoisan peoples to the expansion of the Cape Colony

As the Colony expanded it took away the land of the indigenous Bushmen and Hottentots. Within a few years of the beginning of the Colony a war broke out between the Dutch East India Company and a Hottentot tribe which complained that its lands were being taken away. The war lasted from 1658–60 and the company emerged victorious. After that the Hottentots offered little further resistance to the advance of the settlers. Their weak tribal system easily broke down in contact with European organisation and they were often tempted to sell their land and cattle in return for strong drink and other European goods. Their numbers were also severely reduced by smallpox epidemics. Thus they generally gave up their land without resistance and either entered the service of the settlers as herdsmen or drifted further into the interior.

Origin of the Cape Coloured people

Those who became servants on white farms soon lost their language and their culture and mixed with slaves and children of half European descent to form the present Cape Coloured population.

Migration of the Korana

Of those Hottentot groups who moved into the interior one of the most important were the Korana. They migrated from the Cape to the banks of the Orange river and spread out in small parties north of it around the Vaal and Harts rivers. There they attacked the Tswana tribes and robbed them of their cattle. Their depredations were made worse when they were joined by a German deserter from the company's service called Jan Bloem. He brought guns with him and became the chief of a Korana clan. He died in 1790 after a raid on one of the most powerful Tswana tribes and was succeeded by one of his half-caste sons, also called Jan Bloem, who turned out to be an even greater bandit than his father.

Origin of the Griquas

Another group who moved inland were the Griquas. Some of them were pure Hottentots but most of them were half-caste descendants of white fathers and Hottentot mothers who found themselves discriminated against in the Colony. They established themselves around the meeting place of the Orange and Vaal rivers under a chief called Cornelius Kok. Under missionary influence they settled down and drew up a constitution and made laws. The Kok family fell into disgrace with the missionaries, however, who succeeded in getting a young catechist named Waterboer elected as chief. This led to a split in the community, for some broke away in support of the Kok family; one group followed Cornelius Kok and others Adam Kok who eventually established a settled state of his own higher up the Orange river.

Barend-Barends was another important Griqua leader. Though the missionaries tried to prevent the Griquas from attacking Bantu tribes the temptation of easy profits was too much for some who broke away and came to be known as Bergenaars. Like many of the Korana clans they tended to a life of banditry.

Resistance of the Bushmen to white expansion

Unlike the Hottentots the Bushmen resisted white encroachment on their lands with bitter determination. They retaliated by lightning raids on stock and the murder of herdsmen. In reply the farmers waged a war of extermination against them in the course of which they developed the commando system of local military organisation which was later used in wars with the Bantu. Though the farmers' commandos hunted the Bushmen like wild animals they did not succeed in destroying them. Indeed the Bushmen made some areas so unsafe that several districts had to be abandoned. The farmers then turned to buying peace with gifts of cattle to save the Bushmen from the hunger which forced them to fight. Some became herdsmen on white farms and gradually the settler population increased until the Bushmen could no longer hope to offer effective resistance.

White settlers and Bantu-speaking peoples encounter one another

During the eighteenth century white settlers began to enter the Zuurveld and settle alongside the Bantu who were also just settling the area. The latter belonged to branches of the Xhosa tribe, the southernmost of the Nguni-speaking peoples. This situation did not please the company which feared rightly enough that contact between settlers and Bantu would lead to trouble. In 1778 Governor van Plettenberg made a tour of the frontier and decided that the two races should be kept apart. After discussion with some chiefs on the Fish river he fixed that landmark as the frontier without realising that these chiefs had no authority over the people on the Zuurveld and certainly no right to give their land away. Settlers and Bantu continued to live side by side and soon began quarrelling over land and cattle and in 1779 war broke out between them. This was the first Xhosa resistance war. The Bantu were temporarily driven from the Zuurveld but soon returned and the tension continued.

Republic of Graaf Reinet

In 1786 a magistracy for the eastern districts of the Colony was established at Graaf Reinet. After the first magistrate had proved incompetent he was succeeded by Maynier, a sincere and devoted man who tried to bring law and order and a sense of justice to the frontier. He insisted that farmers must not ill-treat their Hottentot servants and allowed runaway servants with tales of cruelty to find refuge at his court house. He also tried to regulate the behaviour of settlers towards the Bantu. When in spite of his efforts war (the second Xhosa resistance war) broke out in 1793 he made terms which permitted the tribesmen to remain on the Zuurveld on condition of good behaviour, and refused to allow farmers to undertake private expeditions against the Bantu on the pretext of reclaiming stolen cattle. He maintained that the number of cattle reported stolen by Bantu was grossly exaggerated and that the conduct of the settlers was also responsible for the troubles on the Zuurveld. This made him intensely unpopular with the farmers who accused him of pre-ferring the heathens to Christians. Early in 1795 they rose in rebellion, expelled Maynier and proclaimed an independent Republic of Graaf Reinet. The farmers of the neighbouring district of Swellendam followed their example and also proclaimed a republic.

First British occupation of the Cape

The company had not been able to deal with this rebellion when towards the end of 1795 the Cape was seized by the British and the rule of the Dutch East India Company in South Africa was brought to an end.

8 The great nineteenth-century migration

Two great folk movements

The first half of the nineteenth century in southern Africa is dominated by two great upheavals. The first took place amongst the Bantu-speaking peoples. It started in Zululand and gave rise to a chain of movements which affected areas as far afield as the northern part of what is now Tanzania. It is often called the Mfecane, an Nguni word used for the wars and disturbances which accompanied the rise of the Zulu. The second was a sudden movement of expansion of the white settlers at the Cape, known as the Great Trek. It was far less extensive in scale than the Mfecane but is of fundamental importance for the history of southern Africa. As the Mfecane was the earlier of the two movements and the course of the Great Trek was considerably influenced by it, we shall look first at developments in Bantu society and later turn back to take up the thread of the development of the Cape Colony which forms the background to the Great Trek.

Origin of the Mfecane

Zululand and Natal are part of the eastern coastal corridor which runs between the Drakensberg mountains and the sea. They are favoured by relatively abundant rains and were well suited to support a fairly dense Bantu population. We know from the reports of ship-wrecked Portuguese in the sixteenth century that the area was already heavily settled by Bantu at that time. In South Africa moreover the healthy climate and the absence of diseases like malaria encouraged a rapid growth of population, and if we examine the history of South African tribes and see how frequently they split into two or more it is obvious that the population was increasing rapidly. The coastal corridor was a narrow area fenced in by the mountains and Bantu were settled along it as far south as the Fish river. If the Zululand tribes continued to grow, therefore, they were bound to come into conflict with one another over farming and grazing lands.

Four Zulus in traditional costume (but without weapons)
at a modern cattle sale

Military grouping in Zululand

This situation of overcrowding and conflict seems to have developed during the course of the eighteenth century. Wars became more frequent and more severe, and as they did so great leaders emerged who began to build up tribal empires. At the same time there was a need for more efficient military organisation.

About the middle of the eighteenth century three great figures appeared. One of these was Sobhuza, the chief of a tribe then known as Ngwane (but now called the Swazi after Sobhuza's successor Mswati). He had his original home near the Upper Pongola river. The second was Zwide, chief of a very powerful tribe known as the Ndwandwe in central Zululand. The third was Dingiswayo, chief of the Mthethwa, the most powerful and best known of them all.

All these chiefs built up tribal empires and in doing so they developed a new method of military organisation. The traditional initiation ceremonies had always created a sense of fellow-feeling amongst young men of similar age who went through them together. The new development in Zululand, which is often said to have been introduced by Dingiswayo, was to abolish the traditional ceremonies altogether and in their place to form the young men of an age suitable for initiation into a regiment of the tribal army. This had great advantages over the older system, in which local chiefs commanded their own local contingents, because it gave the army more unity. It also provided a means of strengthening tribal empires. The young men of conquered tribes were put into regiments according to their ages, together with boys from other sections of the empire, so that by fighting together they would develop feelings of comradeship and loyalty to the wider unit instead of just to their home group. During Dingiswayo's time, however, the regiments assembled only in times of war, and warfare remained relatively mild.

Origins of the Swazi nation

As the powerful leaders built up their armies they inevitably clashed with one another. First Zwide clashed with Sobhuza and the latter was driven out with his people to settle in the central area of modern Swaziland. There his people found a large number of small tribes of the Sotho-speaking group. These were conquered one after another and incorporated into what is now the Swazi Kingdom.

Death of Dingiswayo and rise of Shaka

After Sobhuza had withdrawn from the scene, Dingiswayo and Zwide clashed with one another. Dingiswayo was victorious on several occasions, but at last Zwide succeeded in trapping him. He walked into an Ndwandwe ambush and was taken prisoner to Zwide's home, where he was put to death. Startled by the loss of their leader the Mthethwa army fled and the tribes who had been conquered by Dingiswayo took the opportunity to declare their independence. Zwide seemed to have emerged supreme, but by this time another leader had appeared on the scene.

His name was Shaka and he was a son of the chief of a small tribe known as the Zulu. His mother had made herself unpopular at his father's home and been driven away, and Shaka had a very unhappy childhood, teased and bullied by his playmates. He grew up with a fierce determination to gain and exercise power, a reckless bravery and a callous indifference to human suffering. He began his career as a warrior in Dingiswayo's army and won the notice of the great chief by his feats of bravery. When his father died Shaka persuaded Dingiswayo to lend him the military support needed to seize the Zulu throne from one of his brothers who was the rightful heir.

 Shaka

Shaka's military reforms

Once established as chief of the Zulu he began to train his followers in accordance with his own military ideas. He saw that the traditional weapons, which consisted of shields and throwing spears, were not suitable for close formation fighting. A warrior who had thrown his spear was bound to fall back. If the warriors kept hold of their spears they could advance in an ordered line, protected by their shields, right up to the enemy and then finish them off. He therefore made his men discard the old weapon and use a short-handled stabbing spear and forbade them on pain of death to leave it on the battlefield. They were carefully drilled to fight in a formation known as the 'cow's horns'. The great mass of warriors would be drawn up in a body several men deep while two regiments, one on each side, advanced in a thin curving line around the enemy. When the two horns met and the enemy was surrounded the main mass would advance to complete the massacre. Such ordered manoeuvres needed considerable training and Shaka introduced a new idea in keeping his age-regiments on permanent duty for many years. They were housed in special military towns each of which was an official homestead of the chief. When not at war they were engaged in practising manoeuvres or ceremonial dances.

Shaka defeats Zwide

When Dingiswayo marched to fight Zwide, Shaka was summoned to go to the aid of his overlord. Whether he deliberately betrayed him, as some believe, or merely arrived too late for the battle, as others maintain, he certainly took no part in the fighting. He withdrew from the scene of the Mthethwa defeat and began at once to build up his own forces by conquering surrounding tribes and putting their young men into his regiments. He even conquered the Mthethwa themselves, killed their new chief and appointed a nominee of his own. As soon as Zwide became aware that Shaka was rebuilding the empire of Dingiswayo for himself he sent an Ndwandwe force to attack the Zulu chief. The superior discipline of the Zulu gave them the victory and the Ndwandwe retired with heavy losses. Zwide then sent his full force in an all-out invasion of Shaka's domain. The Zulu wore them out by constantly retreating, driving away the cattle and destroying the crops as they went. Then as the Ndwandwe turned homewards tired and hungry, Shaka's troops caught them on the banks of the Mhlatuse river and defeated them in a decisive battle. This was probably in the year 1818.

Shaka's kingdom

The victory over the Ndwandwe left Shaka supreme in Zululand. Every year his regiments went out conquering tribes and capturing cattle. They passed right through Natal, forcing almost the entire population to flee to the south, and reached as far as Pondoland. As tribes were conquered Shaka brought them into his expanding kingdom. The conquered tribes kept their own chiefs, though sometimes the existing head was killed and Shaka appointed another member of the royal family. These chiefs continued to administer their own people but their power was greatly reduced as all the young men of fighting age were taken into the age-regiments.

The ever growing army was accommodated at a series of military towns, each under the authority of a military commander. These and the commanders of individual regiments were usually chosen from commoner families and were closely dependent on the King. Each regiment had its own name and its own distinctive equipment. Some had shields of a distinctive colour, others special kinds of head dress. There was keen rivalry between the regiments for honour in war and the favour of the monarch. The arms and equipment were supplied to the warriors by Shaka and each regiment had a section of the royal herds attached to it. As far as possible these herds were made up of cattle with skins of the same colour as the regiments' shields. Each military settlement was also a royal homestead and contained a section of Shaka's family under the authority of a senior female member who had equal powers with those of the military commander. A large proportion of the marriageable girls in the country were brought to the military towns and formed into regiments corresponding to those of the men. They took part in ceremonial dances and agricultural work. Shaka regarded them as his wards and when a regiment had served long enough to be retired from active service he would dissolve a female regiment at the same time and give the girls as wives to the warriors. Shaka himself never officially married and was terrified of having a son who might one day take over his power. Thus the whole way in which his kingdom was organised was designed to increase its military strength and to create among the tribes conquered by his armies a feeling of unity and complete loyalty to Shaka himself.

English traders in Natal

In 1824 a small party of English traders landed at Port Natal (the site of present Durban) and made their way to see the Zulu King. Shaka received them well. He was delighted with the goods they brought and impressed by the medical skill of one of them, Farewell, who treated him successfully for a stab wound inflicted by a would-be assassin. He was also quick to realise the potential military value of firearms and anxious to remain on good terms with the government of the Cape, which he believed to be very powerful. He allowed the traders to settle in Natal and gather together the pitiful remnants of the Natal population around them. In return the traders fought with their guns in some of his expeditions. The settlement was particularly important because it was through its existence that information about the almost deserted state of Natal and the rich farming land there spread to the settlers at the Cape.

The assassination of Shaka, 1828

The way that Shaka's state was organised concentrated all power in his hands. The district chiefs who, in the traditional system, could check the actions of a tribal ruler, lost their power when their fighting men were all in the central army. The only persons who could threaten Shaka's power were the army commanders, and they were commoners raised up by Shaka himself. Thus he did not need to consult the traditional type of council but exercised an autocratic authority. As his reign progressed, however, he became increasingly despotic until even the loyalty of his devoted soldiers was undermined. The climax came after the death of his mother which upset him deeply. He forced his people to undergo severe deprivations as a sign of mourning. Then at the end of a year's mourning period he sent his army out on a great expedition. They travelled to the south as far as Pondoland and ravaged the Pondo tribe but Shaka was warned by one of the traders that he might come into conflict with the colonial forces. Thereupon he wheeled his army round and sent them off immediately to the extreme north of his territory in southern Mozambique. He himself remained behind at one of his military towns and two of his brothers took advantage of the absence of most of the fighting men to plot his downfall. Together with his most trusted induna Mbopa they stabbed him to death.

The assassins quietened the people by assuring them that they had killed the King to put an end to the never-ceasing wars and the hardships that Shaka had imposed on them.

Succession of Dingane

Dingane, one of the assassins and a brother of Shaka, succeeded him on the Zulu throne. He was by nature a rather lazy and peace-loving man and he tried at first to relax the discipline of the Shaka period, but a revolt led by one of Shaka's generals convinced him of the need to keep the army occupied and he sent his regiments out on a number of expeditions.

The sudden rise of the Zulu kingdom led to many peoples being driven from their original homes. Once they had left their crops and their cattle they could only hope to live by plunder and so they tended to move over long distances attacking other tribes as they went and setting them in motion also. After the bloody battle on the Mhlatuse river in 1818, two sections of the defeated Ndwandwe army abandoned their homes and fled northwards into southern Mozambique. They were the Shangane led by Soshangane, and the Ngoni led by Zwangendaba. Both these groups had experienced the value of Zulu fighting tactics at first hand and employed them in conquering other

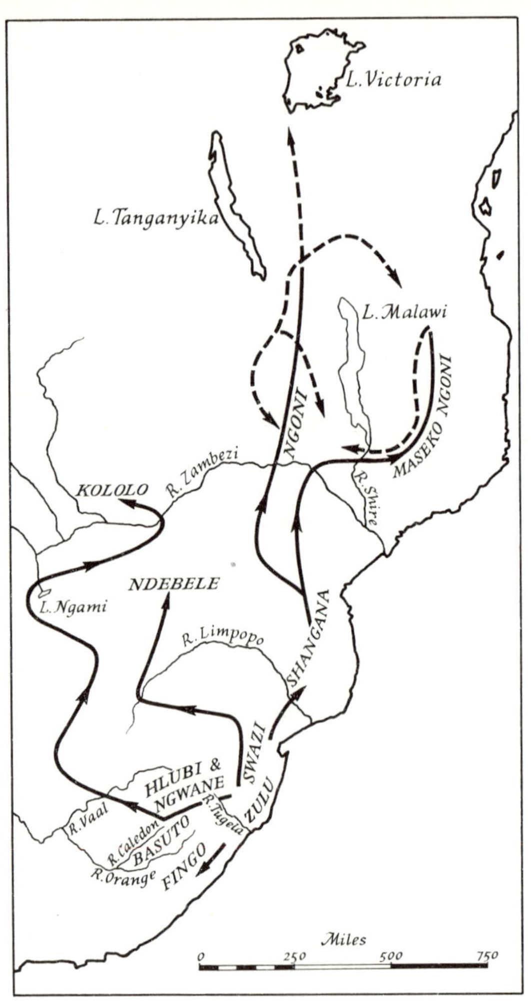

24 The main movements
of people during
the Mfecane

tribes. After a time the leaders clashed with one another. Soshangane
was victorious. He remained in Mozambique and brought almost all
the tribes of the vast area between the Limpopo and the Zambesi
under his control in a Zulu type kingdom. He forced the Portuguese
of Sena and Tete to pay him annual tribute and his forces destroyed
some of the other Portuguese forts where the commanders were
foolish enough to oppose them.

Zwangendaba travelled westward through the Mwene Mutapa
empire wreaking havoc as he went. His warriors hunted down and
killed the last Rozwi ruler and brought the ancient kingdom to an

218

end. When he reached the vicinity of modern Bulawayo, he turned
northwards, and on 19 November 1835, a day marked by an eclipse of
the sun, his regiments crossed the Zambesi. They moved northward
by a series of long stages till they reached a place called Ufipa near
the southern end of Lake Tanganyika, where Zwangendaba died about
1848. Then his army, swollen with captives from many tribes, broke
up into a number of sections.

The Wa-Tuta

One group, known as the Wa-Tuta, cut a path northward into the
country of the Nyamwezi people of northern Tanganyika. They
established their headquarters to the north of modern Tabora and
from there they raided as far as the shores of Lake Victoria.

The Gwangara and the Maseko

Another section known as the Gwangara travelled east and south as
far as the present Songea region of Tanganyika. There they encountered another invading horde, the Maseko Ngoni, who had come up
from Mozambique by a more easterly route than Zwangendaba's
main party. The two groups co-operated at first but then fell to blows.
The Maseko were driven south again and finally established themselves
in the highlands of the Kirk range near the southern end of Lake
Malawi. The Gwangara split into two kingdoms and devastated a vast
area. But they found their match in the warlike Hehe people. Several
bitter battles were fought and then the two sides agreed to make peace
until their children had grown old enough to resume the struggle.

Mpezeni's and Mbelwa's Ngoni

The rest of the Ngoni army split into two main sections, one of which,
under Mpezeni, fought many battles with the Bemba and then finally
settled near Fort Jameson in modern Zambia. The other under
Mbelwa invaded the country of the Kamanga, overthrew the kingdom
and forced the Kamanga and neighbouring Tumbuka, Henga and
Tonga to enter their age-regiments. All these Ngoni groups absorbed
captives into their fighting forces to such an extent that the different
groups came in time to speak different languages, although they all

remembered their common history and kept the main outlines of the Zulu-type political system they had brought from the south. The Ngoni invasions caused untold suffering and destruction, but they also brought into existence a whole series of powerful states which included persons of many different tribes. They encouraged local leaders to arise in self defence and build kingdoms. Undoubtedly they were one of the most important historical developments in East Africa in the nineteenth century before the coming of European colonialism.

The Mfecane on the South African highveld

While the Shangane and the Ngoni were carrying Zulu fighting methods to the north two other tribes, the Hlubi and the Ngwane (a different tribe from the followers of Sobhuza who later became the Swazi), fled across the Drakensberg on to the central plateau between the Orange and Vaal rivers. They spread destruction amongst the Sotho-speaking tribes of the area and also fought bitterly with one another until the Ngwane finally succeeded in destroying their rivals. The Ngwane re-crossed the Drakensberg in 1828 and entered the area near the colonial frontier occupied by the Thembu tribe. They were encountered by a British force which had been sent to protect the tribes against an expected Zulu invasion. The Ngwane were attacked by mistake and the tribe broke up. Many remained in the area as homeless refugees called Fingos. The invasion of the Hlubi and Ngwane drove a powerful Sotho-speaking tribe to take to a life of plunder. These were the Tlokwa under a warrior queen called Mantatisi and her son Sikonyela. They travelled round much of modern Orange Free State creating havoc among the tribes until they finally settled on a fortified mountain top in the north of modern Lesotho.

The migration of the Kololo to Barotseland

The period of warfare and destruction which suddenly descended on the peaceful Sotho peoples between the Orange and the Vaal rivers had two further important consequences. One tribe, known originally as the Fokeng and later as the Kololo, fled across the Vaal and made its way towards modern Kuruman where there was a station of the London Missionary Society. The missionary, Moffat, rode to Griqua-town and called on the Griquas for aid and the invaders were defeated. The Kololo moved northwards, spreading destruction amongst the Tswana tribes, until they reached and crossed the Zambesi. They then moved up the river and invaded the Lozi kingdom in Zambia. The kingdom was overthrown and a Kololo empire established which lasted till it was overthrown in turn by a national uprising which re-established the Lozi kings. By this time the Kololo language had gained so firm a hold that it remains the language used by most of the Lozi.

Kololo kingdoms in the Shire Valley

The Kololo kingdom was visited by the missionary explorer Livingstone who took Kololo porters with him on his journeys of exploration. Some of these remained behind on the banks of the Shire river, which flows from Lake Malawi to the Zambesi. The people of the area were in a pitiful position at the time as a result of Ngoni raids and the activities of slave hunters. The Kololo, with the guns given them by Livingstone and their knowledge of large-scale political organisations, were able to rally the people for their own defence and built up Kololo kingdoms hundreds of miles away from the rest of their tribe.

Moshesh and the Basuto kingdom

The second important consequence of the Hlubi and Ngwane invasions was the creation of the Basuto nation by Moshesh. He was the son of an unimportant member of the royal family of a small Sotho tribe, but early in life he showed evidence of great foresight and powers of statesmanship. He saw that in difficult times a strong defensive position was of the utmost importance and established himself with a few followers on a mountain called Butha Buthe in northern Lesotho. There he beat off a series of attacks from more powerful enemies and increased his following. After experiencing a prolonged siege by the Tlokwa, however, he decided that the mountain was not large enough for his people and moved to the almost impregnable hill of Thaba Bosiu in central Lesotho. There he was able to beat off every attack and gradually gathered the remnants of many Sotho tribes around him to form the Basuto people. In 1833 he invited missionaries of the Paris Evangelical Society to come to his kingdom. They proved very helpful in the long struggles with the Boers of the Orange Free State which followed. Unlike many leaders of his time, Moshesh was essentially a man of peace, who always preferred to attain his objects by diplomacy rather than war. He was one of the most remarkable statesmen in southern African history and the independent state of Lesotho is his memorial.

Mzilikazi and the Ndebele

One of the tribes incorporated in the Zulu kingdom was the Kumalo tribe with its energetic young chief Mzilikazi. Contrary to his usual custom Shaka made the young chief a regimental commander, but in 1821 he rebelled and fled with his warriors into the Transvaal. Mzilikazi and his men, who came to be known as the Ndebele, devastated much land in the Transvaal and built up a powerful kingdom there on Zulu lines. In 1837 after being twice attacked, first by the regiments of Dingane and later by the Boers, Mzilikazi fled and ultimately settled in the Matabeleland area of modern Rhodesia.

The Fingos

As a result of Shaka's campaigns in Natal many refugees poured out of the area and together with the remnants of the Ngwane horde took refuge with the coastal tribes near the colonial frontier. They were known collectively as Fingos.

Development of the Cape Colony

Returning to the history of the Cape Colony, we have seen how the settlers had spread, depriving the indigenous inhabitants of their land and employing them as herdsmen on the white farms. At the same time the white settlers had developed strong colour attitudes and regarded all non-Europeans as intrinsically inferior and not entitled to the same legal rights as whites. This had created a problem of internal tension in the community between white masters and non-white servants but the problems were to become much more serious when the colonists came in contact with the Bantu-speaking peoples. The Hottentots had not offered any serious resistance to the loss of their lands and once on white farms had tended to adopt European language and culture. The Bushmen had fought fiercely but their numbers were tiny. The Bantu on the other hand were far more numerous than any other group. They had strong political systems and they were very strongly attached to their culture. They were certainly not prepared to surrender their lands without a fight. So long, however, as the white population of the Colony continued to increase, and farming remained the main occupation of the settlers, young Boers would continue to need new farming land and labour to work on it. The result could only be the addition of severe border conflict to the already existing tensions of the Colony. In this situation any attempt by the central government to ensure fair treatment for non-whites, or to control the expansion of the farmers, would arouse the resentment of the frontier settlers.

This had already happened by 1795, when the attempts of Maynier in the name of the Colony's government to control the farmers' treatment of their Hottentot servants led to rebellion and the declaration of the Republic of Graaf Reinet and Swellendam. The British occupation of the Colony at the end of 1795 did nothing to alter the basic situation. The British Governor forced the republicans to surrender by threatening to cut off their powder supplies. Soon afterwards, however, another rebellion broke out and this time the government sent troops to suppress it.

The Hottentot uprising

These troops contained a body of Hottentot soldiers and when Hottentot servants saw them coming with the British they assumed that a war with their Boer masters was to be fought. They deserted in large numbers, often stealing their masters' guns, and flocked to the British camp. When the commander tried to disarm them, they fled and formed armed bands which began attacking and pillaging the farms of their former masters. In the general confusion the Bantu gained the impression that they were to be attacked and they too joined in. By the end of the first British occupation in 1803 the eastern frontier districts had been severely ravaged and many farmers reduced to destitution.

British missionaries

The British administration marked the beginning of a new influence with the coming of overseas missionaries to South Africa. The pioneer was Dr van der Kemp of the London Missionary Society who arrived in 1802. He took up work amongst the Hottentots and began to champion their cause. He argued that the chief cause of tension was the fact that Hottentots had no land and were forced to take service with white masters no matter what the conditions. He asked for land to be set aside for Hottentot mission stations where they could support themselves and learn skills which would enable them to command higher wages. This idea was supported by the government but before it could be fully carried out the Colony was handed over to the authorities of the Dutch Republic.

The Dutch at the Cape 1803-6

The three years of the Dutch rule were relatively uneventful. All parties in the frontier area were worn out and anxious for peace. The government continued the policy started by the British of allowing missionaries to establish Hottentot settlements, and kept an eye on conditions of service to which Hottentots were subjected. In these improved circumstances many Hottentots returned to work on white farms, while others settled at the mission stations. Bantu and Boer remained on the Zuurveld and no wars broke out for a time. In 1806 the British recaptured the Cape and this time they kept it.

Second British occupation, 1806

Under the second British administration the government of the Cape was at first strongly conservative. It tended to favour the farmers rather than their servants. Nevertheless the Evangelical movement was gaining force in Britain and missionaries came out to South Africa in ever increasing numbers. They began to extend their work even beyond the frontiers of the Colony, and they became increasingly powerful advocates for the Hottentots' rights. In 1809 the Governor issued regulations defining the position of the Hottentots. These regulations largely confirmed existing customs and were distinctly favourable to the settlers. Every Hottentot was to have a fixed address, which meant an address on a white farm, or he would be liable to imprisonment for vagrancy. If he wished to leave an employer to look for another he must establish a fixed address within fourteen days. If he wished to travel from one district to another he must have a pass from the local magistrate. These regulations made it very difficult for a Hottentot to change his employer or take refuge on a mission station. A later regulation made their lot even more difficult, for it was laid down that if a Hottentot child had been brought up to the age of twelve on a white farm the farmer could keep him as an apprentice for a further three years. Thus if other means failed the farmer could retain a workman by holding his children as apprentices. Nevertheless, inequitable as they were, the regulations did recognise that the Hottentots had rights to fair treatment and payment of wages and that these could be the subject of legal action.

The Black Circuit

In 1811 missionary protests about the failure of the courts to take an interest in Hottentot complaints led to questions being asked in the British Parliament, and the Governor was stung into action. He instructed the Circuit Court to look into every Hottentot complaint in the fullest detail and to try all cases on the basis of strict equality before the law. The Circuit Court of 1812 was a new experience for the frontier farmers and became so unpopular that it was called the Black Circuit. Many were summoned to leave their farms to answer charges brought by their coloured employees, a situation they regarded as intolerable and degrading. Many of the complaints proved trivial but a good deal of evil was uncovered and two farmers were actually convicted of murder.

So bitter was the feeling against the procedure by which coloured persons could bring their employers to court that another frontier rebellion broke out in 1818. A farmer was summoned to answer a charge brought by his Hottentot servant but refused to go. An officer with a party of Hottentot soldiers went to arrest him but he fired at them from a cave where he was hiding. They returned the fire and the farmer was shot. His family then vowed vengeance and rode round stirring up the farmers to rise in revolt. The government forces soon rounded up the rebels and they were publicly hanged at Slagters Nek. In future it would seem safer to leave the Colony in protest against the behaviour of government than to start an armed rebellion.

The Xhosa driven from the Zuurveld

While the affair of the Black Circuit was causing ill-feeling the government was also turning its attention to the frontier. Its idea, like that of its predecessor, was to keep the races apart by drawing a definite line between them, and for this purpose it was decided to make the long-standing Fish river frontier effective. In 1812, 20,000 Xhosa were uprooted from their homes and driven out of the Zuurveld. This did little to resolve the situation, for the arrival of refugees from the Zuurveld caused severe overcrowding on the far bank of the Fish.

Makana and the 1818 war

A prophet named Makana arose who promised supernatural aid to win back the lost territory and in 1818 fighting broke out between his followers and those of Gaika, a Xhosa chief who had always lived outside the frontier and had no quarrel with the Colony. Colonial troops intervened in this affair and the Xhosa then invaded the Colony in force. They were eventually driven back but the only remedy to the situation produced by overcrowding which the government could think of was to take yet another strip of land from the Xhosa to be kept empty of inhabitants as a buffer zone between the two races.

The 1820 settler experiment

After the 1818 war, the government of the Cape attempted a radical solution to the problems of the Colony. It tried to alter the situation in which the farmers were always demanding more land while their population was too scanty to defend itself adequately. A system of more intensive agriculture on much smaller farms which would not need non-European labour would, it was believed, provide a denser population which could defend itself. It would also give rise to villages and towns and create new avenues of employment so that the Colony need not continue to expand in area but could develop a richer and more varied life. Laws were introduced to encourage Boers to divide their farms amongst their children and it was made more difficult to acquire new land by ending the free distribution of Crown lands and putting them up for auction instead. The main means of bringing this about was by the scheme to settle English families on the Zuurveld on farms of about 100 acres instead of the normal Boer farm of 6,000 acres. This plan had additional attractions. It would provide a substantial English element in the predominantly Dutch Colony and it might be a way of relieving unemployment in England. In 1820 about 1,000 English families were settled on the Zuurveld but the experiment failed in its main object. The new settlers did not find it practical to farm on the small farms given them; most drifted away to the towns and the remainder pressed for farms of the Boer type.

Missionary agitation and the 50th Ordinance

In the meantime missionary pressure for an improvement in the lot of the Hottentots was growing. John Philip, the energetic general superintendent of the London Missionary Society in South Africa, launched an all-out attack on the laws governing the movements of Hottentots, which left them at the mercy of white employers and reduced them to a position of semi-slavery possibly even worse than outright slavery. If Hottentots were given equal rights with Europeans, he argued, many would be able to earn better wages and this would create a large market for British goods.

These views, contained in a book called *Researches in South Africa,* created a great stir in England and the acting governor at the Cape was asked to draw up regulations freeing the Hottentots from their legal disadvantages. In fact he had already done so. After consultation with a philanthropically-minded Dutch official named Stockenstroom he had issued the famous 50th Ordinance. The British Parliament simply decreed that the provisions of the 50th Ordinance should not be altered without reference to the King in Parliament.

The 50th Ordinance freed the Hottentots from all their legal disabilities and gave them and all free non-Europeans in the Cape complete legal equality with whites. It was indeed a revolutionary measure for it tried to destroy the whole pattern of racial discrimination which had grown up at the Cape ever since the establishment of the white colony there. It set a pattern of racial equality in the Cape which survived in theory until the unification of South Africa in 1910. But though the 50th Ordinance constituted a legal revolution it did not in practice succeed in destroying the pattern of racial discrimination and the social attitudes which went with it. The Hottentots gained their freedom but they were without property or much skill. Most of them remained the poorest members of society and the general pattern continued to be one of white property-owning masters and coloured property-less servants.

The average white inhabitant of the Colony, and especially the Boers of the frontier areas, objected strongly to the 50th Ordinance. It denied the whole attitude of racial superiority which was the basis of their way of life and it proclaimed an equality between races which they regarded as contrary to the laws of God. It also directly affected their interests, for many Hottentot servants took the opportunity to abandon their masters and flock to the towns or mission stations.

The emancipation of slaves

This blow to the pride and the pockets of the farmers was followed by another. The campaign against slavery had been gathering force in Britain throughout the early years of the nineteenth century. The abolition of the slave trade in 1809 had caused a steady rise in the price of slaves, and their treatment had been subjected to ever increasing regulation. In 1833 came the decision to abolish slavery in British possessions altogether. What is more, it was decided that in South Africa the freed slaves, after a period of three years apprenticeship to their former masters, would fall under the provisions of the 50th Ordinance. That is to say they would have legal equality with their one-time owners. Slave owners were to be compensated for their losses, but the arrangements were mismanaged and many received only a fraction of what was due.

The expanding frontiers

In the meantime tension continued along the eastern frontier, and Boers began to turn away from the fertile lands of the east coast in search of new farms further in the interior. The missionaries also turned their attention to the problem of the expanding frontier. They pleaded for protection for the indigenous peoples and an end to the system of raids to recover supposedly stolen cattle which, they pointed out, caused the innocent to suffer for the guilty and opened the way to many abuses. Governor D'Urban, who came out in 1834 to carry through the emancipation of slaves, also brought with him instructions to reform the frontier system.

The commissie trekke

By that time news of the situation in the interior had been reaching the Cape from the English traders and travellers who visited Natal, and from missionaries and travellers on the central plateau. It became general knowledge that there was excellent farming land virtually unoccupied in Natal and also in the areas around the Vaal and Orange rivers. Finding insufficient land in the Colony to provide for their growing families, and furious at the government's attitude to the racial situation in the Colony and to frontier relations with the Bantu, the farmers began to talk openly of migrating into the interior to occupy the empty lands and set up a government of their own in accordance with their cherished principles. In 1834 three spying parties (commissie trekke) were sent out to discover if the rumours of good land lying empty were really true. One went to Natal, another to the Transvaal and the third to South-West Africa. The third gave an adverse report but the other two were enthusiastic and the Trek would probably have started at once if the farmers had not been engaged in another frontier war.

The Xhosa resistance war of 1835-6

Tension had never ceased on the frontier since the war of 1818 and the decision to take a strip of land from the Bantu as a neutral zone. This had made the Xhosa even more overcrowded and they naturally looked with envy at the rich herds of the white farmers grazing on land they regarded as rightfully theirs. The situation was made worse by the arrival of thousands of refugees from Natal and the interior, who settled with the Xhosa as Fingos. Seeing their plight the government had allowed some chiefs to come back to the neutral strip but insisted that this was dependent on good behaviour. Along such an open and unguarded frontier there were inevitably many complaints of cattle theft and as the settlers looked for new farms for their sons they continually pressed for the Bantu to be driven further back.

When D'Urban arrived he was at first sympathetic to the philanthropic point of view and sent Dr Philip to explain to the chiefs that a new system of regulating the frontier would be put into force which would be more favourable to their people. This produced a good deal of goodwill and the frontier was quiet for a time, but D'Urban, tied down by paper work concerned with emancipation of slaves, kept delaying his journey to the frontier. In the meantime the military authorities did not co-operate with the new scheme, and continued to send punitive parties into Xhosa territory while the settlers demanded that the Bantu be driven back. The chiefs became increasingly convinced that Dr Philip's visit had been a plot to lull them into a sense of security while the whites prepared to attack them and take away still more of their desperately needed land. They therefore prepared for war and in 1835 they invaded the Colony in force.

When D'Urban at last reached the frontier he was so horrified at the scenes of desolation that he declared the Xhosa to be 'irredeemable savages' and decreed that they should be driven out of the whole area from the Fish to the Kei rivers for ever. The farmers and the troops succeeded in turning back the invasion of the Colony but the Xhosa fought for their lands with such determination that the military commander admitted that the policy of driving them out altogether was impossible. At the same time the missionaries and the philanthropists in England raised a storm of protest against the whole policy of D'Urban. He was told to prepare the public mind for the abandonment of the newly annexed area, which he had called Queen Adelaide Province and the philanthropic Stockenstroom was sent to the Eastern Frontier as Lieutenant Governor.

One of the wagons used in the Trek on a modern commemorative occasion

The Trek begins

The farmers had abandoned thoughts of leaving the Colony while they had hopes of gaining new lands in Queen Adelaide Province, but its abandonment was the last straw and during 1836 they poured out of the Colony across the Orange river in ever-increasing numbers. The Great Trek was under way. There were several motives behind it. To some extent it was simply an acceleration of the process of expansion that had brought the settlers from the shadow of Table Mountain to the banks of the Fish river. But the Trek was different from this earlier movement because of its size, and because it was a deliberate attempt to break away from the British government and establish an independent state where there would be no ungodly equality between the races and "proper relations" would be maintained between masters and servants. From this point of view the Great Trek was a revolt against the philanthropic policies of the British government and the spirit of the 50th Ordinance. Finally the decision to embark on the Great Trek, and the direction in which the trekkers moved, depended on information about empty land in the interior resulting from the devastations of the Mfecane. From this point of view the Great Trek was a response by land-hungry Boers to the opportunities offered by the previous movements of the Bantu.

230

The course of the Trek

Turning away from the eastern frontier where the sturdy defence of the Xhosa offered little hope of progress, the trekking parties crossed the Orange river into the plains of the modern Orange Free State. Some lingered on the borders of Moshesh's country but the majority moved on, keeping well clear of the Basuto, towards a meeting place near Thaba Nchu. Then, as they waited for their numbers to increase with new arrivals, some of the first-comers crossed the Vaal to hunt and prospect the land for settlement.

Conflict with Mzilikazi

Unfortunately they gave no notice of their coming to Mzilikazi, the Ndebele king, and his regiments mistook them for hostile Griqua marauders. The waggons were attacked and a number of Boers were killed but the rest gathered together under the leadership of Potgieter and beat off the Ndebele attack at the Battle of Vegkop in October

Voor Trekkers defending themselves against the Ndebele army
at Vegkop, 1836. Under attack the Trekkers formed defensive positions
known as laagers

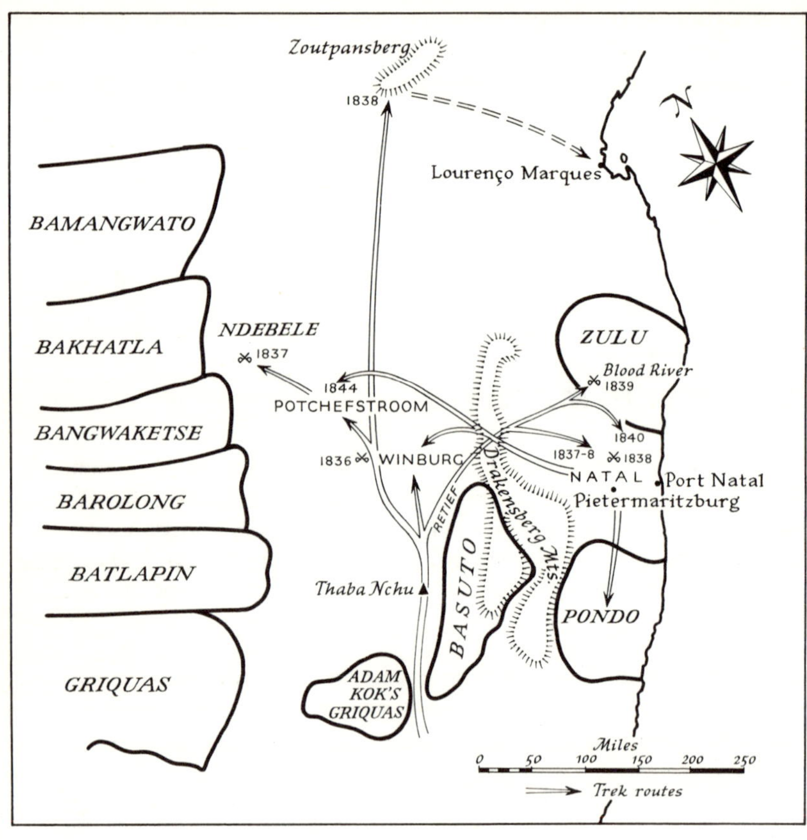

25 Routes followed by the Boers in the Great Trek

1836. The Ndebele seized their cattle, however, and they were
grateful for the help of the Rolong chief, Moroka, who helped them
back to their fellows near Thaba Nchu. In the main trekker camp
there was much discussion whether to move into Natal or continue
the struggle with Mzilikazi. The majority decided to follow Piet
Retief into Natal but a few determined to continue on the highveld.
In January 1837 they made a daring raid on one of Mzilikazi's military
towns and seized a large herd of cattle. Shortly after, Dingane also
sent his regiments to attack the Ndebele. Then in November 1837
the Boers launched an all-out attack. Unable to ward off the hail of
bullets from the Boer guns or to get near enough to attack the mounted
gunmen who used their horses to keep always just out of spear range,
the Ndebele were completely defeated. Their military towns were

captured one after another in seven days of fighting, and Mzilikazi led his people on a flight to the north which took them to modern Rhodesia. The victorious Boers then laid claim to the wide area which had been under Mzilikazi's rule.

A great dance at Mbelebele, a Zulu war settlement. The Zulu used a large number of different dances in connection with many formal occasions in their social life such as marriage, initiation, war and death.
(From a contemporary engraving)

The Trekkers and the Zulu

In the meantime Retief rode to visit Dingane and ask him for the gift of Natal for his people to settle. But the Zulu King was worried and afraid of this horde of armed white strangers. He had heard from a Xhosa interpreter who had come with the English traders how the white men gradually infiltrated the frontier areas and ended up by overthrowing the chiefs and seizing the land. He wished to avoid this fate for himself and his people but he was afraid to refuse the request outright. Accordingly he thought of a plan to buy time. He told Retief that some of his cattle had been stolen by the Tlokwa chief Sikonyela and promised if they were brought back to give Natal to the Boers.

He probably hoped that Retief and his party would be involved in a struggle with the Tlokwa and leave him alone. But further developments proved even more alarming. Retief tricked Sikonyela into trying on a pair of handcuffs and then locked them on his wrists, making him a prisoner. To regain his freedom he had to surrender the cattle asked for by Dingane. Then the news came that the Boers had defeated Mzilikazi and driven his people from their country. Retief wrote in haughty tones to the Zulu King demanding the fulfilment of his promise and then came riding to see him. Even before he arrived the Boers began pouring over the passes in the Drakensberg into the fertile land of Natal.

The coup that failed

Dingane was desperate and felt that the only way to save himself and his people was to catch the Boers unprepared and destroy them before they could establish themselves firmly. He massed his regiments at his main homestead, Ungungindhlovu, and awaited the arrival of Retief and his men. He received them well and made his mark on the paper they asked for. Then he invited them to a farewell dance and when they were standing unarmed amidst his warriors he suddenly gave the order to kill the magicians. Retief and his party were put to death and the Zulu regiments were sent out at once to attack the Boer waggons unawares. But though the first parties met by the warriors were slaughtered, the firing of guns alarmed the others and the regiments were driven back with heavy loss. Dingane's coup had failed. The position of the Boers was not enviable, however, for their numbers were few, they had lost many of their cattle and they dared not disperse to give proper grazing to those that remained. A first Boer counter-attack ended in a retreat from which it got its name, the Vlug Commando (Flight Commando). Many thought of giving up the struggle and returning across the mountains but new reinforcements came from the Cape and some of the Boers on the highveld, including the outstanding leader Pretorius, came to the help of their fellows.

The Blood River Campaign

A large commando with waggons loaded with ammunition was prepared and advanced towards Ungungindhlovu. On 16 December

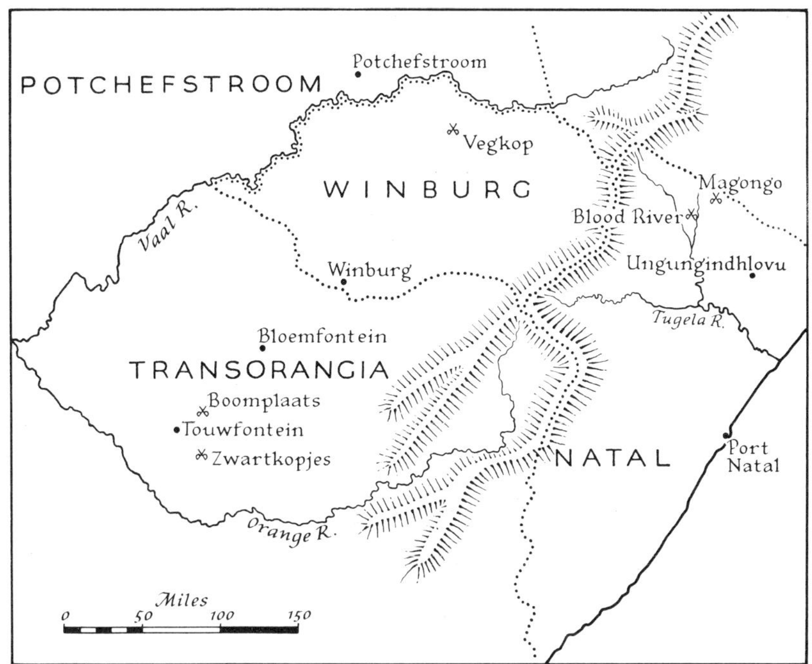

26 Boer-Zulu and Boer-Ndebele battlefields

1838 the decisive Battle of Blood River took place. The superb Zulu discipline proved useless in face of firearms. They were shot down in heaps and heavily defeated. The commando advanced to Ungungindhlovu itself, which Dingane had deserted, and found the bodies of Retief and his comrades together with the piece of paper ceding Natal. By this time the government at the Cape was becoming alarmed at the news from the interior and sent a small force to watch developments at Port Natal. It arrived when the Boers were away on the Blood River Campaign. When they returned victorious there was little the British force could do except try to arrange terms of peace between both sides. Both were by this time ready to negotiate. Dingane did not wish to be involved in another encounter, but although defeated he was still strong and the Boers were still not free to disperse and settle down. A meeting was arranged and a peace treaty drawn up. The Boers drove a hard bargain and in a secret clause of the treaty they forced Dingane to give up not only Natal but a strip of territory across the Tugela in Zululand itself. Satisfied that peace had been made but unaware of the full details, the British force then sailed away.

Zulu civil war

Dingane tried to fulfil his side of the bargain and sent his regiments to clear a way for his retreat by raiding the Swazi. But many of his people grumbled at leaving their land and one of Shaka's surviving brothers, Mpande, seized the opportunity to start a rebellion. He fled with a number of followers across the Tugela and asked for Boer protection. Then as his following continued to grow he proposed to march into Zululand and overthrow Dingane. The Boers were pleased to support him and sent a commando which marched in support of the rebel chief. The two Zulu armies fought a fatal battle at Magongo, and Mpande was victorious. Dingane fled to Swaziland and was captured and killed by a Swazi chief in revenge for his attacks on them. The Boers did not have to fire a shot, but they reaped the fruits of Mpande's victory. They crowned him the new Zulu king and demanded 17,000 head of cattle for their support and as recompense for their past sufferings. At last they were firmly established in Natal and could build up their republic in security.

9 South Africa from the Great Trek to the first Anglo-Boer war

Consequences of the Great Trek

The Great Trek marks the beginning of a new phase in the history of South Africa with important consequences for southern Africa as a whole. Before the Trek, contact between Bantu and white had been restricted to the eastern frontier. In that area a situation had developed in which as we have seen the white settlers, impelled by a constantly rising population, were always trying to gain possession of more of the Bantu's grazing lands. At the same time they were employing more Bantu labour and so turning the Bantu from a member of an independent society into a subordinate member of a multi-racial society, firmly kept at the bottom by barriers of racial prejudice as well as absence of skills and capital. This situation was only slightly improved by the educational work of the missionaries and by the philanthropic pressures which had caused the government at the Cape to insist on the ending of formal legal discrimination.

Before the Great Trek the number of people affected was comparatively small. As a result of the Boer migrations the problems of racial contact and conflict spread over much greater areas. The white settlers were always trying to advance, squeezing the tribesmen off their land and forcing them to enter the ranks of labourers on white-owned farms. This met with brave and determined resistance and was only completed at the end of the nineteenth century after a long series of bitter wars. The wars increased the sense of insecurity among white settlers and strengthened the determination of the trekkers to preserve the principles of racial distinction.

The dilemma of British policy

The Great Trek also presented the British government at the Cape with a difficult problem. The chief value of the Cape to Great Britain,

as to the Dutch East India Company, was as a strategic position on
the route to India and there was a natural reluctance to spend precious
resources on an otherwise poor and unproductive area unless such
expenses were directly related to security. On the other hand Britain
could not avoid responsibility for the behaviour of her subjects who
had trekked into the interior, or for the fate of the indigenous peoples
with whom they were in contact. Still more important, a policy of
leaving the Boers to themselves, which appeared economical in the
short run, might have very expensive consequences in the long run.
The direction which the Trek had taken meant that white settlers
were established on three sides of a great mass of tribes including the
Basuto of Moshesh and the Nguni-speaking tribes along the coastal
corridor between the Cape frontier and the southern borders of
Natal. As these tribes were increasingly short of land and very close
to one another, any conflict along one section of the frontier between
the races was likely to start a chain of disturbance. Thus if the British
left the Boers to themselves in their areas they might find themselves
plunged into war on their own eastern frontier at any time. A similar
situation also prevailed with regard to the white settlements in
Natal and the Transvaal. Both had frontiers with the Zulu kingdom
and either might plunge the other into war at any time. Faced with
this situation British policy alternated between the two opposite
extremes of annexation and withdrawal in accordance with the developing situation in South Africa and shifts of opinion in Britain.

The first stage of British reaction to the Trek

When the Great Trek took place the influence of the philanthropic
movement was at its highest and Britain admitted responsibility
for the conduct of its citizens in the interior by passing the Cape
of Good Hope Punishment Act, under which British subjects who
committed crimes anywhere in South Africa, south of the 35th line
of latitude, were liable for trial at the Cape. The government also
refused to entertain a request from the Natal Boers to be considered
an independent people but insisted that they were and must remain
British subjects. This meant that Britain ought to occupy the areas
in which the Boers were settled, as it was useless to declare them
subject to the law at the Cape but provide no means of enforcing
that law. When it came to taking active steps that would involve
expense, however, the Governor at the Cape found that he could not
get authorisation for even a moderate force to intervene in Natal.

The tiny contingent which was sent to Port Natal at the time of the Blood River Campaign, (1838) was unable to play any major part in influencing events and was withdrawn soon after the Boer victory. The progress of events, however, soon forced the British government to intervene more effectively in Natal.

Conduct of the Natal Republic

The jubilant reception given to an adventurer named Smellekamp who arrived in Natal claiming to be a representative of the King of Holland, as well as the visit of some American ships, created fears lest a foreign power might establish itself on the east coast of South Africa and threaten the route to India. Other reasons for intervention arose from the conduct of the settlers themselves in relation to their Bantu neighbours. The conquest of Natal had given the Boers large areas of excellent farming land, but the heroes of the Zulu war registered so many farms in their names that soon there was no more unallocated land available for newcomers. The cattle paid by the humble Mpande after his victory over Dingane were well in excess of the losses the trekkers had suffered, but their distribution was not controlled firmly enough to prevent the more powerful members of the community from seizing more than their share, so that others did not receive enough to build up a satisfactory herd. When the news of the defeat and death of Dingane became widely known, tribes who had fled out of Natal to the south, or been forced to join the Zulu kingdom, began pouring back to settle in their old homes, now the legal property of Boer settlers. The Natal Boers found the utmost difficulty in coping with this ever-growing influx because they only effectively occupied a small proportion of the farms registered in their names.

The Boers and their neighbours

The government which was called upon to deal with these problems was weak and rickety. When the Boers trekked out of the Cape they regarded themselves as a single body, and this idea was preserved in theory through the life of the Natal Republic. As the main body of settlers had moved into Natal this was the main centre of government. Subordinate governing bodies were established at Winburg in modern Orange Free State and Potchefstroom in the Transvaal.

These were represented on the main governing body in Natal and
supposed to be subject to it though in fact distance and difficulty of
communication meant that the local bodies were virtually self-
governing. In Natal itself power was divided between an elected
legislative body called the Volksraad and the President, who controlled the Executive. Both authorities were supposed to be subject
to the people and this meant in practice any assembly of settlers.

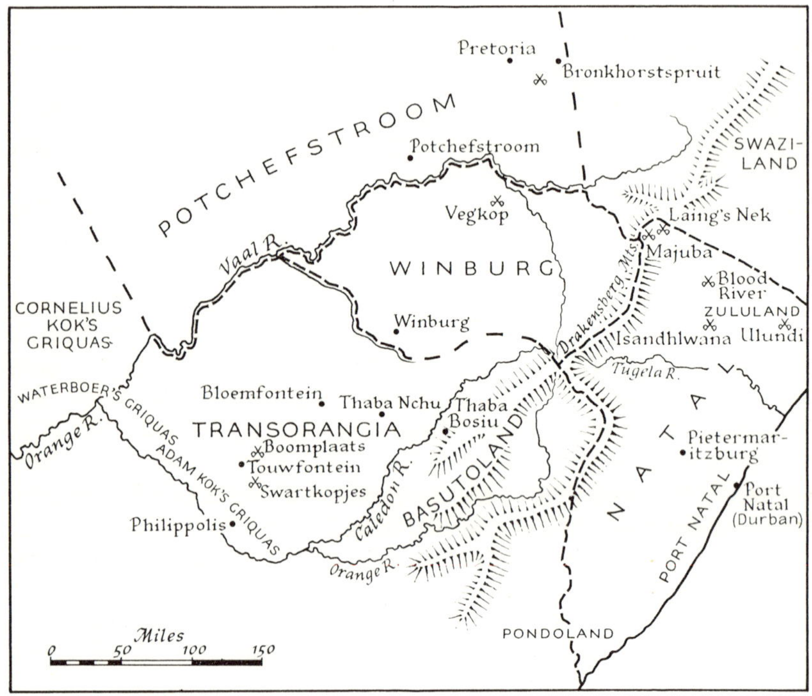

27 The Trekkers' Republic

With such a constitution it was difficult for the Volksraad to prevent
policy being decided by the feeling of the moment. Thus even
though it was aware of the danger that philanthropic opinion in
Britain would exert itself in favour of British annexation of Natal
in order to protect the indigenous peoples, the Volksraad was unable
to prevent its citizens from an aggressive approach to its non-European
neighbours which amply justified the arguments of the humanitarians.
Not satisfied with the herds already extorted from the Zulu the Natal
Republic pressed Mpande for still more cattle and proposed to levy

240

a heavy fine on the Swazi, claiming that they had taken Zulu cattle which belonged to the Boers by right of conquest. A still more shocking development was the behaviour of the Boers towards their southern neighbours. The theft of some cattle by Bushmen was made the pretext for a raid on the Bhaca, a group made up of tribes who had fled from Natal in the time of Shaka and who were living under their chief Ncapayi in the close vicinity of the Pondo. The Boers killed many members of the tribe and seized large booty in cattle. At the same time they proposed to take land from the Pondo to provide for the increasing numbers of Bantu refugees returning to Natal, whom they regarded as a threat to their security. By this time humanitarian feeling was strongly aroused and the procedures of the Natal government also gave cause for grave alarm from the strategic point of view. If they were allowed to push the tribes back from their southern border this must inevitably produce a chain reaction along the closely packed coastal strip, resulting in increased pressure on the frontier of the Cape.

British annexation of Natal

Accordingly, in 1841 a small contingent of British troops was despatched. It halted first at the Pondo and then moved on to Port Natal. When they came in contact with the Boers fighting started and the British government felt too heavily committed to withdraw. In 1845 Natal was formally annexed to the Cape, but already many Boers were leaving the area in disgust to join their fellows on the high veld in modern Orange Free State and Transvaal. The departing Boers were gradually replaced by British settlers, who made Natal the most self-consciously British area in southern Africa, but as they faced the same security problems as the Boers who preceded them they developed almost identical attitudes and policies. Indeed the Natal settlers came in time to exhibit the strongest racial prejudices of any white group in South Africa.

The treaty policy on the eastern frontier
and in Trans-Orangia

With the annexation of Natal the British government had taken a major step in the direction of bringing the areas inhabited by its runaway subjects under British control. In the meanwhile events in the area between the Orange and the Vaal rivers were preparing the way for another step in the same direction. When it decided not to allow the annexation of Queen Adelaide Province the British government proposed to adopt a policy suggested by the philanthropic Dutch official Stockenstroom. The idea of this was to persuade the tribes near the Colonial frontiers to enter into treaties with the Colonial government, under which the chiefs would be made responsible for maintaining peace in the frontier areas, catching and returning runaways and deserters from the Colony, and making good any losses of stock stolen by their subjects. This would end the practice of commandos crossing the frontier to recapture stolen cattle which had proved a grave source of injustice and friction in the past. British Residents would be sent to the more important tribes to help the chiefs understand and carry out their obligations and to represent their views to the British government. The policy was to be applied not only to chiefs in the eastern frontier area but also to others further inland.

The plan was never fully tried out. It was very unpopular with the settlers and the military authorities, and the British government was unwilling to spend enough to make it work. In the area between the Orange and Vaal rivers it was faced by especially difficult problems. There the Griquas and Basuto were living alongside a growing white population, made up partly of Boers who had entered the area before the Trek and who regarded themselves as British subjects, and partly by Trek Boers who denied British authority. This white population was greedy for farms and labour and was subject to no single political authority. Both sections were unwilling to be governed by the non-European rulers that the British government recognised as the legal authorities in the area, and possessed weapons which enabled them to defy these rulers. Seeing the situation, Dr. Phillip urged immediate annexation as the only means of preventing the Boers from seizing the lands of the indigenous peoples and turning them into landless labourers serving on white farms. Nevertheless the British government, anxious to limit expenditure, attempted to apply the treaty system without taking into account the military power of the Boers.

Two Griqua chiefs, Waterboer and Adam Kok, were given treaties in which their authority over their territories was recognised, and they were asked to maintain law and order and return colonial criminals for trial at the Cape in return for small subsidies. A similar treaty was made by Governor Napier with Moshesh, though his request for a Resident to come and live with him was not granted by Napier.

Moshesh, the British, and the Trek Boers

The position of the Basuto ruler was very difficult. He ruled a composite state made up of members of many different tribes. The majority of these had been broken up during the Mfecane and were settled in small groups in his kingdom, under the administration of some members of the paramount's family who had their headquarters in different parts of the kingdom. Others remained substantial tribes governed by their own hereditary rulers under the paramountcy of Moshesh. The majority of the members of this state belonged to the Sotho-speaking group, but there were also considerable numbers who spoke the western Sotho or Tswana tongue. They included the powerful Taung tribe under their brilliant leader Moletsane. Finally there were several groups who spoke Nguni languages and differed considerably in culture from the Sotho-speaking majority. The most important of these were the Phuti or Morosi. On the borders of the kingdom in the north, the Tlokwa of Sikonyela were entrenched in their hill-top position awaiting any sign of weakness to renew their old quarrel and at Thaba Nchu a powerful tribe of Tswana refugees, the Rolong under Moroka, refused to accept the authority of the Basuto King, though they had been allowed to settle in what he regarded as his territory.

The Boers, who began to settle on the borders of Moshesh's country at the time of the great Trek, at first asked for the right to graze their cattle temporarily while they prepared to move further into the interior; but they soon showed signs of settling permanently. They treated the land they occupied as private property which they bought and sold to one another, their numbers increased, and they infiltrated ever deeper into the kingdom. In attempting to preserve the nation he had created Moshesh had to tread very carefully. He was anxious to avoid an all-out collision with the whites, whose superior armaments must in the end give them the victory. On the other hand he could not afford to offend any of his own followers for, lacking the power which a centralised military system gave to rulers like Shaka or Mzilikazi, he could only hope to rule by consent. A concession made for the sake of peace might, if it sacrificed the interests of some of his people, lead to a breakaway and the disintegration of the state he had created and was trying to preserve.

In his difficult dealings with the whites Moshesh had the support and advice of the French missionaries, and this was invaluable to him. But missionary activity also created problems, for the missionary attack on old and revered customs inevitably had a disturbing effect, and produced divisions between Christian converts and more conservative members of the community. In addition, the fact that the Rolong were served by a different mission, the Wesleyans, was an important factor in preventing them from becoming part of the Basuto nation, and differences of opinion between the French and Wesleyan missionaries made matters even more complicated.

Failure of the treaty policy

The attempt by the British government to settle the affairs of the area between the Orange and the Vaal, by recognising the most important chiefs and giving them subsidies, was doomed to failure since it did not give those chiefs any protection against their Boer neighbours. The futility of the arrangement was shown in 1845 when Waterboer attempted to exercise his legal powers under the treaty by arresting a Boer for an alleged crime. The Boers at once flew to arms and threatened to destroy the Griquas once and for all. A hastily assembled colonial force with Griqua support routed the Boers at Swartkopjes, but it was obvious that once it withdrew the problem would arise again. Governor Maitland therefore tried a more realistic plan. The fact was recognised that the Boers occupied, and could not be removed from, much of the area legally belonging to the chiefs. It was also recognised that they would not allow themselves to be governed by the Griqua rulers.

At the same time there was an attempt to protect the chiefs from the loss of any more of their land, to provide a system of government for the whites and to settle any disputes between whites and non-whites. In arrangements drawn up at Touwfontein in June 1845, it was agreed that each chief should divide his land into two sections, an inalienable section in which no whites could acquire rights and an alienable section in which land might be leased to white settlers. The theoretical ownership of the alienable section would still belong to the chief, but he would delegate his powers in that area to a British Resident, who would be responsible for governing the white settlers and deciding any disputes between them and the indigenous peoples. Any whites living in the inalienable area would have to withdraw and the expense of the Residents would be paid from annual rents on the farms of white settlers. The plan had much to commend it, but it depended on the Resident being in a strong enough position to prevent the Boers from settling in the inalienable areas, and forcing them to withdraw if they had already done so. This would require a military force that would cost far more than the rents would bring in, and the British government was not prepared to pay. Moshesh marked out an area to be classified as alienable, but the Boers who were already pushing deeper into his kingdom rejected it as far too small. A British Resident was appointed but without the power to control the situation.

The 1846 Xhosa resistance war on the eastern frontier (The War of the Axe)

While tension rose towards a conflict north of the Orange river the situation on the eastern frontier also grew worse. At first the treaty system seemed to work well. The chiefs were anxious to co-operate and the frontier had a short period of unusual calm but magistrates were far too ready to accept farmers' stories about cattle thefts. The chiefs found themselves faced with a lengthening list of demands for the return of stock, some of which had been killed by wild animals or merely allowed to stray out of carelessness. So bitter was the hostility of the settlers to the whole scheme, and to Stockenstroom, who was appointed Governor to carry it out, that he resigned his position in disgust and disillusion. The situation drifted towards yet another war. It was touched off by a minor incident. In 1846 a relative of the Xhosa chief Sandile was arrested for stealing an axe. He was freed by other members of his family, who killed the Hottentot policeman escorting the prisoner. Sandile refused to return the murderers and war was declared. It proved to be one of the most bitter and costly in the history of the eastern frontier.

Annexation of British Kaffraria and the Orange River Sovereignty

The War of the Axe was brought to an end just as Sir Harry Smith, a new and energetic governor, arrived in South Africa. He speedily decided that the frontier chiefs were unable to control their own people sufficiently to prevent conflicts with the Colony. He therefore annexed the frontier area from the Fish to the Kei river, declared the Bantu living on it to be British citizens, and proposed to introduce direct rule by British magistrates while recognising the rights of the Bantu to their land. The newly annexed area came to be a separate little colony called British Kaffraria.

Sir Harry Smith then dashed off to attend to the situation in Natal, where the Boers were steadily streaming out of the country. On his way he passed through the area of modern Orange Free State, and concluded that so long as there was no common, settled and effective government over the different peoples, conflicts would be inevitable which would endanger the peace of the eastern frontier as well. He summoned the chiefs to a short conference and, when he reached Natal, he announced the annexation of the whole area between the Orange and the Vaal as the Orange River Sovereignty (February 1848).

Reactions to the annexation of the Orange River Sovereignty

Sir Harry Smith's action was welcomed by Moshesh, who saw in it the only hope for protection against the Boers, but it had been undertaken hastily, without authorisation from England and without consideration for the state of opinion there. In Britain the theory of Free Trade was gaining increasing strength. According to this theory prosperity could be increased most by trading with every nation freely and without preferences or restrictions. If this were so then colonies

28 British annexations in Southern Africa up to 1848

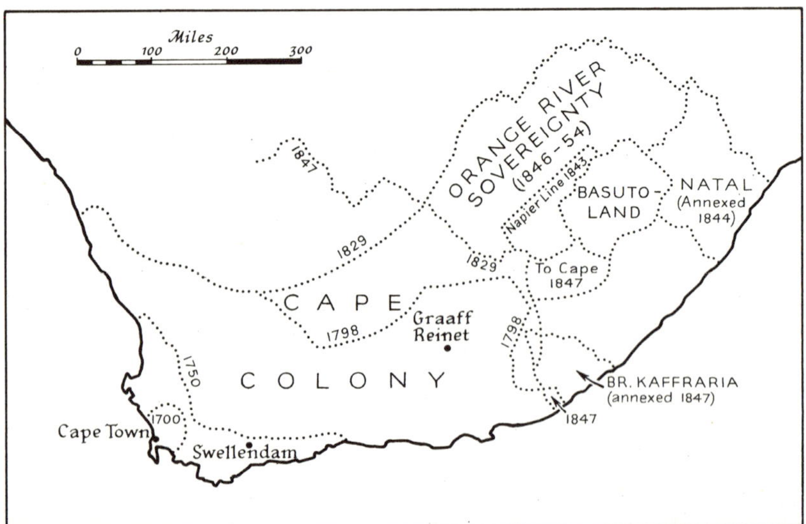

were no advantage since one could trade just as well with independent countries. Expenditure on colonial administration was therefore a sheer waste of resources. Britain should restrict her spending on such matters to a minimum, get rid of colonies where possible and at all costs refrain from acquiring new and expensive responsibilities. In this atmosphere the news of the new annexation was far from popular. It was accepted reluctantly and only on the assumption that it would not involve new expense.

Thus Smith's scheme was doomed from the start. Without funds, a force large enough to enable the Sovereignty government to control Boer as well as Bantu could not be maintained, and the objects of the annexation were unattainable. The first reaction of the Boers in the area was an ill omen for the success of the Sovereignty. While those who had entered the area before the Trek accepted the annexation without enthusiasm, the Trek Boers rose in rebellion, invited Pretorius to come to their aid from the Transvaal, and drove the British Resident out of Bloemfontein. Sir Harry Smith responded promptly, and in August 1848 defeated the Boer forces at Boomplaats. The rebellion collapsed but the Resident was left to exercise a government which would mean arbitrating between the interests of white and non-white without the necessary force.

Warden and Moshesh

Not surprisingly, the British Resident, Warden, tried to conciliate the Boers. He set up a commission to look into the problem of frontiers between Boer and Basuto which contained no Basuto representatives. It proceeded to define a line which left every white farm on the white side of the frontier but cut off whole villages of Basuto from their fellows. Warden tried to get Moshesh to agree to this one-sided arrangement. Aware of Basuto dislike for the frontier proposals, Warden tried to weaken their position. He gave his support to the Rolong, the Tlokwa and other small groups who were jealous of Moshesh. He defined frontiers for them which cut off a good deal of Basuto territory. This led to fighting, and to support his frontier arrangements Warden marched against the Basuto ruler in June 1851. He based his hopes for success on the loyal support of the Boers whose interests he had tried to serve, and on the fighting forces of the Rolong and their lesser allies. But the Boers failed to answer the summons with anything like enough men and the strength of the Rolong had been exaggerated. Warden was defeated at Viervoet and had to fall back. The Orange River Sovereignty fell into chaos and was only saved by the restraint of Moshesh, who held his men back from looting the helpless farmers. Warden called for aid from the Colony but by this time Smith's eastern frontier settlement had also broken down. Yet another frontier war was in progress and no troops could be spared. The Governor of Natal sent a force of Zulus to the aid of the Sovereignty, but they were undisciplined and plundered all sides indiscriminately.

The Xhosa resistance war of 1850

The renewed fighting on the eastern frontier, like that in the Sovereignty, arose from the attempt to do too much without the necessary resources, and from a failure to appreciate the need for a law which would respect the customs of the people. After British Kaffraria was annexed it came in theory under the law of the Cape Colony, and although magistrates in practice modified the law in accordance with common sense and local conditions the prohibition of such a sacred institution as the payment of bride price cattle inevitably provoked violent opposition.

British reactions – war renewed in South Africa

The outbreak of war both in the Sovereignty and on the eastern frontier brought opposition to the forward policy of the British government in South Africa to a head. The wars seemed to reveal the uselessness of annexations undertaken to protect the indigenous people. The voice of the philanthropic movement, which had recently suffered a heavy blow in the failure of Buxton's Niger expedition, was almost silenced. The Free Traders criticised colonial expansion as unprofitable. Others, impressed by the inefficiency of government from a distance and the advantage of giving power to local communities, felt that South African affairs should be left to the settlers. Others again, influenced by the theory of evolution, felt that the conquest of black peoples by whites was an inevitable law of history and that it was a waste of time and resources to oppose it.

There was general agreement that the attempt to follow the trekkers into the interior should be abandoned. No further annexations should be made and if possible the Sovereignty should be abandoned. A commission was accordingly sent out to South Africa to look into the situation. Though the war on the eastern frontier was brought to an end in 1852, and Moshesh still did not take advantage of his victory, the position in the Sovereignty continued to be difficult. The authority of the Resident had broken down, and while some farmers were intriguing with Pretorius in the Transvaal, others were conducting their own negotiations with Moshesh.

The Sand River Convention

The first task of the commissioners was to prevent the Transvaal farmers from taking part in the already complex situation. In view of the changed attitude in Britain they felt able to offer the Transvaalers the legal independence which had always been denied to them in return for a promise not to interfere south of the Vaal river. In 1852 an agreement, known as the Sand River Convention, was drawn up between the commissioners and representatives of the Transvaal Boers. In this convention the British government abandoned its policy of admitting responsibility for the behaviour of its subjects in the interior. The Transvaalers were given complete freedom of action north of the Vaal river, and Britain renounced any right or intention to interfere in that area. Far from attempting to protect the Bantu peoples from the Boers, Britain even sided openly with the white farmers by promising the Transvaalers free access to the gunpowder market at the Cape while not allowing the Bantu to purchase ammunition there. The Sand River Convention put an end to interference from the Transvaal and a measure of peace and order returned to the Sovereignty, but there seemed no way of establishing effective British government without the expense which Britain was determined to avoid.

Moshesh and Cathcart

Moshesh remained the dominant figure in the area, and Governor Cathcart, who succeeded Sir Harry Smith, felt that no settlement was possible in the Sovereignty until Moshesh had been made to accept the over-riding power of British rule. Accordingly, he brought his forces to the borders of Basutoland and demanded payment of a large number of cattle as a fine for the losses caused by Moshesh's men in the recent war. Moshesh begged for time but Cathcart refused to listen, and marched towards Thaba Bosiu. His troops cap-

tured a herd of cattle but they got into difficulties with this booty
when the Basuto launched their counter-attack. Cathcart had to
withdraw, to regroup his forces and wait for more men to arrive.
Moshesh took advantage of this to bring off a diplomatic coup. He
wrote a humble letter to Cathcart saying that as the British had
defeated his people and captured many cattle he hoped that they would
consider it enough and agree to peace. Cathcart was pleased to be
offered an easy way out and agreed. The British forces withdrew
leaving Moshesh victorious.

The Bloemfontein Convention

After this there was no longer any question of holding on to the
Sovereignty, and in spite of the fact that many of the settlers were
reluctant to see the British authority withdrawn, a group was found
who were prepared to accept independence and the Bloemfontein
Convention was signed with them in 1858. This document was
similar to the Sand River Convention. It denied all British responsibilities in the area north of the Orange river and gave the Boers
complete freedom of action. It also included a similar gunpowder
clause. So anxious were the British to be rid of their responsibilities
in the area that they failed even to settle the vital problem of the
frontier between the Boers and the Basuto. Moshesh claimed that the
frontier defined by Warden, to which the Basuto had always objected,
had been cancelled by war and that he could start negotiations afresh.
The Boers maintained that the Warden line stayed the effective frontier.

The Orange Free State

With the departure of the British, the Boers of the Sovereignty area
drew up a republican constitution with an elected Volksraad (parliament) and President. Thus the Orange Free State came into existence,
but in the circumstances it could not be long before it came in conflict with the Basuto.

The disadvantages of the conventions

The Sand River and Bloemfontein Conventions represented the
lowest point of British policy in South Africa. Solemn obligations

250

to the indigenous peoples were cynically given up in the interests of short term economy. The Bantu were left to fight it out with the Boers as best they could, hampered by the gunpowder clauses in the conventions which strengthened the military advantages of the whites. It was not long before this hastily adopted policy was regretted and the British government began to try to undo the consequences of its own acts.

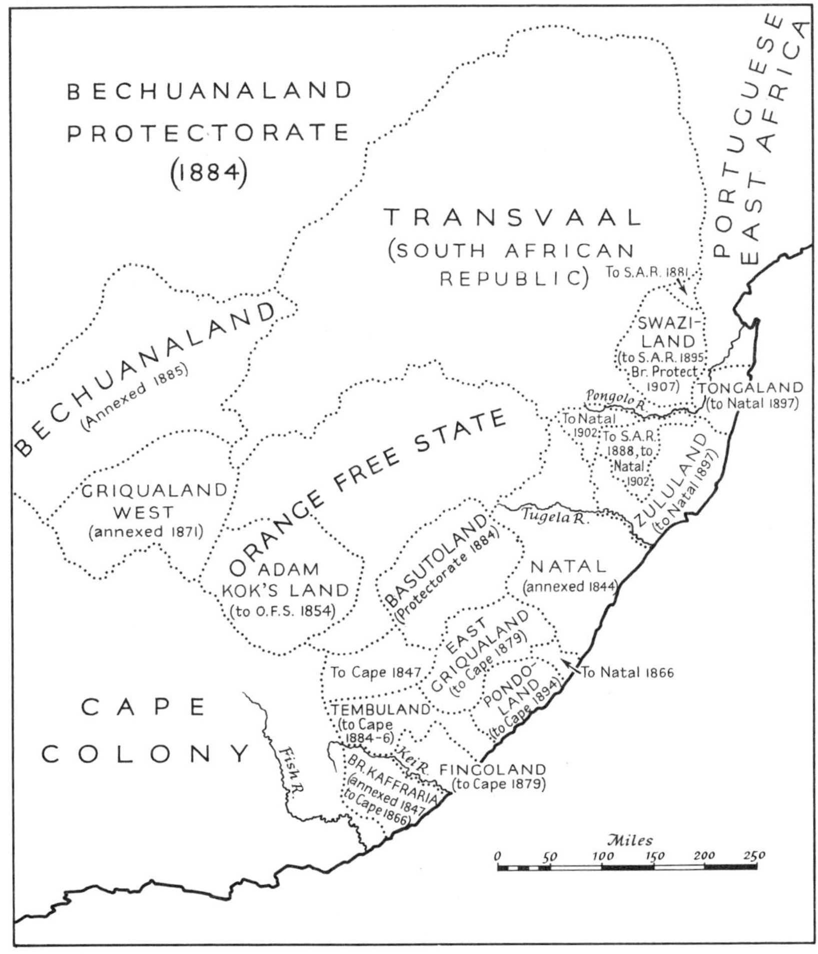

29 South Africa after the Sand River and Bloemfontein Conventions

Unlike other parts of Africa where white people are either temporarily or newly settled, white South Africans have a long separate history represented in this picture by kitchen furniture and equipment in an old Dutch settlers' house in the Cape

Constitutional development of the Cape

Closely related to the Conventions policy was constitutional reform at the Cape. British critics of colonial expenditure, and those who wished to see colonial rule replaced by more independent government, were agreed in the desire to allow settlers to take a larger part in administrative and financial responsibility. The first step in giving administrative powers to the settlers in South Africa had been taken in 1836 when municipal councils were set up. In 1852–3 the next major step was taken when provision was made for the Cape to have an elected parliament.

The Cape Parliament consisted of two houses. The lower house, or House of Assembly, was elected for five years at a time, and the upper house, or Legislative Council, was elected for ten years. When the Cape Parliament was established it was decided to carry on the tradition of legal equality between the races which had been established by the 50th Ordinance, and which had also been applied in the constitution of the municipal councils. There was to be no racial qualification for the vote for members of parliament. The only qualifications required were economic and these were set at a low level to make sure that at least some non-whites would be entitled to vote. This was known as the 'colour-blind' constitution, and under it considerable numbers of Cape coloured people came to exercise the vote, and in time some of the Cape Bantu also acquired the right to vote.

But although the economic qualifications for the vote were low they were unfavourable to non-Europeans, who were generally by far the poorest members of the community. There was always a large majority of white voters, and when the settlers feared that the situation might change they altered the qualifications to safeguard their majority.

When parliamentary institutions were later established in Natal the principle of the 'colour-blind' system was maintained, but so many difficulties were put in the way of Natal Bantu acquiring the vote that they were practically excluded.

The Cape Parliament, whose constitution was decided in 1853, was at first given only legislative powers. Executive power was still in the hands of the Governor and his officials. It was only in 1872 that the Cape acquired a constitution in which the ministers were chosen by Parliament and were responsible to it.

Grey and settlement in British Kaffraria

In 1854 Sir George Grey came to govern the Cape. He had been Governor of New Zealand, where he believed that he had successfully solved the problems of relations between the settlers and the Maori. He was therefore confident that he could solve the problems of racial conflict in South Africa. He had also enjoyed considerable freedom in the exercise of power, and he was impatient of control from Britain. One of his plans was to find a permanent solution to the problem of the eastern frontier. His idea was that if white and Bantu were brought into closer contact the Bantu would learn the farming practices and general culture of the whites, adopt white civilisation and cease to be a threat to security. Accordingly he planned to introduce white settlers into British Kaffraria and in fact settled considerable numbers of German settlers there.

Unfortunately the area was already overcrowded, and by depriving the Bantu of still more of their farming land his measures reduced them to desperate poverty.

The cattle killing

Another war would certainly have broken out if the Xhosa in despair had not looked to supernatural means of salvation. A woman prophet named Nonquase declared that, if all the cattle were slaughtered and the grain destroyed before an appointed day, the sun would rise in the west and the spirits of the ancestors, aided by a mighty wind, would return to help them drive the whites from their land. All who killed their cattle would receive new and better ones. Under her inspiration the Xhosa destroyed their food supplies wholesale, but when the day came no miracle occurred. The disillusioned and starving people were in no condition to fight. Thousands died of starvation though the British government rushed supplies of food to the area. Thousands more took refuge in the colony as workers on white farms. The fighting power of the Xhosa was broken for a time.

The Griquas' Great Trek

Another of Grey's plans was the settlement of Adam Kok's Griquas in a series of valleys at the base of the Drakensberg, between the Basuto and the coastal tribes. Even before the Sovereignty was given up these Griquas, whose territory lay along the Orange river around Philippolis, had been feeling the pressure of land-hungry Boers. After the creation of the Orange Free State the position became steadily worse. Adam Kok and his council made laws forbidding their subjects to lease land to whites but the temptation of immediate gain always proved too much, and once a white farmer was established it was practically impossible to get rid of him again. Though many of the Griquas were comparatively wealthy their territory was steadily shrinking. Adam accordingly decided to look for a new home and Grey proposed that he should settle in the valleys of what was then called Nomansland, where he would act as a buffer between the Basuto and the east coast tribes.

In 1861 Adam Kok sold the Philippolis lands to the Free State and his people undertook their own Great Trek to establish a new state in what is now called Griqualand East. There they built a Griqua republic which flourished for a time, but pressure from the Bantu and the weakness of the Griquas brought about its ruin. The Griqua progressively mortgaged their property to canteen-keepers from the Cape, in return for loans spent on drink and other commodities. Finally, the Griquas lost almost all their land.

Grey's federation scheme

It was with regard to the relations between the Cape and other white settler communities that Grey produced his most ambitious plans. He saw that the peace of the eastern frontier could not be separated from the effects of relations between the Boers and the Basuto and this was particularly impressed upon him by the outbreak of the first Free State-Basuto war.

The first Free State – Basuto war 1858

Though friendly relations between the new white Republic and Moshesh in Basutoland were maintained at first, the problem of the frontier inevitably brought them into conflict. In 1858 war broke out and Free State forces advanced towards Thaba Bosiu, but they were not strong enough to storm its precipitous slopes. In the meantime highly mobile groups of Basuto penetrated deep into the Free State. When the farmers camped in front of Thaba Bosiu learnt that their homes were in danger they suddenly broke up the camp and scattered to defend their families. The Free State President found himself in a desperate situation and appealed to Grey for help in making peace. Moshesh, anxious not to earn the hostility of the British, agreed. Under the first Treaty of Aliwal North, the Basuto gained a slight modification of their territory but not enough to satisfy the needs of their population. Moshesh agreed unwillingly to the arrangement. He felt that his people should have been given more after a successful war.

Grey then began to press with increasing determination for a federation of all the white states in South Africa. He argued that so

Thaba Bosiu, mountain stronghold of Moshesh (from a contemporary drawing)

long as the different white groups conducted their relations with their Bantu neighbours without any co-ordination there could be no stable peace in South Africa. What is more, none of the white states was strong enough on its own to maintain law and order by normal means along its frontiers. Incidents were unavoidable, and the only means such weak states possessed for dealing with them was to attack the Bantu in an all-out war, in the hope of striking terror into them. A federal government would adopt a uniform policy to the Bantu, and would be able to police its frontiers and suppress cattle raids by normal means without recourse to war. It would attract the most enlightened minds from the white population of the sub-continent, and it would be more likely to act impartially and justly towards the Bantu than a small local assembly made up of men whose interests were directly involved in the matters they debated. His arguments fell on deaf ears in the British Colonial Office, where it was felt that his schemes would inevitably involve the British government in the affairs of the interior, and thus in all the trouble and expense that it had tried to avoid by accepting the Conventions.

British rejection of federation

In 1859 Grey received a request from Britain to investigate the possibilities of a federation of the British colonies of the Cape, Natal and British Kaffraria. He took this as an invitation to proceed with his far wider scheme, and without authorisation from Britain he caused the idea of a South African federation to be discussed in the Free State Volksraad and introduced for discussion in the Cape Parliament. This was too much for the British government to tolerate and he was immediately recalled. With a change of government in Britain he was sent back the following year (1860) but with clear instructions not to raise the issue of federation again.

Renewed tension between Boers and Basuto

Although the British government rejected Grey's ideas, it soon found itself forced to go back on the Conventions policy and take the road he had suggested. The decisive factor in this was the developing situation between the Basuto and the Boers. The basis of the quarrel between Moshesh and the Free State was simple. As the Boer population increased they needed more and more land, but the Basuto population was also increasing and much of their land had already passed into Boer hands. The Warden line had left many Basuto settlements on the Free State side of the border, and the changes made after the first Free State-Basuto war did not fundamentally change this situation. The Boers could not tolerate Basuto living in their Republic except as servants on white farms, and as the demand for land became more acute they became increasingly impatient of the continued presence of Basuto villages on their side of the border. Moshesh did not see why the arrangement of frontiers should affect the right of those of his own people who were left on the Free State side to continue to live on their land. He had no room to accommodate them in his own overcrowded kingdom and he feared the effects on public opinion of supporting their expulsion. In 1865 the second Free State-Basuto war broke out.

J. H. Brand, President of the Free State

The second Free State-Basuto war

Brand, the new President of the Free State, was both able and forceful. He took advantage of the gunpowder clause in the Bloemfontein Convention. Moshesh on the other hand was very old, he could no longer keep a firm hold on affairs, and his sons were divided against one another over the question of the succession. The Free State forces were able to overrun most of the fertile areas of the country, and although they failed to capture Thaba Bosiu they were able to reduce the Basuto people to starvation. Moshesh, faced with this state

Moshesh, King of the Basuto

of affairs, decided to buy time, and in April 1866 signed the Treaty of Thaba Bosiu in which he ceded almost all the cultivable area of his kingdom to the Free State. It was only a ruse to enable his people to replenish their food supplies, and as soon as the commandos withdrew the Basuto reoccupied their land and began planting their crops.

British annexation of Basutoland

In the meantime the plight of the Basuto began to attract closer attention from the British government. It was clear that if the terms of the treaty were fulfilled the Basuto kingdom would break up. The Free State on the other hand lacked the means to replace the government it was about to destroy. Instead of a relatively peaceful and stable African kingdom there would be chaos which would undoubtedly affect the eastern frontier area, throwing it into turmoil again. Governor Woodhouse, who succeeded Grey in 1862, urged the British government to respond to the repeated requests of Moshesh and annex the Basuto kingdom. Pressure in the same direction was exercised by philanthropic opinion, which was further inflamed by the fact that the Boers had expelled the French missionaries from their stations in the Basuto kingdom.

The Boers soon realised that the Treaty of Thaba Bosiu was no more than a trick. The first farmers who went to take up land allocated to them in the area ceded under the treaty were immediately murdered by the Basuto. The war then started again, and again the

258

Basuto were reduced to starvation, but Moshesh continued to hold out on his mountain top, addressing ever more pressing requests for annexation to the Governor. Woodhouse secretly urged him to hold on at all costs till he could get the necessary permission. At last, after Natal had shown an interest in taking over the Basuto kingdom, Woodhouse received permission to annex the area provided Natal would take responsibility. The Governor used this to announce the immediate annexation of the Basuto kingdom and sent the Cape police to hoist the British flag. He subsequently stated that annexation to Natal was impossible and the Basuto kingdom became a direct dependency of the British crown.

The Basuto kingdom had been saved and Moshesh died peacefully and content. But the Basuto had suffered grave losses. Woodhouse

30 Basutoland showing the territorial effect of repeated attempts to annexe the territory

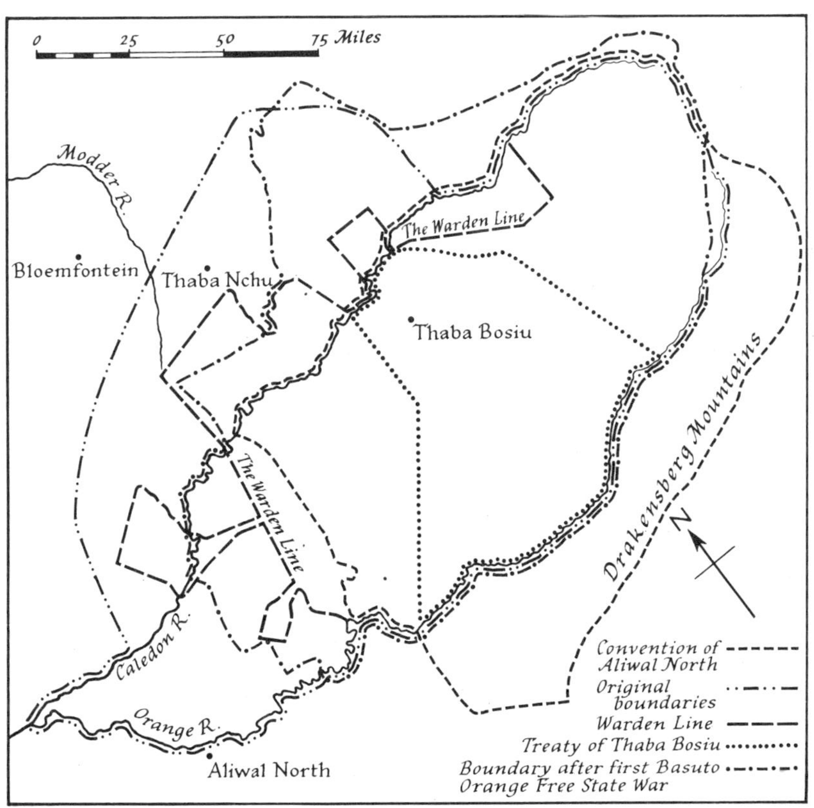

was forced to allow the Free State to keep a large part of their fertile land, and thereafter the Basuto were unable to support themselves on their own territory without a proportion of the population going out to earn their living as workers in the white-controlled parts of South Africa. Though Basutoland (now Lesotho) has been able to survive as a separate political unit in southern Africa it has remained from the economic point of view a satellite of white South Africa.

The diamond fields

The annexation of Lesotho meant a definite reversal of the conventions policy, and was an obvious breach of the Bloemfontein agreement. Another step in the same direction soon followed. The discovery of diamonds in the land round the meeting of the Orange and Vaal rivers had revolutionary effects for the development of South Africa. A country which up to that time had been dependent on agriculture of a relatively unprofitable type was suddenly discovered to possess fabulous mineral wealth. Railways would soon be layed across the vast expanse that had previously known only the groaning ox-waggon, and South Africa would be launched on the first step towards becoming the industrial country it is today. Soon after diamonds were first discovered in 1858, near where the Vaal and Harts rivers meet, the rush began and hordes of enthusiastic diggers of many different nationalities arrived in the diamond fields.

Part of the area in which diamonds were found was claimed by the Orange Free State, and part by the Transvaal. These claims would probably have been accepted by the British government if a lawyer named Arnot had not seen the possibilities of making a claim to the area in the name of the Griqua chief Waterboer. He managed to get himself appointed by the chief as his agent and then advanced claims in his name, strongly supported by the diggers themselves who rejected the authority of the republics.

By this time the British government had begun to feel that the only answer to South Africa's problems was a federation along the lines laid down by Grey, in which the Cape would be the senior partner. It was felt that this should be achieved at Cape expense, however, and for this purpose it would be desirable to give the Colony responsible government. On the other hand if the two Republics became too rich and powerful they might not wish to join a British federation. At the same time philanthropic groups urged British annexation of the diamond fields to save the Griquas from Boer slavery. At the diamond

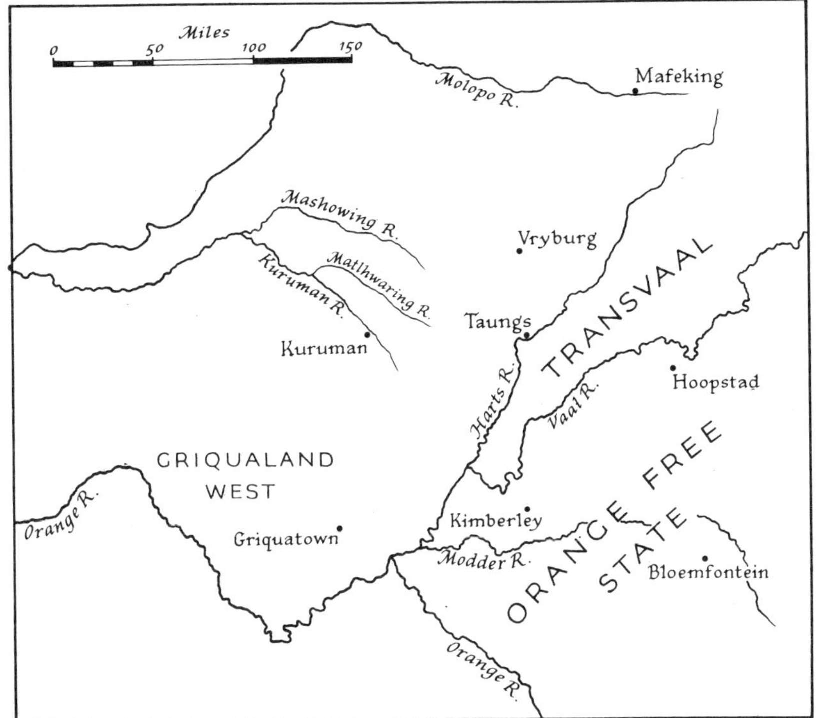

31 The diamond yielding areas of South Africa. The political problems
described in the text resulting from the bordering of three separate
territories on the diamond area are clearly seen

fields the situation became increasingly chaotic, with a turbulent population living under no recognised government. A sailor named Matthew
Parker hoisted a flag and declared an independent Diggers' Republic.

The British annexation of the diamond fields

The Governor at the Cape, Barkly, was given authority to annex the
lands belonging to Waterboer if the Cape Parliament agreed to take
them over, but the Cape Parliament did not give a firm assurance and
the Governor was anxious to act before the situation became still more
difficult. In 1871 he hoisted the British flag. This action was bitterly
resented by the Republics, and public opinion in the Cape largely
supported them. The Cape Parliament refused to take over the
diamond fields which became another direct British responsibility.

Sir James Molteno

Carnarvon's confederation policy

In 1872, shortly after the annexation of the diamond fields, the Cape was given responsible government and Molteno became the first Prime Minister. In Britain the Liberal government fell and was replaced by the Conservatives with Disraeli as Prime Minister and Carnarvon as Colonial Secretary. Carnarvon had a great belief in the value of federal arrangements for creating unity amongst communities of different culture; he had been responsible for bringing about a federal constitution in Canada. He saw a federation of the white states as the obvious answer to South Africa's problems and determined to take an active hand in bringing it about. Another reason for moving in this direction was the feeling that the Free State might have been badly treated over the diamond fields, and federation would be a way for Britain to get rid of its unwanted responsibility for the diamond area.

Carnarvon wanted to go smoothly and therefore wished to be sure of the votes of as many of the white states as possible. He therefore sent Wolseley to try to persuade the settlers in Natal to agree to an increase in the proportion of nominated officials in their legislative council, so that the British government would be in full control. At the same time he sent round a letter to the heads of governments in South Africa suggesting a conference to discuss federation. Finally he sent his friend Froude, the historian, to South Africa to use his influence in the cause of the scheme.

Cape resistance to Carnarvon's plan

Carnarvon's plan met with strong opposition from Molteno, the Cape Prime Minister. He saw it as interference in the affairs of a self-governing state. He did not want to share the revenues of the Cape with the poorer Republics at a time when these revenues were already heavily committed to a programme of railway building, and he was afraid that federation might upset the balance of parties at the Cape and bring about the fall of his government. Froude, however, began a public agitation in favour of federation which almost forced Molteno to change his mind. The Orange Free State was not unwilling to consider the matter. In the Transvaal, Pretorius had been deposed for his failure to get better terms from the British over the diamond fields and the more liberal and cosmopolitan Burgers had been elected President. He was away in Europe trying to raise money for a railway line to be built from Delagoa Bay to the Transvaal but his deputy indicated willingness to consider the proposal. At the crucial moment, however, Carnarvon wrote to suggest shifting the conference to London, and this gave everyone an excuse for not taking part.

British annexation of the Transvaal

Faced with this check Carnarvon looked round for some means of hastening the federation on which he had set his heart, and an opportunity seemed to arise in the Transvaal. The basic situation in that Republic was similar to other parts of South Africa. As the white population increased it occupied more and more land, gradually squeezing out the Bantu and forcing them to become labourers on the white farms. In the north of the Republic, however, the mountains of the Zoutpansberg offered something like the defensive possibilities of the Basuto mountains, and there the Pedi tribe under Sikunyana had built up a paramountcy similar to that of Moshesh. Inevitably, the Pedi and the Boers came into conflict over land, and this was made particularly acute as part of the land occupied by the Pedi had been used as security for the loan which Burgers raised in Europe for the Delagoa Bay Railway. When Sikunyana refused to relinquish this land the Boers marched against him. But the Pedi defended themselves bravely in their mountain strongholds. Horse sickness killed many of the Boer horses. The President was unpopular for his religious views, which were considered too liberal by many settlers. Suddenly the Boers broke up their camp and went home, leaving Sikunyana victorious.

The position of the Transvaal Republic was then desperate. The railway scheme had failed and the state was heavily in debt to Cape banks, which refused further credit. There was a danger that the Zulu would take advantage of the situation to invade the Republic. Carnarvon thought that if he could annex the Transvaal it would be easy to bring about federation, as all the white states except the Orange Free State would then be British. He sent an emissary, Shepstone, to see whether the Volksraad could be persuaded to agree. It did not, but several members confessed privately that it was the only way out of a desperate situation, and Shepstone hoisted the British flag in spite of all protests. Carnarvon then felt sure that his plans were bound to succeed and sent Sir Bartle Frere to South Africa as Governor and High Commissioner to achieve the federation.

Reactions to the annexation of the Transvaal

But instead of federation coming nearer it seemed to become more difficult. The Free State refused to consider it until the Boers of the Transvaal had a representative assembly and were allowed to express their opinions on the annexation. Molteno in the Cape adopted a similar attitude and in the Transvaal the new British government became increasingly unpopular. At first the intention had been to allow the Boers to have a representative council, but Shepstone delayed creating it for fear it might refuse to ratify the annexation. The longer he delayed, the more hostile the Boers became and the greater the volume of protests. Hence the introduction of representative government continued to be postponed. What is more, though the government was generous at first, the British Treasury insisted that the Transvaal must pay for itself, and this meant collecting fairly heavy taxation from a people who were notorious for refusing to pay taxes even to their own government.

The Xhosa resistance war of 1877

In 1878 Sir Bartle Frere seized an opportunity to get rid of one of the main obstacles to federation. In 1877 another war had broken out on the eastern frontier and Molteno asked for the aid of imperial troops. But he refused to allow the Governor to take part in directing the campaign and Frere, aware that the Prime Minister was growing unpopular, dismissed him. A new government at the Cape, under

264

Sir Gordon Sprigg, was favourable to federation, but the problem of the Orange Free State remained. It would never agree to federation until the Transvaalers were given the right to speak their mind, but to allow the Transvaalers to hold a representative assembly while the government was so unpopular would be dangerous.

The 'War of the Guns'

At this time the peoples of all the white states were seized with a deep sense of insecurity for, with the opening of the diamond fields, a tremendous demand for Bantu labour had been created. Workers flocked to the diggings from all parts of South Africa and even from the Ndebele kingdom beyond the Limpopo. At the diamond fields they met their fellows of many different tribes and began to develop a sense of solidarity in face of white dominance. What is more, the greatest attraction of work at the diamond fields was the possibility of acquiring guns, the basis and symbol of the white man's power. A trade in firearms developed, openly tolerated by the Griqualand authorities at first and later conducted illegally, and this seemed to the nervous whites to threaten an alteration in the balance of power.

After the frontier war of 1877–8, Sprigg decided to undertake the major operation of disarming the tribes bordering the eastern frontier, and a law was passed requiring all guns to be surrendered. This applied also to the Basuto, since administration of the Basuto kingdom had been handed over to the Cape in 1871. The measure was bitterly resented by the Basuto, who saw no reason why they should be punished by the confiscation of their weapons and who knew only too well how their military strength had prevented the seizure of their lands in the past. But Sprigg insisted, in spite of the advice of the administrative officers and missionaries in the Basuto kingdom and petitions from the chiefs. The result was the outbreak of the 'War of the Guns' in 1880. This long drawn out struggle was fought entirely by the Cape forces and was perhaps the only war in South Africa to result in a Bantu victory, for not only did the Cape fail to break Basuto resistance and have to agree to a settlement under which the Basuto kept their guns, but the Colonial government relinquished the administration of the Basuto kingdom to the imperial authorities. Henceforth the Basuto kingdom was to remain a separate entity from the rest of South Africa, and on 4th October 1966 became the independent state of Lesotho.

Cetewayo, King of the Zulus

The Zulu war

The Transvaalers had long advanced claims to a strip of land known as the Blood River Territory, which was claimed by the Zulu also. Sir Bartle Frere realised that if the Zulu were defeated the Transvaalers could be given the land and could be expected to become more favourably disposed towards federation. The Cape Province too, would be more willing to accept federation if the burden of defending Natal was lightened. Frere therefore came to see the Zulu kingdom as the key to the South African situation and prepared to bring matters to a head. He set up a commission to look into rival claims to the Blood river lands, confident that it would decide in favour of the Boers and that the Zulu King, Cetewayo, would fight rather than give up his territory. Troops were sent to Natal in preparation for the coming struggle. The commission, however, found in favour of the Zulu and declared the Transvaal claims to be valueless.

This left Frere in an awkward situation and he determined to precipitate war with the Zulu by any means. He took advantage of a violation of Natal territory, by warriors pursuing a runaway wife of the king, to send an ultimatum demanding the break up of the military system on which the Zulu state was based. In 1879 the British troops marched into Zululand for what was expected to be a short and decisive campaign. But almost incredible thoughtlessness and mismanagement led a whole regiment to be trapped by the Zulu at Isandhlwana, with their ammunition in boxes that could not be opened. The Zulu army was able to follow its traditional tactics with

266

success and the regiment was almost completely destroyed. The news of this military disaster produced a great swing of opinion in Britain. Frere was censured for his Zulu policy but not recalled. Instead a lieutenant-governor was sent to Natal who proved incapable of co-operating with Frere. The Zulu war was continued and at the Battle of Ulundi the Zulu armies were finally defeated. Cetewayo was taken a prisoner to Cape Town but British policy in South Africa had lost momentum. Instead of annexing Zululand the government tried to keep it militarily weak by setting up thirteen chieftaincies in place of the old kingdom.

First Anglo-Boer war

Noticing the weakening in British policy the Boers of the Transvaal redoubled their protests and even held open-air meetings condemning the annexation. In Britain an election campaign was under way and

32 The area which the first Boer and the Zulu wars were fought over, showing the positions of the major battles. Battles in the Zulu war are underlined

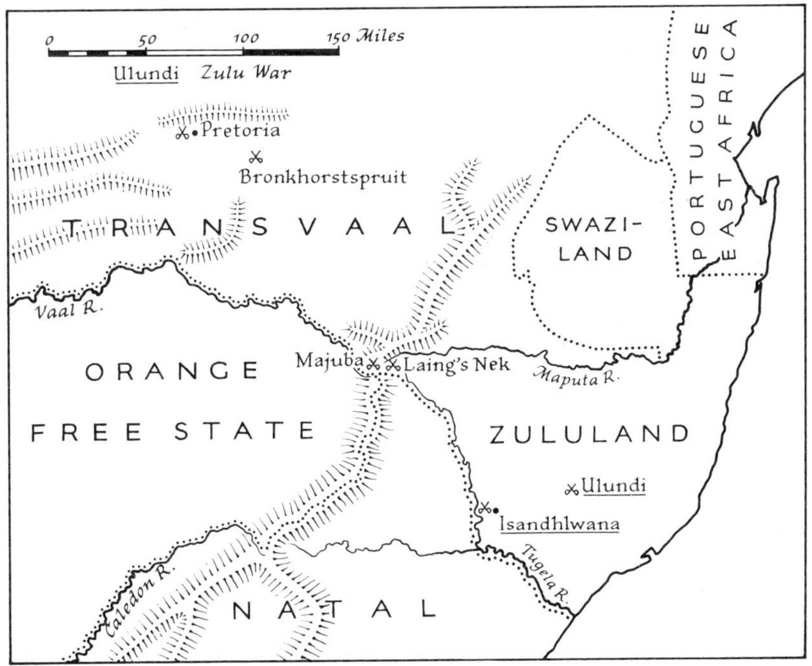

Gladstone then in opposition condemned the annexation and the suppression of Boer freedom. The Transvaal was tense with expectation but later, when he came to form his own government, Gladstone discovered the difficulties of the problem. Queen Victoria was strongly opposed to surrendering British territory and the philanthropic wing of his party disliked the idea of leaving the Transvaal Bantu to the mercy of the Boer. Gladstone decided to hold on, but the Boers were no longer prepared to wait. They rose in rebellion, besieged the British garrison in Pretoria and routed a relief column at Bronkhorstspruit. Troops were rushed up from Natal but they met a severe check at Laing's Nek. Shaken in his resolution Gladstone decided to negotiate, but before any settlement was reached the final battle was fought at Majuba (1881). The British forces were decisively defeated and the commander killed. Gladstone was then prepared to make peace on any terms less than complete surrender.

The Pretoria Convention 1881

By the Pretoria Convention the Transvaal was given self-government under British suzerainty (paramountcy). Foreign policy was to remain under British control and there was to be a British Resident in Pretoria with the right to exercise authority in regard to native policy. In practice the Transvaal had won the war and regained independence in all matters except relations with other European powers. The attempt to produce a British federation in South Africa had ended in failure and a policy of withdrawal which was similar to that of the Sand River and Bloemfontein Conventions. By its lack of resolve and its inconsistent policies in the period after the Great Trek, Britain had failed to exert a decisive influence on the main process of South African history and the type of society growing up there. Throughout the years between the Great Trek and the first Boer war the outstanding historical development had been the steady pressure of the expanding white communities on the Bantu, the restriction of Bantu landholding to areas too small to support their population, and the incorporation of the Bantu as a labouring class in white dominated society. By the time of the first Boer war this process was already reaching its last stages. Officially independent Bantu peoples still occupied large areas in South Africa but they were already to a great extent economically and politically dependent on the white areas. It only remained for them to be formally annexed and placed under white administration.

Part **four**

Middle Africa

10 Middle Africa 1: the prelude

We now turn to the nineteenth century history of the peoples of
'Middle Africa' – that is, that part of the continent north of the Rovuma
river and south of a line drawn from the end of the 'West African bulge'
to the base of the East African Horn. This area is now divided between the states of Angola, Gabon and the two Congos in the west,
and Kenya, Uganda, Rwanda, Burundi and Tanzania in the east.
In the nineteenth century it was divided into an even greater number
of political units large and small. Nevertheless, whatever may be said
of earlier periods, the history of this area in the nineteenth century
had in some ways a natural unity. This does not mean that Middle
Africa was unaffected by events taking place elsewhere on the continent. The wider consequences of Shaka's career in southern Africa
affected people's lives as far north as Lake Victoria. But Middle
Africa was to some extent cut off from events further south by the
empty places of the Kalahari desert, and it was beyond the reach of
the Boer farmer whose presence gave a special twist to the history of
southern Africa.

The Bantu-speaking peoples

To the north, the line defined above is purely artificial. All along it
there has been constant contact between people on either side. Before
the nineteenth century whole peoples had come down into Middle
Africa from the north and this did not stop when the century began.
This line, however, does roughly represent the northern boundary
of the equatorial forest, and beyond it lie the open spaces of the
savannah, in which the civilisations of the Sudan had been built and
prospered. The Sudanic peoples tended to look northward and eastward across parkland and desert to North Africa, the Nile Valley and to

Mecca. The equatorial forest was strange to them, the economy and rhythm of life of its peoples was in many ways different from their own. For them, therefore, the forest was a considerable natural obstacle to their southward progress, and the largest movements of Sudanic and Nilotic cattlemen went round its eastern fringes to Uganda and Kenya. For the Bantu-speaking peoples on the other hand, who formed the overwhelming majority of the population of Middle Africa, the forest was their natural habitat. Most of them lived in or near the forested areas of the Congo basin and around the Great Lakes.

The Bantu were not, however, exclusively a forest people. They might grow their tubers or bananas in forest clearings, but they could equally turn their hands to the cultivation of maize or millet, or the rearing of cattle in the open savannah. For this reason, the southern and eastern edge of the forest, which cut Middle Africa practically in half, did not form the same sort of line of division as it did in the north. On the contrary, the coming together of the two different types of environment seems to have had a stimulating effect upon the people living just inside or just outside the forest, for it was along its fringes that the largest states in Middle Africa were to be found at the opening of the nineteenth century.

The kingly states

In the modern world, where easy communications bring people together, and the division of labour and growth of large cities make man dependent on man, the large, centralised state uniting millions of men is the most usual form of political organisation. The main problem facing statesmen is to ensure that men who cannot live apart from one another should live peaceably together. But in the past, when each village could supply its own wants from the produce of its land, there was no reason for large numbers of men to accept the common rule of a single government. If men consented to belong to one of the larger kingdoms they did so out of belief in the strength of the moral and material power of those who ruled. If that belief waned, the kingdom would crumble and divide into its separate parts – that is into the many self-supporting village communities of which it had been built up. Royal dynasties in Europe before the commercial and industrial revolution were often faced with the danger that their states would fall apart through internal revolt or foreign defeat. Similarly in Middle Africa at the beginning of the nineteenth century some of the

272

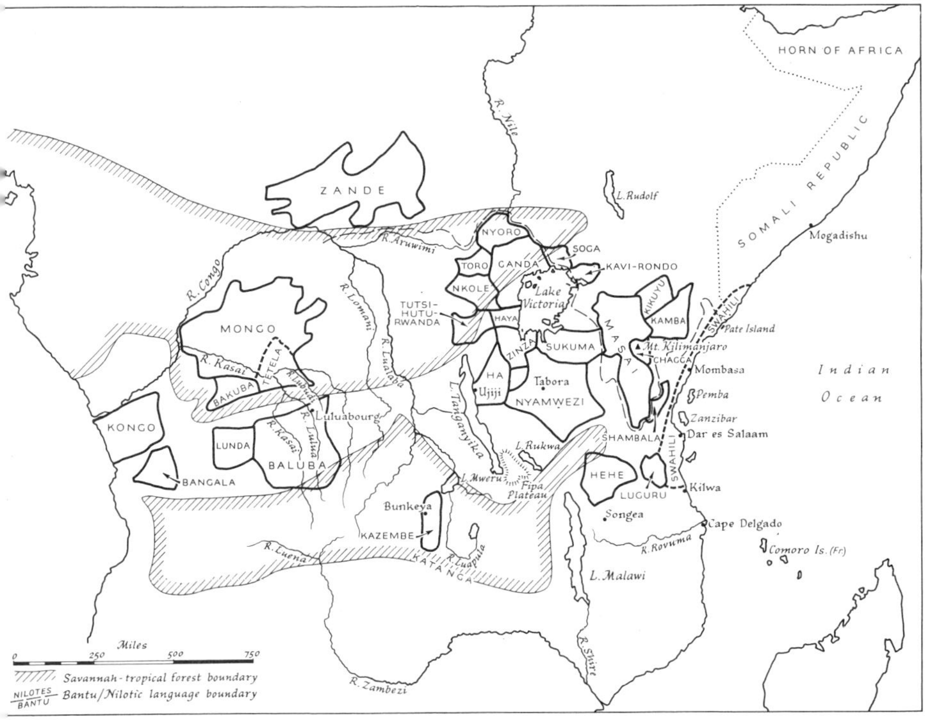

33 The larger groups of Middle African peoples mentioned in the text

A drawing of San Salvadore, the capital of the old Kongo kingdom

kingly states were extending their boundaries while others were losing their power and one in particular had practically disappeared.

The kingdom of Kongo

This was the kingdom of Kongo which in its greatest days in the fifteenth and sixteenth centuries had extended on either side of the Congo river. Since its king's conversion at the beginning of the sixteenth century it had been a Christian kingdom, but this had not won it the permanent friendship of the Christian Portuguese ruling in Angola. In fact it was the Portuguese who by their slave raiding and their assistance to Kongo's enemies were mainly responsible for the kingdom's downfall in the middle of the seventeenth century. From that time the power of Kongo's kings steadily declined, until by the nineteenth century their rule was respected in only a few villages. The Christianity that they had adopted practically died out. By the nineteenth century the kingdom and its religion were only a distant memory among the people of the various self-governing Kongo villages, though neither were entirely forgotten. Both were to be revived in a new form during the nineteenth and twentieth centuries.

The Lunda Empire, Kazembe

About the time that the Kongo Kingdom began to disintegrate, another kingly state to the south east, the Lunda Empire, was rapidly expanding. The original home of the Lunda dynasty lay east of the Lulua river and just south of the present day town of Luluabourg. From there a number of members of the royal lineage branched out to the west in the early seventeenth century to found the state of Bangala in present-day Angola, and to impose themselves as a ruling aristocracy over the peoples in the valley of the Luena river to the south. While these new and separate political systems were being established, the Lunda dynasty at home had linked itself by marriage with the ruling family of the neighbouring Baluba Empire, adopted patrilineal in place of matrilineal succession and began to push eastward. Under Yavo Naweji (c. 1660–75) the first Lunda ruler to take the title Mwata Yamvo, the organisation and ceremonials of the state were established and its borders extended to the Lubudi river.

His successors in the early eighteenth century conquered upper Katanga, crossed the Luapula river and established the tributary

Lunda state of Kazembe, to the south and east of Lake Mweru. Kazembe controlled the copper of the Katanga. Kazembe and the Lunda Empire together formed a great trading system half way across the south of Middle Africa, in commercial contact with the Portuguese both in Mozambique to the east and in Angola to the west. The empire was loosely knit. The governors of Kazembe, for example, were all but independent of the Mwata Yamvo. But the political system of the Lunda Empire nevertheless carried great prestige. At the beginning of the nineteenth century the Lunda Empire and its dependencies were still at the height of their power though they were soon to meet a serious challenge from rising new forces.

A carving representing Chamba Bolongongo,
ninety-third ruler of the Bakuba or Bushongo tribe

Peoples of the Congo Basin

To the north of Lunda and Kazembe lay the old Baluba Empire, large, but by the nineteenth century already beginning to break up into a mass of unorganised small communities. The last great Baluba ruler was Kumwimbu Ngombe who held power in the late eighteenth century. While he was on the throne the state was run efficiently and its borders were extended eastward as far as the west bank of Lake Tanganyika. But after his death his sons quarrelled over the succession and this internal strife left the Baluba state a prey to powerful neighbours during the nineteenth century.

The Baluba's neighbours to the north were the numerous but unorganised Mongo peoples of the equatorial forest, among whom were no kingly states of the size of Lunda or Luba. But to the north-west, in the area enclosed by the Sankuru and Kasai rivers, and just on the edge of the forest, lay the Bakuba state, comparatively small but well organised and famous for its fine carving and raffia work. Bakuba was organised for peace rather than war. The traditions of the state looked back with pride to the hero King Chamba Bolongongo who ruled in the seventeenth century, and who was renowned not for his conquests but for his learning and his introduction of new crops and crafts to Bakuba. In the government the leaders of the craft guilds had an honoured place, and in the eighteenth century the Bakuba extended their trade with their neighbours in the Congo Basin and had little to do with the more warlike commerce with non-African traders on the coast.

The inter-lacustrine kingdoms

To the east and north of the Congo Basin lay another string of kingdoms, most of them smaller in area than those we have just discussed but some equally large in terms of population. They are usually referred to as the inter-lacustrine (between-the-lakes) kingdoms and among them were the kingdoms of the Ha, Zinza and Haya peoples, Rwanda, Nkole, Ganda and Nyoro, and the Avongara kingdoms of Zande country. As these kingdoms resembled each other in various respects it is possible to describe a number of features of their political organisation which were more or less common to all. The king usually possessed very definite, even autocratic, executive powers in addition to the ritual and symbolic eminence accorded to monarchs in other parts of Middle Africa. All authority in the state centred on his person and, though he entrusted a part of that authority to his provincial governors and they in turn to the sub-chiefs in the districts, these officers of the king were only strong because the king allowed them to share his own overwhelming strength. The governors who ruled the provinces on the king's behalf were appointed and dismissed by the king and only in a few kingdoms, such as Rwanda, were they allowed to make their posts hereditary. Another safeguard for the monarch was the fact that in most kingdoms no clear provision was made for the succession to the throne, and thus there was no fear of opposition grouping round the person of a designated heir. In each of the kingdoms, the ruling dynasty was not indigenous, they were not of the same blood with the people they ruled. They had immigrated into their countries either in the recent past as in the case of the Avongara, or several centuries earlier like the Bite dynasty of Nyoro. Whether newcomers or long established rulers, whether their control had been imposed peacefully or by conquest, the royal families of these kingdoms made no attempt to conceal the fact of their separate origin. It was recorded in the tribal histories and often connected with some historical explanation for the superiority of men of royal birth.

Most of the states had a centralised bureaucratic form of administration. The tribute paid to the central government was seldom small, and could amount in some cases to a third of each family's labour. Only the regulation of family matters was left to lineage heads chosen by the local communities; most other affairs were in the hands of chiefs or sub-chiefs appointed directly or indirectly by the king. The royal officials, together with the members of the royal dynasty formed a superior group in society; they were respected throughout the country and stood apart from the ordinary commoners. This group alone could seriously challenge the power of the king. In most cases they did not do so. But in some kingdoms, such as Rwanda and Nkole, the royal officials were mostly chosen from among the members of immigrant aristocratic families – the Tutsi in Rwanda, the Hima in Nkole – who by their birth possessed a status higher than that of the ordinary person. In these cases the royal officials had a double claim to power and they were inclined to regard the king as only slightly superior to themselves. At the other end of the scale was the Kingdom of Ganda where there was no hereditary aristocracy and where the Kabaka or king chose his officials mostly from among the commoners. But even there, as we shall see, a particular set of historical circumstances led to a revolt of the officials against the crown.

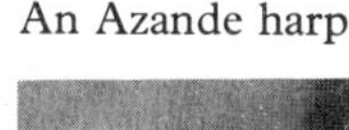

A young Mututsi showing the white robes and traditional hairstyle now rarely worn

An Azande harp

The Zande states

The kingdoms mentioned were of various sizes at the beginning of the nineteenth century and some were expanding while others were on the decline. Among those which were expanding were the Avongara kingdoms of Zande country. The Avongara dynasty with its related Ambomu followers only established itself in the Zande country during the eighteenth century. But by the late nineteenth century Avongara rule had been extended to an area corresponding to much of what is today northern Congo and parts of the south of the Central African and Sudan Republics. One of the motive forces behind this rapid expansion was the lack of provision for a regular succession to the throne. At the death of a king, his sons contended for the succession and those who failed either submitted to their successful brother or carved out new states for themselves. In the early days, when the Avongara were surrounded by weak neighbours, it was comparatively easy for disappointed princes to conquer and create new kingdoms. At their father's death, they could usually command the services of the standing army in the district they governed. They would invade the territories of the nearest small tribes and secure the submission of the chiefs. Then they would infiltrate the chiefdoms with their own Ambomu settlers, the tribesmen would be instructed as to the strength and virtues of the new regime, and when each indigenous chief died he would be succeeded by one of the sons or followers of the newly established Avongara ruler. In this way the Avongara kingdoms multiplied until by 1880 there were about fifteen of them. But by then easy conquests were becoming more difficult to find, struggles for the succession were consequently more bitter and prolonged and the Avongara kingdoms were beginning to weaken just at the time when they came into conflict with powerful forces from the north.

Ganda and Nyoro

East of Zande country the Ganda Kingdom was also expanding at the beginning of the nineteenth century and had been for some considerable time – mostly at the expense of the neighbouring Kingdom of Nyoro. Its methods of conquest were often similar to the Avongara in that the Ganda kings usually confirmed the rule of chiefs of newly conquered tribes, replacing them later by reliable officials from the royal circle. But the Ganda Kingdom did not subdivide on the

Kabaka's death nor was there any hereditary aristocratic clan. The main areas of Ganda expansion in the early nineteenth century were the subdivided chiefdoms of Soga country in the north-west and of Haya in the south. Both of these had formerly been under the influence of Nyoro, which towards the end of the seventeenth century had been a large empire with boundaries extending as far as Zande country on the west and Rwanda on the south. During the eighteenth century Nyoro lost much of its outlying territories, either through successful revolts or war with Ganda and Nkole. In the third decade of the nineteenth century the province of Toro broke away from the Nyoro Kingdom, but failed to secure its complete independence until the intervention of the British sixty years later. Despite this, Nyoro was still a force to be reckoned with in the nineteenth century and it remained one of the largest of the inter-lacustrine kingdoms. In the south the Kingdom of Rwanda was pushing its boundaries northward at the beginning of the period, and continued to do so throughout the nineteenth century at the expense of the small neighbouring Hutu communities.

The Hima aristocracies

The kingdoms of the Ha, Zinza and Haya peoples were mostly small, although the Haya state of Karangwe could rank with Ganda and Nyoro in the early nineteenth century. In fact some of these small states could scarcely be described as more than chiefdoms. Their rulers were mostly drawn from immigrant families of Hima pastoralists – the same who formed the aristocracies of the Nkole and, to a lesser extent, the Nyoro Kingdoms. Here, perhaps the most important historical fact to note is the gradual imposition of Hima rule upon the indigenous communities. At the beginning of the nineteenth century Hima rule was a fairly recent occurrence in much of this area and Hima chiefdoms were beginning to appear among the neighbouring tribes of Sukumaland and many other parts of western Tanzania. At the outset the Hima usually played the role of peacemakers between the various small communities, then through their superior political talents they gradually changed their function from that of judge to that of ruler. In Sukumaland in the early nineteenth century the Hima were still mostly judges but the stirring events of the ensuing years were to enable many of them rapidly to assume full political power.

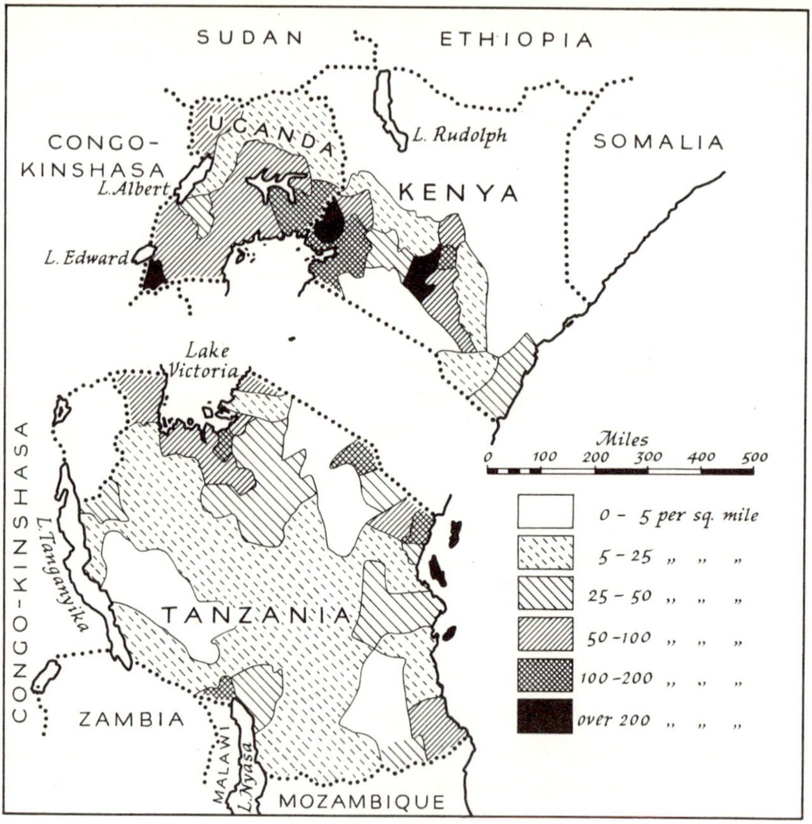

34 Population density in eastern Africa. The map is in two parts as
information from the different countries does not in all cases agree

A Masai with traditional
hairstyle and clothing
at Tabora

Peoples of the east

There were no states of comparable size among the peoples of present-day Kenya and Tanzania at the beginning of the nineteenth century. Over much of the area, particularly of northern Kenya and central Tanzania, one could hardly expect large states to emerge, since the infertility of the land would not support such a large concentrated population as was to be found in Rwanda or on the northern shores of Lake Victoria. The Kikuyu people in the Kenya highlands were numerous and so were the Chagga of Mount Kilimanjaro, but for the most part their village communities regulated their own affairs. They were also to a great extent cut off from events in the inter-lacustrine area by the Masai pastoralists, who tended their herds across a great wedge of territory in central Kenya and north-central

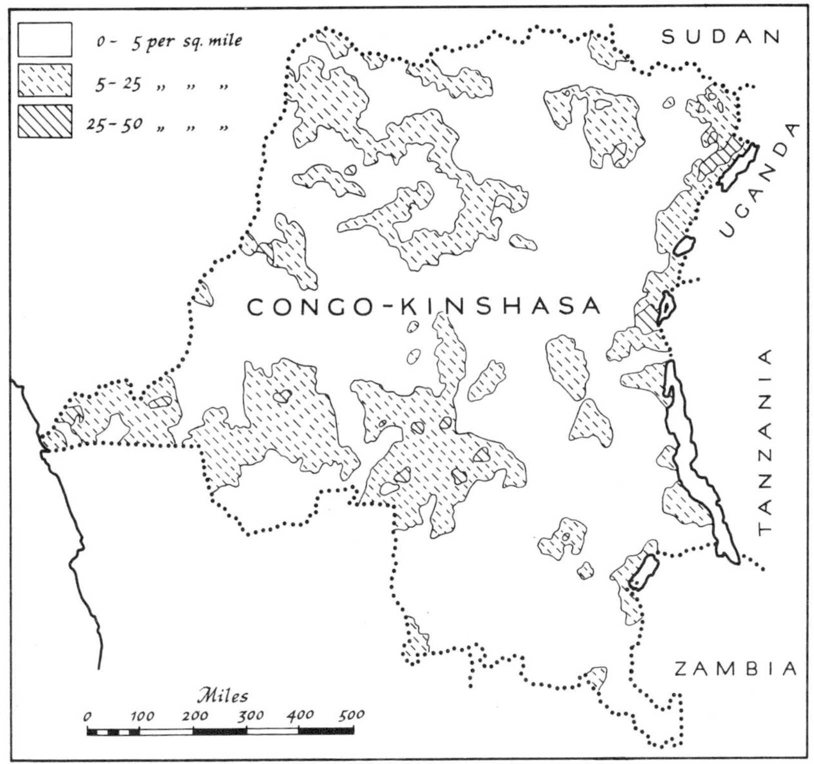

35 Popularity density in the Congo (Kinshasa). Note the low population density in this heavily forested area

Tanzania. The Masai were a warrior race, terrible to their enemies, and their presence obstructed east-west communications over a considerable area of East Africa. By the middle of the nineteenth century however they had begun to retreat northwards, and this made contact easier between the trading communities on the coast and the main populations of Middle Africa to the westward.

Whether the subjects of the larger kingly states, or the inhabitants of autonomous villages, most of the people, like farmers everywhere else in the world at the time, did not concern themselves much with high politics. In the kingly states the struggle for office was left to those born to rule or the adventurous few who were willing to run the very considerable risks of attendance at the royal court in the hope of rising to a position of power. Those who lived in the small self-regulating communities were if anything more politically minded than their counterparts in the kingly states, for there a substantial proportion of the people were involved in dispensing justice and deciding on peace or war. But politics in these communities were on a small scale and did not involve large numbers of men. For the most part people went about their daily tasks, clearing bush, planting crops, cultivating new village land, fending off illness, performing their religious rituals, marrying and raising children. One cannot say in general that there was any wide movement either toward or away from the creation of larger states. In the inter-lacustrine area certainly, the smaller communities were losing ground in favour of wider political organisations. But the history of the Baluba and Kongo Empires showed that the reverse could also happen. If anything it would seem there was a general disposition among the people in favour of unity, which was perhaps related to the widespread belief in the existence of a single High God. Many of the monarchs made use of this belief to consolidate the people's loyalty, and it would seem that when the larger states broke down they did so more because of struggles for power among the ruling groups than because of any general withdrawal of loyalty on the part of the people to the idea of the state.

Weapons used in Middle Africa: the Prussian needle gun and opposite

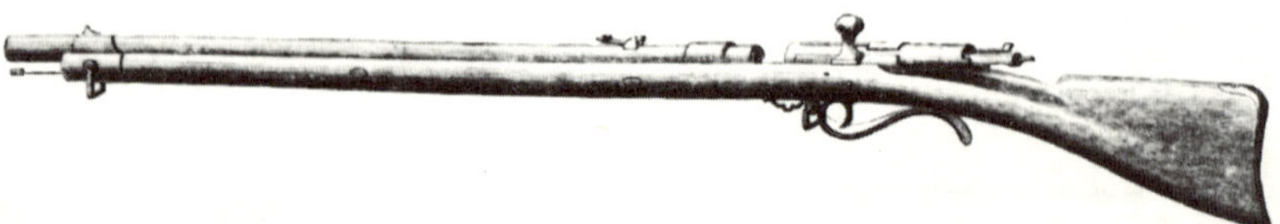

Weapons used in Middle Africa: *right* an eighteenth century musket with fixed bayonet. *Left* a nineteenth century officer of an indigenous East African army armed with a repeater rifle.

Firearms from abroad

While it is difficult to say that the history of Middle Africa was moving in any particular direction at the beginning of the nineteenth century, it is possible to say this of the world outside. There, developments were changing the ways in which government was run. One of the most important of these developments was the improvements made in the manufacture of firearms. People often make the mistake of assuming that all firearms are alike and that the eighteenth century musket was as dangerous a weapon as the nineteenth century rifle. This is very far from being the case. The eighteenth century musket was heavy and unmanageable, slow and difficult to load, and very

the British Snider-Enfield rifle, the first breech loading weapons in general use in the mid-nineteenth century

inaccurate when discharged. Even in the open country of Europe the men who used it also carried a bayonet which enabled them to convert the musket into a stabbing spear, and in the close warfare of the forests and tall grasses of much of Middle Africa it was noisy, but hardly more effective than the spear or the poisoned arrow.

The late nineteenth century rifle was an entirely different gun. It was easily handled, quick to load and when it was aimed and fired at a man at three hundred yards the bullet usually hit him – that is to say, it had much greater precision than the eighteenth century musket. Between these two weapons lay a century of rapid improvement. In the nineteenth century, firearms quickly became out of date and each time inventors designed a new one, the armies of Europe and America bought it and sold off their old ones cheaply. A growing number of these cheap and increasingly effective firearms found their way into Middle Africa during the nineteenth century, particularly after 1860, and this was to have an important effect. All government contains an element of force and if the way in which force is exercised changes, the form of government also is liable to alter. The introduction of firearms on a large scale into Middle Africa in the second half of the nineteenth century brought far-reaching changes.

Maritime peace

Another world development which closely affected Middle Africa in the nineteenth century was the improvement of sea communications. Up to the close of the Napoleonic wars in Europe in 1815, the seas both east and west of Middle Africa were seldom free of pirates and the ships of warring nations. After that date, mainly because the British had secured mastery of the seas, there was a period of unprecedented maritime peace which lasted throughout the nineteenth century. Not only were the great naval powers at peace but piracy of all kinds was rigorously stamped out. The seas to the east of Africa particularly benefited from this. While the Atlantic had known a few periods of peace during the eighteenth century, the Indian Ocean had been the scene of continual piracy and warfare for more than three centuries. Now for the first time merchants could load their vessels in the confidence that they would reach their destinations. Only slave traders had to fear the seizure of their ships at the hands of British anti-slavery squadrons. But even they benefited from the general peace, and the slave trade flourished in the early nineteenth century as never before on both eastern and western coasts. For the anti-slavery squadrons did not operate continuously. They were active on the west coast in the early 1820s, between 1838 and 1841, and again from 1846 until the west coast slave trade practically died out in the 1860s. On the east coast the slave trade was not attacked effectively until the early 1860s and again from 1873 onward to the 1890s when it too came to an end. Before these attacks were made, shipping slaves was an easier business than in any previous century.

Rising foreign trade

Apart from the inestimable advantage of maritime peace, merchants benefited from the greatly improved charts of African waters made in the 1820s and 1830s, and from instruments for navigating at sea. Ships became larger and roomier and were no longer weighed down by guns. Regular postal services established on the west coast in the 1850s and the east coast in the 1870s kept businessmen in African ports in touch with markets in other parts of the world. All this increased the commercial power of the trading communities on the coasts of Middle Africa. In addition, markets in other countries for certain goods which Middle Africa could produce were steadily expanding. The value of slaves sent to the sugar and coffee plantations of Cuba and Brazil tended to rise in the first half of the century until that traffic was put down. The price of the palm-oil produced around the mouth of the Congo river rose rapidly up to the 1860s, the price of ivory which was gathered widely in the heart of Middle Africa rose throughout the century. At the same time, the price of the goods which Middle Africa imported from the outside world was tending to fall. First Indian and then British and American cheap cotton manufactures came flooding into African ports. The price of haberdashery and metalware was also falling as was the price of those deadly imports – guns. In economist's language, the terms of trade were moving steadily in favour of Middle Africa during much of the nineteenth century. On the one hand this gave a considerable incentive to Africans in all parts of the area to organise and to provide themselves with the means to engage in a commerce which year by year yielded increasing profits. On the other hand, the main beneficiaries were the merchants in the coastal towns and those nearest them, who secured the largest share of the rising trade. Throughout the century therefore there was a general tendency for the centres of economic power and initiative to move away from the heart of the continent towards the coast.

Commerce in Middle Africa

The predominant part played by external commerce in the total trade of Middle Africa, which was so evident at the end of the nineteenth century, was something new in the history of the area. At the beginning of the nineteenth century the people mostly provided themselves with their own cloth and manufactured their own tools and weapons. Foreign trade was a fringe affair which affected the lives of only a few in such states as Lunda or Kazembe. The main trade routes were north and south rather than east and west, and the bulk of the commerce was carried on between the populous states of the inter-lacustrine area and the Congo Basin. Much of the trade was on a fairly local basis, such as the manufacture and distribution of hoes and other farming implements by specialist blacksmiths, or the trade in raffia work and bark cloth. Nevertheless, some of the markets for these commodities were to be found hundreds of miles from the place of manufacture, and this was even more strikingly the case with the copper products of the Katanga. Katanga copper was carried as far afield as the Kingdom of Bakuba on the Kasai to the west, and the country of the Nyamwezi on the east.

Of all the African traders of the area in the nineteenth century, perhaps the most enterprising and adventurous were those of Nyamwezi, the neighbours of the Sukuma to the south of Lake Victoria. Many of the trade routes which the Arabs are credited with discovering in the nineteenth century were in fact those which the Nyamwezi had long been using. Their main trade in the early nineteenth century was northward to the Ganda kingdoms and south and westward to Katanga, where they were already well established in the second decade of the century. But they were also interested in the trade eastward with the coast, and that interest grew as they saw what profits they could earn by taking part in it. They were in fact to play a prominent role in the reversal of Middle Africa's trading system and the expansion of commerce with the outside world.

11 Men and Arms

The nineteenth century was a period of revolution and strife in Middle Africa. It has often been suggested that the principal cause of war in Africa in pre-colonial times was the slave trade. But the ending of the export of slaves from Middle Africa was not accompanied by any diminution in the amount of warfare. On the contrary there is abundant evidence that warfare became more widespread after than it was before the foreign slave trade was suppressed. The contrast between the mainly peaceful expeditions led by Livingstone in the 1850s and 1860s and Stanley's violent, heavily armed caravans of the 1870s and after, may have owed something to the differing personalities of the two explorers. It was also partly due to the fact that life on the trade routes was getting tougher as time went by. Historians have tended to place too much emphasis on the export of slaves and too little on the import of guns as a disturber of the peace. Yet it is obvious that the offer of money does not give a man the power to sell his fellow man into slavery, while if he is issued with superior weapons he will have the power either to sell men to others or enslave them to himself.

Though the foreign slave trade diminished after the 1860s, the influx of arms did not. They flowed into Middle Africa in increasing numbers until the 1890s when the colonial powers, fearing that Africans would become too strong for them, banded together to restrict their import. This does not mean that the introduction of firearms was the only cause of war. There were other causes of conflict arising out of specific political situations which will be described later. Nor were war and the slave trade the only causes of devastation. As more ships from other parts of the world frequented Middle African ports they brought with them new diseases. In the second half of the nineteenth century the scourge of war was supplemented by even more deadly epidemics of smallpox, cholera and rinderpest,

An armed caravan fighting its way through Sukumaland in the 1870's.

which swept across the east of the continent attacking man and beast.

The effect of all this was ruinous. In the later nineteenth century a considerable part of Middle Africa presented an almost apocalyptic picture of men fleeing from their homesteads in the plains to seek the safety of stockaded villages in the hilltops or the less comfortable security of marshes. Whole clans and tribes were stampeding from homelands burnt and plundered by marauding bands. Cattle keepers, deprived of disease-stricken herds, wandered in search of new means of livelihood. Whole districts were abandoned through war, famine and plague, and that enemy of man, the tsetse fly, moved in to occupy many of the empty lands. When one understands the extent of the destruction in the immediate pre-colonial period it is easier to see how many people eventually accepted colonial rule out of sheer moral and physical exhaustion.

These stern times threw up a number of outstanding leaders who, by harnessing and controlling the dynamic forces of the age, were able to guarantee security and prosperity to their followers – though, be it said, often at the expense of their less fortunate neighbours. Some were traditional rulers, either long established like the Kabaka Suna of the Ganda kingdom, or more recently so, like Kimweri, the King of the Shambala in the Usumbara mountains to the east. Others were self-made men, men from small isolated clans, who

An engraving of an ivory caravan in 1891

would have had a very limited future had the traditional scheme of things prevailed. These men were real innovators with little time to create royal traditions. They depended on their military skill and the enterprising use of every new military, political or trading device that came to hand to maintain their power. Among them may be counted M'siri and Mirambo of the Nyamwesi.

There were many others. As we shall see these men were to become the dominant figures in the history of Middle Africa in the second half of the century.

The century opened comparatively peacefully. There were wars, of course, on the frontiers of the expanding kingdoms in the interlacustrine area, within the Baluba Empire in the south, and wherever the Masai cattlemen came in conflict with their agricultural neighbours. There were squabbles also between the various small selfgoverning village communities. But these conflicts were local and there is no reason to suppose that they were worse than anything that had gone before. More ominous was the increasing slave trade on the east coast around Kilwa, where men were being carried off to work on the developing plantations on French islands in the Indian Ocean. But this too was a mainly local affair, for these slaves were drawn from the main east coast slaving area behind Kilwa. The first half of the century was a comparatively peaceful period during which the

289

forces of change and strife were gradually building up. If we wish to
know more of these forces we must look especially to the east coast
and to southern Africa.

Coastal traders

The trading communities of the eastern coast had remained where
they were for several centuries, without making any significant
attempt to move inland and make contact with the populous African
areas around the Lakes. They were mostly of mixed African and
Arab blood, representing several waves of immigrants who, over a
long period of years, had settled in such places as Kilwa, Mombasa
and Zanzibar, intermarried and made their homes there. But in the
early nineteenth century, especially after 1820, things began to stir
in the seaport towns. The community of Indian traders, already
well-established when the century began, swelled in numbers and
became more active. Many of them were agents of firms established
in the large commercial and manufacturing cities in north-western
India. Those firms were well-organised and enterprising concerns.
Many were linked indirectly with the growing economic power of
Britain. They had money to invest and as the Indian Ocean became
safe for peaceful businessmen they were able to take a closer interest
in East Africa. Then there were the Arabs of the Persian Gulf, warlike
men who were being squeezed out of their own waters by British and
Indian pressure. Omani Arabs had a long history of shipping and
trading contact with East Africa but in the nineteenth century they
came in larger numbers and with more warlike intent than before.

Sayyid Sa'id and Zanzibar commerce

The influx of these new elements into the seaport towns was presided
over and controlled by Sayyid Sa'id, the Sultan of the town and district
of Masqat in Arabia, and successor to Masqati dynasties who had held
important possessions on the coast of East Africa since the seventeenth century. In the early years of his reign, between 1806 and
1820, Sayyid Sa'id tended to neglect his East African dominions.
But after 1820, when his efforts to enlarge his empire in the Persian
Gulf were visibly failing, he switched his attention from his Arabian
homeland. His visits to Zanzibar became more frequent and in 1840
he established his capital there. By that time he had consolidated his

Sayyid Sa'id, Sultan
of Zanzibar

control over most of the ports between Mogadishu and Cape Delgado. He had also, by his diplomacy, cemented an alliance between the enterprising Indian businessmen and the Arab soldiers and sailors, and directed the energies of both toward the economic exploitation of the interior. Extensive clove plantations were established on the islands of Pate and Zanzibar, most of them owned and run by Arabs, backed by Indian capitalists who provided the money to buy slaves to work on them.

The trade inland was also developed by the same combination of Arabs and Indians. Indians provided goods on credit which enabled caravans to go out from the East African ports laden with articles to exchange with the peoples of the interior. Indians also provided the money to stock trading depots, for example that at Tabora in central Tanzania. The leadership of the expeditions to the interior was mostly in the hands of immigrant Arabs and men from the Arab families established at Zanzibar. By 1825 men from the coast were trading near Tabora, by 1844 Arabs had reached the court of the Kabaka in Ganda, and by 1850 they were established at Ujiji on the east coast of Lake Tanganyika, whence they traded with the people of the Congo basin beyond. Others swung south of the Lake and by the same date (1850) two of them had traversed the continent to reach the western coast. The Arab caravans went out mainly in search of slaves and ivory. Slaves were wanted to provide labour for the Zanzibar clove estates, and for export to Arabia and islands in the Indian Ocean and Somaliland – indeed, to any place where newly rich men were anxious to acquire the services of others. Ivory found a ready market in Europe and America, and it was shipped off with the cloves by the American, French, German and British Indian vessels which

congregated in increasing numbers in the port of Zanzibar from the
1830s onward.

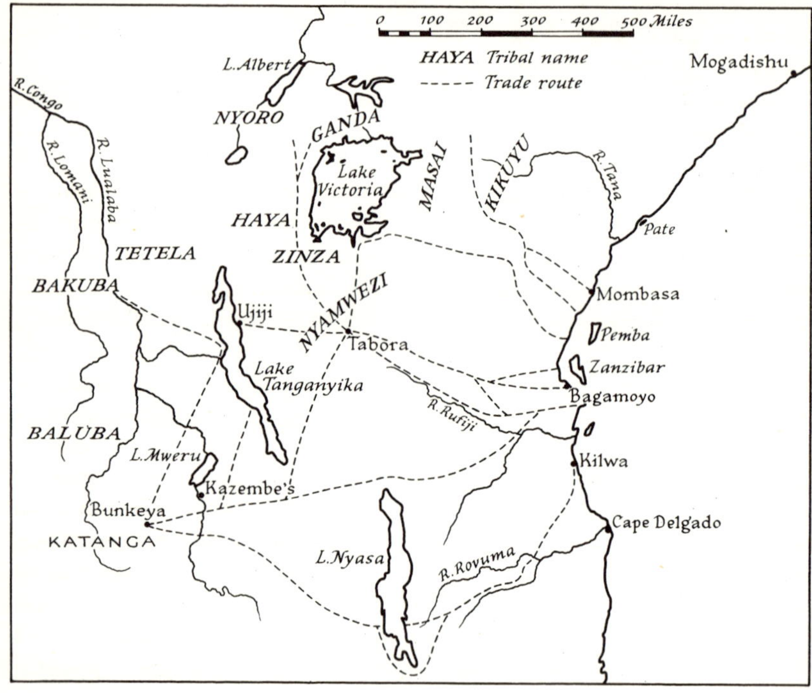

36 Trade routes in Middle Africa

Arab and Nyamwezi traders

The spectacular extension between 1820 and 1850 of Zanzibari
trading activity, along the thousand mile route from the coast to the
populous areas from Ganda to Katanga, was not a purely Indo-Arab
affair. Men from the coast may have led the caravans, but the guides
and the men who actually carried the goods came mostly from Nyamwezi country in the middle west of Tanzania. The Nyamwezi, as has
already been seen, were one of the greatest trading peoples of Middle
Africa. They had already developed trading routes north and south
from Ganda to Katanga and east and west from Lake Tanganyika
to the coast. Indeed Zanzibar's first contacts with the far interior had
been through their agency. They had come down with the produce
of their own and neighbouring countries for barter in the seaport

292

towns. But, as more Indian capital was invested in the trade, the commercial initiative passed from the Nyamwezi to the people of the coast. The Indians were able to send thousands of pounds worth of trade goods to the interior, and sit and wait for a year or more until their caravans returned with produce they could sell to European shippers. Thus, instead of beginning in Nyamwezi, business deals now began at Zanzibar and those entrusted with their execution were people of that town.

Yet the commercial expertise and co-operation of the Nyamwezi was still essential to the trade. They provided most of the porters, both for Arab caravans and for those they continued to run on their own account. They were also more or less in command of the trade routes. In 1839 Sayyid Sa'id signed a commercial treaty with them, and probably about the same time the Nyamwezi agreed to the passage, free of tolls, of caravans flying Sa'id's flag. For a time the agreement worked, but it came under strain as the caravans grew larger and ate up more of the food supplies of villages they passed through. Food was hard to come by in the badly watered areas of central Tanzania. Droughts and local famines were common and, when they came, people sold off their cattle to buy provisions from more fortunate neighbours. It was not to be expected that people would take kindly to the constant passage of hungry caravaners, and quarrels over tolls became exceptionally serious in the 1850s.

The result was trouble between the Arabs and their Nyamwezi hosts, and to maintain their position the Arabs began to interfere in local politics, backing one clan of the fragmented Nyamwezi against another and involving themselves in chieftaincy disputes. The Arab depot at Tabora became a stronghold rather than a group of warehouses, and by 1860 it was fighting a regular war with Manua Sera, one of the principal Nyamwezi Chiefs. Manua Sera was defeated and beheaded in 1865, and the Arabs thus secured control of the central point of communications in this area. But they were not to remain undisturbed for long, for while they were quarrelling with their one time allies, the Nyamwezi, the whole of western Tanzania was being torn apart by new forces advancing from the south.

The Angoni

The effects of the great Mfecane already mentioned in connection with the history of southern Africa, were not confined to that part of the continent alone. Zwangendaba's Ngoni warriors moved northward as far as the Fipa plateau between Lakes Tanganyika and Rukwa, and when that leader died, around 1848, his followers set off on a typical Ngoni career of conquest across the grasslands to the north and east. It is difficult to give exact dates to the movements of the swift-footed Ngoni, or Angoni as they are called in Tanzania. But it is possible to say that they began their operations close to the Fipa Plateau and then struck northward towards Ujiji, which they devastated in the 1850s. From there they moved north again but failed to make any headway against the solidly organised Ha people and the kingdom of Rwanda. Instead they struck eastward, made a devastating tour of Zinza country and western Sukumaland, and then made off south-westward again to the neighbourhood of Ujiji, where they were active late in the decade of the 1880s. While this was going on in the north another larger body of Angonis had pushed in a solid mass across the Rovuma river in the 1850s and struck out on all sides against the peoples of southern Tanzania from their bases in the Songea area.

Angoni imitators

The impact of the Angoni cannot be measured simply in terms of the number of men in their marauding bands. Wherever they went they disturbed the societies with whom they came into contact. Some communities were scattered or absorbed into the Angoni armies. Others reorganised themselves along Angoni lines in order to survive. When a community did this it became a menace to its neighbours and so the torch which the Angoni lit was carried further afield by others until much of western Tanzania was ablaze.

Among the imitators of the Angoni was Chief Mugumba who ruled the Hehe people to the north east of Lake Rukwa roughly between 1855 and 1879 – that is, during what might be called the Angoni period. A brief description of the methods by which Chief Mugumba built up his empire will give some impression of how an Angoni imitator worked and what sort of revolution the Angoni brought about. Mugumba's conquest of a sub-tribe, of which twenty-nine or so were eventually absorbed into his state, may be divided into three phases. Phase one – the 'break-in' – was achieved by force of arms. Mugumba's soldiers would attack a neighbouring tribe, carry off its cattle and force the traditional leaders to accept his rule. During phase two the traditional rulers would either be driven out and replaced by a younger brother or they would be confirmed in their positions and made sub-chiefs under Mugumba's control. At

294

the same time members of Mugumba's large 'school' of young twelve- to twenty-year-old followers, trained in the ideology of the new state, would be planted out as military colonists among the tribe to spread the idea of loyalty to the king. By the end of the second phase the tribesmen would be completely absorbed. In the third phase, they would be called on to provide warriors for the central army and some of their young men would be selected for training in the royal school. They would render obedience to the king, who controlled the collection of ivory and distributed the coastal trade goods to each according to his rank. The king also monopolised the function of rain-making, and his ancestors were made the object of special ritual offering by the whole state.

A striking feature of Mugumba's work was its amazing permanence. Although it was a very recent creation, the Hehe state stood solidly together against the Germans when they came, and thirty years of direct rule after 1898 failed to make the people forget the idea of unity and loyalty to the dynasty.

The Ruga-Ruga

The Hehe state has been described at some length, not because of its size or the importance of its contribution to the history of Middle Africa, but because, although it was a comparatively small state, the system Mugumba built up contained features similar to those of the Angoni groups and their imitators to the south, east and west of Hehe country. In many cases those who wished to follow his example had no need to break in to the territories of their neighbours. The breaking had already been done for them by the ravages of the Angoni. During the period between 1850 and 1880 thousands of villages were destroyed and burned by raiding forces, and the young men wandered off in search of a new way of making a living. Some became hemp-smoking hooligans, 'ruga-ruga' as they were often called, who formed small groups and sallied forth with assegai and musket to rustle cattle and terrorise peaceful villages like their contemporaries in the American West after the Civil War. Others joined one or other of the emerging states or the trading caravans. Even in peaceful villages in the Nyamwezi area there was a growing urge among the adventurous youths to take to the roads in search of a fortune. Men of this type combined with others from the shattered west to form the backbone of the great trading empires established by two outstanding Nyamwezi leaders, Mirambo and M'siri.

Mirambo

Mirambo, a tall, sinewy, soft-spoken man, was born around 1830. He spent his youth as a caravan porter, then, succeeding to the chiefdom of the small district where he lived, he expanded his territory with the assistance of the Angoni. By 1871 he had become so powerful and so well provided with guns plundered from passing caravans that he was able to defeat an Arab force of a thousand gunmen sent against him from Tabora. From then until his death in 1884 he dominated a wide area of north-west Tanzania, from near Lake Victoria on the north to beyond Tabora on the south, and from near Lake Tanganyika on the west to the limits of Nyamwezi country on the east. His empire was less compact than Mugumba's Hehe state; one might say also that it was less traditional in its character. Mirambo had his 'school' of young trainees about his person, but they were turbanned, gun-bearing warriors, not very different in appearance from the Arabs' Swahili followers. Mirambo himself was favourable to new influences. It is true that he spent much of his life fighting the Arabs but his disagreements with them were mainly political.

One of Mirambo's gun-bearing warriors

The main issue was whether he or they should control the trade routes, not the way in which control should be exercised. He copied many Arab methods. He was friendly with such of them as were prepared to co-operate with him, like Tippu Tip who was of half African parentage. He also welcomed Europeans and wished to have a Christian mission established in his territory. His empire was closely geared to commerce. It was above all an empire of the trade routes, far-flung

296

but also loose-knit and vulnerable. It was not sufficiently well-established in the minds of the people to survive Mirambo's death in 1884.

Mirambo's work was more spectacular but less lasting than Mugumba's. But while he lived Mirambo's name was feared along all the approaches to the inter-lacustrine kingdoms from the east, and his activities contributed to the revolution in men's ideas and their way of life, which was going on over much of Middle Africa in the two decades before the European colonial powers arrived upon the scene.

M'siri

There are striking similarities between Mirambo's career and that of his fellow Nyamwezi, M'siri. M'siri was born around the same year (1830) as Mirambo and was the son of a Nyamwezi trader whose main business lay in the region of Katanga. M'siri too became a porter and caravan leader, and about 1858 he established himself in the country to the west of Lake Mweru, which was rich in copper and in ivory. His own people, called by the local inhabitants Bayeke, were already trading there in considerable numbers. But it was M'siri who conceived the idea of turning from trade to politics. He brought in guns from the east coast and a flood of uprooted youths from western Tanzania. With these tough warriors at his back, he interfered in the quarrels of local chiefs, forced the settlement of disputes and imposed

M'siri

his own rule on the successful parties. By 1869 he was powerful enough to declare himself Mwami or king of the area he controlled. He established a large capital town at Bunkeya, stopped and thrust back the Baluba who had been slowly advancing from the north, and cut the communications between Kazembe and the main Lunda empire to the west. By 1870 he was in contact with the Portuguese slave and ivory traders from the west coast, and he also traded northward with the Arabs established on the west coast of Lake Tanganyika.

His empire, situated between the Lualaba and Luapula rivers in Katanga, was if anything larger than Mirambo's. It was slightly different in nature in that M'siri controlled the sources of production while Mirambo concentrated on the command of the trade routes. But basically it had the same commercial character. M'siri's governors and sub-chiefs were mainly concerned with the collection of the ivory in their districts. His rule was insecurely based and after his death in 1891 his state failed to survive; little but the memory of it remains today. M'siri however, was one of the agencies by which the revolution of western Tanzania was carried to the Congo basin and his empire conveyed onward to its neighbours the shock of the new forces.

Arabs in the Congo

While M'siri was building up his kingdom in the southern Congo, Arab traders from Zanzibar were penetrating the country west of Lake Tanganyika from their base at Ujiji. There they met with the fragmented communities of the middle Congo, who could not offer concerted resistance to the invaders. The latter of course were not entirely Arab. Only the caravan leaders and a few followers were from Arabia or the coast. The force which thrust across Lake Tanganyika was composed of essentially the same elements as had helped to found the empires of Mirambo and M'siri. There were perhaps more Swahilis among the porters, but the bulk of the Arabs' followers were Nyamwezi and other western Tanzanians with, in addition, new recruits raised from among the remnants of broken Congo villages. The men were largely the same, but the Arab system was somewhat different from that of the Nyamwezi rulers. Mirambo's type of government was one step away from Mugumba's mainly traditional Hehe state; Arab rule went one large step further. There were some superficial resemblances, for the Arabs, like Mirambo, were surrounded by their young uprooted followers, and they monopolised the collection of ivory and appointed sub-chiefs to control the trade in subjected districts. But the spirit of their rule was different. If the young men about them were trained in any ideology it was not one which was focused on the ruler. It was rather the ideology of Islam, which proclaimed loyalty to one God, to the Koran and to the body of Muslim learning. The link with the traditional was all but snapped.

Tippu Tip

Tippu Tip

But between the Arab state and M'siri's empire to the south, there lay another state neither Arab nor wholly traditional in its organisation. This was the kingdom which the brilliant Afro-Arab, Hamed bin Abdalla, alias Tippu Tip, created among the Tetela people. When Tippu Tip approached the ivory rich Tetela country from the south in the 1870s, he had the wisdom to construct for himself a genealogy which made him the alleged descendant of a Tetela princess. The Tetela were at the time under heavy pressure from their Baluba neighbours, and to make himself acceptable to his prospective subjects Tippu Tip defeated a Baluba force. On arrival among the Tetela he delivered to them some of their captured sons whom he had released from Baluba captivity. According to Tippu Tip's own account the chief resigned his rule immediately in his favour. Tip became a Tetela ruler and soon set his people off in a career of conquest against their neighbours. Tip's Tetela state however was an exception. Few other Arabs or Swahilis put forward such traditional claims to rule. Nevertheless their power extended over a wide area of what is now the eastern Congo. Based on a number of fortified strongpoints, from near Lake Mweru in the south to the Aruwimi river in the north, they extended their operations up to and beyond the Lomami river on the west and were still expanding when they clashed with King Leopold of Belgium's men and were defeated between 1891 and 1894.

The northern trade routes

North of a line from Mount Kilimanjaro westward along the south bank of Lake Victoria, people were not affected by the same destructive combination of Angoni raids and Arab penetration as those further south. It is true that Arabs traded in these parts. The first Arabs reached the Ganda kingdom from their base at Tabora in the south in 1844. In the 1860s they began to take over the routes leading from the coast opposite Pemba island to western Kenya – routes which had up to then been monopolised by Kamba traders. But the quality of the Arab impact was different. They were dealing for the most part with heavily populated districts. Some of the societies certainly were fragmented like the Kikuyu. But most of those to the east of Lake Victoria had been toughened by incessant combat with the marauding Masai without being broken by them. And there are indications that numbers of the Kikuyu and Kamba clans united from time to time behind outstanding leaders for purposes of defence. To the west of Lake Victoria lay the inter-lacustrine kingdoms, most of them much too large to be dominated by the strongest Arab trading caravans. The Angoni had, by interfering in succession disputes, managed to make havoc in the kingdoms of Zinza. But this was as far north as they reached.

The Arabs had managed to penetrate further afield and they interfered in a succession dispute in the Haya kingdom of Karangwe. But beyond that they were within the sphere of influence of the powerful Ganda kingdom. There they traded successfully, but they did so within the framework of the Ganda state. Instead of playing the role of itinerant caravan leaders, many of them settled down and switched from war and transport to commerce pure and simple, spiced with a certain amount of political intrigue. The goods they ordered from Tabora and Zanzibar were mostly carried from the frontier by Ganda porters.

300

Mutesa

Ganda expansion

This does not mean that conditions were much more peaceful or less dynamic in the inter-lacustrine area in the second half of the nineteenth century than they were further south. Important changes were taking place, even though the broad political fabric of the area with its large and small kingdoms did not alter radically. The principal disturbing factor was the centrally placed Ganda state. Under two powerful Kabakas important reforms were effected in Ganda, the effect of which was to enhance the power of the ruler and his administration and weaken all competing elements in the state. The army was overhauled and its efficiency improved, and in the 1870s a striking force of musketeers was formed from among the youth at court to supplement the main body of tribal levies.

Bark cloth had always been much in demand in Ganda. When the Arabs came, their cotton cloth replaced it as the fashionable wear for men about the court. The new textiles were much sought after and so were the muskets which the Arabs also brought. But Ganda had little ivory to offer in return. Instead the Baganda earned the wherewithal

 Kabarega of Nyoro

to pay for their imports by war. The Ganda kingdom made little effort to extend its frontiers in the period between 1850 and the time of European colonisation, but it sent out military expeditions to plunder its neighbours on every side. Ganda military forces made no fewer than sixty raids on the country's neighbours in the twenty-seven years of Mutesa's reign. These exploits brought Ganda into conflict with another powerful inter-lacustrine state, Nyoro, which after 1870, under the leadership of Kabarega, was also becoming more aggressive after over a century of decline. In many of the areas which Ganda attacked, Nyoro claimed control of trade relations. The result was twenty years of intense conflict between the two kingdoms which ended in Ganda's favour when the British joined in on the Kabaka's side in 1893.

Egyptian pressure

In both Ganda and Nyoro the power of the rulers tended to increase as a result of the growing importance of firearms, most of which passed into the kings' hands. These firearms came mostly from the Zanzibari Arabs, but some also were brought in from the north. For the inter-lacustrine kingdoms were situated at the edge of the commercial empire which the Egyptians built up between 1841 and 1884 on the upper Nile. The Egyptians never acquired the same sort of influence as the Zanzibaris in either kingdom; for example Islam in present-day Uganda came from the east coast rather than from the Nile. The Zanzibaris were for the most part regarded as friendly traders, while the Egyptians were representatives of a territorial power close enough to be a serious threat to either state. This was how they were regarded and Nyoro carefully sought to avoid hostilities with them, while Ganda tried to secure their alliance against Nyoro. In fact, although Egyptian officials claimed to have annexed both states formally in the 1870s, and although Egyptian posts were established in northern Nyoro, the two kingdoms were too large and too far south to be in any way dominated by Egypt.

This was not the case however with the Zande kingdoms to the west. They had begun to feel the effect of Egyptian penetration from the Bahr al Ghazal area from the 1860s onward. Their divisions and succession disputes made it easy for the Egyptians to intervene. The Egyptians controlled the import of firearms and firearms gave each man who received them a decisive advantage over his rivals. Had the Zande rulers combined they could easily have resisted the invaders since the Egyptians were operating far from their main bases. But internal jealousies and bitter competition for power and office was the main characteristic of the Avongara ruling class and one by one they fell under Egyptian rule, paying tribute in the form of slaves and ivory in order to win support against their neighbours. On the other hand the existing form of society and political relations was not broken up by foreign intervention as was the case further south. The Egyptians left the Avongara states intact and recognised the rulers as 'Sultans' of their respective kingdoms. The main consequence of Egyptian intervention, and that of their Mahdist Sudanese successors, was an increase in the amount and intensity of interstate warfare and a certain weakening of the idea of Avongara kingship.

Middle Africa in perspective

Looking at the history of Middle Africa as a whole in the pre-colonial nineteenth century it is possible to note three distinct periods amid the varied experiences of the many different peoples in the vast area. Up to about the middle of the century life went on very much as it had done before. The bulk of the trade ran north and south. There was a growing trade between the interior and the coast but much of it ran along traditional lines. The Portuguese carried on their usual commerce with the Lunda Empire. The Arabs drew their slaves from the

Commercial Zanzibar in 1885 showing the waterfront and harbour,
with dhows and steamships of the period

old slaving areas behind Kilwa and in the north the Kamba traders did
not break through Masai country to trade with Kavirondo until
about mid-century. The Nyamwezi trade with the coast was larger
than before but the indications are that it was carried on in mainly
peaceful conditions.

Then in the quarter century after 1850 there was widespread dislocation, as new forces interfered with traditional organisation. Angoni
raids became exceptionally severe across the whole of Tanzania south
and west of a line from Dar es Salaam to the south-western tip of Lake
Victoria. Arab caravans made wider use of firearms, they became
larger and more menacing and relations between them and the
Nyamwezi began to break down. Nyamwezi and Arab operations
beyond Lake Tanganyika carried disorder to the Congo basin, and
in the north the Egyptians began to penetrate Zande country. Everywhere after 1860 imported firearms were beginning to affect the
organisation of government and this was the period when major

reforms were made in the Ganda military system. The disorder in the interior was probably one of the main reasons for the trade depression which ruined the prosperity of Zanzibar roughly between 1860 and 1875. This in its turn, and the weak leadership offered by Sayyid Sa'id's successor Majid (1856–72), led to a breakdown of the partnership between Indians and Arabs at Zanzibar and a danger of Indian expulsion which brought about British intervention in 1873. The fate of much of Middle Africa lay in the balance in these years.

Then after 1875 the new forces began to get the upper hand. Trade revived at Zanzibar. Chiefs who monopolised the collection of ivory and the import of firearms were everywhere in the ascendant, whether they were successors of old dynasties like Mutesa in Ganda or new men like M'siri in Katanga. From the east coast to the Lomami river in the Congo basin, the strongholds of the African and Arab warlords, some of them regular stone fortresses, others surrounded by palisades, ditches or thorn bushes, were scattered across the plain. Sultan Barghash of Zanzibar joined in the work of state building, and his system of direct rule began to extend outward from the coast opposite Zanzibar into the Angoni-ravaged Luguru country. At the other end of the trade route, he appointed a governor over the scattered Vinza peoples in Ujiji on Lake Tanganyika. This revolution was in full flood when the colonial powers arrived on the scene, and when they sought to impose their rule they met the severest opposition not from traditional society but from the rising political power of these new forces – the Arabs, the Hehe, the Angoni, the Tetela and M'siri.

Questions

Chapter 1

1 Explain the significance of the following dates in Egyptian History: AD 643, 1798, 1801, 1811, 1827, 1849.
2 Account for the success and failures of Mameluke rule in Egypt.
3 What improvements did Egypt experience under Ottoman rule? Explain why and how the Mameluke system revived in Egypt.
4 Give reasons why Napoleon Bonaparte's invasion of Egypt was bound to succeed and state the consequences of that invasion.
5 Assume that you were an Egyptian in the period of the conflict between Britain and France over Egyptian sovereignty. Write a reasoned account of your opposition to the encroachment of two European powers on your country.
6 Write short notes on the following: Copts, Mamelukes, Fellahin, The Diwan, Institut de L'Egypte (Egyptian Institute), Wali (governor), The Treaty of Unkiar-Skell'esi (1833), Ferdinand de Lesseps, Berne Conference (1877).
7 Give reasons why you would regard Mohammed Ali as a great statesman and innovator in Egypt. Why were his endeavours not always successful?
8 'Said's reign laid the foundation for Egyptian financial difficulty under his successor, Ismail Pasha.' How was this state of affairs arrived at and extended?
9 'British occupation of Egypt created nationalism in Egypt.' Describe the events following the occupation and justify or modify the above statement.

Activities
1 Conduct a debate in class by splitting up into two groups – one group advancing the argument for Britain and the other the argument for France over the claim to overlordship of Egypt.

2 Use an encyclopaedia and find out more about Arabi Pasha.

Chapter 2
1 Trace briefly the career of Mohammed Ahmad until his death in 1885. What were the main achievements of his reign?
2 What internal upheavals rocked the Mahdist state after the death of Mohammed Ahmad and how were they overcome?
3 In the light of later events would you say that the Khalifa Abdullahi's refusal to unite with the Emperor Menelik against the designs of European imperialists was short sighted?
4 Account for the rise and fall of the Emperor Theodore II of Ethiopia.
5 From which quarters did threats to Ethiopian independence come between the years 1875 and 1896?
6 'Menelik II was a master tactician.' Explain how he used this special quality not only to secure the Ethiopian monarchy but also to defeat the machinations of outsiders.
7 'As the victor of the Battle of Adowa in 1896, Menelik II not only confirmed his assertion of Ethiopian independence but compelled the Europeans to recognise it.' Discuss.
8 Write short notes on the following: The Funj Sultanate, Mohammad Ahmad (the Mahdi), General Gordon, Amils, the Fashoda Incident, the Anglo-Egyptian Condominium, The Emperor John IV of Ethiopia, Battle of Matemma (1889), Treaty of Ucciali (1889).

Activities
Hold a debate justifying or criticising the Khalifa's war strategy at the time of the British invasion of the Sudan in 1898.

Chapter 3
1 Account for the emergence of Turkish rule in the Maghreb before 1800.
2 Comment on the activities of Warrington in Libya between 1814-35.
3 Why was the year 1830 a turning point in Maghreb history? Account for the stages leading up to this climax.
4 'From the single experience of Algeria we see that European imperialism in Africa was not an easy walkover.' Discuss the truth of this assertion.
5 Give reasons for the change in tactics by the French in the colonization of North Africa after the Algerian experience of

resistance and say how European interference drove the Tunisians into the clutches of the French.

6 Explain the stages by which Ahmed Bey's successor, Mohammed es Sadek, as ruler of Tunisia, aided the tightening of the French grip on the country.

7 Write short notes on the following: the fly-whisk incident (1827), Abdel Kader and the resistance to France, the Colons of Algeria, the theory and practice of French citizenship in Algeria, Ahmed Bey as ruler of Tunisia.

8 'External perfidy was the undoing of King Abdul Aziz'. Do you agree?

9 Account for the founding and influence of the Senussiya brotherhood in Libya in the nineteenth century. What was their attitude to European imperialism?

Chapter 4

1 Account for the importance of the trans-Saharan Trade routes before the commencement of the trans-Atlantic slave trade.

2 'The West Sudanese played the role of middlemen for many centuries before their trade was disrupted.' Explain how this was done indicating the products traded in and the benefits to the Sudan.

3 What would you say were the temporary and lasting benefits resulting from the coming of Islam to West Africa?

4 Is it right to assume that the trans-Saharan trade gave rise to the impulses which created the trans-Atlantic trade and that the latter eventually stifled the former?

Chapter 5

1 Why were the coastal states of West Africa able to preserve their independence before the nineteenth century?

2 It has been suggested that British motives for abolishing the slave trade were mixed and not purely humanitarian. Discuss this viewpoint.

3 Write short notes on: Olaudah Equiano (alias Gustavus Vassa), Chief Justice Mansfield, Granville Sharp, Equipment Treaties, the Black Poor, King Obi Ossai of Abo.

4 Suggest reasons why the transition from the slave trade to trade in other commodities did not come readily especially in West Africa. (As a guide use the following headings: habit (both of Europeans and Africans), moral attitude of the people in the nineteenth century, fear of the unknown, self-interest, national

rivalries of European participants.) What final effect had the
abolition of the slave trade in West Africa?

5 Account for the failure of the expeditions of MacGregor Laird
(1832) and Thomas Fowell Buxton (1841) and the success of Dr.
William B. Baikie's in 1854.
6 Give an account of the French effort to gain a foothold in West
Africa and explain the contributions of governor Louis
Faideherbe.
7 'African reaction to European penetration of West Africa was
based partly on the policy of ensuring that the newcomers did
not tamper with the middlemen or local vested interests.' Do you
agree?
8 Outline the activities of the various foreign Missionary Societies
in West Africa from the late eighteenth century to the third
quarter of the nineteenth.

Activities
Hold a debate in class on the merits and demerits of repatriating
African slaves from the New World to Africa. In this debate
consider carefully the motives of the British Sierra Leone Company
(St. George's Bay Company), the American Colonization Society,
and the attitude of the Royal African Company.

Chapter 6

1 'Uthman dan Fodio was a Fulani rebel.'
'Uthman dan Fodio was a Fulani patriot.'
Reconcile these statements.
2 What were the main effects of the nineteenth-century jihads on
the peoples of the West Sudan? Use the following headings:
political, religious, social, and cultural effects.
3 Account for the rise, success, and later failure of Samori in the
West Sudan during the nineteenth century.
4 What internal and external factors rocked the edifice of the
Yoruba kingdom of Oyo from about 1770 and contributed to its
eventual downfall?
5 Why and how did King Gezo of Dahomey and his son Glele try
to extend their empire eastward?
6 Present both the Asante case and that of the British for the series
of wars which came to be known as the Asante Wars.
7 Write short notes on the following: Sir Frederick Hodgson,
Agyeman Prempe I, Sir Garnet Wolseley, Sir Charles MacGarthy,
Captain George Maclean.

Hold discussions in class using a member or a few members to:
1 Present the Asante case as to why the wars between Asante and the British were not of Asante's own creation.
2 As the chief spokesman for the Asante cause, present the arguments for direct trade with the Europeans rather than through intermediaries.

Chapter 7

1 Why are the following dates important in the history of Central and Southern Africa: 1652, 1657, 1779, 1793, 1795?
2 Describe the political and social organisations of the Bantu-speaking people of Southern Africa before the advent of European rule.
3 Trace the growth of foreign influences in Central and Southern Africa between the fifteenth and nineteenth centuries.
4 Account for the development of a superior-inferior attitude among the races at the Cape colony after 1715. What contribution did religious dogma make to this deteriorating situation?
5 Give an account of the reactions of the peoples of Southern Africa to European penetration of Africa from the south. What was the final outcome?
6 'Southern Africa was not immune from the kind of resistance offered by Africans in other parts to European penetration.' Describe the nature and areas of this resistance between the seventeenth and eighteenth centuries and account for their failure.
7 Write notes on the following: The Mwene Mutapa Empire, the Malawi Empire, the Dutch East India Company and the Cape, Jan Bloem (Snr.), the Korana, Griquas, Maynier.

Chapter 8

1 Give a brief account of how the rivalries between these three Southern African potentates were resolved: Sobhuza, Dingiswayo and Zwide; and explain the factors at stake.
2 Account for the rise of Shaka as king of the Zulus. How did he consolidate his successes?
3 Use a sketch-map to indicate the main lines of migration of people during the Mfecane and outline the factors contributing
4 to this movement of people.
   Write short notes on the following: Moshesh, Mzilikazi, The

Black Circuit, Dr. John Philip, Xhosa resistance war of 1835-6, Dingane.

5 Suggest reasons for the Boer Trek beyond the Orange and Vaal rivers in the early nineteenth century. What were the experiences of the Trekkers and how were they overcome?

6 Describe the events which led up to the Battle of Blood River in 1838.

7 'The Boers played on the rivalries of the Africans to secure a firm foothold in Natal (Zululand).' Discuss the validity of this assertion.

Chapter 9

1 'Moshesh had an almost impossible task to accomplish.' Consider this statement in the light of his experiences with Britain, the Boers, the European missionaries, and his subjects.

2 What was the treaty policy on the eastern frontier of South Africa and why was it not successful?

3 'The series of conflicts and upheavals which took place in Southern Africa during the nineteenth century were conditioned by the conflict of interests between the British and the Boers. The Africans were merely onlookers.' Is this a fair assessment of the then prevailing situation?

4 Discuss the major factors which made the collapse of African resistance to European encroachment in Southern Africa inevitable.

5 'Between the years 1818 and 1877 the Xhosa people fought wars of resistance against European ascendency in Southern Africa.' State in each case the reasons for those wars. What alternatives would you have suggested?

6 Write short notes on the following: The War of the Axe (1846), Sir Harry Smith, Warden, the Sand River Convention (1852), the Griquas, the Treaty of Thaba Bosiu, Lord Carnarvon, Sikuyana, the War of the Guns, Sir Bartle Frere, The First Anglo-Boer War, and the Pretoria Convention (1881).

7 What were the causes and effects of the Free State-Basuto wars?

8 What effect had the discovery of diamonds in 1858 near the Vaal and Harts rivers?

9 'It was a British official rather than the Zulus who precipitated the Zulu wars in the reign of Cetewayo.' Discuss.

Activities

Assuming that you were the Zulu King Cetewayo, prepare a

statement to be read before your subjects explaining the justice
of the Zulu cause.

Chapter 10

1 By means of a sketch-map show the states which formed the area
  known as Middle Africa.
2 'While the old Kongo Kingdom was disintegrating the Lunda
  Empire was rapidly expanding.' How were these opposing trends
  brought about?
3 Describe the common characteristic features of the inter-lacustrine
  kingdoms of Middle Africa before the coming of the Europeans.
  What were the weaknesses and strength of their organisations?
4 Show how the following factors: firearms, improvement of sea
  communications, and foreign trade changed the pattern of life in
  Middle Africa during the first half of the nineteenth century?
5 Write short notes on: The Zande States, Ganda and Nyoro, the
  Hima Aristocracies, the Masai and their neighbours, fire arms,
  and Middle Africa in the nineteenth century, and the Nyamwezi.

Chapter 11

1 Describe the external and internal factors which lead to far-
  reaching social change in Middle Africa after 1850?
2 Is it true to assert that people of Middle Africa succumbed to
  colonial rule from sheer exhaustion created by internal factors?
3 Sketch the lines of internal trade in Middle Africa in the
  nineteenth century.
4 Account for the growth of middlemen traders on the east coast of
  Middle Africa in the nineteenth century.
5 Assess the importance of the following in the history of Middle
  Africa: (a) Chief Mugumba, (b) Mirambo, and (c) M'siri.
6 'The man of the moment.' Is this an apt description of the rise of
  Tippu Tib (Hamed bin Abdalla)?
7 Write short notes on the following: Sayyid Sa'id, The Agoni,
  Ruga-Ruga, Kabaka Mutesa, and Kabarega.

A list of suggestions for further reading for both Volumes I and II
of The Making of Modern Africa is provided at the end of Volume
II.

Index

Abbas I: 50, 57
Abdel Kader: 92–4, 101
Abdel Aziz: 102–4
Abdel Rahman: 101
Abdul-Karim-al-Naqil: 165
Abdullab, The: 8, 58
Abdullah (Brother of Uthman): 159, 161
Abdul-Rahman ibn Hammada: 159
Abdullah (the Khalifa): 66–72, 80, 84
Abeokuta: 150, 174–5, 179–181
Abiodun: 172–3, 178
Abo: 124, 130, 145
Abomey: 114–5
Aboukir Bay: 41
Abu Likeilik: 58
Abuna, Theodore: 75–6, 78–9
Accra: 153, 183
Acre: 41, 49
Adowa, Battle of: 82–4
Afonja: 173, 175, 179
African Association: 137–8
Agaja Trudo: 18
Ahmaddiyya: 25
Ahmad Seku: 166–7
Ahmadu Ahmadu: 165
Ahmadu Seku: 165
Ahmed, Bey of Tunis: 96
Aja: 8, 114
Akan States: 18, 114, 181, 190
Akwamu: 114, 182
Akwapim: 182
Akyem: 114, 182
al Baida: 105
Alexandria: 47, 52, 56–7
Alfa Ibrahim b. Nuhu: 158
Algeria: 2, 11–13, 85, 87–8, 90–6, 99–101, 104–5, 111, 147
Algiers: 87–8
Ali b. Ghadhahim: 98
Ali, (Khalifa): 66
Ali Pasha: 104
Almoravids: 16
al-Sayyid Muhammad al-Mahdi: 106
al Tijani: 167
Amara Dunkas: 8, 58
American Soc. for Colonising the Free People of Colour, 134–6
Amils: 69
Anamaboe: 183–4
Andi: 201
Angola: 19, 28–9, 194, 271, 274–5

(A)nkole: 21, 276–7, 279
Ansar: 64
Arabia: 5, 9, 17, 23, 47, 105, 290, 298
Arabi Pasha: 44, 55–6
Aro: 129
Aruwimi R.: 300
Asante (Ashanti): 18, 56, 114, 151, 181–8, 190
Asantehene: 18, 182–4, 188, 190
Asante Kotoko: 182–3
Asante Union: 182, 190
Ashmun, Jehud: 34
Assab, Bay of: 79
Atiba: 174–5, 177
Atlas Mts.: 2, 12, 85
Avongara: 276, 278, 303
Awdaghast: 111
Awori: 179–80
Axum: 8–9, 57, 73
Ayyoubids: 36
(A)zande: 58, 276, 278–9, 303–4

Bachwezi: 21
Bacri & Busnach: 90–1
Badagry: 180
Baggara: 68–9
Bagirmi: 17, 172
Bahr al Ghazal: 63, 303
Baikie, Dr. W. B.: 139, 145
Bakongo: 19
Bakuba, Kingdom: 20, 275–6, 286
Bambara: 17, 141, 166, 168
Bangala: 274
Baraka: 106
Barend–Barends: 208
Bargash, Sultan: 305
Bariba: 174
Barkly, Governor: 261
Barotseland: 201
Barth, Dr. Heinrich: 141, 143
Basuto, see Lesotho
Batedo, Battle of: 176
Bathurst: 153
Bauchi: 168
Bawa, Sultan of Gobir: 159
Bayeke: 297
Beecroft, John: 144
Begho: 114
Bello, Sultan Mohammed: 139, 149, 160, 165, 168
Bemba: 22, 201, 219
Benin: 18, 28, 113–4, 118–9, 149, 176

Benue, R: 3, 19, 144
Berbers: 5, 10–12, 86–7, 91, 94, 111
Bergenaars: 208
Berne Convention: 53
Bhaca: 241
Bisandugu: 171
Blue Nile: 2, 8, 57–8, 61, 64
Bloemfontein, Convention of: 247, 250
   257, 260, 268
Blood River, Battle of: 235, 239
Boer War (1st): 268
Boers, The: 221–271
Bond of 1844, The: 130, 187
Bondu: 158
Bonny: 129–30
Boomplaats: 247
Borgu: 174
Bornu, see Kanem
Botswana: 15
Bouët-Willaumez, Governor: 147
Bou Hamara: 104
Brand, J. H.: 257
Brass: 129
Brazil: 28–29, 126, 129, 285
British Kaffraria: 245, 248, 253, 256
British S.A. Co.: 54
Bronkhorstspruit: 268
(Bu)ganda: 21, 276–9, 286, 288, 291–2,
   300–303, 305
Bugeaud, General: 94
Bulawayo: 219
Bunkeya: 298
(Bu)nyoro: 21, 276, 278–9
Burundi: 271
Bushmen: 14–15, 30, 193–4, 196–8,
   207, 209, 222, 241
Busoga: 21
Bussa: 142–3
Butha-Buthe: 221
Buxton, T. F.: 144, 248

Caillie, Réné: 146
Cairo: 17, 25, 36, 40, 42–3, 46, 56, 71,
   138, 140, 165
Calabar: 130
Caliph (Khalifa): 24–6, 36, 64, 66–7,
   69, 101, 149, 160, 165–8
Cameron, Consul to Ethiopia: 76
Cameroun: 3, 129
Cape Coast: 183
Cape Coloureds: 208, 253
Cape of Good Hope: 28, 30, 71, 196,
   202, 205
Cape Mesurado: 134
Cape Parliament: 252–3, 256, 261

Cape Province: 193–4, 204–8, 210,
   216, 222, 230, 234–5, 237–9, 241–2,
   245, 248, 252, 255–6, 259–64, 266
Cape Town: 15, 267
Cape Verde: 113, 127
Carnarvon, Lord: 262–4
Cathcart, Governor: 249–50
Cave, Stephen: 54
Cayor: 147
Cazembe: 20, 201
Central African Mission: 139
Cetewayo: 266–7
Chagga: 281
Chamba Bolongongo: 276
Chamberlain, Joseph: 190
Charles X: 91
Chewa: 21
Chikura-Mayembe: 201
Chitimukulu: 201
Church Missionary Society: 150–3, 181
Clapperton, Hugh, 141–3, 149
Clarkson, Thomas: 123
Comité du Maroc: 103
Commissie Trekke: 228–9
Congo (Kongo): 19, 274, 282
Congo (Brazzaville): 19, 71, 271
Congo River: 3–4, 14, 19, 28, 113,
   272, 274, 276, 285–6, 291, 298, 304–5
Congress of Berlin: 99
Constantinople: 42, 48–9, 98, 105
Copts: 35, 47
Corsairs: 88, 91
Crabites: 51
Creek Town: 130
Cromer, Lord: 51, 56, 65
Cyrenaica: 104–5

Dagomba: 182
Dahomey: 18, 29, 114–5, 121, 218–9,
   151–2, 175–81, 184
Dakar: 147
Dar es Salaam: 304
Darfur: 17, 60, 63–4, 68
Davidson, Capt.: 136
Degeli: 159
Delagoa Bay: 202, 207, 263
Delgado, Cape: 29
Denham, Major D.: 141–2
Denkyira: 182
Desmichels (Treaty): 92
Deval, Consul: 91
Diamonds: 260–3, 265
Diggers Republic: 261
Dingane: 217, 222, 232–6, 239
Dingiswayo: 212–3, 215
Dinguiray: 165

Dinka: 58
Disraeli, Benjamin: 53–4, 262
Diwan: 40
Dodowa: 186
Dogali: 80
Dongola: 63
Drakensberg: 193, 211, 220, 234, 254
Duke Town: 130
Durban: 228–30
Dutch East India Co.: 30, 202, 205–7, 210, 238
Dwaben: 182

École des Otages: 147
Edo: 18, 114
Efik: 115
Egba: 152, 173–7, 179–81
Egbado: 179–80
Egypt: 2, 4–8, 10, 16, 24–5, 27, 35–47, 56–61, 64–5, 68, 69, 71, 75, 79–80, 84, 87, 90–92, 96, 105–6, 111, 165, 302–3
Ekiti: 177
Elmina: 28, 114, 187
Emin Pasha: 61
Equiano, Olauda (Gustavus Vasa): 123–4
Equipment Treaties: 126
Eritrea: 79
Essaka: 124
Ethiopia: 2, 4–5, 8–10, 32, 52, 57, 69, 73–84
Ethiopia, Church of: 10, 75
Ethiopian Highlands: 5
Ezana, King of Axum: 8–9, 57, 73

Faideherbe, Louis: 147–8
Fante: 19, 114, 130, 154, 181, 183, 186–8
Fante Confederecy: 187
Fashoda: 69, 71
Fellahin: 37, 44, 50
Felou Falls: 119
Fezz: 101
Fezzan: 17, 90, 104
Fingos: 220, 222, 229
Firearms: 283–5, 287, 296, 301, 303–5
Fish River: 196, 206, 212, 226, 230, 245
Fort Jameson: 219
Fourah Bay College: 152
Freeman, T. B.: 151
Free State: 255
Free State-Basuto War: 257
Freetown: 132, 153

Frere, Sir Bartle: 264, 266–7
French Somaliland: 79
French Equitorial Africa: 71
Fulani: 14, 64, 110, 158, 160–1, 163, 165, 167, 169, 173–7, 179
Funj Sultanate: 8, 16–7, 27, 43, 47, 58: *Black Sultanate*, 60–1
Futa Jallon: 3, 158, 165
Futo Toro: 158, 165

Ga: 181–2
Gabon: 271
Gaika, Chief: 226
Gallas: 10, 74, 79–80
Gambia: 113, 120, 140–1, 149
Gambia, River: 119, 146
Geba, River: 119
Geez: 9
Gezo, King: 179–80
Ghadames: 139
Ghana (modern): 19, 28, 113–5, 120, 150, 154, 177, 184, 186–7, 190,
Ghana (Empire): 16, 167
Gladstone (Prime Minister): 65–6, 268
Glele, King: 129, 181
Gobaze, ras of Amhara: 78
Gobir: 158–60
Gold: 11, 16, 110, 114, 119
Goldie, Rev. H.: 153
Goletta: 98–9
Gondar: 75
Gonja: 182
Gordon, General G.: 63, 65–6
Goree: 146
Grand Bassa: 135
Greeks, (Ancient): (2, 6, 9, 11), 47, 57, 92
Grey, Sir James: 253–6, 258, 260
Griffith, Brandford: 190
Griqualand East: 254
Griquas: 208, 220, 231, 242, 244, 254, 260, 265
Grigua-Town: 220
Groundnuts: 146
Gudu: 159
Guinea: 3, 110–11, 114, 117–9, 155
Guinea, Gulf of: 113
Guinea, Republic of: 171
Gwandu: 160–1, 164, 173
Gwangara: 219

Ha (Kingdom): 276, 279, 294
Hamad (Ahmad, Ahmadu, Hamadu), Shaikh: 164–8
Hamdullahi: 165, 167

Hamed, of Libya: 89
Hanafis: 24, 62
Hapta Giorgis: 83
Harper, General: 134
Harris, Walter: 102
Hausa States: 17, 19, 106, 114, 139, 157–61, 163–4, 169
Harts, R.: 208, 260
Haya: 276, 279, 300
Hehe: 219, 294–5, 296, 298, 305
Henga, The: 201, 219
Herero, The: 198
Hicks Pasha: 65
Hijra: 23, 64
Hima: 277, 279
Hlubi: 220–21
Hodgson, Sir F.: 190
Hoggar: 3
Houghton, Major: 140
House System: 115, 136
Hottentots: 15, 30, 193–4, 196–8, 205–10, 222–5, 227–8, 245
Hussein b. Ali Agha, Bey of Tunis: 87, 96
Hussein, Dey of Algeria, 90, 91, 96
Hutu, The: 279

Ibadan: 150–1, 174–7, 179
Ibos: 19, 123
Ibrahim Bey: 38
Idris Alooma, Mai of Bornu: 17, 111
Ife: 18, 173–4
Igbeji: 180
Ijaye: 174–6
Ijebu: 173–4, 176–7, 179
Ijo: 115
Ikorodu: 176
Ilorin: 173–4, 177, 179
Ilaro: 180
Imam: 24, 40, 158
Indigo: 60, 122, 128, 146
Indunas: 199–200
Inhambane: 202
Institut de l'Egypt: 41
d'Isalguier, Anselme: 112
Isandhlwana: 266
Isieke: 124
Islay, Battle of: 101
Ismail Pasha: 51, 53–5, 61–3, 65, 79, 103
Ivory: 11, 110, 122, 128–9, 285, 291, 295, 297–300, 303, 305
Ivory Coast: 171

Jamieson: 144
Jefferson, Thomas: 134

Jenne: 17, 114, 148
Jibril: 159
Jihad: 31, 80, 87, 155, 157–60, 163–5, 167–9, 173
Jihadiyya: 60
Jizya: 24
Joal: 146–7
John IV, Emperor of Ethiopia: 67, 79–81
Jones, Commander: 136

Kaarta: 17, 141, 153, 166
Kabarega: 302
Kabylie Mts.: 12–3, 94
Kalahari: 193–4, 197–8, 271
Kalanga: 198, 200–201
Kalonga: 201
Kamanga: 201, 219
Kamba: 300, 304
Kamil Pasha, Son of Mohammed Ali: 60
Kanem: 17, 90, 106, 111, 139, 149, 161, 163–5, 168, 172
Kanemi, al: 139, 149, 163–5
Kanuri: 163
Kaolack: 147
Karamanli, Osman: 88, 104–5
Karamanli, Yusuf: 89–90, 104–5, 139
Karangwe: 279, 300
Kasai, River: 4, 275, 286
Katanga: 4, 19, 21, 201, 274–5, 286, 292, 297–8, 305
Kavirondo: 304
Kazembe: 22, 275, 286, 298
Kei, River: 230, 245
Keniera: 171
Kenya: 4, 70, 271–2, 281, 300
Ketu: 181
Khatt, Khatt Hakimi: 60
Khartoum: 57, 60, 64–7, 69, 81
Khoisan: 194
Kikuyu: 281, 300
Kilimanjaro, Mt.: 4, 281, 300
Kilwa: 20, 289–90, 304
Kirshid Pasha: 42
Kitchener, General H. H.: 71–2
Koelle, Rev. S. W.: 153
Kok, Adam: 208, 242, 254
Kok, Cornelius: 208
Kokofu: 182, 188
Kololo: 220–21
Konieh: 49
Koran: 23–4, 64, 66, 92, 105, 157, 159, 299
Korana: 208
Kordofan: 58, 64–5

Kufra: 106
Kumasi: 114, 151, 182–3, 188, 190
Kumwimbu, Ngombe: 275
Kurshid: 61
Kuruman: 220
Kurunmi: 174–5
Kush: 8–9, 16, 57
Kwara: 75
Kwonni: 158
Kwororafa: 19, 161

Lagos: 150–1, 153–4, 176–7, 179, 181
Laing, Major Gordon: 139, 141, 146
Laing's Nek: 268
Laird, Macgregor: 144–5
Lake Bangweulu: 22, 201
Lake Chad: 4, 14, 17
Lake Kivu: 4, 21
Lake Kyoga: 4
Lake Malawi: 4, 201, 219, 221
Lake Mweru: 275, 297, 300
Lake Rudolf: 81
Lake Tanganyika: 4, 21, 219, 275, 291–2, 294, 296, 298, 304–5
Lake Victoria: 4, 57, 61, 219, 271, 281, 286, 296, 300, 304
Lander, John: 141, 143–4
Lander, Richard: 141–4, 149
Leopold II of Belgium: 70, 300
Lesotho (Sotho): 194, 197, 200, 213, 220–2, 231, 238, 242–4, 247, 249–50, 254–60, 263, 265
Lesseps, F. de: 51, 99
Liberia: 130–1, 133–6, 150–1, 154, 171
Liberia Herald: 135
Libya: 17, 40, 85, 87–8, 90, 104–6
Likimdars: 60, 61
Limpopo, River: 218, 265
Liverpool Merchants: 148
Livingstone: 221, 287
Lomami, River: 300, 305
London Missionary Society: 220, 223, 227, 150
Louis XVIII of France: 90
Lozi: 22, 201, 221
Lualaba, River: 298
Luanda: 28
Luapula, River: 20, 22, 201, 274, 298
Luba: 19, 21–2, 274–5, 282, 289, 298–9
Lucas, Simon: 140
Luguru: 305
Luluabourg: 274
Lunda: 19–22, 201, 274–5, 286, 298, 303

MacCarthy, Sir Charles: 186
Maclean, Captain George: 186–7
Maclean, Harry: 102
McQueen, James: 137, 144
Macina: 148, 164–8
Madagascar: 204
Madrasa: 24
Magdala: 76
Maghreb: 2–3, 5, 10–13, 16, 27–8, 85–106, 109, 112
Magongo: 236
Maitland, Governor of Cape Colony: 244
Majid, Sultan of Zanzibar: 305
Malawi: 4, 21–2, 32, 201
Mali (Kingdom): 16–7, 167
Mali (Republic): 140
Malikis: 24, 63, 92, 157
Malinke: 170
Maltese: 94
Mamelukes: 7, 25, 36–8, 40, 42–4, 48, 52, 59, 87
Mampong: 188
Mande: 158
Mandingoes: 148
Mangasha: 81–2
Mansfield, Chief Justice: 125, 131, 133
Mansour, El: 12, 13, 17
Mantatisi, Queen: 220
Maravi (Malawi): 21, 201
Marchand, Major J. B.: 71
Masai: 281–2, 289, 300, 304
Maseko Ngoni: 219, 221, 220
Masqat: 290
Massawa: 53, 79–80
Matabeleland: 222
Maynier: 209–10, 223
Mbelwa: 219
Mbemba-a-Nzinga (Dom Affonso): 19
Mecca: 17, 23–5, 64, 105, 165, 272
Medea: 101
Medina (Saudi Arabia): 23, 25, 64, 105
Medina (Senegal): 147–8, 166
Menelik: 69, 78–84
Meroe: 8, 16
Mesopotamia: 5–6, 8
Metemma: 69, 80
Mfecane: 211, 230, 242, 293
Mhlatuse, River: 215, 217
Miambana, King of Thetemne: 131
Miliana: 101
Mills, Samuel J: 134
Milner, Sir Alfred: 51
Mirambo: 289, 295–8
Moffat: 220
Mogadishu: 20, 291

Mogador: 101
Mohammed (the Prophet): 23–6, 64, 67, 92, 100, 105, 155
Mohammed Ali: 42–52, 60–1, 69, 92, 96, 105
Mohammed Gran: 10, 74
Mohammed es Sadek: 97, 103
Moletsane: 243
Mollien, G: 146
Molteno: 252–4
Mombasa: 290
Monrovia: 135
Montserrado: 135
Moors: 146, 148
Morocco: 2, 11–13, 17, 85–7, 92–3, 100–105
Moroka: 232, 243
Morosi: 243
Moshesh: 221, 231, 238, 242–3, 245–250, 255–9, 263
Moulay Hassan: 101–2
Moulay Ismail: 13, 100, 102
Moulay Suleiman: 101
Mozambique: 20–1, 28–9, 32, 196, 198, 200–202, 217–9, 275
Mpande: 236, 238, 240
Mpezeni: 219
Msiri: 289, 295, 297–9, 305
Mswati: 212
Mthethwa: 212–3, 215
Muawiya: 25
Mudirs, The: 60
Muftis: 46
Mugumba: 294–8
Muhammad Ahmad, the Mahdi: 63–9, 79
Muhammad Sharif: 66
Muslim Brotherhood: 35, 105
Mutesa: 302, 305
Murad Bey: 38
Murzuk: 90, 139
Mwata Yamvo: 20, 22, 201, 274–5
Mwene Mutapa: 22–3, 28, 200–202, 218
Mzilikazi: 222, 231–4, 243

Nafata: 159
Napier, Governor: 242
Napier: 76, 82
Napoleon: 37–41, 53, 90–1, 146, 184
Natal: 211, 215–16, 222, 228–9, 232–6, 238–240, 241, 246, 248, 253, 256, 259, 262, 266–8
Navarino: 47
Ndebele: 222, 231–2, 265
Ndwandwe: 212–3, 215, 217

Ngoni (Angoni): 219–20, 293–6, 300, 304–5
Nguni: 197–8, 206, 209, 211, 238, 243
Ngwane: 220–222
Niger, Delta: 3, 19, 212, 136, 143–4, 148, 177
Niger, River: 3, 13–14, 16, 100, 110, 114, 137–9, 141–5, 170, 208
Nigeria: 3, 19, 27, 54, 129, 154
Nigeria, Eastern: 115, 124, 129
Nigeria, Mid-West: 18, 124
Nigeria, Northern: 16–18, 168–9
Nigeria, Western: 18, 114
Nile, River: 2–5, 7–9, 14, 16–17, 27, 32, 40, 43, 45, 47, 52, 57–8, 60, 65, 70–1, 86, 142, 271, 302–3
Nilotes: 15, 21, 197, 272
Nizam Jadid: 44
Nova Scotia: 132
Nsuta: 182, 188
Nuba Mts.: 58, 69
Nubia: 8, 16, 48
Nun River: 143
Nupe: 19, 139, 164
Nyamwezi: 219, 286, 289, 292–3, 295–8, 304
Nyoro: 302–3

Obi Assai, King of Abo: 130
Ofinso: 182
Oke Odan: 180
Omanis: 20, 290
Omdurman: 68–71
Onitsha: 145
Orange Free State: 194, 220–221, 231, 239, 241, 246, 250, 254–8, 260–63, 269
Orange River: 196, 208, 220, 228, 230–1, 242, 244–6, 250, 254, 260
Orange River Sovereignty: 246–250, 254
Osei Tutu: 18
Oshogbo: 176
Osman Digna: 64
Ottoman Empire: 7, 13, 25, 36, 39–40, 42–3, 47–9, 52–3, 87, 96–7, 99, 105–6 (see also Turks)
Oudney, Walter: 141–2
Overweg, Dr.: 141
Owu: 173–4, 179
Oyo: 18, 114, 151, 164, 172–4, 177–9
Oyo Mesi: 172–3
Oyoko: 182

Park, Mungo: 141, 148–9
Parker, Mathew: 261

Paris Evangelical Soc.: 221
Pedi, The: 263
Philip, John: 227, 229, 242
Philippolis: 254
Plowden: 76
Pondoland: 215, 217, 241
Port Natal: 216, 235, 239, 241
Porto Farina: 97
Porto Novo: 114
Potchefstroom: 239
Potgieter: 231
Prempe I: 188, 190
Pretoria: 268
Pretoria Convention: 268
Pretorius: 234, 247, 249, 263
Preventive Squadron: 125–7, 129, 132, 136, 284–5
Pyramids, Battle of: 38

Qadi: 24, 26, 40, 46, 92, 95
Qadiriyya: 168
Qish Naziri: 60
Queen Adelaid Prov.: 230, 242

Raban, Rev. J. T.: 153
Rabeh ibn Fadl Allah: 171–2
Raisuli: 104
Reciprocal Search Treaties: 126
Red Sea: 9, 51, 53, 60, 70–1, 79–80
Reinet, Graaf: 209–10, 223
Retief, Piet: 232, 234–5
Rhodes, Cecil: 71
Rhodesia: 21–2, 32, 54, 196, 198, 200, 222, 233
Richardson, Jas.: 141
Rolong: 232, 243–4, 247
Rovuma, River: 271, 294
Royal African Co.: 131
Royal Niger Co.: 54
Rozwi: 22, 29, 198, 201–2, 218
Rufisque: 146
Ruga Ruga: 295
Ruwenzori Mts.: 4
Rwanda: 21, 271, 276–7, 279, 281, 294

Saadian Dynasty: 12
Sahara: 2–4, 11–12, 13, 14, 16, 27, 30, 32, 85, 106, 109–113, 117, 138–9, 140, 169, 271
Saidu Tall: 165
St. Louis: 146–7
Salisbury, Lord: 54
Sammaniya, Brotherhood: 64
Samori Toure: 170–2
Sand River Convention: 249–50, 268
Sankuru River: 275

São Thomé: 28–9, 119–120
Said: 51
Sayyid Muhammad bin ʼAli al Sanusi: 105
Sayyid Saʼid: 20, 290, 293, 305
Schmaltz, Col: 146
Sefawa Dynasty: 163–4
Segu: 17, 141, 148, 157, 164–7
Sekondi: 121
Sena: 22, 202, 218
Senegal: 51, 113, 120, 138, 140, 148–9
Senegal River: 16, 110, 119, 146–7, 158, 166–7
Sennar: 8, 58
Senussiya Brotherhood: 105–6
Seres, Capt.: 44
Shafiis: 24
Shaiqiya: 58, 60
Shaka: 213–17, 222, 236, 241, 243, 271
Shambala, The: 288
Shangamire: 22, 201
Shangane: 217, 220
Sharia: 24, 26, 66
Sharifs (Sayyids): 26, 100, 104–5
Sharpe, Granville: 123, 125, 131–2
Shepstone: 264
Sherbro Is.: 134
Shiites: 25–6
Shilluks: 58
Shire Highlands: 4
Shire River: 221
Schon, Rev. J. F.: 153
Shona: 198
Soshangane: 217–8
Sidi Muhammad al Ghali: 165
Sierra Leone: 126–7, 130–6, 149–154, 171, 186–7
Sierre Leone Committee of Correspondence: 154
Sierre Leone Company (St. George's Bay Co.): 132
Sikonyela: 220, 233–4, 243
Sikunyana: 263
Slave Trade: 15, 29, 97, 110, 113–115, 117–119, 122–134, 136–7, 144, 149, 152, 169, 177–9, 181–3, 186, 207, 229, 274, 284–5, 287, 291, 298, 303
Smeathman, Dr. Henry: 131
Smith, Sir Harry: 245–9
Sobhuza: 212–3, 220
Sofa: 171
Sofala: 20, 22, 200, 202
Sokoto: 139, 149, 160, 163, 165, 167–8
Somaliland: 291
Somalia: 4, 20, 40, 74, 84
Songea: 219, 294

Songhay (Empire): 13, 17, 31, 158, 161(ai), 167
Sori Birama, King of Bisandugu: 170
South Africa: 21-2, 30-2, 71, 193, 196-8, 200, 205, 210-11, 223-4, 227-8, 238-9, 237, 241, 245, 248, 250, 252-3, 255-6, 260, 262-8
South West Africa: 15, 194, 196, 198, 200, 229
Sprigg, Sir George: 265
Stanley, H. M.: 287
Stel, Simon van der: 204, 207
Stockenstroom: 227, 230, 242, 245
Suakin: 53
Sudan Republic: 8, 27, 40, 47-8, 57-8, 60-2, 65-72, 75, 80, 84, 115, 171-2, 190, 278, 303
Sudanic Belt: 13-14, 16-18, 27, 40, 111-13, 118, 138-9, 143-4, 155, 157-8, 161, 164-5, 167-8, 271
Suez Canal: 51-4
Sufi, The: 26, 68
Sukumaland: 279, 286, 294
Suleiman Bal: 158
Suna, Kabaka: 288
Swahili: 296, 298, 300
Swartkopjes: 244
Swazi: 220, 236
Swazi Ngwane: 212-3, 241
Swellendam: 210, 223

Table Mountain: 230
Tabora: 219, 291, 293, 296, 300
Tanganyika: 20, 70, 201, 219
Tanzania: 211, 271, 279, 281-2, 291-4, 296-8, 304
Tangier: 101, 104
Tantumkweri: 121
Taung, The: 243
Tayib, Sheik: 63
Tessama: 83
Tete: 22, 202, 218
Tetela, The: 299, 305
Tewfik: 54-6
Thaba-Bosiu: 249, 255, 257
Thaba-Bosiu, Treaty of: 258
Thaba Nchu: 231-2, 243
Thembu, The: 220
Thonga, The: 198
Tigre: 78-9, 81
Tijanniya, Brotherhood: 93, 105, 165, 168
Timbuctu: 17, 110, 141, 146, 165
Tippu Tip (Hamed bin Abdallah): 296, 299
Tlokwa: 220, 221, 233-4, 243, 247

Tonga: 201, 219
Toro: 21, 279
Toronkawa, The: 158
Touwfontein: 244
Transkei: 196
Transvaal: 194, 222, 229, 238-9, 241, 247, 249, 260-1, 263-8
Traza: 146-7
Treaty of Aliwal North: 253
Treaty of Bardo: 100
Treaty of London (1840): 49
Treaty of Marsa: 100
Treaty of Tafna: 92
Treaty of Ucciali: 81
Treaty of Unkiar-Skellesi: 48
Trek, Great: 211, 229-30, 237-8, 242-3, 247, 254, 268
Tripartite Treaty (1906): 84
Tripoli: 17, 88, 90, 104-5, 117, 138-140, 143
Tswana: 197, 208, 221, 243
Tuareg: 14, 16-17, 86, 161
Tugela, River: 235-6
Tumbuka: 201, 219
Tunisia: 2, 11-12, 85, 87, 92-3, 96-100, 103, 106
Tunis: 98-9
Turks: 10, 44-5, 55-6, 60-2, 64-5, 68-9, 79, 84, 88, 91, 139 (see also Ottoman Empire)
Tutsi, The: 277

Uganda: 4, 61, 70, 271-2, 303
Ujiji: 291, 294, 298, 305
Ulama: 24
Ulundi, Battle of: 267
Umar, al Hajj: 147-8, 164-8, 171
Ungungindhlovu: 234-5
Urundi: 21
Usumbara Mts.: 288
Uthman dan Fodio: 149, 158-9, 160-1, 163-5, 167-8, 173

Vaal River: 196, 208, 220, 228, 231, 242, 244, 246, 249, 260
Van Plettenberg: 209
Vegkop, Battle of: 231
Vice-Admiralty Court: 132
Victoria, Queen: 76, 268
Viervoet: 247
Vinza, Peoples: 305
Vlug Commando: 234
Volksraad: 240, 250, 256, 264

Wadai: 17, 106
Wadi Halfa: 60
Wahhabis, The: 47
Walo, Kingdom: 146–7
War of the Axe: 245
War of the Guns: 265
Warden: 247–8, 250
Warden Line: 250, 257
Warri: 118, 149
Wassa: 182
Waterboer: 208, 242, 244, 260–1
Warrington: 89, 104
Wa-Tuta, The: 219
Wesleyan Methodist Missionary
    Society: 150–1, 244
West Indies: 15, 29, 124, 131–2, 147
Whydah: 114–5
Wilberforce, William: 123
Wilmot, Commodore E.: 129
Winburg: 239
White Nile: 2, 57–8, 61
Wolseley, Sir Garnet: 56, 188
Woodhouse: 258–9
Wolsely, General: 66

Xhosa: 209–10, 226, 229–231, 233,
    245, 254

Yao: 21, 201
Yavo Naweji: 274
Yevogan: 121
Yoruba: 18, 114, 151, 153–4, 172, 181
Yunfa: 159, 161

Zambezi River: 4, 21–2, 193, 202,
    218–9, 221
Zambia: 20–2, 32, 201, 219, 221
Zamfara: 159
Zanzibar: 20, 290–3, 298, 300, 302–3,
    305
Zimbabwe: 22, 201
Zinza: 276, 279, 294, 300
Zubair Pasha: 172
Zulus: 31, 197, 211–8, 220, 222–36,
    238–41, 248, 264, 266–7
Zuurveld: 196–7, 206, 209–10, 224, 226
Zwangendaba: 217–9, 293
Zwide: 212–13, 215